BIG VEGAN

D0752029

BIG VEGAN

MORE THAN 350 RECIPES
NO MEAT / NO DAIRY
ALL DELICIOUS

PHOTOGRAPHS BY KATE SEARS

VEGAN

BY ROBIN ASBELL

CHRONICLE BOOKS
SAN FRANCISCO

Text copyright © 2011 by Robin Asbell.
Photographs copyright © 2011 by Kate Sears.

All rights reserved. No part of this book may be reproduced in any
form without written permission from the publisher.

Library of Congress Cataloging-in-Publication Data available.

ISBN 978-0-8118-7467-0

Manufactured in China.

Designed by Alice Chau.

10 9 8 7 6 5 4 3 2

Chronicle Books
680 Second Street
San Francisco, California 94107
www.chroniclebooks.com

Acknowledgments

I'd like to thank my sweetheart, Stan, for accompanying me on this and all my journeys. As always, my family and friends were a source of joy and support in the work of making this book.

My agent, Jennifer Griffin, was invaluable as an editor, advisor, and hand-holder, and I am truly grateful. All the wonderful people at Chronicle Books made the process fun and contributed to the final product in ways great and small. Special thanks to Bill LeBlond, Amy Treadwell, Doug Ogan, Alice Chau, Tera Killip, Peter Perez, and David Hawk, who brought the book to life.

My recipe testers—Lisa Genis, Crystal Grobe, Marge Porter, Liz Nerud, Joy Harris, Jane Gordon, and Kristine Vick—gave me invaluable feedback, and I can't thank them enough. Special thanks go to Deanne Klevander, for volunteering her very sharp eyes and organized mind.

A collection of my colleagues also contributed to this project, with wit, advice, and support: Sandra Gutierrez, for Guatemalan recipe advice and more; Zoe Francois and Jeff Hertzberg, for their bread techniques; Tara M. Desmond, for support and almost-vegetarian things; Antonia Allegra, for constant inspiration; Jill O'Connor, Nancie McDermott, Cheryl Sternman Rule, and my IACP friends, for keeping me laughing—a very valuable thing.

I am also grateful for all the wonderful cooking schools that have hosted my cooking classes and helped me get real food to the people.

Introduction to the Vegan World

Vegan is getting bigger all the time, so welcome to the party!

Some of you may be committed, long-time vegans, and some of you may just be starting to investigate this way of eating. Some of you may just want some great plant-based recipes to help you cut back on animal foods. You are all welcome, and there should be something for everyone in this book. Eating great foods that just happen to be animal-free is good for your health, good for the environment, and good for the animals, so every time someone chooses vegan, we all win. With even just one plateful, clean plant-based food makes a difference.

Eating this way is a celebration—a celebration of you nourishing yourself while reveling in the sensuous cuisine that springs from a nourished planet. It's a celebration of the colors, tastes, scents, and textures that emerge from the soil and all the energy they possess. Feeling great, looking good, and doing good for the planet is just one big party, with no hangover the next day. As much as we look to food for pleasure, the ultimate hedonism is great health. Sure, junk food has its fleeting buzz, but living in a nourished body is a long-term plan for serious fun. Who doesn't want to have more energy and avoid chronic disease? The most powerful tool for accomplishing a vibrant state of being is your plate.

The plant-based food party is coming into its own place in the world. Good food is good food, transcending labels. Anyone who has ever eaten a crispy-hot slice of hearty bread spread with melting peanut butter and jam for lunch was enjoying a vegan meal with no label attached. Sublime pleasures like a perfect, ripe peach; a just-picked juicy tomato still warm from the sun; or a handful of crisp pistachios come from plant cuisine at its most basic. Hand those over to creative chefs, and a whole world of flavors and textures begs to be explored. Many of the most respected culinary minds, including Thomas Keller and Charlie Trotter, now explore plant-based cuisine in their world-famous restaurants. Making amazing food from pure, simple ingredients gives them a chance to show that they really understand food. Working without animal products makes them stretch, drop old ways of thinking, and work a little harder to produce something that people will pay top dollar to experience. And, like me, they look to the history and the ancient traditions of eating low on the food chain. We have come full circle.

Eating well has always involved plants. Every great cuisine of the world has dishes that revel in the textures and flavors of vegetables, fruits, nuts, beans, and good oils. Peasants ate this way out of poverty—the *cucina povera* of Italy is the source of some of the most robust, decadent, animal-free dishes on the planet. Every country that touches the Mediterranean Sea has its own form of vegetable worship—from Spanish romesco to Greek *hortika* in olive oil to Lebanese hummus and Syrian eggplant in pomegranate molasses. The Mediterranean diet, that lifelong prescription for pleasure and health, goes vegan without skipping a beat. The real Mediterranean diet was flexitarian before we had a word for it. Hardscrabble living consisted of eating things you could grow most of the time, since eating animals was expensive. Luckily, one of their native plants was the olive, so they could drench their healthful food in its richness and in the process, create a life-saving cuisine that we aspire to today. Wine, plant foods, and song—how can you go wrong?

Looking to the East, we see the influences of Buddhism and other peaceful philosophies have planted seeds for plant-loving cuisines that flourish to this day. In the traditional Chinese kitchen, we find masterpieces made from plants. Can you imagine a world with no soy sauce? There must be a bottle of that simple, fermented black elixir in every kitchen in the world by now. Like the Mediterranean way, traditional diets all over Asia are plant-based—a little bit of animal, stretched across an expanse of rice and a crisp-tender jumble of stir-fried vegetables, or perhaps simmered into a miso soup with the best vegetables available for the season. It's easy to go vegan with such a plant-filled plate. A few thousand years ago, China turned away from dairy foods. It's unclear whether it was to differentiate from the Mongol herders, or perhaps an emperor was secretly lactose intolerant. Either way, one of the world's most ancient civilizations has been making magic without dairy for quite awhile, and we still reap the benefits. Tofu is also attributed to the Chinese, so tip a hat to those soybean alchemists.

More tropical Asian cultures, like Thailand, Malaysia, and the Pacific Rim, bring us light, plant-based food born of sizzling heat and tropical plants. Coconut milk and chiles, exotic spices, and fermented beans make a light, summery meal taste rich and satisfying. In tropical climates, everybody wants to eat foods that won't weigh them down—and vegans like that feeling, too. How sexy is a rich coconut sauce, spiked with heat and spice, punched up with touches of sweet and sour, flecked with fresh herbs? You could put it on anything and it would sing, but it really speaks when gentle plants hold it high.

India, where vegetarian traditions are strong to this day, has much to teach us about making satisfying plant cuisine. After a few thousand years, they have worked out complex spice and flavor balances that elevate the simplest potato to gourmet fare. Dal and rice are the national dish, and variations are endless. We can borrow many of their classic, time-tested cooking techniques and combinations, and work around their yogurt and cheese. A symphony of spice, a subtle play between soft and crisp, a teasing touch of sweet, then a hint of sour—the experience in a mouthful of curry is so intense that it needs only simple plants to carry it.

As much as we depend on Europe and Asia, we can also travel the globe, discovering the creative ways in which cooks prepare plant foods. South America, with its amazing quinoa, amaranth, rice, and corn, and the home of the chile and so many varieties of beans, has a vast treasure trove of plant dishes. Many islands, from Jamaica to Hawaii, are home to tropical flavors, many based on abundant fruits and vegetables that soak up that sunshine and heat. Jamaica even has its own vegan religion, the Rastafarians, who happily simmer up the fruits of the island with coconut and *callaloo*.

The melting pot of our global kitchen brings us exciting access to the dishes of far-flung islands and faraway steppes. This is the great vegan harvest. The down-to-earth foods that people have made from plants for years build the base of our cuisine. Don't be fooled by restaurant fare. When you eat in a restaurant that serves another country's food, you usually get the celebration food, the meat dish they only serve on feast days, the richest, sweetest things that are meant to seduce you. In everyday life, there have to be plant-based, inexpensive foods. Look to the old ways, the agrarian traditions, and there you will see how that culture expresses its love of plants. Learn from it; take it home.

The vegan way of life is also about fusing global tastes with local foods, to keep our carbon footprint as small as possible. Vegans are cutting edge in that regard, in the food world. I attended a panel discussion featuring Elizabeth Andoh, a Japanese food expert and anthropologist; Rick Bayless, Mexican food expert; and Vikram Vij, an Indian chef running a wildly popular Indian restaurant in Canada. The topic was which was more authentic, importing the foods of the homeland for each immigrant popu-lation, or applying the cooking style and flavors of a cuisine to the fresh, local foods? While the whole notion of authenticity is always changing, all agreed that the true expression of a cuisine involves using the best indigenous foods, even if they did not exist in a recipe's homeland. While vegan food was the last thing they thought they were discussing, I think that adapting foods of the world to plant-based dishes, and even using local, nontraditional substitutions, results in a vibrant new cuisine. Food culture is always evolving, and evolving away from animal agriculture and Big Food is the way of the future.

What Is Vegan Food Anyway?

The label "vegan" essentially means you are participating in a food chain with no animals in it. Not cows, not chickens, not even bees. It's not a new idea, but it is one that is making more sense all the time. Here in the Western world, where diet-related diseases are common, turning to plants is a delicious way to dance right past health issues that might slow you down. People are finding that eating vegan makes them feel and look better, and that it can really be quite delicious and fun. As consumers, more of us are looking at where our food comes from and the impact that our consumption has on the planet. Once you start looking into the ramifications of your food choices, choosing to go vegan is a simple way to live lightly on the earth.

While vegan cooking is often defined by what you *don't* eat, it's not about deprivation. It may take a little creativity to get beyond the idea of a plate anchored by a piece of protein, but it is not difficult. Your friends and family may need a little help and patience. Be gentle with them—they know not what they do. Eating is a deeply emotional, personal choice, and most people are very attached to their food. Saying yes to a tasty felafel burger may well mean saying no to a cheeseburger, but there is no need to try to convert anyone beyond serving and enjoying. Every plant-based meal makes a difference. We can help our friends the most by eating and sharing vibrant, tasty foods that are plant-based. When you are living vegan and showing the people around you how great you feel and how good the food really is, you may just nudge them to make better choices.

The foods that vegans eat are the lively ones. Move past the meat counter and look to the veggies, fruits, beans, grains, nuts, and seeds and you are looking at energy and health. You may have noticed that when the latest list of "super foods" hits magazine covers, it usually involves plants. Headlines about the newest ways to prevent cancer or diabetes always recommend eating more plants. Striving for nine servings of plant foods a day is the government recommendation for vegetable and fruit consumption, and most people fall far short.

What is so unimaginable to your standard-diet friends is that once you stop eating animal foods, you genuinely appreciate the flavors and textures of your new diet even more. It's as if animal and processed foods were shouting all the time, but when they are gone, you can suddenly hear all the gentle sounds of the plants. Instead of overwhelming your palate, entertain it with the rich, crunchy experience of a walnut, harmonizing with all the subtle flavors of a tender bowl of greens and a zingy citrus dressing. A perfectly tender bean bathed in a lush, herbal vinaigrette melts in your mouth, spilling its simple comforts. Cooks find it hard to give up the way that meat and animal fat flavor things so intensely, but it's so easy! An animal has transformed all the plants he ate into something with lots of complexity, and you need to learn a few tricks to get similar complexity with vegan dishes. But your palate will change, if you will only turn down the volume and listen.

Living a plant-based life is like traveling light. Your system adjusts to foods that don't weigh you down and take forever to digest. You may find that maintaining your weight gets easier, as long as you don't hit vegan desserts too hard. The vegan mainstream has food manufacturers taking notice: Vegan-friendly packaged foods multiply daily. While that makes it easier to eat vegan, don't become a junk-food vegan. The upside? Options in dairy-free milks, ice creams, and vegan-friendly sweeteners are growing. The downside? You can construct a vegan diet out of pudding cups, fake bologna, and white bread, but you will not be all that healthy doing it. You still have to seek balance and listen to your body. It will tell you how things are going, if you just pay attention.

In the years I have spent cooking for vegans, it seems to me that what they craved most was special food—food for celebrations and shared dinners; food that really tastes great. It's not that difficult to put together a big salad or sandwich on your own. Restaurants will happily strip down dishes and leave off the cheese. You can eat vegan and survive, but it's the special foods that you crave. After going to the same sandwich shop a few times and having a sandwich with just veggies and no cheese, vegans want recipes for genuinely interesting food. A virtual world exists on the Internet, where vegans swap sources for marshmallow crème and recipes for mock cheese sauces. This book is my best effort for plant-based diners who want food that rocks.

Why Vegan?

Vegetarianism has been practiced in many forms for thousands of years. Spiritual and religious groups all around the world, from Buddhists and Brahmins to Seventh-Day Adventists, have adopted "thou shalt not kill" as a dietary guideline. Veganism follows that line of logic to its end and asks why animals should be used at all to provide food for us. Any ingredient of animal origin, from gelatin and Worcestershire sauce to milk and eggs to honey from bees is not vegan. The official birth of the vegan movement was in 1944, when a group broke away from the Leicester Vegetarian Society in England to form a vegan group. They wanted to live harmlessly and followed the vegetarian ideal to its logical end.

Health

It's OK to act out of self-interest when you are going vegan. Many vegans get into it purely for their health, looks, and energy level. All that other stuff is a side benefit. The popularity of a vegan diet as a means to lose or maintain weight has brought a lot of people to the practice. Svelte vegan celebs who go public undoubtedly convert plenty of folks— why not try it if it works for them? If your body is a temple, fuel it with nutrient-rich, pure plant energy to purify it. Obesity is running rampant among omnivores, who just can't seem to eat any vegetables. Dumping the junk food and eating more plants is a simple strategy for getting and staying lean and healthy.

Then there are people who are well along the way to serious illness, due to the standard American diet of refined foods, fatty meat, and sweets, and who go vegan to heal themselves. Dr. John McDougall and Dr. Dean Ornish are just two of the better-known proponents of this kind of veganism. They take people who are on track for the quadruple bypass because their bloodstream is so blocked and completely turn them around with a very low-fat, vegan diet. It works: Check out the research. Good food is serious medicine. The National Cancer Institute estimates that three out of four deaths in contemporary Western society are diet-related, including heart disease, cancer, and diabetes. The risks from all those diseases are markedly lower for vegans. If heart disease or diabetes runs in your family, you would do well to head them off at the pass by eating defensively. Vegetarians who avoid meat because of cholesterol and saturated fat are cutting back, but eggs and dairy still contain the same fats as the animals that made them.

The medical establishment has been slow to come around to the healthfulness of vegan diets, so don't be surprised when your doctor voices concern about your choices. Myths about complete protein coming only from animals have been debunked, and fears that a vegan diet will inevitably lead to B_{12} deficiency, anemia, or brittle bones can be put to rest. Considering that the American Dietetic Association gave vegan eating its stamp of full approval in 2009, you can feel confident that a vegan diet can be healthful. A balanced vegan diet can certainly provide all the nutrients you need, especially with fortified foods that are available now. Beyond that, loading up on plant foods delivers the protective elements they contain in abundance, like antioxidants, fiber, essential fatty acids, and vitamins and minerals. It does take some planning, though, like all healthful diets do.

The Environment

Now that you know how well you are taking care of Number One, you might as well consider the effect that your lifestyle has on the planet. It's no longer just a hippie thing to search out ways to minimize the damage to the earth from our food consumption. In 1996, the United Nation's Food and Agriculture Organization released "Livestock's Long Shadow," a report detailing the environmental impact of animal husbandry. At that time, 30 percent of the world's surface was used to raise livestock and their food, and 70 percent of the Amazon rainforest had been cut down to raise cattle. Livestock runoff still dumps tons of pollutants into waterways, choking and killing streams and even large swaths of the ocean.

For many vegans, animal rights are the big issue. Steering clear of animal foods is one way to leave the critters alone. When you can live a healthy, happy life eating plants, why not?

How to Cook Vegan

I turned on the TV the other day, just in time to see a scene from a movie in which the characters go to a vegan restaurant because the guy mistakenly believes that his date is vegan. They are offered kelp pizza described as "earthy, with a taste of dirt" and are served "a yeast ball for the table," which looks like a cross between taffy and bread dough. Neither can pretend to like it, so they spit it out and the camera cuts to the sizzling beef they are about to order at a street truck. Unfortunately, vegan food has an image problem.

In the omnivorous world we live in, some consider the label "vegan" a flashing red warning sign for bad taste. Chefs spend years mastering their craft, and vegan cuisine is not generally covered in culinary school, so they may well be baffled by requests for it. I am hopeful that this image (at least in big cities) is changing with more exciting restaurants serving plant-based cuisine that even food critics rave about. When we share vegan food, we should pick things that are entry-level, not too challenging but infused with flavor and texture. You may not even want to say it's vegan, at least not before they try it, just so that they will have an open mind. One of the highest compliments that I have received many times over the years is "I could be a vegetarian, if I had food like this every day." Of course, they *can* make food like this every day, and so can you!

To cook without animal foods can be looked at in two ways. One is just to adapt your favorite dishes and use soy cheese, soy burgers, and soy sausages. You don't need a cookbook to do that—so I don't use them here. Tofu, seitan, and tempeh are as close as we get to processed food, and they are all real foods that you can make in your own kitchen; they are not really trying that hard to be meat, and that's okay. The only dairy substitutes we use are a little tofu "cream cheese" and Earth Balance margarine and a variety of plant milks. A second way to approach vegan cooking is to work with recipes that were mostly animal-free to begin with. Indian dal or Jamaican rundown are already close to vegan as long as you use vegan sweeteners. The challenge for most beginning vegan cooks is to get the level of flavor, texture, and satisfaction that they remember from using animal foods. Your palate will adjust, but it will be easier if you know how to harness the flavor and texture of the new foods you will be using. Armed with the plant-based traditions of the world and the food chemistry tool kit I've put together for you, you will be ready to win over friends and family with your enviable, delicious lifestyle.

The Tool Kit

Balancing the Five Tastes

Putting food together in the kitchen is many things, but at its essence, it is chemistry. When you put vegetables in a hot pan, all sorts of processes occur, and suddenly cells collapse, chemicals that were separate in the living plant mix together, and the taste changes. As organisms go, plants are simple. When animals eat plants, they concentrate all sorts of chemicals into the complex constructs that are muscle, milk, or eggs. That is why cooking a piece of animal food is so easy: There is a lot going on in there, and cooks can fall back on the fats, amino acids, and browned sugars from a piece of beef to flavor a whole dish. Melted cheese is a complicated sauce because cheese itself is complex, and you can't really create it without the cow. When you cook without animal products, you can still use culinary chemistry to replace some of the flavors and sensations that animal foods have. As vegans, we can layer flavors and use plant-based chemistry to give the palate well-rounded flavors and sensations. Like all chefs, we work with the five tastes: sweet, salty, bitter, sour, and—a new one for Western chefs—*umami*.

Vegans would do well to understand umami. It is the Japanese word for "meaty," or the experience of well-rounded mouthfeel. The Japanese have made an art form out of harnessing the amino acids and other molecules that spark this fifth taste. It was a Japanese scientist who isolated the most common and basic umami chemical, monosodium glutamate (MSG), and started the manufacture of it in crystalline form. In recent years, a taste receptor for umami was located, and scientists believe that we evolved to feel pleasure when we eat umami-rich foods because they are good for us. Basically, all foods that contain protein contain a collection of amino acids, some of which are bound together in a protein molecule, and some of which are free. When proteins break apart through fermentation or cooking, amino acids are freed to trigger your umami receptor. This kind of umami comes from fermented foods like miso, soy sauce, fermented bean pastes of all kinds like Chinese and Korean black bean sauces, and tempeh. Other sources are mushrooms, and drying them or any vegetable concentrates the taste of umami. Ripe vegetables and fruits, like vine-ripened tomatoes, develop maximum umami. Sweet corn, peas, beans, winter squash,

walnuts, sunflower seeds, and almonds all have varying levels of umami. Sea vegetables, like the kombu used in miso soup, are full of umami chemistry—and the first isolated MSG was made from kombu. Even nutritional yeast is loaded with umami, and the actions of active yeast give baked goods more umami. Fermented drinks like wine and beer, as well as pickled foods, develop umami, too. Tea has theanine, its very own umami chemical, which makes the brew more appealing. Beyond the intrinsic food ingredients, smoking foods gives them more umami.

To add umami to recipes throughout this book, I have used small amounts of miso, nutritional yeast, and other ingredients. It may not be traditional to use miso in a Southeast Asian recipe, but because it adds flavors the recipe once got from umami-rich fish sauce, miso is a great vegan stand-in.

So now that you know which vegan foods are rich in umami, you can use it to give plant-based dishes a satisfying fullness in the mouth. Then you can play with the other four tastes: sweet, sour, salty, and bitter. Taste combined with aroma makes flavor. When you look at the cuisines of India, the balancing of tastes is an art form that makes vegetarian food sing. Learning to make a curry with toasted and raw spices; combinations of beans, vegetables, and grains; and the play between sweet, sour, and hot will make you a better cook. Chinese, Japanese, Thai, and Southeast Asian cuisines make light foods intense by balancing tastes and flavors. The balance of salty, sweet, and sour are the backbone of many Asian dishes. You may not realize how much you like a little bitterness, until you think about dark chocolate, coffee, and even some spices and vegetables. Your palate wants just a touch, balanced with other tastes and sensations. Bitter chocolate is better with some sweet and fat. A tomato sauce might seem flat until a shot of wine adds acid and another kind of umami, and a hint of salt brings up the sweetness of the fruit at its base. Herbs add complexity, aroma, and often a touch of bitter.

Textures

As much as we crave taste, we crave texture. Humans love the sensations that butter, cream, and cheese bring to their mouths, as the umami chemicals and fats that melt at body temperature cascade sensations to the brain. We can trip the same triggers without the cow, though. Vegans have the amazing coconut to provide rich milk and a fat that behaves a lot like butter. Nondairy milks have become better and better, with choices proliferating every day. Where once we had only rice and soy, we now have hemp, almond, hazelnut, and coconut milks as well. Nondairy creamers have also appeared in flavors designed for coffee, but they can be used to make vegan "ice creams," too. Nondairy "yogurts," "sour cream," and "cream cheese" are stand-ins when you crave the old standards, and you can make your own. Liquid oils are generally best for health, but some margarines with no hydrogenated fat or trans fat have become readily available. I often use a little cold-press corn oil to get a buttery taste, or simply switch to a mild, buttery olive oil for a whole new experience.

The texture of cheese has been the hardest thing to mimic, with plenty of icky, nonmelting soy "cheeses" on the market, but those are getting better, especially as the rising number of vegans makes an impact on manufacturers. Cheese brings fat, fermented complexity, and often a hefty dose of sodium to dishes, so you may find that a little sour and a bit of salt help make up for its absence. In this book, purees of lightly fermented, raw, or toasted nuts create cheese-like sensations. In a sandwich, sliced avocado or melted nut butters can provide both the holding power and the intensity that a slice of cheese would. In a pasta, a puree of beans, nuts, or even veggies can make a rich, creamy sauce. Of course, a nondairy béchamel or pureed veggie soup with soy milk is a great stand-in for dairy.

When you want meat's heft and chewiness in a dish, you can thank Asia for gluten. Mock duck, mock chicken, and even Tofurkey are made from forming the springy proteins extracted from wheat into tasty forms. You can purchase convenient canned, frozen, and even dried gluten products, and it is not that difficult to make them at home. Soy foods like tempeh add chunky texture and nutty flavor, and tofu can be frozen or crumbled and cooked to give dishes a chewier feel. Textures that can be used to replace meat include the granular chewiness of bulgur wheat or chunkily chopped mushrooms or beans. Nuts and seeds can also create a meaty texture. If you want to try processed foods like vegan "sausages" and "burgers," that is up to you, but they are not in this book. Of course, you may be able to buy some minimally processed burgers, so just use your judgment about how real they are. As with soy cheeses, manufacturers are coming out with better ones every day.

Techniques

There are times when a leaf of lettuce or a spear of steamed broccoli is just the thing: light, simple, and satisfying. But when you want to amp up the flavor, you need some methods for intensifying, layering, and deepening the plant flavors in the pot. Many a classic dish starts with a sauté of onions and other aromatics. The magical chemistry of the *Allium* genus gives onions, leeks, shallots, and garlic a potent sweet chemical that comes forward with long, slow cooking. Caramelized onions and roasted garlic are two ingredients that add depth, sweetness, and complexity to dishes. In the same vein, roasting also brings out sugars, shrinks and condenses vegetables, and tempers bitter and vegetal flavors. A root vegetable like a beet can lose half its weight during a long roast, shrinking down to an earthy, butter-soft nugget.

Similarly, flavorful liquids can become even more intense when simply simmered to cook off the water and reduce their volume. Reduction is a chef's trick for quickly making the juices from a dish into a sauce and intensifying flavors. It's also a tried-and-true technique to use alcohol as a flavor enhancer. Adding wine or liquor to vegetables actually does more than add flavor: The alcohol in the liquid acts as a solvent, breaking open molecular bonds and extracting flavors that were locked in plant tissues. Once the alcohol has done its job, simmering the liquids also evaporates the alcohol, leaving the precious extractions behind.

Grilling/barbecuing, broiling/grilling, and searing also work to layer flavor. A mushroom or a piece of marinated tofu is really quite wet inside, and when the surface hits higher heat, the crust or skin that is created is very pleasing to bite into. Browning also develops sugars into more interesting flavors. Grill marks, with their hint of carbon, also give a little bitterness to the overall impression.

Smoke is such a powerful flavorizer it is really an ingredient. As it adds umami, it can add strong aroma and the taste of the plant being burned, from mesquite to rosemary stems. It should be handled judiciously, as a little goes a long way. Liquid smoke, used in some of the recipes in this book, is a convenient way to add a hint of smoke without burning anything. It's manufactured by burning wood and infusing the smoke into water, then reducing the liquid. Always go slow with liquid smoke, though—just a few drops go a long way.

Equipment

Vegan food is just food, after all, and the usual pans and stoves are all you need. There are only a few pieces of equipment that you might want to add to your kitchen.

For breads and pizzas, you need a baking stone. I keep one in the oven all the time: Just put it on the bottom shelf and leave it there. Everything you bake will be better on stone, with a crisper crust and a better rise. A side benefit is that you can remove it after it cools and scrub it gently, so if there are spills, you don't have to clean the whole oven.

Cast-iron pans should have a place in every vegan kitchen. Cooking in cast iron adds measurable nutritional iron to cooked foods, which vegans need. When well-seasoned, cast iron can be a healthful alternative to coated nonstick pans and the chemicals that they bring to the table.

For baking, I find that air-bake sheet pans are superior for cookies/biscuits and buns. They have a layer of air sandwiched between two sheets of metal, which makes them a little gentler in browning the bottoms of your baked goods. Use parchment/baking paper or silicone baking mats to avoid contact with the aluminum, if you are concerned.

For many of the recipes, a food processor or blender is necessary. For the best, smoothest, nut-based sauces, a serious blender like a Vitamix is a good investment. They are a bit pricey, so if you can't spring for one, get the best blender you can. You'll just have to scrape down the jar and repeat the pureeing a few more times.

For steaming, you can either invest in a bamboo steamer or something like it, or you can rig up your own. For steaming dumplings or larger foods, you can place a cake rack or even wads of foil in a pot, simmer water in the bottom, not touching the rack, and put a plate on top, as long as there is room around the plate for steam to circulate, and a tight lid on the pot to hold it in. For vegetables, a folding steamer or a perforated steamer insert pan will do.

For some of the seitan recipes, you will need to invest in some cheesecloth/muslin, a light cotton fabric that is often used in canning.

A bamboo mat, or sudare, for rolling sushi is helpful, especially for making inside-out rolls. It's simply thin strips of bamboo stitched together. For inside-out rolls, look for a larger bamboo mat.

An electric rice cooker is a conveniece that you may find worth the investment. These cookers range from inexpensive, "cook and turn off"–style cookers, to "cook and keep warm" ones, on up to pricier "fuzzy logic" cookers. Since you will be cooking brown rice and whole grains in yours, look for one that has a setting for them and always measure the water—don't rely on markings on the sides of the container.

A slow-cooker or crockpot is another convenience. Instead of simmering beans or seitan on the stove, you can put them in a crock and let them gently cook all night or all day when you are at work.

A pasta rolling machine is used to make fresh pasta in one recipe in this book. If you love fresh pasta and want to show your friends how great eggless pasta can be, you may want to invest in one. A simple manual crank one is perfectly adequate and will last for years.

Baking

If cooking is chemistry, baking is advanced chemistry. A muffin or a cake batter is a carefully balanced formula in which leaveners mix with liquids and react to create bubbles. Then the wet starches and proteins in the dough trap the bubbles and harden into an open structure as the heat removes moisture, and fats and sugars keep the whole thing tender and sweet. Yeasts, as they come to life and colonize in a bread dough, break molecules apart and consume starches, liberating all kinds of flavors that were trapped in the grain. Yeasts give off alcohols and gases, which evaporate during baking, as gluten fibers harden around the holes where they expanded and changed form. In vegan baking, we harness all those things but replace the standard butter, milk, cream, and white sugar (which is often processed using animal by-products) with animal-free ingredients. Since all our favorite cakes, pies, and pastries are usually made with dairy and eggs, we have to be a little clever and find ways to do the same kinds of things with vegan ingredients.

So, when you look at a recipe with eggs and dairy, look at the roles they play in the recipe. Something like a meringue or an angel food cake is almost all egg whites, and there is really no vegan product that will act the same way. On the other hand, something like a cookie/ biscuit, in which there is one egg in the recipe, is a prime candidate for veganization. Your egg-free pantry includes several options. One is egg replacer powder, such as Ener-G Egg Replacer. It's a mixture of starches and leaveners that does some of the binding and lifting that eggs do. It's best for cakes and muffins, in which ingredients are pretty light. Flax seeds are another natural binder, because when ground and mixed with water, they form a kind of glue that holds the batter together and can help trap gases as they rise. Flax doesn't make things rise, though, so you still need baking soda/bicarbonate of soda and baking powder. Flax can also be heavy, so it's more of a cookie or scone

ingredient. You can also replace the richness and binding of eggs with a puree of bananas, applesauce, dried fruit, sweet potato, or squash.

Cream and milk provide liquid, richness, and flavor, but you may not have realized that they also act as acids to spark chemical leaveners like baking soda/bicarbonate of soda. So when you replace dairy in a quick bread, you will often need to add some vinegar, lemon, or other acid to have the same leavening effect. Take your pick from the nondairy options for baking. I usually pick the ones with the mildest, whitest milks—usually rice, almond, or coconut. If there is just a little in a whole-wheat/ wholemeal muffin, it doesn't matter, but in an ice cream or white cake, you don't want a strong taste or a beige tint. In something like caramel that is made from cream added to a hot syrup, coconut milk from a can or a nondairy creamer from a carton works well.

Sugar is the next challenge. Because the Vegetarian Resource Group estimates that 20 percent of the refined cane sugar sold in the United States is purified by passing it through filters made from cow-bone char, it's not considered vegan. When I first got involved with vegan baking in the '80s, it was just assumed that all vegan baking involved alternative sweeteners like brown rice syrup, molasses, fruit juice concentrates, crystalline fructose, and, a relative newcomer, Sucanat (sometimes called rapadura). Sugar was seen as the white menace, sucking nutrients out of your body and contributing to chronic disease, and that was before the new drug of choice, high-fructose corn syrup. In recent years, some vegans have decided to go ahead and use refined sugar, because it is inexpensive and easy. It's up to you. A good middle ground can be found in vegan sugars, dried cane juices, and organic sugars that promise all the ease of sugar with no bone char involved. Keep in mind that baking with liquid sweeteners always requires that you reduce the amount of liquid in a recipe, and often these syrups are strong tasting. Brown rice syrup gives a charming, caramel quality to some dishes, and a shot of molasses goes a long way in gingerbread. A recent addition in the liquid sweeteners category is agave syrup—made from the cactus that gives us tequila. Agave is a great choice, because it is mostly fructose, a kind of sugar that has less of a metabolic impact. It also has a clean, sweet taste and dissolves easily into liquids. Using dry, crystallized sweeteners allows you to do the creaming step that many baked goods require, in which margarine is beaten with a sugar until fluffy. This is an important step for some recipes, because the bubbles formed in the fluffy mixture are the only spots for the leavening to do its lifting. If you don't get tiny bubbles in the fat, you don't get any lift. Granular cane sugars are the only sugars that can be browned for a caramel, and they melt into syrups as well. Their pure, sweet flavor is what we are used to.

In the recipes in this book, the word *sugar* refers to granular cane products like dried cane juice, vegan sugar, Florida Crystals products, Wholesome Sweeteners products, and the like. In those recipes, you can use conventional sugars as well.

Vegan Nutrition

It's great to hear that dietitians endorse a vegan diet. They don't mean chips/crisps and candy instead of beef; they mean a well-planned diet. It's not rocket science, but if you are going to eat exclusively vegan foods, you do need to make sure you are not missing out on some nutrients. Luckily, the bounty of fortified foods available just for vegans—from breakfast cereals to soymilks—makes it really easy. Nutrients like B_{12}, calcium, vitamin D, iron, and a few others that you absolutely need and that omnivores get from animal foods can be obtained from eating unprocessed plant-based foods, with only a few additions like fortified "milks" or nutritional yeast to your diet.

While the average omnivore struggles to eat enough vegetables and fruits, the vegan solves that problem by going all-plant. Your body is awash with healing antioxidants, and most vitamins and minerals fall into place effortlessly. You might have to monitor your B_{12} intake, but fiber and good, heart-healthy fats are easily incorporated in your daily fare.

The vegan lifestyle can be easy. Once you understand which foods you need, it all becomes second nature. The Vegan Food Guide Pyramid is a good tool for keeping the big picture in mind. In general, that means that you eat more vegetables and fruits as the base of your diet. Even vegans forget this one. Make sure you eat a variety of fruits and vegetables, consciously emphasizing leafy greens, which you need for calcium. Make most grains whole, and eat a variety: Each kind of whole grain has its own charms and special nutrient bonuses. The legumes/pulses, beans, and seeds group, as well as the fortified nondairy products, can make up your concentrated protein sources. The top of the triangle is the stuff you make sure to keep in balance—like sweeteners and fats. Your body needs some fats and oils, so don't think that lesser quantities means total elimination.

The Vegan Pyramid

For many years, the food pyramid published by the USDA was not vegan-friendly and gave the impression that vegan diets were unhealthful. Thanks to the work of vegan-friendly dietitians, the nutrition community has come around to the soundness of an animal-free diet.

VEGAN FOOD GUIDE PYRAMID

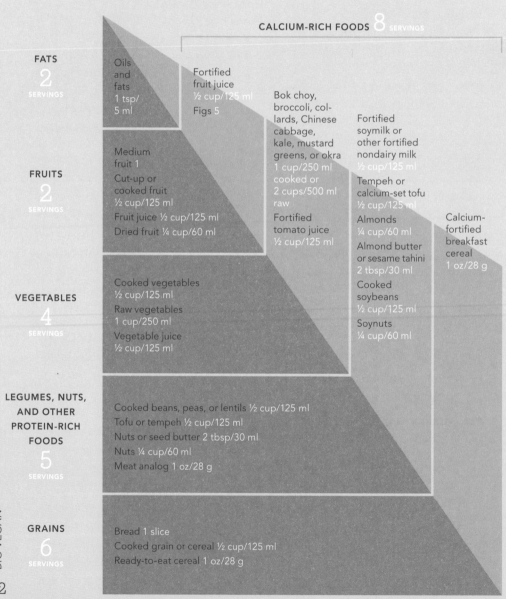

CALCIUM-RICH FOODS 8 SERVINGS

FATS 2 SERVINGS
Oils and fats 1 tsp/ 5 ml

Fortified fruit juice ½ cup/125 ml
Figs 5

Bok choy, broccoli, collards, Chinese cabbage, kale, mustard greens, or okra 1 cup/250 ml cooked or 2 cups/500 ml raw
Fortified tomato juice ½ cup/125 ml

Fortified soymilk or other fortified nondairy milk ½ cup/125 ml
Tempeh or calcium-set tofu ½ cup/125 ml
Almonds ¼ cup/60 ml
Almond butter or sesame tahini 2 tbsp/30 ml
Cooked soybeans ½ cup/125 ml
Soynuts ¼ cup/60 ml

Calcium-fortified breakfast cereal 1 oz/28 g

FRUITS 2 SERVINGS
Medium fruit 1
Cut-up or cooked fruit ½ cup/125 ml
Fruit juice ½ cup/125 ml
Dried fruit ¼ cup/60 ml

VEGETABLES 4 SERVINGS
Cooked vegetables ½ cup/125 ml
Raw vegetables 1 cup/250 ml
Vegetable juice ½ cup/125 ml

LEGUMES, NUTS, AND OTHER PROTEIN-RICH FOODS 5 SERVINGS
Cooked beans, peas, or lentils ½ cup/125 ml
Tofu or tempeh ½ cup/125 ml
Nuts or seed butter 2 tbsp/30 ml
Nuts ¼ cup/60 ml
Meat analog 1 oz/28 g

GRAINS 6 SERVINGS
Bread 1 slice
Cooked grain or cereal ½ cup/125 ml
Ready-to-eat cereal 1 oz/28 g

The pyramid on the facing page was developed by Virginia Messina, MPH, RD, member of the ADA's Vegetarian Nutrition Dietetic Practice Group. It's a nice, visual way to understand healthful eating, with a special emphasis on calcium, which can be an issue in vegan diets.

Protein

The single biggest myth about vegetarian and vegan diets is that they don't contain enough protein. Cows are vegans and build all that muscle mass and make all that milk with only plant-based proteins! We aren't set up to digest a diet of grass, but we can get all the protein we need from plants. Proteins are made up of twenty-two different amino acids, and of those, nine must be supplied by food. These are called the "essential" amino acids. The remaining amino acids can be made by the body. The misunderstanding about vegan diets being protein-poor came about because animal foods have all nine essential amino acids, while plant foods contain varying proportions. That led to the theory of "protein combining," put forward by Frances Moore Lappé in her book *Diet for a Small Planet* (1971). In the book, Ms. Lappé developed the idea that if beans have one set of amino acids and whole grains have another, combining the two would form a complete protein. To this day, people think that plant foods must be combined carefully for our bodies to get complete protein. This has been proven to be unnecessary, and Ms. Lappé has done her best to set the record straight since then. It turns out that all plant-based amino acids count as part of complete

protein, and when eaten over the course of the day they add up to usable, nourishing protein.

It is instructional to look at protein-per-calorie ratios when comparing proteins. Per 100 calories, spinach has 13 grams, broccoli has 10.6, and tofu has 11.1. In contrast, Cheddar cheese has 6.4 grams, ground/minced beef has 8, and chicken has 12.5. That means that 400 calories of spinach has twice as much protein as 400 calories of cheese—but everyone thinks of cheese as a rich source of protein. All plant foods contain a little protein, so if you are eating sufficient calories with plant foods alone, you can easily hit your RDA of protein unless you are really eating junk. Even if you subsisted on plates full of vegetables, as long as you got enough calories, you would probably get enough protein. You would, of course, lack a lot of other important nutrients, but you would not be short on protein.

PROTEIN IN SOME VEGAN FOODS	
Food	Protein
½ cup/100 g **extra-firm tofu**	19.9 g
1 cup/240 g **cooked chickpeas**	14.5 g
3 tbsp **tahini paste**	8.1 g
2 slices **whole-wheat/ wholemeal bread**	5.4 g
½ cup/80 g **cooked brown rice**	4.5 g
1 medium/175 g **baked potato**	4 g
½ cup/80 g **rolled oats**	3 g
1 cup/160 g **raw broccoli**	2.6 g
½ cup/120 ml **soymilk**	2.5 to 4 g
1 medium **banana**	1.2 g

Fats

Just like everybody else, vegans need to keep an eye on fats. Because plants are naturally low in saturated fat, you don't have that to worry about. However, because plant-based fats are just as calorie-dense as any other fat, keep your consumption under control. There are many schools of thought about fat, ranging from those experts who think you should keep it extremely low to the Mediterranean diet—where good fats are used more liberally. I'm more in tune with the latter, which has plenty of great research backing it up; just look to Oldways, a great group that promotes ancient ways of eating with current science. If you are trying to lose weight, though, reducing fat is a good place to start. You can always modify recipes to use less oil; just cut the quantity in half and see how it comes out.

You might have heard that coconut oil is an unhealthful fat, and therefore you'll be surprised to see it in this book. In fact, the fats in coconut are classified as saturated like animal fats, but they are different in some crucial ways. Unrefined coconut oil is rich in medium-chain triglycerides, which the body burns more like carbohydrates. It can play a role in a healthy vegan diet, when eaten in moderation.

Essential Fatty Acids

To maximize production of DHA and EPA (healthful omega-3 fatty acids), vegans should include good sources of alpha-linolenic acid in their diets. These include flax seeds, flax seed oil, canola oil, tofu, soybeans, and walnuts, and to a lesser extent, green leafy vegetables.

If not taking supplements, adult males need 2.2 to 5.3 g per day and adult women need 1.8 to 4.4 g omega-3s in the form of ALA. The omega-3s in fatty fish are actually extracted from algae that the fish consume. The salmon eats smaller fish that eat smaller fish that eat algae, and that original, plant-based source is where all the good fats come from! Supplement manufacturers are now making an omega-3 supplement extracted only from algae. The omega-3s in all animal foods originally come from either algae or grass or greens.

Ideally, you should be eating plenty of foods from the list below, but if you don't always hit your mark, consider supplements.

OMEGA-3 SOURCES

Food	Omega-3
¼ cup/30 g **chopped walnuts**	2,655 mg
1 tsp **flax seed oil**	2,400 mg
3 oz/85 g **firm tofu**	814 mg
1 tsp **ground flax seed**	570 mg
1 tsp **walnut oil**	470 mg
1 tsp **canola oil**	411 mg
¼ cup/30 g **pecans**	240 mg
1 medium **avocado**	221 mg
1 cup/175 g **cooked kale**	130 mg
3 oz/85 g **tempeh**	120 mg
1 cup/160 g **cooked broccoli**	92.8 mg

B_{12}, the Bacteria Vitamin

The most controversial vitamin in the vegan diet is B_{12} (thiamine). It is made by bacteria and is not present in any food unless that food has been a host to B_{12}-producing bacteria. The reason there is B_{12} in animal foods is because the bacteria lived in the animal's body.

Before there were water-treatment plants, we probably got B_{12} and the bacteria that make it from unsanitary water. Vegans have no plant-based sources of B_{12} except fortified foods, nutritional yeast, and supplements. B_{12} deficiencies in the general population often arise from poor absorption, so anyone with bad digestion is at risk of not getting enough B_{12} and other nutrients. Make sure to keep a balance of good bacteria in the gut to help with that. People who drink a lot of alcohol, take antibiotics, or suffer from depression (as well as women on birth control pills) should take extra care to get plenty of B_{12}.

B_{12} is so important to your brain and nervous system that you should make sure that you are getting 2 to 3 mcg (micrograms) every day. Nutritionists recommend that practicing vegans get 10 mcg to make sure enough is absorbed. Nutritional yeast, fortified nondairy milks, and supplements can make it very easy to do.

B_{12} SOURCES

Food	B_{12}
2 tbsp **nutritional yeast, large flake**	8 mcg
1 cup/240 ml **fortified soymilk**	about 3 mcg

Calcium and Vitamin D

Calcium is crucial to your bone health and much more. It is essential to muscle contraction, hormone secretion, and the nervous system. You may not realize that your body is constantly remodeling your bones, taking calcium out and putting it back in, to keep proper levels circulating throughout your body. Animal foods are very acidic. If your body has an acidic environment because you drink a lot of alcohol or caffeine (for example), you excrete more calcium. Eating a lot of vegetables and less animal foods makes you more alkaline, which decreases calcium loss. Calcium needs change throughout your lifetime, but for men and women between 18 and 50 years old, 1,000 mgs per day is recommended. Vegans have to be mindful that they get enough calcium in addition to the vitamin D that is its partner in remineralizing bones. Exposing your skin to the sun for 5 to 30 minutes, at least twice a week, is thought to give you enough vitamin D (but this is compromised by the widespread use of sunscreen!). You need 5 mcg per day, so if you don't get out in the sun, you should eat fortified foods or take supplements.

CALCIUM SOURCES

Food	Calcium
2 tbsp **blackstrap molasses/treacle**	400 mg
1 cup/175 g **cooked collard greens**	357 mg
1 cup/240 ml **calcium-fortified orange juice**	300 mg
4 oz/115 g **silken tofu, processed with calcium sulfate**	200 to 330 mg
1 cup/240 ml **soymilk or rice milk, commercial, calcium-fortified, plain**	200 to 300 mg
1 cup/175 g **cooked kale**	179 mg
2 tbsp **tahini paste**	128 mg
¼ cup/30 g **whole almonds**	91 mg

Iron

You need iron, especially if you are a woman of childbearing age. The recommended daily intake is 13 mg per day for women, 10 mg per day for other adults. Throughout this book, you will see recipes that call for a cast-iron pan. Vegans would do well to cook in cast iron almost exclusively, as this adds nutritional iron to food. Foods like tomato sauce/puree, because of the acids in the tomatoes and the long simmering time, will go from 0.6 mg to 5.7 mg in a 3-ounce serving when cooked in cast iron. Beans and greens are good food sources of iron. Always eat some foods that contain vitamin C when you eat foods high in iron, to help you absorb it.

IRON SOURCES

Food	Iron
1 cup/170 g **edamame**	3.5 mg
1 cup/300 g **cooked soybeans**	8.8 mg
2 tbsp **blackstrap molasses/treacle**	7.0 mg
1 cup/250 g **cooked lentils**	6.6 mg
1 cup/300 g **cooked kidney beans**	5.2 mg
1 cup/300 g **cooked chickpeas**	4.7 mg
1 cup/300 g **cooked lima beans**	4.5 mg
1 cup/175 g **cooked Swiss chard/silverbeet**	4.0 mg
1 cup/175 g **boiled spinach**	6.4 mg
1 tbsp **tahini paste**	3.1 mg

Vegan Foods You Should Know

Sweeteners

White sugar and high-fructose corn syrup rule the processed food world, but they don't have to rule your kitchen. To bake and cook without them, you have a lot of options. The world of sweetness falls into two categories: liquid and granular. Each one has differing balances between sucrose, fructose, maltose, and other sugar molecules, and that is where the debate begins.

Liquid sweeteners include agave, grain sweeteners (like brown rice syrup and barley malt), maple syrup, and fruit juice concentrates.

Agave syrup or nectar is used frequently in this book, because it is such a pure product. Made from the cactus variety used to make tequila, agave is a fructose-based sweetener with minimal processing. It's delicious and kind of expensive, but when you are eating just a few fabulous sweets, it's worth it.

Grain sweeteners are made from sprouted whole grains, which are rich in maltose, another kind of sugar molecule. My favorite grain sweetener is brown rice syrup, which has a caramel taste. Barley malt is a grain sweetener often used in baking bread. All grain sweeteners have strong, grainy flavors, which can be intense.

Maple syrup is the concentrated sap of the maple tree, and one of the finest sweeteners you can buy. Grade B maple syrup has a distinctive flavor and dark hue, but if you want pure sweetness, use grade A (which is also the least flavorful).

Fruit-juice concentrates, which can be as basic as the kind you add water to for juice, can be used in baking. Fruit, which is high in fructose, can also be concentrated and purified into clear or golden syrups. Whole-fruit juice concentrates are full of all the fruit's nutrients; they add a lot of flavor and acid to a recipe. Pure fruit syrups act like honey in recipes. They are difficult to find, so I didn't use any in this book. Fruit-sweetened jams and sorbets that you buy at the store are made with these refined syrups.

In general, using liquid sweeteners means subtracting some liquids in a recipe in addition to adjusting the acids so the leavening will work. You can follow the old honey advice: Subtract ¼ cup/60 ml of total liquid in a recipe for each cup/230 ml of liquid sweetener used, but that is not a hard-and-fast rule. You can do pretty well using agave or maple syrup instead of honey in recipes. As with acidic honey, you need to add ¼ tsp baking soda/bicarbonate of soda per 1 cup/230 ml of liquid sweetener to make the chemistry work.

For textures that fall between liquid and granular sugars, you have to look at palm sugar, date sugar, and various fruit pastes. Palm sugar is a moist and grainy sweetener from tropical Asia, often eaten in Thai and Vietnamese food. It's made simply by boiling the sap of the sugar palm and is sometimes called coconut sugar. It is a really delicious, nuanced sweetener. The jaggery or *gur* of India is another traditional and whole sweetener made from boiled sugarcane juice. Look for chunks of it in Indian groceries and use it in curries and sauces that call for a little brown sugar.

Granular and other dry sweeteners include cane and beet sugars, granular fructose, and maple sugar. The vegan issue with white cane sugar is that 20 percent of the white cane sugar sold in the United States is purified using cow-bone char as a filter. That means that an animal product was used in its production, even though none of the animal material remains in the sugar.

It's up to you if this is a problem for you personally—some people don't care as much about this one as they do about eggs and dairy. Another aspect to the sugar debate is in the refined qualities of the end product. Taking sugarcane's whole juice and stripping away everything but pure sucrose makes it a very un-whole food. There are many forms of cane sweeteners, which all attempt to be a little more complete than sugar while still being sweet. Rapadura is the least refined of the cane products and consists of whole cane juice, dried and pulverized. It has a light molasses flavor and does not melt or get creamy like other granular sweeteners, but it can be a great whole sweetener. Mexican *piloncillo*, often sold molded into little cones for grating, is also made from whole cane juice. Beige, granulated sugars like Florida Crystals and dried cane juice are slightly refined but have a little more of the molasses that is removed from white sugar, and they are not purified with bone char. Vegan versions of white, powdered, and brown sugars have become available, and they are often labeled as organic as well. Nutritionally they are the same, they behave the same in recipes, and they taste the same as their less-expensive commercial counterparts.

GRIND YOUR OWN POWDERED SUGAR

If you can't find a vegan powdered sugar, grind a vegan white sugar in the blender, mixing in 2 tbsp of cornstarch/corn flour per 1 cup/110 g. Don't try to grind too much at a time, or it will be hard to get it as fine as you need it to be.

Oils

You will notice that the recipes in this book depend on two workhorses of the kitchen: extra-virgin olive oil and canola oil. These are considered the most healthful oils for cooking, and each has different uses. Extra-virgin olive oil is a lower-heat oil, so it is a good sauté or salad oil, but it is not for high-heat stir-frying. It's also very flavorful and pairs best with non-Asian foods. Canola oil is a neutral, flavorless oil that can be used with higher heats. It's great for stir-frying, curries, and sweet baking, where the other flavors should dominate.

Beyond these two oils, your pantry should contain some toasted sesame oil, hot or chile-infused sesame oil, cold-press corn oil, and coconut oil. Sesame oil is a nutty, very flavorful oil that gives Chinese food a distinctive taste. It's a very low-heat oil, so don't stir-fry with it. Hot sesame oil is used as a seasoning. Cold-press corn oil is an invaluable ingredient for its buttery taste. It's pricey, but a little bit gives your vegan baking a hint of butter flavor, keeping it from being flat tasting. If you can't find it, use a buttery olive oil or nut oil or canola oil. Coconut oil, which is emerging from under the cloud of nutritional suspicion, is a healthful, solid fat. I recommend reading up on coconut, if you have questions about its chemistry. For our purposes, coconut oil acts like butter, making phyllo desserts crisp and rich, and pie crusts flaky. If you don't mind a hint of coconut flavor, buy unrefined; for a neutral taste, go for refined. If you don't want to use it in baking, use vegan margarine.

In some baking recipes, Earth Balance buttery sticks are the best fat. You can use other margarines, but Earth Balance is the brand that combines the more healthful, cleaner fats and flavors and works the best as a substitute for butter. The hydrogenated and trans fats in some margarines are worse than lard, so avoid any trace of them.

If you have room in your fridge, walnut, hazelnut, cold-press peanut, and other nut oils are fabulous additions to your repertoire. A drizzle of a flavorful nut oil and a squeeze of lemon are all you need to dress some greens with intense flavor. Pumpkin seed oil is a dark green elixir of *pepita* flavor. The upside is that all these oils are chock-full of healthful fats, delivering omega-3s and other goodies. For maximum flavor, look for oils made from toasted nuts.

Flax and hemp oils are great sources for essential fats, so it is a good idea to keep a bottle in the refrigerator to dress salads and warm grains. Some people like to take these in supplement form, but as long as they taste good, why not get the satisfaction of eating them?

Nuts and Seeds

Nuts and seeds are the fun foods of the plant kingdom. While many of your omnivorous friends have crossed them off their list as being "too high-fat," you know better. Dropping all those fatty animal foods means that you can eat nuts and seeds to your heart's content. Nuts and seeds have high satiety factors, which means they satisfy and keep you full longer than the same amount of calories from other sources. The good fats, phytosterols and lignans and other heart-healthy compounds or chemicals in nuts and seeds, are exactly what your body needs. Keep your nuts and seeds in the refrigerator or freezer to prevent their oils from going rancid. Look for organic nuts whenever possible, especially when buying peanuts. We think of peanuts as a nut, but they are a legume/pulse that grows underground, and conventionally grown ones are often heavily treated with both pesticides and fungicides.

Flax seeds are a unique part of the vegan pantry, providing essential nutrition and acting as an egg replacer in baking. Flax and flax oil provide omega-3 fatty acids, so adding a little to recipes is a good thing. A splash of flax oil in a salad dressing or a spoon or two of ground flax seeds will help keep your essential fats at a good level. When ground and mixed with water, flax seeds form an egg-like paste that will bind baked goods and help hold the bubbles that leaveners produce.

Flours

A whole-foods life includes whole grains and whole-grain/wholemeal flours. Whole grains contain all the minerals and fiber that nature provides, and we all need a minimum of three servings a day—but more is better. Like nuts, whole grains contain healthful fats, which can be affected by heat and air. Keep whole flours in jars or heavy zip-top bags in the refrigerator or freezer. If you don't have room there, only buy what you will use up in a month, and keep the flour in a cool, dark place.

The most important thing to understand about flours is that they vary in gluten content. Gluten is the springy protein that traps gases and then stiffens into the structure of bread, cake, or pastry. For

SCOOP-AND-LEVEL MEASURING

In this book, I measure flours by the scoop-and-level method, which means that a cup of flour weighs a little more than it would if you had sifted it first. I don't believe that an average baker is going to get out a sifter and sift flour into a cup. It just doesn't happen, and pretending that home bakers will do it sets them up to fail.

bread making, we want higher-gluten flour, but when we make pastry, we want lower-gluten flour. Flours labeled as bread/strong flour or simply as whole-wheat/wholemeal flour will be made from high-gluten, hard winter wheat. Because whole-wheat/wholemeal flour still has the bran and germ in it when it is ground, the percentage of gluten is lower than it is in refined flour. To make up for the higher density and achieve good breads, we can add some higher-gluten flour. Gluten flour is simply made from the wheat protein, and a little added to whole-grain bread recipes helps them hold a good rise and also adds to the protein content. Vegans also use gluten flour to make seitan and to bind burgers and loaves, so keep some in the pantry.

Whole-wheat/wholemeal pastry/soft-wheat flour is lower-gluten flour and is best for muffins, cakes, pie crusts, and other applications that are meant to be tender. It's also finely ground, with none of the flaky bran that some stone-ground whole-wheat/wholemeal flours have. While the world of flours is worth exploring, for the purposes of this book, I've only used one other flour besides wheat, and that is spelt.

Spelt is a fabulous, medium-gluten flour. If you can't get whole-wheat/wholemeal pastry/soft-wheat flour, you can use spelt. Kamut and farro flours are also delicious members of the wheat family that can be tolerated by some people who are allergic to or intolerant of conventional wheat. However, all of them contain gluten and are not safe for celiacs or other gluten-intolerant people.

In this book, I use a judicious amount of unbleached wheat flour in some of the recipes. My goal is to make foods that strike a balance between nutrition and flavor, and that are comparable to their nonvegan counterparts. You should eat desserts occasionally, so it's okay if you don't make them 100 percent whole-wheat/wholemeal. You should be getting your whole grains all day long, and a slice of cake is a treat that should be light and fluffy and even a little buzzy with carbs.

Soy

Soy is an important part of a balanced vegan diet. You don't have to eat it every day, but unless you are allergic to it, it's a great food for you. In recent years, anti-soy advocates have been spreading rumors that soy causes men and boys to become feminine and might accelerate the growth of breast cancer. These are all theories based on the very weak estrogen-like substances (phytoestrogens) in soy. As of this writing, an abundance of evidence refutes these theories. Most experts say that eating a few servings of soy a day is really good for you and is associated with lowered risks of many kinds of health problems.

The many forms of soy include soymilk, whole green soybeans (edamame), black and yellow soybeans, soy flour and protein powders, tempeh, tofu, miso, soy sauces, and the many mock meats made from soy protein. Fortified soymilk is a recommended source of several nutrients that vegans need, so it is easy to get off on the right foot with your B vitamins and calcium when you have soymilk with cereal for breakfast.

Mastering the art of cooking with tofu is easy—just remember that there are two basic kinds of tofu with two different textures. For creamy dressings and puddings, silken tofu is the best. It is made like a pudding by thickening whole soymilk. The other kind of tofu, sometimes called Chinese-style, *nigari* tofu, or just firm tofu, is made by adding nigari (a calcium salt that coagulates the soymilk) and then lifting the curds out of the "whey," which makes a product with a spongy texture and much less water. You want this spongy, firm tofu for sturdy stir-fry cubes, chewy crumbles in scrambles, and slabs that can stand up to the grill.

WORKING WITH TOFU

Throughout this book, you will see instructions to "drain and press" tofu. There are now tofus out there that are already so firmly pressed that you hardly need to do much more than pat them dry. For regular, firm tofu, wrap the block in a kitchen towel, then place it on a cutting board and put another board on top. Set a heavy pot or another weight on top of that. For most recipes, 10 to 15 minutes is plenty of time, but if you leave it longer it will just keep getting thinner and denser.

Tempeh is another soy food, although it is often made with additions like grains or veggies for flavor. It's basically whole beans that have been cooked and inoculated with a culture, which ferments the beans slightly and holds them in a chewy cake. That bit of fermentation makes many of the nutrients in soy more absorbable and the beans easier to digest. Some people find the chewy, nutty taste and texture more appealing than soft tofu, so work it into your rotation for some variety.

Misos also benefit from fermentation. Of Japanese origin, miso is a salty paste that is fermented long enough to break out amino acids and antioxidants that are bound up in whole soy. It's a miracle food, and there is good evidence that it protects against cancer and radiation damage. It also contains active enzymes that aid digestion, so don't boil miso soup or you will inactivate the active enzymes. White miso is the mildest and sweetest miso, and red and brown rice misos are stronger tasting, while dark misos like *hatcho* are very intense.

Soy sauces are delicious condiments, full of umami and, of course, salt. They are comparable to wine in that you get what you pay for: Cheap soy sauces are made quickly with soy flour and chemicals, while good-quality tamari and *shoyu* are made with whole soy and brewed to ferment and develop rich flavors. Shoyu, or most soy sauce, is made with wheat as well as soy and has a characteristic wheat flavor. You can buy wheat-free tamari, but don't assume it is wheat-free unless it says so.

Nutritional Yeast

If there is one food that is identified as Vegan with a capital *V*, it is nutritional yeast, also known as *Saccharomyces cerevisiae*. It comes in larger flakes or fine powder, and it has a cheesy taste and gives foods a boost in umami. It's not brewer's yeast, which is brown and much stronger tasting.

Nutritional yeast is grown on molasses/treacle that has been enriched with minerals and bacteria-grown B_{12}. It's the only vegan, food-based source of B_{12}, other than supplements or enriched foods like soymilk.

Nutritional yeast is 52 percent complete protein and packed with B vitamins, minerals, fiber, and even some trace compounds like beta-glucans, glutathione, trehalose, and mannan—all of which are good for balancing blood sugar. It is also high in chromium, a big helper for blood-sugar balance. Vegetarians, diabetics, and women on birth control pills are all prone to B_{12} deficiency. Otherwise known as thiamine, it is necessary for the nervous system. Nutritional yeast is also high in B_6, which supports antibodies and red blood cells, as well as your nervous and musculoskeletal systems. B_{12} prevents nerve damage, anemia, digestive problems, infertility, and depression.

Just 2 tbsp a day is all you need to meet your RDA for B vitamins. Overall, the miracle of nutritional yeast is that it boosts immunity, lowers cholesterol, prevents cancer, and supports blood-sugar balance.

Sea Vegetables and Agar

You'll see recipes calling for various sea vegetables in this book, from *nori* to *wakame*. Vegans need to get familiar with these, since they are awash in all the healthful minerals of the sea. Calcium, carotenoids, vitamin C, and a host of antioxidants are mixed with digestible protein and lots of filling fiber in sea vegetables. They are a tasty part of many Asian and fusion dishes, from sushi to the Sea Veggie and Brown Rice Pasties (page 350).

Agar is a unique sea vegetable, one that you will use like gelatin. Agar comes in bars, flakes, and powders, but for most of the recipes in this book, agar flakes are the preferred form. Flakes are easy to get and use and seem to give the most consistent results. Powdered agar is convenient, but magazine editors tell me that they get the most complaints about recipes with agar powder—they turn out completely differently in different parts of the country.

MEASURING AGAR

In general, 1 agar bar (7 g) is equal to 2 tbsp of flakes or 2 tsp of powder. That amount is enough to gel 2 cups/ 16 oz of low-acid liquid, so if you are working with something more acidic, use more agar.

How to Really Practice the Vegan Diet

You have in your hands a big book of recipes, many of them simple and quick. Still, few people these days cook three meals a day. If you are looking for weight management in your life, you will have to adopt some plant-collecting strategies. Think like a hunter-gatherer who doesn't hunt, and collect real, unaltered veggies, grains, and fruits, and you will be on track. Everybody is unique. You may be going vegan to get skinny, so you will want to steer toward the leanest way. On the other hand, pale and gaunt vegans give the diet a bad name, so if you have a hard time keeping weight on, eat more nutrient-dense foods like nuts, avocados, and soy.

Big Breakfasts

Even if you forgot to make the Hemp-Cherry Muesli (page 60) or Fruit-Sweetened Chai-Spice Granola with Pecans (page 66) this week, do not ever skip breakfast. Starting your day hungry sets you up to feel lethargic, and you will probably overeat later. If you are eating for weight management, you should stop eating when you are done with dinner, and when you get up in the morning, you should be hungry. It's OK to exercise first, but breakfast shortly afterward is a must to refuel your body and repair the microscopic tears in muscle caused by exercise. A serving or two of some kind of whole grain and a large amount of fruit is essential, and protein is a good addition to keep you feeling full. This can be as simple as a purchased whole-grain cereal or some leftover cooked grain or some toast. Finding a good protein-enriched packaged cereal and eating it with fortified soymilk and fruit is a decent strategy for making a fast and easy morning.

Snacks

Not every hunger must be answered with a vegan sweet. A plant-based diet means packing some fruits, veggies, and other high-volume, low-calorie foods for hunger attacks. Nuts, seeds, and dried fruit are portable, easy, and nutrient dense. That means just a few pack a caloric punch, though, so if you feel ravenous, eat a handful and then fill up with vegetables and lean whole grains.

Lunch

If you have been indulging a lot, a great fallback meal is a big salad. I know that it is a stereotype that vegetarians only eat salads. We should eat a lot of them, though, if only to set an example! When navigating the lunch counter at your job, you may find few vegan options. Try to bring food as often as possible so you don't get in a nutritional rut with that one bean burrito over and over. Bringing food can be as simple as a bagged salad with tahini and whole-wheat/wholemeal bread, or you can cook an extra serving the night before and have "planned-overs." Think creatively about your options, as you may be able to bring some nuts or marinated tofu slabs to add to a commissary salad or soup, making a meal from someone else's side dish.

Dinner

If you have eaten on the run all day, dinner is when you get to sit down and focus on your food. If you have eaten simple and light during the day, you deserve to sit down with something satisfying and delicious. This is the time to cook and share your food with family and friends. Whether you try one of the fast sandwiches or a more elaborate main course, take the time to eat mindfully. Even vegans can fall into mindless eating. Preparing your food with care and eating it with focus and enjoyment will do more for your health than just keeping your weight under control.

On the other hand, if you had a decadent lunch with dessert and didn't move from the desk all day, tonight might be a good time for a vegetable soup with a salad and a walk around the block. It's all about balance. The balanced vegan life is a high-energy experience, and if you do it right, worrying about weight issues may just become a thing of the past.

Pantry Staples

Call them pantry essentials, basics, or whatever you want. Following is a collection of DIY recipes for the vegan essentials that you will want for great cooking. Sure, you can buy seitan and mock duck, but making your own is really quite easy. And amping up the beefiness for a mock beef is a neat trick to know how to do. Baking some marinated tofu or simmering some lentil "sausages" will stock you up for multiple meals. Don't buy factory-made mock meats when you can make your own with easy-to-pronounce, real-food ingredients. And you can freeze them for later.

The recipes for nut "cheeses" are simple and direct and, in most cases, soy free. The only soy "cheese" that I use in this book is the "cream cheese." Newer and better soy cheeses come out every day, and you can use those without recipes from me. In this book I'm making "cheeses" with a whole-food base, like cashews or tofu. Soy cheese is not trying too hard to be dairy cheese; instead it stands alone as good food. A jar of the Almond-Cashew "Chèvre" (page 44) in the fridge means you are ready to make pizza, sandwiches, and many of the foods you once made with cheese. Give them a try—you will be pleasantly surprised.

Throughout this book, vegetable stock is added to recipes for a little more veg flavor. If you want to make your own stocks, these recipes make great ones. Stock freezes beautifully, and if you stock up (so to speak!), you can add it to all your recipes with great success.

12 large dried mushrooms, such as button or portobello

6 garlic cloves, halved

1 in/2.5 cm fresh ginger, chopped

4 black tea bags

¾ cup/180 ml shao xing rice wine

7 tbsp/105 ml dark miso

½ cup/150 g cooked chickpeas

¼ cup/60 ml tamari or soy sauce

2 tbsp tahini paste

2 tbsp tomato paste/puree

1 tbsp toasted sesame oil

2 tsp Kitchen Bouquet/ Browning Sauce

2 cups/255 g gluten flour

½ tsp onion powder

½ tsp granulated garlic

MAKES ABOUT
2 LB / 910 G

This version of homemade seitan is extra hearty and filled with umami and flavor boosters. The bouncy strands of gluten in the mix cook to a chewy, porous texture that has been standing in for meat for hundreds of years in China. It's great in the Tibetan "Beef" Fried Noodles (page 395) or just about any recipe that calls for beef.

Mock Beef

1 In a 2-qt/2-L pot, combine 8 cups/2 L water, the mushrooms, garlic cloves, and ginger. Bring to a simmer and cover; cook on low heat for 20 minutes to make a stock. Uncover, remove from the heat, add the tea bags, and let them steep for 4 minutes. Discard the tea bags. Measure out 1 cup/240 ml of the liquid and set it aside to cool to room temperature. Whisk the wine and 3 tbsp of the miso into the remaining stock and mushrooms and cover to keep warm.

2 In a blender, pulse the chickpeas to mince them, then add the remaining ¼ cup/60 ml miso, the tamari, tahini, tomato paste/puree, sesame oil, and Kitchen Bouquet. Process until smooth. Add the cup of cooled stock gradually to make a smooth puree. In a large bowl, mix together the flour, onion powder, and granulated garlic. Dump in the contents of the blender and stir to mix. It will quickly become a dough; knead it for about 5 minutes, until springy and spongy. Divide the dough into 16 pieces. Pull and flatten as much as you can to form 4-in-/10-cm-long pieces before dropping them into the warm stock with the mushrooms. Bring to a very low simmer, preferably not bubbling except around the edges, watching carefully that it doesn't boil. Cover and cook for 1 hour, until firm.

3 Take the pot off the heat and let the contents cool completely, then refrigerate the seitan in the cooking liquid for up to 1 week. To use, wring out each piece and slice or chop as needed.

2 cups/255 g gluten flour

½ cup/65 g
chickpea flour

2 tbsp nutritional yeast

2 tbsp dark miso

7 tbsp/105 ml tamari or
soy sauce

1 tbsp vegetarian
bouillon/stock paste
or granules

2 tsp toasted sesame oil

4 garlic cloves

3 bay leaves

MAKES APPROXIMATELY
1¾ LB / 800 G

Making your own seitan is easy, now that gluten flour is readily available. Make a big batch on the weekend and put it in the slow-cooker, then you can keep some in the refrigerator and freeze some for later. Slice or tear the logs into pieces and simmer them in flavored broth or sauce, if desired.

Mock Duck or Seitan

1 In a stand mixer with a dough hook or in a large bowl by hand, mix together the gluten flour, chickpea flour, and yeast. Measure 1½ cups/360 ml water. Put the miso in a cup and whisk in a little of the water to make a smooth paste. Whisk in the remaining water, 3 tbsp of the tamari, the bouillon/stock paste, and the sesame oil. Stir the mixture into the dry ingredients, then knead for 2 minutes, until spongy.

2 Cut two 10-in-/25-cm-long pieces of cheesecloth/muslin. Divide the dough into two pieces, then form each into an 8-in/21-cm log wrapped in cloth, smoothing the outside as well as you can. Twist the ends and tie or twist-tie to secure them well.

3 In a large pot or 2-qt/2-L slow-cooker, combine 2 qt/2 L water with the remaining ¼ cup/60 ml tamari, the garlic, and bay leaves. Bring to a simmer, then add the seitan bundles. Simmer for 2 hours on the stovetop or for 5 hours in the slow-cooker, until firm to the touch. Let the seitan and broth cool to room temperature before unwrapping. This freezes well for up to 3 months.

8 oz/225 g tempeh

2 tbsp maple syrup

1 tbsp canola oil,
plus more for pan

½ tsp liquid smoke
flavoring

½ tsp salt

MAKES 8 SLICES

Sweet and smoky tempeh strips are a nice way to sub for bacon at breakfast, with way less grease. The chewy, nutty tempeh gets crisp edges but stays moist in the middle. Tempeh is an ancient food invented in Indonesia that will nourish you naturally.

Smoky Maple-Tempeh "Bacon"

1 Set up a steamer and bring the water to a simmer. Steam the tempeh for 5 minutes to moisten it, then let it cool completely. Thinly slice the tempeh lengthwise into eight strips. In a bread pan/tin, whisk together 2 tbsp water with the maple syrup, 1 tbsp oil, smoke flavoring, and salt. Add the tempeh and gently mix to coat without breaking the strips. Marinate overnight in the refrigerator.

2 To cook, heat a large cast-iron frying pan over medium heat. When hot, add a drizzle of oil, then transfer the tempeh slices to the pan, preventing them from touching. Fry until the glaze is absorbed and the slices are browned. Remove to plates and serve hot.

8 oz/225 g tempeh

2 tsp extra-virgin olive oil

¼ cup/30 g minced onion

2 garlic cloves, minced

1 tsp chili powder

1 tsp paprika,
preferably smoked

1 tsp red pepper flakes

½ tsp ground cumin

½ tsp fennel seeds

½ tsp dried oregano

1 tsp salt

4 tsp dark miso

¼ cup/60 ml white wine

¼ cup/30 g gluten flour

Vegetable oil spray

MAKES ABOUT
2 CUPS / 450 G
CRUMBLES

Once you try this tasty, spicy mock chorizo, you will want to keep some around in the fridge for impromptu tacos and burritos, or to adorn rice and beans. The Spanish Fideua Pasta with Saffron (page 376) calls for 1½ cups of this, leaving you with ½ cup for lunch the next day.

Tempeh "Chorizo"

1 Set up a steamer and bring the water to a simmer. Chop the tempeh into 2-in/5-cm pieces and steam them for 5 minutes to moisten them. Let the tempeh cool until it stops steaming, then transfer it to a food processor and grind it into a chunky mince.

2 In a medium saucepan over medium heat, heat the olive oil. Add the onion and cook until softened. Add the garlic, chili powder, paprika, pepper flakes, cumin, fennel, and oregano and cook for 1 minute. Add the tempeh and salt and stir, cooking for a few minutes to brown.

3 In a small cup, mash the miso with the wine until well dispersed. Sprinkle the flour over the tempeh mixture in the pan and stir, then stir in the liquids. Stir vigorously over the heat until the mixture is quite stiff. Transfer the mixture to a large bowl and let it cool slightly. (To cook later, store tightly covered in the refrigerator.)

4 To cook, either crumble the mixture and sauté it over high heat to brown, or form two disks from 2 tbsp of the mixture. Spritz a baking sheet/tray with vegetable oil spray and put the "chorizo" disks on it, then spritz the "chorizo." Bake at 400°F/200°C/gas 6 for 20 minutes, turning the patties at 10 minutes, until they are browned.

½ cup/120 ml Basic Vegetable Stock (page 49)

¼ cup/60 ml tamari or soy sauce

1 tbsp agave syrup

1 tbsp toasted sesame oil

2 small, whole dried mushrooms (any kind)

12 oz/340 g firm tofu, drained and pressed (see page 68)

Vegetable oil

3 tbsp nutritional yeast

MAKES 8 SLICES

Dried mushrooms and nutritional yeast give this savory tofu a meaty crust, as well as a sprinkling of vitamins and minerals. Cooking it this way really concentrates the flavors and drives them just a little deeper into the tofu.

Savory Tofu "Steaks"

1 In a small saucepan, combine the stock, tamari, agave, sesame oil, and mushrooms. Put the pan over high heat and bring to a boil, then reduce to a simmer and cook for about 5 minutes, until slightly reduced. Slice the tofu lengthwise into four slabs, then cut those in half to make eight squares. Place the tofu in a shallow heat-resistant bowl and pour the hot marinade over them. Let cool to room temperature, then turn the tofu in the marinade, and cover tightly. Refrigerate it overnight, turning the tofu a few times.

2 Preheat the oven to 400°F/200°C/gas 6. Spread some vegetable oil on a baking sheet/tray. Drain the tofu and sprinkle half of the yeast over the tofu pieces. (Save the marinade and refrigerate it for another batch, or discard.) Transfer the tofu to the baking sheet/tray, coated-side down, then sprinkle the remaining yeast over the tofu.

3 Bake for 20 minutes, flip the "steaks," and bake until golden, 10 minutes more. Let cool in the pan on a rack. Store, tightly covered, for up to 1 week in the refrigerator.

8 oz/225 g
sea vegetable tempeh

½ cup/60 g unbleached
all-purpose/plain flour

2 tbsp nutritional yeast

2 tsp baking powder

½ tsp salt

½ tsp freshly cracked
black pepper

¼ cup/60 ml Basic
Vegetable Stock
(page 49)

2 tbsp Dijon mustard

1 garlic clove, crushed

1 tsp white miso

1½ cups/170 g panko or
other dry bread crumbs

Canola oil or
vegetable oil spray

MAKES 8 STICKS

You can call these sea sticks if you want to be more accurate, especially if you use tempeh made with sea vegetables mixed right in. You can also use regular tempeh. Serve these hot in sandwiches, or with a tartar sauce for dipping. They have a crispy crust and chewy center and make great finger food for kids and adults alike.

Crunchy "Fish" Sticks

1 Set up a steamer and bring the water to a simmer. Slice the tempeh into eight sticks ½ in/12 mm thick and 4 to 5 in/10 to 12 cm long. Steam them for 5 minutes over boiling water to moisten them. Drain them on a paper towel/absorbent paper and pat dry.

2 In a large bowl, whisk together the flour, yeast, baking powder, salt, and pepper. In a cup, whisk together the stock, mustard, garlic, and miso. Spread the crumbs on a plate. Whisk the wet mixture into the flour mixture, then dredge the tempeh in it, and roll each slice in panko. Place the panko-coated pieces on a plate.

3 In a large frying pan, pour enough oil in the bottom to generously coat it. Heat the oil over high heat until shimmering, then add the tempeh pieces. When the oil returns to a sizzle, lower the heat to medium. Turn the pieces when they are crisp and browned. Alternatively, preheat the oven to 425°F/210°C/gas 7. Place a heavy baking sheet/tray in the oven for 5 minutes. Take out the sheet/tray, coat with oil spray, place the tempeh on the sheet/tray, and spritz the tempeh. Bake for 15 minutes, until lightly browned and crisp.

1 cup/250 g red lentils, soaked overnight

1 cup/155 g rolled oats

½ cup/60 g unbleached all-purpose/plain flour

½ cup/60 g gluten flour

½ cup/120 ml plain soymilk or other milk

¼ cup/10 g nutritional yeast

¼ cup/60 ml canola oil, plus more for the cloth

2 tbsp tamari or soy sauce

2 tsp liquid smoke flavoring

1 tsp salt

1 tsp dried sage

1 tsp fennel seeds

½ tsp granulated garlic

½ tsp dried oregano

½ tsp red pepper flakes

MAKES 4 "SAUSAGES"

If you crave something with the heft and chew of sausage, look no further. Liquid smoke gives these chewy, high-protein links a meaty quality, and you will love them with your morning scramble, or even sliced on a pizza.

Smoky Red Lentil "Sausages"

1 Drain the lentils and finely grind them in a food processor. Transfer the paste to a large bowl and stir in the oats, both flours, soymilk, yeast, canola oil, tamari, smoke flavoring, salt, sage, fennel, garlic, oregano, and pepper flakes. Knead to combine.

2 Set up a steamer and bring the water to a simmer. You may want to keep a teapot of hot water handy to replenish as it goes. Cut four 8-in-/20-cm-long pieces of cheesecloth/muslin. Rub oil on the cloth to prevent sticking. Form four sausages about 5 in/12 cm long. Wrap them in cheesecloth/muslin and tie the ends with string. (Alternatively, divide the mixture between four 6-oz/180-ml oiled ramekins and drizzle the tops with oil.) Steam for 1 hour, until the "sausages" are firm to the touch. Let cool before unwrapping. Store tightly wrapped in the refrigerator for up to 1 week, or freeze for up to 1 month.

1 cup/115 g raw cashews

1 acidophilus capsule (see page 520; check to make sure it is dairy free)

Canola oil

½ cup/55 g slivered/flaked blanched almonds, soaked in water overnight

1 tsp freshly squeezed lemon juice

½ tsp salt

Olive oil, for drizzling (optional)

MAKES ABOUT
1¼ CUPS / 300 G

This creamy, slightly fermented nut "cheese" is a very nutritious and tasty stand-in for a soft cheese. You can leave it soft and creamy and enjoy the active acidophilus cultures as well, or you can bake it for a firmer, sliceable cheese.

Almond-Cashew "Chèvre"

1 In a heavy-duty blender or food processor, finely grind the cashews, then add ½ cup/120 ml water and the contents of the acidophilus capsule and puree until very smooth. Transfer the mixture to a storage container or bowl and cover loosely with plastic wrap/cling film or a towel. Leave it at room temperature for 24 hours to ferment. The mixture will bubble slightly, have tiny holes in the surface, and smell lightly sour. If it is a hot day, don't leave it out any longer than 24 hours, or it may sprout mold.

2 The second day, oil an 8-oz/240-ml ramekin. Drain the almonds and puree them in a blender or food processor. Add the fermented mixture, lemon juice, and salt and process to mix. Scrape the mixture out into the oiled ramekin and either refrigerate it (for a soft texture) or bake (for a firmer texture). To bake, drizzle the top with olive oil and bake at 300°F/150°C/gas 2 for 30 minutes, until lightly toasted and dry on top. Refrigerate, tightly covered, for up to 1 week.

Canola oil

1 cup/115 g raw pine nuts

½ cup/55 g raw cashews

2 tsp freshly squeezed lemon juice

1 tsp white miso

½ tsp salt

½ cup/120 ml plain almond milk or other milk

2 tbsp cornstarch/ cornflour

MAKES
1 CUP / 295 G

If you don't have time to wait for the Almond-Cashew "Chèvre" (facing page) to ferment, you can make this quicker cheese. Pine nuts are soft enough to puree with no soaking, and rich enough to give you a cheesy, spreadable texture.

Pine Nut "Cheese"

1 Oil an 8-oz/240-ml ramekin. In a food processor, finely grind the pine nuts and cashews, then add the lemon juice, miso, and salt and process until very smooth.

2 In a small saucepan, whisk together the milk and cornstarch/ cornflour. Put the pan over medium heat and, whisking constantly, bring the mixture to a boil. As soon as it boils, it will be very thick. Cook for a few seconds, then quickly scrape the mixture into the processor with the nuts. Process and scrape down the sides, repeating until the mixture is very smooth. Transfer the "cheese" to the oiled ramekin and cover. Refrigerate, tightly covered, for up to 1 week. Slice or spread like soft cheese.

¼ cup/30 g slivered/
flaked blanched almonds

6 slices white baguette,
crusts removed

¼ tsp salt

1 tbsp nutritional yeast
(optional)

½ tsp grated lemon zest
(optional)

¼ tsp granulated garlic
(optional)

MAKES ABOUT
¾ CUP / 55 G

Sometimes you just want something on top of your
pasta or sprinkled on a salad for crunch. Bread
crumbs are actually a traditional Italian topping
that soaks up sauce and clings to pasta. This vegan
version adds the mild crunchy presence of almonds.

Almond-Crumb "Parmesan"

1 Preheat the oven to 300°F/150°C/gas 2. On a baking
sheet/tray, spread the almonds at one end of the pan and
put the bread slices at the other. Bake for 10 minutes, just to
lightly toast the almonds. If the bread is still moist enough to
sink in when you poke it in the middle, use a spatula to transfer the almonds to a bowl and return the bread to the oven
for another 5 minutes. The bread should be dry and crisp, but
not browned.

2 Put the almonds, bread, and salt in a food processor and
pulse until the nuts are finely chopped and the bread is in
large crumbs. Transfer to a small bowl, and if using yeast,
lemon zest, or garlic, stir them in. Store in a jar or tightly
sealed plastic bag in the refrigerator for up to 2 weeks.

2 tsp cold-press corn oil

¾ cup/120 g
minced shallots

½ cup/120 ml Basic
Vegetable Stock
(page 49)

2 tsp cornstarch/
cornflour

2 tbsp very smooth
carrot puree or carrot
baby food

¼ tsp salt

MAKES ABOUT
¾ CUP / 145 G

This sunny orange spread is a handy stand-in for
butter, great for spreading on toast or drizzling on
steamed veggies. Make a double batch to keep on
hand for all your buttering needs. Not for baking,
this is all about spreading, topping hot veggies,
and dolloping on plain brown rice. Carrots make a
beautiful buttery color, as well as add sweetness.

Veggie "Butter"

1 In a small frying pan, heat the oil over medium heat. Add
the shallots and stir. When the mixture starts to sizzle, reduce
to the lowest heat and stir every few minutes. Cook until the
shallots are golden and soft, about 10 minutes.

2 In a small cup, stir together the stock and cornstarch/corn-
flour. When the shallots are caramelized and shrunken, stir
the stock mixture and add it to the pan. Stir and simmer until
thickened. Stir in the carrot puree and salt and heat through.
Remove the "butter" from the heat. If desired, puree it thoroughly in a food processor, or simply use as is. Store, tightly
covered, for up to 1 week in the refrigerator.

1 large, ripe avocado

12 oz/340 g silken tofu

1 tbsp canola oil

2 tbsp freshly squeezed lemon juice

2 tsp rice vinegar

1 tsp sugar

½ tsp salt

MAKES ABOUT
1¼ CUPS / 300 ML

Most vegan "sour creams" are tofu based, so I amped up the fabulousness of this one by putting in some creamy avocado. Since you will probably be using it on top of nachos or salsa, it is a tasty and nutritious addition that works well with the flavors of Mexican cuisine.

Tofu-Avocado "Sour Cream"

In a blender or food processor, puree the avocado flesh and tofu until smooth, scraping down the sides several times to make sure all the tofu is processed. Add the oil and process until smooth, then add the lemon juice and process again, scraping down the sides. Add the vinegar, sugar, and salt and puree. Transfer the "sour cream" to a wide-mouthed jar or storage tub and refrigerate, covered, for up to 4 days.

1 tsp extra-virgin olive oil

2 onions, skin on, coarsely chopped

12 garlic cloves, smashed

8 oz/225 g shallots, skin on, coarsely chopped

1 rib celery, coarsely chopped

1 small carrot, peeled and sliced

4 large leeks, cleaned and sliced

8 oz/225 g fresh button mushrooms, halved

4 large Roma tomatoes, roughly chopped

1 big handful/45 g fresh parsley stems

10 sprigs thyme or other twiggy herb (optional)

2 small bay leaves

1½ tsp salt

1 tsp black peppercorns

MAKES ABOUT
14 CUPS / 3.4 L

Making your own stock is a great way to save money and to make sure that you use good ingredients. This makes a large enough amount for you to freeze portions for later use.

Basic Vegetable Stock

1 In a stockpot, heat the oil over medium-low heat, then add the onions, garlic, shallots, celery, and carrot. Cover and cook, stirring frequently, until the onions are soft and turning golden, about 15 minutes. Add the leeks and mushrooms and keep cooking, stirring occasionally, for about 10 minutes. Add 5 qt/4.7 L water, the tomatoes, parsley, herbs (if using), bay leaves, salt, and peppercorns. Increase the heat to medium-high and bring the stock to a simmer. Reduce to medium-low and simmer gently, covered, for 45 minutes, until the stock is flavorful.

2 Strain the liquid, but do not press on the solids—it might make the stock bitter. After straining, the liquids can be boiled to reduce, if desired, for a more intense flavor. The stock can be refrigerated for up to 6 days, covered, or frozen for up to 2 months.

5 large carrots

5 large ribs celery

2 medium parsnips

1 large onion

1 large leek, green part reserved

½ large sweet potato

6 large garlic cloves, peeled

1 tbsp extra-virgin olive oil

1 big handful/45 g fresh parsley stems

2 tbsp white miso

2 bay leaves

1 tsp salt

1 tsp peppercorns

MAKES ABOUT
10 CUPS / 2.4 L

This is a special stock, full of roasted veggie intensity, designed to go with the Roasted Vegetable Ribollita (page 234). It's a bit more effort to roast all the veggies first, but it is an exercise in building flavor. The time in the oven brings out the sweetness of the vegetables and deepens the flavor in the final stock.

Roasted Vegetable Stock

1 Preheat the oven to 425°F/220°C/gas 7. Slice the carrots, celery, parsnips, onion, white parts of the leek, and sweet potato into slices ¼ in/4 mm thick. Toss them with the garlic and oil and spread them in a roasting pan/tray and cover with foil. Roast for a total of 40 minutes, stirring halfway, until the vegetables are browned.

2 Transfer the vegetables to a large soup pot and add the leek greens, parsley, miso, bay leaves, salt, and peppercorns. Add 3 qt/2.8 L water and bring to a boil, then reduce to a low simmer. Cover and simmer gently for 40 minutes, until the stock is flavorful and golden. Strain the stock and discard the solids. Use the stock immediately or boil to reduce it for more concentrated flavor. Refrigerate, covered, for up to 1 week or freeze for up to 2 months.

1 tsp extra-virgin olive oil

1 large leek, sliced

4 small shallots, sliced

2 ribs celery, chopped

8 oz/225 g fresh button mushrooms, coarsely chopped

2 oz/55 g dried mushrooms (any kind)

½ cup/120 ml white wine, rice wine, or red wine

½ cup seasonings (such as minced ginger, garlic, lemon grass, lime leaf, thyme, rosemary, etc.)

Salt

MAKES ABOUT
6 CUPS / 1.4 L

Mushrooms, especially dried ones, are a concentrated source of umami. They also give great flavor to this stock, which is a perfect one to use in Asian soups or anything with mushrooms. Use a wine that will complement your dish, like a white for light French soups, red for a bean stew, or rice wine for Asian fare.

Mushroom Stock

1 In a large pot over medium heat, heat the oil, then sauté the leek, shallots, and celery until soft and golden. Add 9 cups/2.2 L water, the mushrooms, wine, and seasonings. Bring the liquid to a simmer, then simmer gently for 45 minutes, until the stock is flavorful.

2 Strain the stock, discarding the solids. For a more concentrated stock, simmer the liquid to reduce it to the desired strength. Season with salt after you have the desired strength. Refrigerate, covered, for up to 1 week or freeze for up to 2 months.

Breakfast

Breakfast really is the most important meal of the day. Think of it as a foundation, the base from which you spring, full of energy and inspiration. If you were building a house, you couldn't start without a solid square on which to put everything to come. Luckily, there is not as much heavy lifting involved in breakfast each day. It's easy to plan for a good square meal every day of the week. In this chapter, there are recipes for on-the-go foods that you can set up the night before, as well as tasty treats that make a weekend morning into a vegan feast.

It's no coincidence that the base of the food pyramid is made up of whole grains and that breakfast is usually grain based. That foundation of energy from complex carbohydrates will fuel you for the day ahead. Starting the day off with whole grains is smart. Whole grains burn more slowly, and the fiber keeps you fuller for longer than white products. Adding some protein and fruits or vegetables also makes that breakfast last longer.

You might be a pastry lover, or perhaps you prefer a savory style of morning meal. Both tastes are represented here, with decadent sticky buns on the sweet side and savory hashes and wraps on the other. If you are cooking for family, eating a lovely breakfast like one of these is a great way to spend time together before everyone scatters. If it's just you, take care of yourself and make sure you get your RDA of flavor as well as nutrients.

You can certainly start the day with cereal from a box, but when that gets boring, try homemade granola or a scone. You will surely start the day with a smile on your face.

1 cup/240 ml chocolate or vanilla soymilk or other milk

1 large frozen banana, sliced

¼ cup/120 ml cold-press or espresso-brewed coffee

2 tbsp agave syrup (optional)

2 tsp unsweetened cocoa powder

¼ tsp vanilla extract

SERVES 2

This is a healthier version of the famous frozen coffee drinks that seem to be in everyone's hands in the summertime. If you are avoiding caffeine, try it with decaf or a grain beverage like Kaffree or Teeccino instead.

Mocha Frappé

Combine all the ingredients in a blender and puree, then serve immediately.

1 cup/180 g sliced peeled kiwi fruits

6.25 oz/175 g silken tofu

½ cup/120 ml soymilk

¼ cup/60 ml brown rice syrup or agave syrup

1 tbsp matcha tea powder

1 tsp almond extract

SERVES 2

Eating kiwi is a fun way to get vitamins C, E, and K, as well as potassium and copper. A little matcha green tea adds crazy-good flavor and antioxidants as well.

Kiwi–Green Tea Smoothie

Combine all the ingredients in a blender and puree, then serve immediately.

2 cups/330 g chopped
peeled fresh mango

1 cup/165 g chopped
peeled fresh pineapple

1 cup/240 ml coconut milk

4 ice cubes

2 tbsp/28 g vegan
protein powder (optional)

1 tsp vanilla extract

½ tsp ground cinnamon

SERVES 2

You will feel like you are on the beach if you close
your eyes as you drink this delicious smoothie. You
can add a scoop of protein powder for a heartier
breakfast that will keep you full a bit longer.

Tropical Coconut-Mango Smoothie

Combine all the ingredients in a blender and puree, then
serve immediately.

1 large frozen banana

2 cups/330 g peeled cubed papaya/pawpaw

½ cup/120 ml fresh carrot juice

½ cup/120 ml vanilla almond milk or other milk

4 ice cubes

2 tbsp agave syrup or all-fruit jam

1 tbsp freshly squeezed lime juice

SERVES 2

I created this for a class on eating for beautiful skin. Papaya is famously high in vitamins A and C—both good for fighting free radicals that promote premature aging. Rub the insides of the papaya skin on your face for a mild exfoliant!

Beautiful Papaya-Carrot Booster

Combine all the ingredients in a blender and puree, then serve immediately.

2 cups/290 g frozen
strawberries

1 large frozen banana

1½ cups/360 ml vanilla
almond milk or other milk

¼ cup/40 g rolled oats

2 tbsp all-fruit strawberry
spread (optional)

½ tsp almond extract

SERVES 2

Strawberry and banana is a classic flavor combo, and in this creamy smoothie, they make a pink breakfast you will want to make again and again. A sprinkle of oats makes it a little thicker and more substantial in your belly. Don't thaw the strawberries and banana—putting them in frozen will make the smoothie thick and luscious like a milkshake.

Strawberry-Banana Blender

Combine all the ingredients in a blender and puree, then serve immediately.

½ cup/65 g hulled hemp seeds

1 cup/155 g thick rolled oats

1 cup/155 g rolled barley

½ cup/85 g dried cherries

1 cup/240 ml vanilla soymilk or other milk

1 cup/240 ml unsweetened dark cherry juice

2 tbsp agave syrup (optional)

SERVES 4

Muesli is a no-cook way to have great grain cereals for breakfast—just soak the rolled grains in flavorful liquids overnight. Dark cherry juice is packed with sweet, fruity flavor and antioxidants and gives the oats a purplish hue. It has a little more texture than your typical oatmeal, which makes it even more satisfying to eat.

Hemp-Cherry Muesli

1 Put the hemp seeds in a small frying pan and place it over medium heat. Stir and swirl the seeds until they are just fragrant and toasted.

2 In a large bowl or storage tub, combine the seeds, oats, barley, and cherries and toss. Stir in the soymilk, cherry juice, and agave syrup (if using). Cover tightly and put in the refrigerator overnight, or for at least 1 hour.

3 Stir and serve cold, or microwave for 2 minutes per bowl.

1 cup/200 g whole farro, wheat berries, or kamut

1 cup/160 g steel-cut oats

2 cups/480 ml apple juice

1 cup/170 g chopped dried apricots

½ tsp ground cinnamon

1 cup/240 ml coconut milk yogurt (optional)

½ cup/55 g coarsely chopped toasted hazelnuts or walnuts

SERVES 4

This may be the ideal way to cook whole-wheat berries of all kinds, as they take so long on the stove. Just load the slow-cooker the night before, and your hot cereal will be ready when you are. This is the most chewy, hearty hot cereal you have ever had. The combination of slightly crunchy farro grains with the softer chunks of steel-cut oats gives it far more texture than oatmeal. Don't use rolled oats, though; they will melt overnight and might stick to the bottom of the pot.

Overnight Slow-Cooker Farrotto

1 In a small slow-cooker, combine 1 qt/960 ml water, the grains, apple juice, apricots, and cinnamon. Turn the cooker on low and cover. Cook for 7 to 8 hours, or until the farro is tender. To leave it cooking longer, add ½ cup/120 ml more water when you put it on to cook.

2 To serve, portion the grain into bowls and swirl in the yogurt, if desired. Sprinkle with the nuts.

½ cup/90 g quinoa

½ cup/100 g millet

1 cup/240 ml apple juice

½ cup/85 g raisins or other dried fruit

½ cup/50 g shredded carrot

1 pinch salt

½ cup/30 g pumpkin seeds

Agave syrup, for drizzling (optional)

SERVES 4

Quinoa is such a perfect food for vegans, because it's so high in protein and calcium. It's good to have it at breakfast, as well as lunch and dinner. Make a big batch and keep this in the refrigerator to warm up throughout the day.

Sweet Quinoa– Pumpkin Seed Pilaf

1 In a 4-qt/4-L, heavy-bottomed saucepan, dry-toast the quinoa and millet over high heat. Swirl the grains until they are crackling and fragrant. Take off the heat and carefully add 1 cup/240 ml water and the apple juice. It may boil up, so stand back. Add the raisins, carrot, and salt and bring back to a boil. Cover tightly, reduce the heat to low, and cook for about 25 minutes, until the liquids are all absorbed.

2 In a small frying pan, dry-toast the pumpkin seeds over medium-high heat. Swirl and toss the seeds until they are toasted and popping. Pour them onto a plate to cool. Serve the pilaf topped with the crunchy seeds and drizzled with agave syrup, if desired.

Canola oil

1 cup/175 g steel-cut oats

⅛ tsp salt

8 slices Smoky Maple-Tempeh "Bacon" (page 39)

¼ cup/60 ml maple syrup

SERVES 4

While a bowl of oatmeal is great, making a polenta-style slab of the creamy grain and then frying it is an extra-special way to eat your oats. It's a fun way to use up leftover oats, too, so make a big batch and chill them overnight, then slice and cook.

Griddled Oat Polenta
with Smoky Maple-Tempeh "Bacon"

1 Start the polenta the day before you want to eat it. Lightly oil a 9-by-4-in/23-by-10-cm loaf pan/tin. In a 4-qt/3.8-L saucepan, bring 3 cups/720 ml water, the oats, and salt to a boil, then reduce the heat to low. Stir often and cook for 25 minutes. When the timer goes off, take the pan off the heat and let it stand for 5 minutes. Scrape the oats into the loaf pan and spread the mixture evenly. Cover and refrigerate until completely cold.

2 To prepare, invert the loaf onto a cutting board and cut the polenta into slices 1 in/2.5 cm thick. Heat a ridged grill pan or a cast-iron frying pan over high heat. When hot, brush the pan with oil and place the oat slices in the pan. Cook for about 5 minutes per side, until the outside of the pieces develops a nice crust. Turn until the polenta is heated through and firm. In the same pan, spread a little oil and heat the tempeh "bacon." Serve two polenta slices with the tempeh on the side, drizzle with the maple syrup, and eat hot.

5½ cups/850 g rolled oats

1 cup/200 g sugar

½ cup/40 g vegan protein powder

½ cup/60 g whole-wheat/ wholemeal flour

½ cup/55 g ground flax seeds

½ cup/50 g unsweetened cocoa powder

1 cup/240 ml apple juice concentrate, thawed

½ cup/100 g creamy peanut butter

½ cup/120 ml canola oil or coconut oil, plus extra for the pans

2 tsp vanilla extract

1 tsp almond extract

½ tsp salt

SERVES 12

Two great tastes that taste great together, chocolate and peanut butter make this a breakfast you will jump out of bed for. Cocoa is also a great source of all the antioxidants and heart-healthy chemicals in dark chocolate.

Cocoa–Peanut Butter Granola

1 Preheat the oven to 300°F/150°C/gas 2. In a large bowl, mix together the oats, sugar, protein powder, flour, flax, and cocoa. In a food processor or a medium bowl, mix together the apple juice concentrate, peanut butter, oil, vanilla, almond extract, and salt. Stir the two mixtures together; your hands will work best for this.

2 Lightly oil two baking sheets/trays with rims. Scrape the mixture onto the pans and crumble it into chunks. Bake for 15 minutes, then use a metal spatula to turn the layer, and reverse the position of the pans in the oven. Repeat every 15 minutes for a total of 1 hour, until the granola is toasted and chunky.

3 Let the granola cool in the pans on racks until completely cool and dry. Store in an airtight container for up to 2 weeks.

2 cups/310 g rolled oats

2 cups/310 g rolled barley flakes

2 cups/60 g brown rice cereal

1 cup/115 g pecan pieces

½ cup/60 g whole-wheat/wholemeal flour

½ cup/40 g vegan protein powder

1 cup/240 ml maple syrup

½ cup/120 ml canola oil, plus extra for the pans

2 tsp vanilla extract

½ tsp salt

SERVES 16

Oats reign in the cereal world, but did you know that barley has more of the heart-healthy starches that make oats the recommended grain? Beta-glucans are a kind of starch that lowers cholesterol, and barley has more of them. It also makes a hefty, tasty rolled flake that you can make into a delicious granola.

Maple-Barley Granola

1 Preheat the oven to 300°F/150°C/gas 2. In a large bowl, mix together the oats, barley, rice cereal, pecans, flour, and protein powder. In a large bowl or a blender, combine the maple syrup, oil, vanilla, and salt. Lightly oil two baking sheets/trays with rims and spread the oat mixture on the pans.

2 Bake for 20 minutes, then turn the granola with a spatula and bake for 20 minutes more, until it is lightly toasted. Let the granola cool completely on the pans on racks. Store in airtight containers or zip-top bags for up to 2 weeks at room temperature.

6 cups/930 g rolled oats

½ cup/60 g whole-wheat/wholemeal flour

¼ cup/30 g gluten flour

½ tsp salt

12 oz/360 ml frozen apple juice concentrate

½ cup/120 ml canola oil, plus extra for the pans

½ cup/100 g brown sugar (optional)

1 tbsp ground cinnamon

1 tsp ground cloves

1 tsp ground ginger

½ tsp ground cardamom

½ tsp freshly cracked black pepper

2 cups/230 g pecan pieces

SERVES 12

You can make this all fruit-sweetened by leaving out the brown sugar. The cinnamon, cloves, ginger, cardamom, and black pepper that make chai so warming and energizing also make granola taste great.

Fruit-Sweetened Chai-Spiced Granola with Pecans

1 Preheat the oven to 300°F/150°C/gas 2. In a large bowl, mix together the oats, both flours, and salt. In a blender or a bowl, combine the apple juice concentrate, oil, brown sugar (if using), cinnamon, cloves, ginger, cardamom, and pepper. Mix well and pour over the oat mixture; add the pecans. Stir thoroughly to mix.

2 Oil two baking sheets/trays with rims. Distribute the oat mixture over the pans. Bake the granola for 15 minutes, then stir it and switch the position of the pans. Do this every 15 minutes for a total of 1 hour, until the granola is golden. Break up the granola into small pieces as you stir and turn.

3 The granola will be soft, but it will firm up when cool. Let the granola cool on the pans on racks until completely cold. Store in zip-top bags or storage tubs for up to 2 weeks at room temperature.

- 3 cups/465 g rolled oats
- 2 cups/160 g quinoa flakes
- ½ cup/60 g whole-wheat/ wholemeal flour
- 1 tbsp ground cinnamon
- ¼ tsp salt
- 1½ cups/360 ml all-fruit lemonade concentrate, thawed
- ½ cup/50 g brown sugar
- ½ cup/120 ml vegetable oil
- 2 tsp vanilla extract
- ½ tsp almond extract
- 1 cup/115 g whole almonds, coarsely chopped
- Vegetable oil spray
- 1 cup/170 g dried apricots, chopped

SERVES 9

Using all-fruit lemonade is a great way to add fruity nutrition, sweetness, and moisture to this granola. Don't overbake it, though; if it looks like it is browning faster than it should, take it out and let it cool.

Lemony Quinoa-Almond Granola

1 Preheat the oven to 300°F/150°C/gas 2. In a large bowl, mix together the oats, quinoa, flour, cinnamon, and salt. In a small bowl, stir together the lemonade concentrate, brown sugar, oil, vanilla, and almond extract. Pour the liquids over the oat mixture and stir thoroughly with your hands. Let stand for 10 minutes to absorb the liquids, then stir in the nuts.

2 Coat a baking sheet/tray with a rim with vegetable oil spray. Spread the oat mixture on the pan and bake for 15 minutes, then use a metal spatula to turn over portions of the mixture on the pan. Bake for another 15 minutes and repeat for a total of 1 hour, until the granola is golden. Let the granola cool on the pan on a rack until completely cool and dry. Mix in the apricots. Store in an airtight container or zip-top bag for up to 2 weeks at room temperature.

10 oz/280 g extra-firm tofu

3 scallions/spring onions, slivered

¼ cup/40 g rolled oats

¼ cup/25 g grated carrot

2 tbsp nutritional yeast

1 tbsp sherry vinegar

1 tsp salt

1 garlic clove, pressed

1 tsp Dijon mustard

1 tsp freshly cracked black pepper

1 pinch saffron, crumbled

Olive oil spray

2 large tomatoes, seeds squeezed out, chopped

1 cup/30 g chopped fresh basil

8 slices whole-wheat/wholemeal baguette, toasted

Tahini paste or nut butter (optional)

SERVES 4

Go Mediterranean with the flavors in this substantial scramble. Don't discount basil as just a seasoning—it is a nutritious leafy green that just happens to taste divine.

Tomato-Basil Tofu Scramble
with Toasted Baguette

1 Drain the tofu and wrap it in a kitchen towel, then place a cutting board on top. (If you do this at night and put the tofu, tightly wrapped in the towel, in the fridge, it will be ready when you get up.)

2 In a large bowl, crush the tofu with your hands. Mix in the scallions/spring onions, oats, carrot, yeast, vinegar, salt, garlic, mustard, pepper, and saffron.

3 Place a large cast-iron or nonstick frying pan over high heat. Let it heat up thoroughly (cast iron takes a couple of minutes). Coat the pan with olive oil spray. Dump in the tofu mixture and begin stir-frying over high heat. Stir, scraping the bottom of the pan, until the tofu is dry and firm, with golden brown spots. Add the tomatoes after the tofu is well browned. Add the basil just before serving.

4 Smear the baguette slices with tahini, if desired, and serve alongside a plateful of scramble.

1 cup/110 g grated carrots

½ cup/120 ml
cooked quinoa

½ medium yellow bell
pepper/capsicum, thinly
sliced

12 oz/340 g extra-firm
tofu, drained and
pressed (see facing page)

3 tbsp nutritional yeast
(optional)

2 tsp vegan
Worcestershire sauce

1 tsp dried thyme

1 tsp tamari or soy sauce

½ tsp paprika

½ tsp salt

⅛ tsp ground turmeric

2 tsp canola oil

2 cups/60 g spinach
leaves

½ cup/55 g toasted
sunflower seeds

SERVES 4

Wake up with a bright and sunny scramble, sans eggs and cholesterol. Quinoa adds some texture and nutty flavor, as well as all the protein, minerals, and fiber of that amazing grain.

Sunshine Carrot-Tofu Scramble
with Spinach

1 In a large bowl, combine the carrots, quinoa, and bell pepper/capsicum. Crumble in the tofu, then add the yeast, Worcestershire, thyme, tamari, paprika, salt, and turmeric. Mash the mixture together with your hands until it is well mixed. The mixture can be made up to this point and refrigerated overnight.

2 Put a large cast-iron frying pan over high heat. When hot, smear it with the oil. Dump in the tofu mixture and scramble, using a spatula to turn the mixture. Scrape the pan to release bits on the bottom; if it sticks, add a little more oil. Scramble until the tofu is firm and golden. Stir in the spinach and take the pan off the heat, stirring until the spinach is just wilted. Serve topped with the sunflower seeds.

2 cups/480 ml mashed baked sweet potatoes (about 1 lb/455 g)

2 tbsp red miso

½ tsp freshly cracked black pepper

Four 8-in/20-cm or larger whole-wheat/wholemeal tortillas

2 cups/320 g cooked brown rice

2 recipes Smoky Maple-Tempeh "Bacon" (page 39)

SERVES 4

Put a meal in a wrap—with the veggies, grains, and tempeh all together. Savory and filling, this is a sturdy sandwich to take to work or on the bus, so you can get your breakfast no matter what.

"Bacon," Sweet Potato, and Brown Rice Breakfast

1 In a medium bowl, mix the sweet potatoes with the miso and pepper. Lay out the tortillas and portion the sweet potato mixture in the center of each, then top with the rice and 4 slices of tempeh "bacon."

2 Fold in the sides and roll up the tortillas. Wrap each in wax/greaseproof paper if you plan to microwave later, or foil to bake in the oven or toaster oven. Refrigerate until serving.

3 To microwave, take off the paper and place a wrap, seam-side down, on a plate and heat for about 2 minutes. Or bake the wraps in a 375°F/190°C/gas 5 oven for 15 to 20 minutes to heat through.

Four 8-in/20-cm whole-wheat/wholemeal tortillas

8 tsp all-fruit apricot jam

8 tbsp/100 g almond butter

1 medium apple, chopped

16 large dates or other dried fruit

¼ cup/30 g toasted slivered/flaked almonds

½ tsp ground cinnamon

SERVES 4

If you have to run out the door in the morning, make these the night before. Just remember to grab it on the way out and you will have a calcium-rich, high-fiber breakfast to go.

Almond-Apple-Date Breakfast Burrito

1 Place each tortilla on a piece of wax/greaseproof paper or foil about 1 ft/30 cm long and spread with 2 tsp jam. Then put 2 tbsp almond butter in the center third of the tortilla, leaving ½ in/12 mm or so bare at each end.

2 In a small bowl, mix together the apple, dates, almonds, and cinnamon, then divide the mixture among the tortillas. Fold in the bare ends and then roll up each burrito. Lay, seam-side down, on the paper or foil and wrap each burrito, pulling the wrap in from the short sides first, so you can unwrap the end at which you start to eat the burrito and the paper or foil will hold it neatly as you go.

3 Refrigerate for up to 3 days until serving.

1 lb/455 g boiled red or yellow potatoes

1 lb/455 g boiled beets/beetroot, skins slipped off

4 oz/115 g smoked tempeh, diced

½ cup/50 g chopped scallions/spring onions

½ tsp salt

Freshly cracked black pepper

2 tbsp Earth Balance margarine

Vegan ketchup/tomato sauce, for serving

SERVES 4

This is a breakfast that will stick with you, packed with high-protein tempeh and sizzling root vegetables. Beets for breakfast is actually an old idea that works wonders for your iron levels, especially if you use cast iron for cooking.

Red Flannel Hash
with Smoked Tempeh

1 Shred the potatoes and beets/beetroot, then mix them in a large bowl with the tempeh, scallions/spring onions, and salt. Season with pepper. This step can be done the night before and the mixture refrigerated, covered.

2 Heat a large cast-iron frying pan over medium heat. Add the margarine and swirl the pan to coat. Add the potato mixture and press to make a single flat cake. Cover and cook for 20 minutes, until the bottom is crusty and browned. Turn the hash over in large sections with a spatula and pack it down again; cook for 10 to 15 minutes more, until it is well browned. Serve with ketchup/tomato sauce.

1 cup/115 g unbleached all-purpose/plain flour

½ cup/60 g whole-wheat/wholemeal pastry/soft-wheat flour

½ cup/30 g wheat bran

2 tbsp sugar

2 tsp baking powder

1 tsp ground cinnamon

½ tsp baking soda/bicarbonate of soda

½ tsp salt

1 ripe, medium banana

2 cups/480 ml vanilla rice milk or other milk

2 tsp egg replacer powder

2 tbsp canola oil

Vegetable oil spray

¾ cup/85 g chopped walnuts or berries

Maple syrup, for serving

MAKES 12 PANCAKES

Making homemade pancakes doesn't take long—you can even set up the night before, mixing the dry ingredients and leaving the bowl on the counter. Wait until the last minute to mix up the egg replacer, and enjoy the hot cakes drenched in pure maple syrup.

Fluffy Banana-Bran Pancakes
with Maple Syrup

1 Preheat the oven to 200°F/95°C/gas ¼, so you can keep the cakes warm as you finish cooking the rest. In a large bowl, mix together both flours, the bran, sugar, baking powder, cinnamon, baking soda/bicarbonate of soda, and salt. In a glass measuring cup, mash the banana. In another cup, whisk together the milk and egg replacer powder until frothy, then whisk in the canola oil. Add the milk mixture to the bananas to make 2½ cups/600 ml. With a spoon, quickly stir the liquids into the dry mixture, leaving some small lumps.

2 Heat a large nonstick frying pan or griddle until hot; a drop of water should sizzle on the surface. Grease the pan with vegetable oil spray and measure ¼ cup/60 ml of batter for each cake. Drop the batter onto the pan and quickly sprinkle 1 tbsp of nuts evenly over each cake; pat with a large spatula to sink them in. Lower the heat to medium and cook each side for about 1 minute, until lightly browned. Place each pancake on an oven-safe platter and keep it in the oven until all are done. Serve with maple syrup.

1½ cups/170 g unbleached all-purpose/plain flour

1 cup/115 g buckwheat flour

¼ cup/50 g sugar

2 tsp baking powder

½ tsp baking soda/bicarbonate of soda

½ tsp salt

2 tsp egg replacer powder

2½ cups/600 ml vanilla rice milk or other milk, plus more as needed

2 tbsp canola oil

1 tbsp rice vinegar

Rhubarb Compote

4 cups/490 g chopped rhubarb

2 cups/250 g raspberries, fresh or frozen

1 cup/240 ml maple syrup or agave syrup

2 tsp ground cinnamon

Vegetable oil spray

SERVES 4

Buckwheat, with its earthy flavor and deep brown hue, is an underappreciated grain. Pancakes are the only place that most Americans ever see it. Enjoy these happy little cakes in spring when the rhubarb is good, then look for buckwheat groats to cook later and serve like rice.

Buckwheat Silver Dollar Cakes
with Rhubarb Compote

1 Preheat the oven to 200°F/95°C/gas ¼, so you can keep the cakes warm as you finish cooking the rest. In a large bowl, mix together both flours, the sugar, baking powder, baking soda/bicarbonate of soda, and salt. In a glass measuring cup, mix the egg replacer powder with 3 tbsp of the milk until dissolved, then add the remaining milk, the oil, and vinegar. With a spoon, quickly stir the liquids into the dry mixture, leaving some small lumps. Let stand for a couple of minutes to absorb the liquids.

2 TO MAKE THE COMPOTE: Combine the rhubarb, berries, maple syrup, and cinnamon in a 4-qt/4-L saucepan. Over low heat, slowly bring the mixture to a simmer, stirring often. Cook until thick, but pourable, about 10 minutes.

3 While the compote is cooking, heat a large nonstick frying pan or griddle until hot; a drop of water should sizzle on the surface. Grease the pan with vegetable oil spray and measure 2 tbsp of batter for each cake. Do one tester cake, and if the batter is too thick to spread out easily, stir in 1 to 2 tbsp of milk. Lower the heat to medium and cook each side for about 1 minute, until lightly browned. Place each pancake on an oven-safe platter and keep it in the oven until all are done.

4 Serve the pancakes with the warm rhubarb compote.

1 cup/115 g unbleached all-purpose/plain flour

1 cup/115 g whole-wheat/wholemeal pastry/soft-wheat flour

1 tsp baking powder

¼ tsp salt

2 ripe, medium bananas

1 cup/200 g raw sugar

½ cup/120 ml rice milk or other milk

½ cup/120 ml canola oil

2 tbsp ground flax seeds

1 tsp cider vinegar

10 tsp/40 g peanut butter

10 tsp/50 ml jam

MAKES 10 MUFFINS

Pack these muffins for lunch, and you will not need to bring peanut butter and jelly, because it is already concealed in the center of every one. It's also a great way to use up potassium-rich bananas and stock up on tasty snacks.

Peanut Butter and Jelly Banana Muffins

1 Preheat the oven to 375°F/190°C/gas 5. Line 10 cups in a muffin pan/fairy cake tin with muffin papers. In a large bowl, mix together both flours, the baking powder, and salt. In a food processor or bowl, puree the bananas until smooth. Add the sugar, milk, oil, flax, and vinegar. Stir the banana mixture into the flour mixture just until combined.

2 Scoop a scant ¼ cup/60 ml of batter into each muffin cup. Drop 1 tsp of peanut butter in the center of each, then top that with 1 tsp of jam. Use the remaining batter to cover the filling in each cup.

3 Bake for 25 to 30 minutes, or until a toothpick inserted in the center of a muffin comes out with only peanut butter and jelly on it. Let cool on racks. Store in an airtight container in the refrigerator for up to 1 week.

Vegetable oil spray

1 cup plus 2 tbsp/130 g unbleached all-purpose/plain flour

1 cup/115 g whole-wheat/wholemeal pastry/soft-wheat flour

½ cup/100 g granulated sugar

1 large lemon, zested and juiced

1 tsp baking powder

1 tsp baking soda/bicarbonate of soda

½ tsp salt

2 tsp egg replacer powder

1 cup/240 ml rice milk or other milk

¼ cup/60 ml canola oil

1½ cups/230 g frozen blueberries (do not thaw)

8 tsp turbinado sugar

MAKES 8 MUFFINS

Blueberries and lemon go together so well because the tart lemon brings out the sweetness of the juicy berries. Blueberries are the darlings of superfood lists, with their concentrated antioxidants and vitamin C.

Blueberry-Lemon Muffins

1 Preheat the oven to 375°F/190°C/gas 5. Line 8 cups of a muffin pan/fairy cake tin with muffin papers, then coat the top of the pan between the cups with vegetable oil spray to prevent sticking. In a large bowl, combine 1 cup/115 g of the all-purpose/plain flour with the pastry/soft-wheat flour, granulated sugar, lemon zest, baking powder, baking soda/bicarbonate of soda, and salt; whisk to combine. In a 2-cup/480-ml measure, whisk the egg replacer powder with 2 tbsp warm water until well mixed. Add milk to make 1 cup/240 ml, then add the canola oil and 1 tbsp of the lemon juice. In a medium bowl, toss the frozen blueberries with the remaining 2 tbsp all-purpose/plain flour. Stir the liquids, then dump them into the dry mixture and stir just until combined. Fold in the frozen blueberries just to distribute. Portion the batter into the 8 muffin cups, and sprinkle each with 1 tsp of the turbinado sugar.

2 Bake for 40 minutes, or until a toothpick inserted in the center of a muffin comes out with a little blueberry juice, but no wet batter on it. Let cool on racks. Store tightly covered in the refrigerator for up to 1 week.

Vegetable oil spray

1 cup/115 g whole-wheat/wholemeal pastry/soft-wheat flour

1 cup/115 g unbleached all-purpose/plain flour

2 tsp ground cinnamon

1 tsp baking soda/bicarbonate of soda

½ tsp salt

1½ cups plus 4 tbsp/175 g turbinado sugar

1 cup/240 ml mashed cooked sweet potatoes (about 7 oz/200 g)

12 tbsp/180 ml rice milk

½ cup/120 ml canola oil

2 tbsp ground flax seeds

2 cups/340 g raisins

MAKES 12 MUFFINS

Plump muffins studded with sweet raisins always hit the spot—and the nutrient-dense sweet potato batter is full of antioxidants. You can always try other dried fruit for variety.

Sweet Potato and Raisin Muffins

1 Preheat the oven to 375°F/190°C/gas 5. Line 12 cups of a muffin pan/fairy cake tin with muffin papers, then coat the top of the pan between the cups with vegetable oil spray to prevent sticking. In a large bowl, mix together both flours, the cinnamon, baking soda/bicarbonate of soda, and salt. In a food processor or blender, combine 1½ cups of the sugar, the sweet potatoes, milk, canola oil, and flax. Blend until well mixed. Pour the wet mixture into the flour mixture, stir just until combined, and then quickly stir in the raisins. Fill the muffin cups to the top, then sprinkle the tops with the remaining 4 tbsp of the sugar.

2 Bake for 35 to 40 minutes, or until a toothpick inserted into the center of a muffin comes out with no wet batter clinging to it. Let cool on racks. Store in an airtight container in the refrigerator for up to 1 week.

Vegetable oil spray

½ cup/45 g shredded/desiccated unsweetened coconut

1 cup/115 g whole-wheat/wholemeal pastry/soft-wheat flour

1 cup/115 g unbleached all-purpose/plain flour

1 cup/200 g sugar

1 tsp ground cinnamon

½ tsp baking powder

½ tsp baking soda/bicarbonate of soda

¼ tsp salt

½ tsp ground allspice

½ tsp ground cloves

1 cup/240 ml rice milk or other milk

1 tbsp cider vinegar

¼ cup/60 ml canola oil

1 tsp vanilla extract

1 tsp almond or coconut extract

¾ cup/130 g chopped dried mango

MAKES 9 MUFFINS

Go tropical with these fruity, spiced muffins, spiked with toasted coconut. Keep dried mango in the pantry, and you can always whip up some fresh muffins and get your fruit servings in.

Coconut-Mango Muffins

1 Preheat the oven to 300°F/150°C/gas 2. Line 9 cups of a muffin pan/fairy cake tin with muffin papers, then coat the top of the pan between the cups with vegetable oil spray to prevent sticking. Spread the coconut on a baking sheet/tray and place the pan in the oven. Toast the coconut for 5 minutes, stir, and continue to toast until lightly golden, 3 to 5 minutes more. Let the pan cool on a rack and increase the oven to 375°F/190°C/gas 5.

2 In a large bowl, mix together both flours, the sugar, coconut, cinnamon, baking powder, baking soda/bicarbonate of soda, salt, allspice, and cloves.

3 In a medium bowl, combine the milk, vinegar, canola oil, vanilla, and almond extract. Stir quickly into the dry mixture, and when almost combined, fold in the mangoes. Scoop into the prepared muffin cups and bake for about 25 minutes, until a toothpick inserted in the center of a muffin comes out with no wet batter clinging to it. Let cool on racks. Store tightly covered in the refrigerator for up to 1 week.

1 tbsp Earth Balance margarine, plus extra for the pan

½ cup/120 ml agave syrup

½ cup/120 ml brown rice syrup

1 tsp vanilla extract

1 cup/155 g rolled oats, ground

3½ cups/520 g prepared trail mix

MAKES 8 BARS

It's a good idea to carry something energy packed when you are out on the trail, which is what trail mix is all about. These delicious bars will sustain you on any path you choose, no matter how urban.

Trail Mix Bars

1 Liberally grease an 8-in/20-cm square cake pan/tin with the margarine. In a 4-qt/4-L pot, mix together the agave and rice syrups, 1 tbsp margarine, and the vanilla. Bring to a boil over high heat, then monitor the heat as you stir the boiling mixture for 5 minutes; be careful not to let it boil over. Take the pan off the heat and stir in the ground oats and trail mix. Stir until coated, then scrape the mixture into the prepared pan. Flatten as well as you can with a greased spoon, then place wax/greaseproof paper on the top and press firmly into the pan. Refrigerate until firm.

2 Bring to room temperature to slice. Store in the fridge in an airtight container for up to 1 week.

Canola oil for the pan, plus 2 tbsp

2 cups/310 g rolled oats

¼ cup/30 g whole-wheat/wholemeal flour

¼ cup/30 g vegan protein powder or gluten flour

½ tsp ground cinnamon

¼ tsp baking powder

¼ tsp salt

1 tbsp ground flax seeds

½ cup/100 g almond butter

½ cup/120 ml agave syrup

1 tsp vanilla extract

1 cup/170 g chopped pitted dates

MAKES 8 BARS

Steer clear of the commercially made breakfast bars—they have all sorts of weird ingredients. These are easy to put together on the weekend, so you can enjoy them all week.

High-Protein Oat Breakfast Bars

1 Preheat the oven to 350°F/180°C/gas 4. Lightly oil a 9-in/23-cm square cake pan/tin. In a large bowl, mix together the oats, flour, protein powder, cinnamon, baking powder, and salt. In a cup, whisk the flax with ¼ cup/60 ml water and let stand while you prepare the rest, stirring occasionally.

2 In a small bowl, whisk together the almond butter, agave syrup, 2 tbsp oil, and vanilla until smooth. Stir the flax mixture into the almond butter mixture. Stir the wet mixture into the dry, and use your hands to combine it thoroughly. Stir in the dates.

3 Scrape the mixture into the prepared pan and use wet hands to pat it evenly in the pan. Bake for 25 minutes, until the mixture is golden brown around the edges and slightly puffed in the middle. Let cool on a rack. Cut into eight bars. Wrap individually and refrigerate for up to 1 week or freeze for up to 3 months.

2 cups/255 g whole-wheat/wholemeal pastry/soft-wheat flour

1 cup/115 g unbleached all-purpose/plain flour, plus extra for the counter

1 tsp baking powder

1 tsp baking soda/bicarbonate of soda

1 tsp ground cinnamon

½ tsp salt

½ cup/120 ml coconut oil, frozen

1 cup/155 g rolled oats

2 tsp egg replacer powder

¾ cup/180 ml rice milk or other milk

½ cup/120 ml maple syrup

2 tbsp cold-press corn oil

1 tsp cider vinegar

1 tsp vanilla extract

1 cup/170 g dried sweet cherries

¼ cup/50 g turbinado sugar

MAKES 8 SCONES

Dried cherries and maple syrup make these scones into a taste sensation. It's best to measure the coconut oil while it's soft, put it in the freezer until firm, then knock it out of the cup to grate it. Corn oil adds a buttery flavor to these hearty, filling wonders.

Whole-Wheat Maple-Cherry Scones

1 Preheat the oven to 400°F/200°C/gas 6. Line a large baking sheet/tray with parchment/baking paper. In a large bowl, whisk together both flours, the baking powder, baking soda/bicarbonate of soda, cinnamon, and salt. Grate the cold coconut oil over the dry ingredients or cut it in using a pastry blender. Add the oats and mix with your hands. In a large measuring cup, stir the egg replacer powder into the milk, then stir in the maple syrup, corn oil, vinegar, and vanilla. Add the liquid mixture to the dry mixture and stir just until mixed. Let stand for a couple of minutes for the oats to soak up moisture. Stir in the cherries.

2 Transfer the dough to a floured counter and form it into a disk about 1 in/2.5 cm thick. Using a bench knife or large knife, cut the disk into eight wedges. Sprinkle the tops with turbinado sugar, pressing lightly to make it stick. Transfer the wedges to the prepared pan, 2 in/5 cm apart, and bake for 15 minutes, until the edges are golden brown. Transfer to racks to cool. Store in an airtight container for up to 1 week.

2½ cups/315 g pastry/soft-wheat flour, plus extra for the counter

¼ cup/50 g sugar

1 tbsp matcha green tea powder

2 tsp baking powder

½ tsp salt

¼ cup/55 g Earth Balance margarine, frozen

1 cup/240 ml coconut milk, plus extra for brushing

¾ cup/130 g golden raisins/sultanas

MAKES 8 LARGE OR 16 SMALL SCONES

For a treat, try these pale green scones, made with cake flour—the whitest flour of them all. It shows off the delicate color and flavor of the tea. You can get back to whole-wheat tomorrow!

Matcha Scones
with Golden Raisins

1 Preheat the oven to 400°F/200°C/gas 6. Line a baking sheet/tray with parchment/baking paper. In a large bowl, mix together the flour, sugar, matcha, baking powder, and salt. With a pastry blender or grater, cut the margarine into the dry ingredients and work it in with your fingers. Pour the milk into the flour mixture and stir until just combined. Add the raisins and mix with your hands.

2 Scrape the dough out onto a lightly floured counter and form it into a disk about ¾ in/2 cm thick for eight scones (or make two rounds for sixteen smaller scones; slice each round into eight wedges). Place the scones on the baking sheet/tray, 2 in/5 cm apart, and brush with milk. Bake for 12 to 14 minutes, until the bottoms are browned and the edges are golden brown (bake smaller scones for about 10 minutes). Let them cool on the pan for 10 minutes before removing to cool on racks. Store in an airtight container for up to 1 week.

1 cup/115 g unbleached all-purpose/plain flour, plus extra for the counter

1 cup/115 g whole-wheat/wholemeal pastry/soft-wheat flour

¼ cup/50 g granulated sugar

1 tsp baking powder

1 tsp ground cinnamon

½ tsp baking soda/bicarbonate of soda

½ tsp salt

6 tbsp/85 g Earth Balance margarine, frozen

½ cup/100 g whole amaranth

½ cup/120 ml vanilla rice milk or other milk

2 tsp egg replacer powder

¼ cup/60 ml maple syrup

1 cup/170 g sliced pitted dates

¼ cup/50 g turbinado sugar

MAKES 8 SCONES

Amaranth is an ancient Aztec treasure, loaded with protein and minerals. The tiny grains were a staple food for the Aztec people, and now you can enjoy them in a scone. The uncooked amaranth gives these scones a crunchy, nutty texture and flavor.

Crunchy Amaranth-Date Scones

1 Preheat the oven to 400°F/200°C/gas 6. Line a baking sheet/tray with parchment/baking paper.

2 In a large bowl, mix together both flours, the granulated sugar, baking powder, cinnamon, baking soda/bicarbonate of soda, and salt. Grate in the margarine, then use your fingers to work it throughout the mixture, leaving rice-size chunks. Stir in the amaranth. In a measuring cup, whisk together the milk and egg replacer/powder to make a smooth, bubbly mix. Stir in the maple syrup, then add to the dry mixture. Stir just until mostly mixed, then add the dates and press together to make a dough.

3 Transfer the dough to a floured counter and form it into a disk about 1 in/2.5 cm thick. Using a bench knife or large knife, cut the disk into eight wedges. Sprinkle the tops with the turbinado sugar, pressing lightly to make it stick. Transfer the scones to the pan, 2 in/5 cm apart, and bake for 15 minutes, until the edges are golden brown. Let cool on the pan for 5 minutes. Transfer to racks to cool. Store in an airtight container for up to 1 week.

Caramel

½ cup/100 g brown sugar

3 tbsp coconut milk

2 tbsp Earth Balance margarine

2 tbsp agave syrup

Dough

2½ cups/300 g unbleached all-purpose/plain flour, plus more if needed

¼ cup/50 g granulated sugar

2½ tsp bread-machine yeast

Zest of ½ lemon

¼ tsp salt

6 tbsp/85 g Earth Balance margarine, melted

¾ cup/180 ml rice milk or almond milk

1 tsp egg replacer powder

1 tsp vanilla extract

¼ cup/50 g brown sugar mixed with 1 tsp ground cinnamon

½ cup/85 g raisins

Looking for a very special breakfast treat? These tender rolls are packed with raisins, cinnamon, and sugar; drenched in sticky caramel; and will satisfy any kind of sticky-cinnamon cravings you might have. They are perfect for when you have guests; just make them the day before and get them out to rise and bake in the morning.

Sticky Cinnamon-Raisin Rolls

1 TO MAKE THE CARAMEL: In a small saucepan, combine the sugar, milk, margarine, and agave syrup. Bring to a boil over medium heat, then reduce to a strong simmer and cook for 3 minutes to melt the sugar. Take the pan off the heat and let it cool, then divide the caramel evenly among the twelve cups of a muffin pan/fairy cake tin. Set aside. The caramel will harden as it cools.

2 TO MAKE THE DOUGH: In a stand mixer or a large bowl, mix together the flour, granulated sugar, yeast, lemon zest, and salt. Whisk the margarine into the milk and then whisk in the egg replacer powder and vanilla. With a dough hook or by hand, mix the milk mixture into the flour mixture. Add more flour if necessary to make a soft but not too sticky dough. Knead for 5 minutes after all the flour has been added, until you have a smooth dough. Place the dough on a floured counter and let it rest for 5 minutes.

3 On the floured work surface, press the dough out into a square, about 12 in/30 cm wide and almost as long. Cover with the cinnamon-sugar mixture and the raisins and roll up tightly into a log, pinching the seam to seal it. Slice the log into twelve rolls and place each in a prepared muffin cup. Cover the finished rolls with plastic wrap/cling film and refrigerate overnight to develop flavor.

4 The next morning, put the pan/tin in a warm place and let the dough come to room temperature; it will take 1½ to 2 hours, or longer if the room is cool. Preheat the oven to 375°F/190°C/gas 5. When the rolls are warm to the touch and are expanding to fill the cups, put the pan on a larger baking sheet/tray to catch any caramel overflows. Bake for 20 to 25 minutes, until the caramel is bubbling and the rolls are firm to the touch. Let the rolls cool in the pan for 10 minutes and then carefully place a large baking sheet/tray over them. Flip to drop the rolls onto the sheet/tray. Lift the pan off the rolls and use a small spatula to scrape any remaining caramel from the cups onto the rolls. As they cool, scoop any extra caramel back onto the rolls as it thickens. Serve with lots of napkins.

1 cup/165 g chopped peeled fresh mango

1 cup plus 2 tsp/250 ml maple syrup

1½ cups/360 ml coconut milk

6 tbsp/20 g nutritional yeast

2 tbsp cornstarch/cornflour

1 tsp vanilla extract

½ tsp ground cinnamon

⅛ tsp ground nutmeg

Canola oil

8 slices whole-wheat/wholemeal bread, slightly stale if possible

SERVES 4

Mango and coconut milk give this French toast an exotic flair, adding hints of the tropics to your breakfast table. This is a great way to use up slightly old bread and pretend it's not winter.

French Toast
with Mango-Maple Syrup

1 In a small saucepan, combine the mango and 1 cup/ 240 ml of the maple syrup. Put over high heat, bring to a boil, then reduce to medium-low and simmer for 5 minutes to let the flavors marry. Let cool slightly.

2 In a pie pan/tin, whisk together the milk, yeast, cornstarch/ cornflour, the remaining 2 tsp maple syrup, the vanilla, cinnamon, and nutmeg. Heat a large cast-iron frying pan or griddle over high heat. When hot, spread it with oil. Dip each slice of bread in the coconut milk mixture to coat, letting it soak for about 1 minute. Drop the slices on the hot pan and cook for about 2 minutes per side, reducing the heat to medium or medium-low as they start to sizzle. Flip the slices until they are well browned. Be patient; it may take 8 minutes total. Serve the French toast with the warm mango syrup.

2 tbsp Earth Balance margarine, plus extra for the pan

4 large Granny Smith apples, chopped

1 cup plus 1 tsp/245 ml maple syrup

½ tsp ground cinnamon

¾ cup/180 ml vanilla soymilk or rice milk

3 tbsp nutritional yeast

1 tbsp cornstarch/cornflour

½ tsp vanilla extract

⅛ tsp ground nutmeg

24 thin slices whole-wheat/wholemeal baguette

1½ cups/340 g tofu "cream cheese"

SERVES 4

Looking for a special breakfast treat, with very little effort? Golden brown French toast filled with creamy "cheese" and topped with a quick sauté of apples looks like you really fussed. Sautéed apples are a delicious, nutritious alternative to syrups.

Baguette French Toast
with "Cream Cheese" and Apples

1 In a small frying pan over medium heat, melt the margarine. Add the apples and sauté, tossing and stirring, until they are soft and juicy. Add 1 cup/240 ml of the syrup and the cinnamon and toss. Bring the syrup to a boil, then take it off the heat. Let cool.

2 In a pie pan/tin, whisk together the soymilk, yeast, cornstarch/cornflour, remaining 1 tsp syrup, the vanilla, and nutmeg. Heat a large cast-iron frying pan or griddle over medium-low heat. When hot, spread it with margarine. Dip each slice of bread in the milk mixture to coat, letting it soak for about 1 minute. Drop the slices in the pan and cook for about 4 minutes per side, reducing the heat to medium as they start to sizzle. Flip the slices and cook until they are well browned.

3 Sandwich two cooked slices with 1 tbsp of "cream cheese." Serve the French toast sandwiches with the warm apples and syrup.

CHAPTER

Breads

3

Baking your own bread is such a pleasure that I hope you will come to love it. Sure, you can buy some good breads, but there is nothing like the aroma of freshly baked loaves or buns hot from the oven. The scent triggers some primal, collective part of the human brain and calls everyone to the kitchen. No matter what is going on, people will come together to tear into a hot loaf and slather it with veggie "butter." Hearty whole-grain breads are at their deliriously seductive best when freshly baked and delivered with a loving hand. Then there are quick and easy rolls, which are fast enough to make on a weeknight. A hot, fragrant bread and some soup makes a deeply satisfying repast, no matter who you are. Flatbreads and crackers are another easy way to make your grains into tasty breads. Your guests may never have seen a homemade cracker, and the fact that the crackers are vegan makes them even more appealing.

Like many working people, I am a weekend bread baker. It's a healthy habit, getting up in the morning and throwing some yeast and flour together to get things started. Overnight breads make it even easier, and there are recipes in this chapter for no-knead doughs that ferment in the fridge while you sleep. Baking your own means you can control what goes into them. Organic, whole-grain, and vegan—your ingredients are up to you, not someone else.

While it's not that hard to find breads that don't contain dairy or eggs, finding loaves that eschew white sugar and additives can be more challenging. Vegan drop biscuits are something you just have to make for yourself, since fresh and hot is the only way to go. These vegan recipes make use of nondairy milks, alternative sweeteners, and fruits and veggies in a way that suits the plant-based diet. Some even have additional nuts or soy for a little protein boost. All of them are delicious and satisfying.

6 cups/690 g white whole-wheat/wholemeal flour

¼ cup/45 g soy flour or vegan protein powder

2 tbsp gluten flour

4 tsp bread-machine yeast

2 tsp salt

2 cups/480 ml oat milk

½ cup/120 ml canola oil, plus extra for bowl and pans

1 tbsp brown rice syrup or malt syrup

1 cup/110 g grated carrots

3 large scallions/spring onions, chopped

1½ cups/45 g baby spinach, finely chopped

MAKES 2 LOAVES

It's hard to pile enough veggies on a sandwich—you might as well pack a few into the bread itself! Don't worry if it seems like a lot of veggies, though. As long as you roll them up inside, they will have the added effect of keeping the bread moist.

Veggie Sandwich Loaves

1 In a stand mixer or a large bowl, combine 4 cups/460 g of the whole-wheat/wholemeal flour, the soy flour, gluten flour, yeast, and salt.

2 In a small saucepan over low heat, warm the milk and oil to no warmer than 110°F/45°C and then add the brown rice syrup.

3 Pour the milk mixture into the flour mixture and stir, then knead until the dough is supple and not sticky, adding the remaining 2 cups/230 g flour as needed. When the dough is well mixed, knead for 5 minutes more, until the dough is smooth and springy. Add the vegetables and knead them in. You may have to remove the dough from the bowl and fold the dough over the veggies and keep folding until they are well distributed. Transfer the dough to an oiled bowl and cover it with oiled plastic wrap/cling film. Let the dough rise in a warm, draft-free place for 1 hour, until doubled in bulk.

4 Preheat the oven to 350°F/180°C/gas 4. Oil two 4-by-10-in/10-by-25-cm loaf pans/tins. Punch down the dough and form it into two cylinders to fit into the pans. Cover the pans lightly with the plastic wrap/cling film again and let the dough rise on top of the oven for 45 minutes to 1 hour, until the top is puffed up and above the pan. Uncover and bake for about 30 minutes, until well browned on top and, when tipped out of the pan, the loaf sounds hollow when tapped with a finger.

5 Let the bread cool in the pans for about 10 minutes before knocking out and letting them cool completely on a rack before slicing to serve, or storing in a zip-top bag for up to 1 week.

BREADS

91

1 cup/115 g unbleached all-purpose/plain flour

2 tsp active dry yeast

2 tbsp barley malt

3½ cups/445 g white whole-wheat/wholemeal bread/strong flour

2 tsp bread-machine yeast

2 tsp salt

Vegetable oil

2 tbsp/15 g medium-grind cornmeal

MAKES 2 LOAVES

The white wheat flour in these loaves will give you an attractive golden loaf, with a slightly milder flavor than conventional whole-wheat flour and with all the nutrition. If you can't find white wheat flour, use standard whole-wheat flour made from hard winter wheat, which is very similar, just brown. Using regular active dry yeast in the first rising and quicker yeast in the second makes this loaf just a little faster to finish.

Rustic White Wheat Baguettes

1 Four hours before mixing the dough, make the sponge: In a ceramic bowl, mix together 1 cup/240 ml room-temperature water, the all-purpose/plain flour, and the active dry yeast. Cover the bowl with a dampened kitchen towel and set it somewhere warm to ferment for 4 hours.

2 After 4 hours, the sponge should be bubbly. Dump it into a stand mixer bowl fitted with the dough hook or a large mixing bowl. Mix 1 cup/240 ml warm water (no warmer than 110°F/45°C) with the malt and stir it into the sponge on low speed.

3 Mix 1 cup/115 g of the bread/strong flour with the bread-machine yeast and salt, add to the sponge, then raise the speed to medium and beat for 2 minutes to activate the gluten. If mixing by hand, beat until thick and stringy looking, about 2 minutes.

4 Continue to knead the dough on medium speed, adding the last 2½ cups/315 g of flour as needed to make a soft, slightly sticky dough. This should take about 10 minutes. Oil a large mixing bowl to prevent sticking and transfer the dough to the bowl. Cover the bowl tightly with plastic wrap/cling film and put it in a warm, draft-free place to rise for 2 hours, or until doubled in bulk.

5 On a baking sheet/tray with no rim or a pizza peel, spread the cornmeal to make a nonstick surface to place the loaves on. The two loaves will be at a right angle to the edge, where they can easily slide off into the oven.

6 Punch down the dough and cut the mass in half. Flatten each half into a rectangle about 1 ft/30 cm long, then roll up the dough, starting at a long edge to form a baguette. Roll each cylinder on the counter to shape and seal it. Place the baguettes on the cornmeal at least 4 in/10 cm apart, with the tips just touching the edge of the pan so they will be easy to slide off onto the stone. Cover the pan loosely with plastic wrap/cling film and let the bread rise for at least 1 hour, until the loaves are doubled in bulk.

7 Put a small pan of water on the bottom of the oven and get a water misting bottle. This will create steam to form a good crust on the bread. Preheat the oven with a pizza stone for 30 minutes at 425°F/220°C/gas 7. When the oven is hot, make a few diagonal slashes in the tops of the loaves with a very sharp knife or razor blade, and then use a long metal spatula to help slide the loaves onto the stone, trying not to deflate them. Spritz the surfaces of the breads with water and bake for about 15 minutes.

8 When the loaves sound hollow when tapped with a finger, they are done. Let cool on racks completely before slicing. Store in a zip-top bag for up to 1 week.

2½ cups/315 g whole spelt flour or whole-wheat/wholemeal flour

1½ cups/170 g unbleached all-purpose/plain flour

1 tbsp gluten flour

2¼ tsp bread-machine yeast

1 tsp salt

2 tbsp canola oil

Earth Balance margarine or shortening/vegetable lard

Vegetable oil spray

MAKES 1 LOAF

An effortless way to make bread, this no-knead technique relies on a long, slow rise in the refrigerator for all its chemistry to happen. If you have time but feel lazy, this is the loaf for you. Just be sure to let the chilled dough sit out until it is fully warmed to room temperature before baking.

No-Knead Spelt Sandwich Loaf

1 In a storage container or bowl that will hold 6 cups/1.5 L, mix together all three flours, the yeast, and salt.

2 In a bowl, mix together 2 cups/480 ml warm water (no warmer than 110°F/45°C) and the canola oil.

3 Stir the wet ingredients into the dry until a shaggy mass forms. Don't knead or worry if it is not perfectly mixed. Loosely cover the container with a damp kitchen towel and let the dough sit at warm room temperature for 2 or 3 hours, until the dough rises and bubbles.

4 Use at least 1 tbsp of margarine to heavily grease a 4-by-10-in/10-by-25-cm loaf pan/tin. The dough should be very soft; just scrape it into the pan.

5 Spritz a sheet of plastic wrap/cling film with vegetable oil spray and place it, oiled-side down, over the dough, trying not to have it airtight or touching the dough. Put the pan/tin in the refrigerator for at least 20 hours and up to 30 hours, for a slow, flavor-developing rise.

6 After 20 to 30 hours, take out the dough and let it come to room temperature for at least 2 and up to 3 hours, depending on the room's temperature; the dough needs to be warm all the way through. When it bubbles up to the top of the pan but no higher, it is ready to bake. Remove the plastic wrap/cling film.

7 Preheat the oven to 375°F/190°C/gas 5. Bake for 25 to 30 minutes, until golden brown on top. Run a paring knife around the edges of the pan to loosen the loaf. When turned out of the pan, it should sound hollow when tapped on the bottom. Let the bread cool thoroughly in the pan on a rack before slicing. Store in a zip-top bag for up to 1 week.

Vegetable oil

3½ cups/400 g white whole-wheat/wholemeal flour, plus extra for counter

2 tbsp gluten flour

2 tsp bread-machine yeast

1 tsp salt

1½ cups/360 ml hazelnut milk

½ cup/120 ml canola oil

¼ cup/60 ml agave syrup

½ cup/55 g toasted hazelnuts, skinned and chopped

MAKES 1 LOAF

Chunky hazelnuts make this bread irresistible and add some extra protein and crunch. It makes great toast, slathered with nut butter and jam.

Savory Hazelnut Bread

1 Grease a 4-by-10-in/10-by-25-cm loaf pan/tin with vegetable oil. In a large bowl or stand mixer fitted with the dough hook, combine 3 cups/345 g of the whole-wheat/wholemeal flour, the gluten flour, yeast, and salt.

2 In a small pot, heat the milk, canola oil, and agave syrup to no warmer than 110°F/45°C. Gradually add the liquids to the dry ingredients, stirring them in using the dough hook or a sturdy spoon. Add the remaining ½ cup/60 g flour to make a soft but not too sticky dough.

3 On a floured counter, knead the dough until it is smooth and elastic, 6 to 8 minutes. Knead in the hazelnuts.

4 Grease a large bowl with vegetable oil and turn the dough in the bowl to coat it. Loosely cover with a damp kitchen towel and let rise in a warm, draft-free place until doubled in bulk, 45 to 60 minutes.

5 Punch down the dough and move it to the lightly floured counter. Roll it out to a 12-by-7-in/30-by-17-cm rectangle. Beginning at the short end of the rectangle, roll up the dough tightly as for a jelly/Swiss roll. Pinch the seam and ends to seal.

6 Place the dough, seam-side down, in the greased loaf pan/tin. Cover with oiled plastic wrap/cling film or a damp kitchen towel and let rise in a warm, draft-free place until doubled in size, about 90 minutes.

7 Preheat the oven to 375°F/190°C/gas 5. Bake for 35 to 40 minutes, or until the loaf is golden brown and sounds hollow when tapped on the bottom. Remove from the pan and let cool thoroughly on a wire rack before slicing. Store in a zip-top bag for up to 1 week.

1½ cups/170 g whole-wheat/wholemeal flour, plus extra for counter

1½ cups/170 g unbleached all-purpose/plain flour

2¼ tsp bread-machine yeast

1 tsp ground cinnamon

¾ tsp salt

¾ cup/180 ml almond milk or other milk

½ cup/120 ml canola oil, plus extra for the bowl and pan

¼ cup/50 g sugar or ¼ cup/60 ml agave syrup

1 cup/170 g raisins

MAKES 1 LOAF

This gorgeous loaf is studded with raisins, and it's just a little sweet with the scent of cinnamon. If you want to give someone a gift of bread, make this one and they will think you really fussed.

Cinnamon-Raisin Braid

1 In large bowl or stand mixer, mix together both flours, yeast, cinnamon, and salt.

2 In a small pot, warm the milk, ½ cup/120 ml water, the oil, and sugar to no warmer than 110°F/45°C, and then stir the mixture into the flour mixture.

3 With the dough hook attachment or a sturdy spoon, knead the dough for about 5 minutes to make a soft, fairly smooth dough. Scrape out the dough onto a floured counter, flatten it out to a 12-by-8-in/30-by-20-cm rectangle, and cover with the raisins. Fold the dough over onto the raisins and then form it into a ball with the seam on the bottom. Grease a large bowl and turn the dough in the bowl to coat it. Cover loosely with oiled plastic wrap/cling film. Let it rise in a warm, draft-free place for 45 minutes, or until doubled in bulk.

4 Punch down the dough and divide it into three equal pieces. Roll out each piece into a snake about 12 in/30 cm long, tapering each so it is fat in the middle and skinny on the ends.

5 On a greased baking sheet/tray, lay out the three ropes, pressing them together at one end, with one rope on top. Braid the three ropes loosely and tuck the ends under. Cover loosely with the oiled plastic wrap/cling film and let rise in a warm, draft-free place until doubled again, about 60 minutes.

6 Preheat the oven to 375°F/190°C/gas 5. Bake for 30 minutes, or until the top is dark golden and the loaf sounds hollow when tapped on the bottom. Remove from the sheet/tray and let cool completely on a rack before slicing. Store in a zip-top bag for up to 1 week.

BREADS

97

2 cups/230 g white whole-wheat/wholemeal flour

1 cup/115 g whole spelt flour

2¼ tsp bread-machine yeast

½ tsp salt

2 tbsp olive oil, plus extra for bowl and pan

2 tbsp agave syrup or maple syrup

½ cup/80 g hemp seeds

MAKES 10 ROLLS

Hemp seeds provide essential fats and protein and have a unique taste that you will grow to crave. Making rolls is easy and faster than loaves, so you can start these in the afternoon and have them for dinner. All hemp seeds sold in the United States are sterilized, so that they can't be used to grow hemp, and most are hulled. Look for hulled seeds and keep them in the refrigerator.

Hemp Seed Dinner Rolls

1 In a stand mixer or large bowl, combine both flours, the yeast, and salt. Mix well.

2 Measure 1¼ cups/300 ml warm water (no warmer than 110°F/45°C). Add the oil and agave syrup to the water and then stir into the flour mixture. With the dough hook attachment or a sturdy spoon, knead until the dough is smooth and slightly sticky and then knead in the hemp seeds. Grease a large bowl and turn the dough in the bowl to coat it. Cover with oiled plastic wrap/cling film. Let it rise in a warm, draft-free spot until doubled in bulk, about 1 hour.

3 Preheat the oven to 375°F/190°C/gas 5. Oil or lay parchment/baking paper on a baking sheet/tray. Divide the dough into 10 pieces and form each into a ball. Place them, seam-side down and 2 in/5cm apart, on the prepared pan, covering loosely with the oiled plastic wrap/cling film. Let rise until almost doubled, 45 minutes to 1 hour.

4 Uncover and bake for 15 minutes, until the rolls are golden brown and they sound hollow when turned over and tapped. Remove them from the pan to racks and let cool. Serve slightly warm or at room temperature. Store in a zip-top bag for up to 1 week.

4 cups/510 g whole-wheat/wholemeal flour

2 cups/255 g unbleached all-purpose/plain flour

½ cup/55 g toasted wheat germ

1 tbsp bread-machine yeast

2 tsp salt

1½ cups/300 ml hemp milk or nut milk

¼ cup/60 ml agave syrup

1½ tbsp cider vinegar

¼ cup/60 ml olive oil, plus extra for bowl

1 cup/120 g chopped onions

¼ cup/7 g chopped fresh sage and thyme

1 tsp coarsely cracked black pepper

MAKES 18 ROLLS

These savory rolls are a big hit at the holidays… or anytime! They have enough flavor so you don't need any kind of adornment. People love them plain, right out of the oven.

Herb and Onion Whole-Wheat Rolls

1 In a stand mixer or large bowl, mix together both flours, the wheat germ, yeast, and salt.

2 Measure ½ cup/120 ml warm water (no warmer than 110°F/45°C). Mix in the milk, agave syrup, and vinegar. Set aside.

3 In a medium frying pan over medium-high heat, heat the oil. Add the onion, lower the heat to medium-low, and sauté, stirring constantly, until soft and golden, 5 to 10 minutes. Add the herbs and pepper and cook for a few more minutes, until the herbs are fragrant. Remove from the heat and stir in the milk mixture, then take the temperature. If necessary, let the mixture cool to 110°F/45°C.

4 Stir the onion mixture into the flour mixture, kneading as it thickens. With the dough hook attachment or your hands, knead to produce a soft, supple dough, about 5 minutes. Grease a large bowl and turn the dough in the bowl to coat it. Cover with oiled plastic wrap/cling film. Let it rise in a warm, draft-free place until doubled in bulk, about 45 minutes.

5 Preheat the oven to 375°F/190°C/gas 5. Divide the dough into three even portions, and then divide them into six pieces each. Form each piece into a ball and place it on an oiled baking sheet/tray with 2 in/5 cm of space between each. Cover loosely with the oiled plastic wrap/cling film and let the rolls rise until almost doubled, about 30 minutes.

6 Uncover and bake for 15 to 17 minutes, or until the tops are golden brown and the bottoms sound hollow when tapped with a finger. Remove them from the pan to racks and let cool. Serve slightly warm or at room temperature. Store in a zip-top bag for up to 1 week.

1 cup/115 g white whole-wheat/wholemeal flour

½ cup/80 g rolled oats

1 tsp bread-machine yeast

¼ tsp salt

¼ cup/60 ml brown rice syrup

2 tbsp canola oil or melted Earth Balance margarine, plus extra for bowl and pan

½ cup/85 g pitted, chopped dates

MAKES 12 ROLLS

These are no-knead, almost effortless little rolls. Simply stir the ingredients together and allow them to sit in the refrigerator overnight! They are subtly sweet and studded with sweet dates. If you want to take them over the top, sprinkle the tops with cinnamon and turbinado sugar before they rise in the muffin tins.

Overnight Oat-Date Rolls

1 In a stand mixer or large bowl, mix together the flour, oats, yeast, and salt.

2 Measure 1 cup/240 ml warm water (no warmer than 110°F/45°C). Mix in the brown rice syrup and oil, then stir into the flour mixture with the dough hook attachment or a sturdy spoon. When a dough starts to form, stir in the dates. The dough will be very soft and sticky. Transfer to an oiled bowl and let it rise in a warm, draft-free spot until doubled in bulk, about 90 minutes, then cover tightly with plastic wrap/cling film and refrigerate overnight, or for up to 2 days.

3 Preheat the oven to 375°F/190°C/gas 5. Oil twelve cups of a muffin pan/fairy cake pan/tin and reserve.

4 Without stirring or disturbing the dough, scoop ¼-cup/60-ml portions into the muffin cups. Cover the pan lightly with oiled plastic wrap/cling film, then let the dough rise in a warm, draft-free place until doubled, 45 minutes to 1½ hours, depending on the temperature of the room.

5 Uncover and bake for 15 minutes, or until the buns sound hollow when tapped on the bottom. Let them cool in the pan for 5 minutes, then carefully remove them to a rack. Let cool completely before storing in a zip-top bag for up to 1 week.

1 cup/195 g brown whole teff

½ cup/120 ml agave syrup

½ cup/120 ml canola oil, plus extra for bowl

2½ cups/315 g whole-wheat/wholemeal flour

½ cup/60 g teff flour

2 tsp bread-machine yeast

2 tsp salt

Coarse cornmeal

MAKES ABOUT 24 BREADSTICKS

Teff is the tiniest grain available, and the teensy seeds are powerfully nutritious. In these dramatically cocoa-colored breadsticks, the teff is just partially cooked—long enough to soften a little but not make it into porridge. Originally grown in Ethiopia, teff coaxes concentrated nutrients from the poorest soils, with very little water.

Teff Breadsticks

1 In a 1-qt/960-ml saucepan, bring 2 cups/480 ml water to a boil. Add the whole teff, stir, return the liquid to a boil, then reduce the heat to low. Cover tightly and simmer for 10 minutes. The teff will still be crunchy. Remove the pan from the heat and stir in the agave syrup and oil to help cool the mixture to 110°F/45°C.

2 In a stand mixer or large bowl, mix together 2 cups/255 g of the whole-wheat/wholemeal flour, the teff flour, yeast, and salt.

3 When the wet mixture is the proper temperature, stir it into the dry mixture, then knead with the dough hook attachment or a sturdy spoon for 5 minutes. If the dough is still sticky, gradually mix in the remaining ½ cup/60 g whole-wheat/wholemeal flour to make a soft dough. Grease a large bowl and turn the dough in the bowl to coat it. Cover with oiled plastic wrap/cling film. Let it rise in a warm, draft-free place until doubled in bulk, about 1 hour.

4 Preheat the oven to 400°F/200°C/gas 6. Punch down the dough and divide it into four portions. Divide each portion into six pieces, then roll each out into a snake about 10 in/25 cm long. Coat two baking sheets/trays with cornmeal, then place the snakes on the pans with 2 in/5 cm between them.

5 Cover the breadsticks with the oiled plastic wrap/cling film and let them rise until doubled, about 20 minutes. Uncover and bake for about 12 minutes, until browned and cooked through. Transfer the breadsticks to racks to cool. Store tightly wrapped for up to 1 week.

Vegetable oil spray

1 cup/85 g raw
buckwheat groats

1 cup/115 g
whole-wheat/wholemeal
pastry/soft-wheat flour

¾ cup/85 g unbleached
all-purpose/plain flour

¼ cup/10 g nutritional
yeast

1 tsp baking powder

1 tsp baking soda/
bicarbonate of soda

½ tsp salt

½ cup/120 ml coconut oil
or margarine, frozen

1 tbsp rice vinegar

¾ cup/180 ml plain rice
milk or other milk

MAKES 10 BISCUITS

Whole buckwheat groats act like crunchy nuts in these biscuits, adding an earthy flavor and lots of nutritious whole grain. These biscuits are quick and easy to stir up for serving with soups and salads. A bit of nutritional yeast adds a cheesy taste and a hit of B_{12}, for both yum factor and health benefits.

Crunchy Buckwheat Drop Biscuits

1 Preheat the oven to 400°F/200°C/gas 6. Coat a baking sheet/tray with vegetable oil spray.

2 In a large bowl, mix together the buckwheat groats, both flours, the yeast, baking powder, baking soda/bicarbonate of soda, and salt.

3 Using the large holes on a grater, grate the coconut oil into the flour mixture, tossing the shreds to coat with flour. Use your fingers to work the shreds into bits the size of corn kernels.

4 Quickly stir the vinegar and milk into the flour mixture, just until the flours are moistened—don't overmix or the biscuits will be tough.

5 Scoop a scant ¼ cup/60 ml of dough to create each round, and tap it out onto the prepared pan, leaving 2 in/5 cm between each biscuit.

6 Bake for about 15 minutes, or until the bottoms are browned and the tops are golden. Transfer the biscuits to wire racks and let them cool for 5 minutes before serving. Store in a zip-top bag for up to 1 week.

Vegetable oil spray

2¼ cups/275 g whole-wheat/wholemeal pastry/soft-wheat flour

1½ tbsp sugar

1½ tsp dried thyme

¾ tsp baking powder

¾ tsp baking soda/bicarbonate of soda

¾ tsp salt

¼ cup/60 ml cold-press corn or canola oil

5 tbsp/75 ml plain soymilk or other milk

1½ tsp cider vinegar

1½ cups/300 g mashed or pureed baked sweet potatoes

MAKES 12 BISCUITS

These are a hybrid of two Southern culinary classics: sweet potatoes and biscuits. Unlike standard biscuits, these are vegan and made with liquid oils for a much more healthful result. The golden corn oil adds a hint of buttery flavor.

Sweet Potato Drop Biscuits

1 Preheat the oven to 400°F/200°C/gas 6. Lightly coat a large baking sheet/tray with vegetable oil spray or line it with parchment/baking paper.

2 In a large bowl, whisk together the flour, sugar, thyme, baking powder, baking soda/bicarbonate of soda, and salt.

3 In a medium bowl, stir to combine the corn oil, soymilk, and vinegar, then stir in the sweet potatoes.

4 Stir the wet ingredients into the dry just until mixed.

5 Use an oiled ¼-cup/60-ml measure to scoop and drop portions of the dough onto the prepared pan with 2 in/5 cm between the biscuits. Slightly flatten the dough to make each biscuit 1 in/2.5 cm thick.

6 Bake for 15 minutes, or until the edges and bottoms of the biscuits are golden brown. Transfer the biscuits to racks and let cool, or serve warm. Store in a zip-top bag for up to 1 week.

2 cups/310 g rolled oats

6 tbsp/45 g white whole-wheat/wholemeal flour, plus extra for counter

1 tsp salt

¾ tsp baking powder

¼ cup/55 g coconut oil or Earth Balance margarine, frozen

9 tbsp/105 ml unsweetened rice milk or other milk

1 tbsp coarse salt or sesame seeds (optional)

MAKES ABOUT 24 CRACKERS

If you have only had boxed crackers before, prepare to taste the real thing. These are classic, mostly oat crisps that have been a tradition in Scotland for centuries but made vegan for your munching pleasure. Be sure to roll them thinly and bake them until they are crisp.

Scottish Oat Crackers

1 Preheat the oven to 375°F/190°C/gas 5. Line two large baking sheets/trays with silicone baking liners or parchment/baking paper.

2 In a food processor, pulse to finely grind the oats, flour, salt, and baking powder. Add the coconut oil and pulse until it is cut into tiny bits, then add 6 tbsp/90 ml of the milk and pulse just to barely bring the mixture into a ball. Place the dough on a lightly floured counter and knead just to mix, adding milk if needed to hold it together.

3 Scatter more flour on the counter and roll out the dough to ⅛ in/3 mm thick. Cut the dough into 2-in/5-cm squares— or whatever size you desire. If you like a crunchy topping, brush the crackers with the remaining milk and sprinkle with coarse salt. Place the crackers on the prepared pans. Bake for 12 to 15 minutes, rotating the pans midway, until the crackers are completely stiff when you remove them from the pan. If they bend or flex at all, put them back in for another 5 minutes. Transfer the crackers to racks and let cool completely before storing them in airtight containers for up to 1 week.

1½ cups/170 g whole-wheat/wholemeal pastry/soft-wheat flour, plus extra for counter

¼ cup/30 g ground flax seeds

¼ cup/30 g whole flax seeds

¼ cup/10 g raw pumpkin seeds, finely chopped

1 tsp sugar

½ tsp baking powder

¼ tsp salt

½ cup/120 ml unsweetened almond milk or other milk

¼ cup/60 ml extra-virgin olive oil

Coarse salt (optional)

MAKES ABOUT 30 CRACKERS

Give your homemade crackers even more snap with crunchy seeds, which also pack essential fats and minerals into every tasty bite. These are so hearty they stand alone, or they can complement a spread like Almond-Cashew "Chèvre" (page 44).

Flax and Pepita Crackers

1 Preheat the oven to 325°F/165°C/gas 3. Line two baking sheets/trays with parchment/baking paper.

2 In a large bowl, mix together the flour, ground and whole flax, pumpkin seeds, sugar, baking powder, and salt.

3 In a cup, mix together the milk and oil, then stir them into the flour mixture until well combined.

4 On a well-floured counter, roll out the dough to ⅛ in/3 mm thick. Cut it into squares or rectangles and sprinkle with coarse salt, if desired.

5 Transfer each square or rectangle to the prepared pans and bake for 20 minutes (longer if they are thicker), until the edges are golden brown and the crackers quite firm when you take them out. Transfer the crackers to racks to cool before storing them in airtight containers for up to 1 week.

¾ cup/85 g unbleached all-purpose/plain flour

¾ cup/100 g chickpea flour

½ tsp ground cumin

½ tsp freshly cracked black pepper

¼ tsp salt

1 cup/240 ml plain almond milk or other milk

1 tbsp cider vinegar

Vegetable oil, for pan

MAKES 5 FLATBREADS

The delicious dosas served at your local Indian restaurant are quite time consuming to make, so I created these, which take hardly any time at all. Like thin, savory pancakes, they make a great alternative to serving the same old rice with curries. Serve the flatbreads warm with soup, or roll them up with chutneys and sautéed onions inside.

Quick Indian Flatbreads

1 In a large bowl, combine both flours, the cumin, pepper, and salt.

2 In a cup, whisk ½ cup/120 ml water with the milk and vinegar, then stir them into the dry mixture. Add additional water, if needed, to make a batter the consistency of heavy cream. Cover with plastic wrap/cling film and let stand for half an hour for the flours to hydrate fully.

3 Heat a nonstick, 10-in/25-cm frying pan over high heat, and use a paper towel/absorbent paper to smear just a bit of oil on the pan.

4 Scoop ½ cup/240 ml of the batter onto the hot pan, then tilt and swirl the pan to spread the batter into a round about 8 in/20 cm across. If the first one is too thick, thin the batter a bit with water.

5 Cook, reducing the heat to medium as the bread starts to bubble around the edges. When the edges look firm and toasty, flip the bread with a spatula and cook until golden spots appear. Slide it onto a plate and continue with the rest of the batter, raising the heat to high again each time. Store in an airtight bag or container for up to 2 days.

3 cups/385 g unbleached all-purpose/plain flour, plus extra for counter and pan

3 cups/385 g whole-wheat/wholemeal flour

1 tbsp bread-machine yeast

2 tsp salt

1 tbsp extra-virgin olive oil, plus extra for bowl

MAKES 16 PITA BREADS

If you thought there was a trick to getting that pocket in the bread, there really isn't. Any bread that isn't given very long to rise will create a big pocket of air under the top crust, so it is almost a happy mistake.

Whole-Wheat Pita Bread

1 In a large bowl or stand mixer fitted with a dough hook, mix together the all-purpose/plain flour, 2 cups/255 g of the whole-wheat/wholemeal flour, the yeast, and salt. Mix in 2½ cups/600 ml warm (no warmer than 110°F/45°C) water, then add the oil. While mixing the dough, add the remaining 1 cup/130 g wheat flour to make a soft dough. Knead for 5 minutes, until supple and springy. Wash, dry, and oil the bowl, then put the dough in it, turn to coat, and cover with oiled plastic wrap/cling film. Let it rise in a warm, draft-free place until doubled in bulk, about 1 hour.

2 Preheat the oven with a pizza stone inside to 450°F/230°C/ gas 8 for 30 minutes.

3 On a lightly floured counter, divide the dough in half, then divide one half into eight pieces, while keeping the other half covered. Roll each piece into a round 8 to 10 in/20 to 25 cm in diameter. Place them on a pan or counter, not touching. Continue until the remaining dough is formed into rounds. Cover the rounds with damp cloths or plastic wrap/cling film for 15 minutes to let them rise slightly.

4 Slide one or two rounds onto a rimless baking sheet/tray sprinkled with flour and then slide them onto the hot pizza stone. Bake until they have ballooned, 2 to 3 minutes. Remove them with the baking sheet/tray and tongs to cool on a wire rack. Repeat with the remaining rounds. Let them cool thoroughly before storing in a zip-top bag for up to 1 week.

1 cup/130 g
chickpea flour

½ tsp salt

¼ cup/60 ml tahini paste

3 tbsp extra-virgin olive oil

2 tbsp untoasted hulled
sesame seeds

SERVES 8

This savory bread is actually eaten as a sandwich filling in parts of Italy, where it is cooked by street vendors. The soft, dense socca has the hint of eggy flavor that chickpea flour imparts, as well as the added protein of beans. You can eat it any way you want—smeared with a tasty spread or layered inside crusty breads. Serve warm with a salad.

Sesame Socca

1 Preheat the oven to 400°F/200°C/gas 6. Place a 12-in/30.5-cm cast-iron frying pan in the oven for 5 minutes.

2 In a large bowl, whisk together the flour and salt. Whisk in 1½ cups/360 ml water, a little at a time, making a smooth paste. Whisk in the tahini.

3 Pour 2 tbsp of the oil into the frying pan and swirl to coat, then sprinkle in half of the sesame seeds. Pour the batter into the pan, sprinkle with the remaining seeds, and drizzle with the remaining 1 tbsp oil.

4 Bake for 30 minutes, until the socca is browned on top and pulls away from the sides of the pan. Carefully invert it onto a cutting board (watch out for hot oil) and slice it into wedges. Store, tightly wrapped, in the refrigerator for up to 1 week.

½ cup/60 g white whole-wheat/wholemeal flour

½ cup/60 g spelt flour

¼ cup/30 g wheat germ

¼ tsp baking soda/bicarbonate of soda

¼ tsp salt

2 tbsp extra-virgin olive oil

½ cup/60 g chopped onion

½ tsp cider vinegar

SERVES 4

Your trusty cast-iron pan will bake this savory onion-slathered bread to perfection. If you don't have a cast-iron pan, you can sauté the onions in a frying pan, then transfer them to a cake pan to complete and bake. Serve it hot with dips or soups.

Skillet Onion Flatbread

1 Preheat the oven to 400°F/200°C/gas 6.

2 In a large bowl, mix together both flours, the wheat germ, baking soda/bicarbonate of soda, and salt.

3 In a 12-in/30.5-cm cast-iron frying pan, heat the oil and then sauté the onion for 10 minutes, until golden and soft.

4 Whisk 1½ cups/360 ml water and the vinegar into the flour mixture, then pour the batter over the onion in the pan. Bake for 30 minutes, until the bread pulls away from the sides of the pan and is golden brown on the top and bottom. Slice the bread into wedges and use a pizza spatula to serve. Store, tightly wrapped, in the refrigerator for up to 1 week.

Sauces and Condiments

What would life be without sauces? Many a food has been lifted from fine to fabulous by the magical qualities of a well-chosen sauce. All sorts of dips and condiments can make things as simple as a chunk of bread or a bowl of rice into a gourmet meal.

Eating simple, plant-based foods will be much more exciting and tasty once you master a repertoire of saucy embellishments. Every cuisine in the world has their sauces, from the simplest salsa to the haute cuisine of French reductions and emulsions. Making all kinds of delicious sauces with vegan ingredients is easy and will satisfy even the most gourmet among us.

Finding the best pairing for a sauce with a dish is the first step. What kind of cuisine are you having? A creamy Béchamel Sauce (page 123) complements French and Italian meals. Thai Peanut Sauce (page 128) is a surefire hit with Thai food—even take-out that needs a little extra oomph. Basic spaghetti sauce (see page 120) goes everywhere, from a pot of pasta to pizzas and even sandwiches like grinders and meatball subs. Everybody knows what to do with Vegan "Mayonnaise" (page 113), don't they?

Once you pick your culinary territory, think about what you might call the "weight" pairing of the food and the sauce. A subtle, understated white asparagus would be overwhelmed by a dose of spaghetti sauce but will be perked up considerably by Spanish Salsa Verde (page 119) or even Chinese Sesame Sauce (page 127). The White Wine and Herb Reduction (page 132) would also be a nice touch. The fiery, tart Bengali Curry Simmer Sauce (page 130) will make a feast of anything, so put your sturdiest, most flavorful beans and veggies into that pot and make sure you have some raita (see page 114) on the side to cool it off.

Get saucy with plant foods and celebrate life—with flavor!

6 oz/170 g silken tofu

2 tsp Dijon mustard

2 tsp freshly squeezed lemon juice

1 tsp agave syrup

½ tsp salt

¼ tsp paprika

⅛ tsp ground turmeric

¼ cup/60 ml extra-virgin olive oil

MAKES ABOUT

1 CUP / 240 ML

First off, I have to admit that Vegenaise vegan "mayo" is pretty good, so if you have a jar of that, you may well have met your mayonnaise needs. However, this tofu-based "mayo" gives it a run for the money and is full of jazzy flavors.

Vegan "Mayonnaise"

In a food processor or blender, puree the tofu. Scrape down the sides and repeat until it is completely smooth. (Unless you are using a powerful blender, it will not get any smoother once you add the remaining ingredients.) Add the mustard, lemon juice, agave syrup, salt, paprika, and turmeric and process until smooth and combined, scraping down the sides and repeating if needed. With the machine running, slowly drizzle in the oil to make a smooth emulsion. Take the lid off and stir from the bottom with a spatula to bring all the tofu into the mixture, then process to get it all mixed. Transfer the "mayo" to a jar, cover, and refrigerate for up to 1 week.

1 tbsp coarsely chopped peeled fresh ginger

1 cup/50 g peeled, seeded, diced cucumber

½ cup/120 ml coconut milk

2 tbsp freshly squeezed lemon juice

½ tsp salt

MAKES ABOUT
1 CUP / 240 ML

Raitas are the cooling sauces that you put alongside hot and spicy Indian food, so that you can dive in for a calming spoonful when the heat is just too much. Cucumber is a classic cooler, so whip this up to go with your next curry.

Cucumber Raita
with Coconut Milk

In a food processor, mince the ginger finely, scraping down the sides after pulsing. Add the cucumber, milk, lemon juice, and salt. Pulse a few times to make a coarse puree. Transfer the raita to a small bowl and refrigerate for 1 hour before serving. Raita keeps for 3 days in a covered container in the refrigerator.

1 lb/455 g globe
eggplant/aubergine

1 onion, slivered

2 tbsp extra-virgin olive oil

1 tbsp pomegranate
molasses or juice
concentrate

1 tbsp brown sugar

½ tsp salt

Pomegranate seeds

MAKES ABOUT
3 CUPS / 720 ML

If you have not tried pomegranate molasses, find a bottle and make this dish. It's not molasses at all, but a thick, boiled-down syrup made from pomegranate juice. The result is dark and tangy, and adds a burst of Middle Eastern intrigue to this eggplant spread. Serve with pita wedges or in sandwiches, or as a relish alongside Middle Eastern food.

Mediterranean Eggplant Relish
with Pomegranate Molasses

Preheat the oven to 400°F/200°C/gas 6. Peel and cut the eggplant/aubergine into ½-in/12-mm cubes. Put them in a deep roasting pan/tray with the onion; drizzle with the oil, and toss to coat. Cover the pan tightly with aluminum foil and roast for 20 minutes. Uncover, stir the vegetables, and roast for 20 minutes more, until butter soft and moist. Drizzle with the pomegranate molasses and mix well with the brown sugar and salt. Let the mixture cool to room temperature, then serve it sprinkled with pomegranate seeds. Store leftovers in an airtight container in the refrigerator for up to 1 week.

3 cups/90 g fresh basil leaves

1 cup/30 g fresh spinach

½ cup/55 g pine nuts, toasted

2 garlic cloves, peeled

½ tsp salt

½ cup/120 ml extra-virgin olive oil

MAKES ABOUT

1 CUP / 240 ML

Pesto is great tossed with hot pasta or stirred into a bowl of soup. You might want to start putting it in everything, once you know that basil is a potent source of B_6 and lots of other valuable nutrients.

Basil Pesto

Put the basil, spinach, pine nuts, garlic, and salt in a food processor and process until they are finely ground. Scrape down the sides and process until smooth. With the motor running, drizzle in the oil and process to make a smooth paste. Use immediately or cover the surface of the pesto with plastic wrap/cling film to prevent it from browning. Refrigerate for up to 2 days.

- 2 cups/60 g fresh spinach
- ½ cup/55 g hazelnuts, toasted and skinned
- 2 tbsp minced fresh sage leaves
- 2 tbsp minced fresh parsley leaves
- 1 garlic clove, peeled
- ¼ cup/60 ml extra-virgin olive oil or hazelnut oil
- ½ tsp salt

MAKES ABOUT
¾ CUP / 180 ML

Summertime belongs to fresh basil, but when it's cold outside, try this one made with the sturdy herbs we associate with roasting and stewing. Hazelnuts add toasty flavor and even boost your essential fats at the same time. This is great tossed with hot penne and roasted veggies, or spread on pizza for a sauce.

Sage-Hazelnut Winter Pesto

In a food processor, combine the spinach, hazelnuts, sage, parsley, and garlic and process until the mixture is finely ground. Scrape down the sides and process until smooth. With the motor running, drizzle in the oil and process to a creamy paste. Add the salt and adjust the seasoning. Use immediately or cover the surface of the pesto with plastic wrap/cling film to prevent it from browning. Refrigerate for up to 2 days.

1 cup/185 g chopped
fresh tomato

¼ cup/30 g chopped
onion

¼ cup/7 g chopped
cilantro/fresh coriander

1 large jalapeño or
chipotle chile, seeded
and minced

1 tbsp freshly squeezed
lime juice

1 garlic clove, minced

¼ tsp salt

½ cup/about 100 g diced
avocado, black beans,
chopped green bell
peppers/capsicums, or
corn (optional)

MAKES ABOUT
2 CUPS / 480 ML

Salsa is a great way to get your veggies; just scoop
large amounts of this tasty sauce onto chips and
munch away. It's also a good way to use a ripe
avocado or some leftover cooked beans and make
a meal of it.

Basic
Tomato Salsa

In a medium bowl, combine the tomato, onion, cilantro/fresh
coriander, chile, lime juice, garlic, and salt. Toss to mix. As
desired, add any of the add-ins. Serve immediately or cover
and refrigerate for up to 2 days.

2 garlic cloves, peeled

¾ cup/20 g fresh flat-leaf parsley, well dried (see Note)

4 green olives, pitted and chopped

2 tbsp capers, rinsed

2 tbsp champagne vinegar

¼ cup/60 ml extra-virgin olive oil

MAKES ABOUT
½ CUP / 120 ML

When a sprightly green sauce is called for, this is the one. The Spaniards use it as a classic topper for fish; it is also great on a slab of polenta, on a tortilla, over tofu, or on toast.

Spanish Salsa Verde

In a food processor, mince the garlic. Add the parsley and process to finely mince it. Add the olives, capers, and vinegar and pulse into chunks. Scrape down the sides and process again. With the motor running, pour in the oil and thoroughly puree the salsa. Serve immediately or cover tightly and refrigerate for up to 4 days.

NOTE: *It is important for the leaves to be very dry so the sauce is not diluted by water clinging to them.*

2 tbsp extra-virgin olive oil

2 ribs celery, chopped

1 cup/120 g chopped onions

½ cup/50 g grated carrot

2 garlic cloves, sliced

14 oz/400 g canned tomato puree/tinned sieved tomatoes

14 oz/400 g canned/ tinned diced tomatoes

2 tbsp Tapenade (facing page) or store-bought

1 tsp dried basil

1 tsp dried oregano

1 tsp agave syrup or other sweetener

½ cup/15 g chopped fresh parsley

Salt

Freshly cracked black pepper

MAKES

As long as you are making a tomato sauce, you might as well pack it with more veggies than the usual stuff in a jar. Carrots give it a mild crunch and a sweetness that counters the slightly acidic tomatoes.

Basic Veggie Spaghetti or Pizza Sauce

1 In a 4-qt/4-L pot, heat the oil and add the celery, onions, and carrot. Over medium-high heat, bring them to a sizzle, then reduce the heat to medium-low and slowly sauté until the vegetables are very soft. Add the garlic and cook, stirring until fragrant, about 4 minutes. Add the tomato puree/sieved tomatoes, diced tomatoes, tapenade, basil, oregano, and agave syrup. Bring to a simmer, then reduce the heat to a low simmer and cook until thick, stirring every 10 minutes or so.

2 When the sauce is thick, stir in the parsley and cook for another couple of minutes. Taste and season with salt and pepper. Use immediately or cover and refrigerate for up to 1 week. Reheat in a pot over low heat.

1 cup kalamata or other Mediterranean black olives, pitted

6 tbsp/20 g minced fresh basil

2 tbsp capers, rinsed and drained

2 tbsp fresh thyme

2 tbsp minced orange zest

2 garlic cloves, peeled

2 tbsp extra-virgin olive oil

MAKES ABOUT
1 CUP / 240 ML

The health benefits of the Mediterranean diet are abundant in this classic spread. Crushed olives, herbs, and a spike of orange zest taste so delicious you will want to slather this tapenade on bread, stir it into plain rice, or use it to jazz up tomato sauces.

Tapenade

In a food processor, finely mince the olives, basil, capers, thyme, orange zest, and garlic. Add the oil and scrape down the sides, then process until the olives are chopped and mixed but still chunky. Cover and refrigerate the tapenade for up to 2 weeks.

3 tbsp extra-virgin olive oil, plus extra as needed

½ cup/55 g slivered/flaked almonds

Three 1-in/2-cm slices white baguette

2 garlic cloves, peeled

2 large/240 g roasted red bell peppers/capsicums, peeled

1 tbsp chopped fresh parsley

2 tsp paprika

2 tbsp sherry vinegar

½ tsp salt

MAKES ABOUT
1½ CUPS / 360 ML

Romesco is the perfect topper for all sorts of Spanish-flavored items, from tapas like roasted potatoes to Spanish Saffron Tortilla (page 423). It's a great change from tomato-based sauces, with sweet peppers and almonds that nourish your very essence.

Romesco Sauce

In a large frying pan, heat the oil over medium heat, then add the almonds and baguette slices. Stir, cooking until the nuts are golden and the bread is toasted, about 5 minutes. In a blender or food processor, mince the almonds, bread, and garlic. Add the bell peppers/capsicums, parsley, and paprika and process to make a paste. Add the vinegar and salt and process, then drizzle in more oil, 1 tbsp at a time, to make it the desired consistency. If you are cutting back on oil today, stir in water to thin it. Cover and refrigerate for up to 1 week.

2 tbsp extra-virgin olive oil or cold-press corn oil

2 tbsp unbleached all-purpose/plain flour

1 tbsp chickpea flour

1½ cups/360 ml unsweetened rice milk or other milk

¼ cup/60 ml white wine

½ tsp salt

MAKES ABOUT
2 CUPS / 480 ML

This all-purpose white sauce can be used in many ways, from simply pouring it over a plate of pasta and veggies to layering it in lasagna or making it the base for a quick creamy soup. Since béchamel is usually all about milk and butter, nondairy milks, flavorful oil, and a bit of chickpea flour work alchemy to make a creamy plant-based sauce that is just as tasty.

Béchamel Sauce

1 In a 4-qt/4-L saucepan, whisk together the oil, all-purpose/plain flour, and chickpea flour to make a smooth paste. Put the pan over medium heat and stir constantly, making sure to reach into the corners of the pan. When the mixture starts to bubble, reduce the heat to low and keep whisking for 1 minute, until the paste is thoroughly cooked. Take off the heat and whisk in the milk, a little at a time, making a thick paste. Stir in the wine and salt and, over medium-low heat, bring the sauce to a low simmer, until it bubbles around the edges of the pan. Take it off the heat.

2 Serve warm or let cool and refrigerate for up to 1 week. Reheat very gently; do not boil, or it may separate.

2 tbsp canola oil or Earth Balance margarine

4 oz/100 g fresh button mushrooms, coarsely chopped

¼ cup/30 g chopped onion

3 tbsp unbleached all-purpose/plain flour

1 cup/240 ml plain rice milk

1 cup/240 ml Basic Vegetable Stock (page 49) or Mushroom Stock (page 51)

3 tbsp nutritional yeast

1 tbsp tamari or soy sauce

1 tsp crumbled dried sage leaves

¼ tsp dried thyme

¼ tsp dried marjoram

¼ tsp salt

Freshly cracked black pepper

MAKES ABOUT
2¼ CUPS / 540 ML

Sometimes gravy just hits the spot—with mashed potatoes, with Homemade Mock Turkey Roast with Stuffing (page 422), or over biscuits at breakfast. All our umami lessons pay off in this creamy gravy, where mushrooms, soy sauce, and nutritional yeast add complexity and "meatiness." This updated classic will become a family favorite.

Basic Mushroom Gravy
with Herbs

1 In a medium saucepan over medium-high heat, warm the oil, then add the mushrooms and onion. Sauté until the mushrooms are shrunken and wet. Sprinkle on the flour, then stir to make a paste. Keep cooking and stirring until the mixture starts sticking to the pan. In a large measuring cup, combine the milk, stock, yeast, tamari, sage, thyme, and marjoram. Whisk to combine.

2 Over medium heat, continue to stir the mushroom mixture constantly, scraping the pan with the spatula, until the mixture bubbles and turns a shade darker and the mushrooms brown. Take the pan off the heat, add a little of the milk mixture, and work it into a paste with the spatula. Keep adding the liquid a little at a time and working it in, switching to a whisk as it gets incorporated.

3 Put the pan back over medium-high heat. Whisk constantly until the gravy boils, then immediately reduce the heat to low and cook for a couple of minutes, until thickened. Add the salt and season with pepper and take the gravy off the heat. Serve warm or let cool and refrigerate for up to 1 week. Reheat gently over low heat.

¼ cup/30 g shredded/desiccated unsweetened coconut
¼ cup/30 g raw cashews
1 tbsp cumin seeds
1 tbsp brown mustard seeds
1 tbsp ground coriander
1 cup/30 g cilantro/fresh coriander
½ cup/15 g fresh mint
1 jalapeño, seeded
1 tbsp sliced peeled fresh ginger
6 tbsp/90 ml coconut milk
1 tbsp freshly squeezed lemon juice
1 tbsp brown sugar or jaggery
½ tsp salt

MAKES ABOUT
¾ CUP / 180 ML

Chutneys add excitement to an Indian meal, and it is best to have at least one with any kind of curry. This is a creamy, herbal one—bright with mint and lemon. It would make an excellent condiment alongside Bengali Curry of Cauliflower and Kidney Beans (page 418) or Saag "Paneer" (page 420).

Cilantro-Mint Chutney
with Coconut Milk

1 Preheat the oven to 300°F/150°C/gas 2. Toast the unsweetened coconut on a baking sheet/tray with sides for 5 minutes, then stir and toast for another 5 minutes, until it is golden. In a food processor, grind the coconut and cashews together to make a paste.

2 In a frying pan over high heat, toast the cumin and mustard seeds, shaking and stirring constantly, until they are fragrant, 30 to 60 seconds. Add the ground coriander and toast for a few seconds; remove from the heat.

3 Put the spices in the food processor with the coconut mixture. Puree, then add the cilantro/fresh coriander, mint, jalapeño (starting with a small amount and adding more to taste), and ginger. Puree the mixture thoroughly. Add the milk, lemon juice, brown sugar, and salt and process to combine thoroughly. Adjust the spiciness and seasoning as desired. Cover and refrigerate for up to 3 days.

SAUCES AND CONDIMENTS

¾ cup/90 g shredded/
desiccated unsweetened
coconut

2 tbsp coconut oil

4 oz/115 g tempeh,
finely chopped

2 tsp soy sauce

Paste

1 stalk lemon grass,
chopped

2 small shallots, peeled

2 tbsp sliced peeled
fresh ginger

2 garlic cloves, peeled

1½ tsp dried fennel seeds

1 tsp red pepper flakes

½ tsp ground turmeric

Coconut oil as needed
for grinding, plus 1 tsp

2 tsp freshly squeezed
lime juice

½ tsp sugar

¼ tsp salt

2 large kaffir lime leaves,
or the zest of 1 lime

MAKES ABOUT
1 QT / 960 ML

Everyone who tries this calls it "addictive," and you will see why. Turning tempeh into a spicy, crispy topping for rice is brilliance. Tempeh was invented by the Indonesians, and clearly that region of the world has mastered the coconut as well. Put out a bowl of this with Indonesian food, or use it to turn a simple bowl of brown rice and veggies into a delicious meal.

Coconut and Tempeh Serunding
(Malaysian Condiment)

1 In a medium frying pan over medium heat or in an oven at 300°F/150°C/gas 2, toast the unsweetened coconut until it is fragrant and golden brown, about 10 minutes. Set it aside to cool in a bowl.

2 Place the frying pan over high heat and add the coconut oil. Sprinkle the tempeh with the soy sauce. Fry the tempeh until it is dry and crisp, about 4 minutes. Transfer the tempeh to the bowl with the toasted coconut and reserve.

3 TO MAKE THE PASTE: In a spice grinder or large mortar, grind the lemon grass, shallots, ginger, garlic, fennel, pepper flakes, and turmeric, using a little coconut oil if necessary to get it to grind thoroughly.

4 Heat the 1 tsp coconut oil in a large frying pan and fry the spice paste. When the paste is fragrant and has become a shade darker, add the lime juice, sugar, and salt and mix well. Add the tempeh mixture and keep stirring constantly over low heat until the oil is absorbed. Add the lime leaves and cook for 3 minutes, until fragrant. Let the serunding cool completely before serving. Store in an airtight container in the refrigerator for up to 1 week.

4 garlic cloves, peeled

2 in/5 cm fresh ginger, peeled

½ cup/120 ml tahini paste

¼ cup/50 g smooth peanut butter

6 tbsp/90 ml tamari or soy sauce

¼ cup/60 ml rice vinegar

2 tbsp sesame oil

2 tbsp agave syrup

1 tsp red pepper flakes

MAKES ABOUT
1½ CUPS / 360 ML

This sauce is great in stir-fries, on noodles or rice, or even drizzled on green salads. Keep a jar of it in the fridge, and you will be ready to whip up fast and flavorful meals. This makes a thick sauce, but it can be thinned with water for a salad dressing.

Chinese Sesame Sauce

In a food processor, mince the garlic and ginger. Add the tahini and peanut butter and pulse to mix well. Scrape down the sides and process again. Add the tamari, vinegar, oil, agave syrup, and pepper flakes and process until smooth. Transfer the sauce to a bowl, cover, and refrigerate for up to 2 weeks.

1 cup/240 ml coconut milk

1½ to 2 tsp red curry paste

¼ cup/55 g smooth peanut butter

2 tbsp palm sugar or brown sugar

2 tbsp freshly squeezed lemon juice

2 tsp soy sauce

MAKES ABOUT
1½ CUPS / 360 ML

Make this sauce to serve with grilled tofu or noodles, and keep the remainder in the refrigerator for quick meals all week long. Slather it on sandwiches, dip veggies in it, or serve it with spring rolls. Red curry paste should be in the Asian section of your supermarket; be sure to read the label and buy a brand with no fish sauce or mysterious ingredients.

Thai Peanut Sauce

Pour the milk into a small saucepan over medium heat and whisk in the curry paste. Bring it to a simmer, then whisk in the peanut butter, palm sugar, lemon juice, and soy sauce until smooth. Simmer until the sauce thickens, but if the oil starts to separate, take it off the heat and whisk to combine. Use immediately or cool and refrigerate for up to 2 weeks. Reheat over low heat.

½ cup/120 ml canola oil

6 tbsp/20 g thickly sliced garlic, cut lengthwise

6 tbsp/20 g sliced shallots

6 large dried Thai red chiles, seeded and chopped

¼ cup/50 g palm sugar

2 tsp salt

MAKES ABOUT
¾ CUP / 180 ML

Make this sauce with the stove fan cranked, or some windows open. Scorching the chiles results in a deep, char-flavored sauce that is out of this world; it also sends a certain amount of the capsaicin heat airborne, where it will make you cough if you breathe too much of it. This sweet, hot, burnt sauce is a fine accompaniment to any spring roll or Thai dish, to dab a little accent here and there.

Thai Blackened Chile Sauce

1 In a small saucepan, heat the oil over medium-high heat. Add the garlic and quickly fry until it is golden; remove it with a slotted spoon to a heat-safe bowl to cool. Do the same with the shallots. Then fry the chiles until almost blackened, leaving some red still visible. Take off the heat and transfer the chiles and oil carefully to the bowl with the garlic and shallots to cool.

2 When the garlic mixture is well cooled, transfer it to a food processor and puree with the palm sugar and salt. (If you have a sturdy mortar and pestle, you can use that instead of the processor; just scoop out the garlic mixture, leaving the oil in the pan, and grind manually, then add the paste to the oil in the pan with the sugar and salt.) Store tightly covered in the refrigerator for up to 2 weeks.

1 tbsp canola oil

1 tbsp cumin seeds

1 tbsp black mustard seeds

½ tsp red pepper flakes, plus extra if desired

1½ cups/180 g chopped onions

1 tbsp ground coriander

2 tsp ground turmeric

½ tsp ground cardamom

14 oz/400 g canned tomato puree/tinned sieved tomatoes

1 tsp brown sugar or jaggery

¼ tsp salt

MAKES ABOUT
2 CUPS / 480 ML

The secret to most Indian menus is that they have a host of "mother sauces," which are the premade sauces made by hard-working prep cooks. When you order your tikka masala or vindaloo, there is a base sauce with lots of complexity that gets cooked into your chosen dish, with some additions to make it just so. This recipe can act as your premade mother sauce, in which you can simmer any number of tasty things. Serve over rice or another grain or with Quick Indian Flatbread (page 106).

Bengali Curry Simmer Sauce

1 Heat a large frying pan over high heat, then add the oil. When the oil is hot, add the cumin, mustard seeds, and pepper flakes and stir until the spices are fragrant, 30 to 60 seconds. Add the onions, stir, and lower the heat so they don't stick or burn. Cook, stirring over medium heat, until the onions are soft and golden. Add the ground coriander, turmeric, and cardamom and keep stirring until those spices are fragrant, another 1 minute. Add the tomato puree/sieved tomatoes, brown sugar, salt, and ½ cup/120 ml water. Stir and cook until the sauce starts to thicken. Season with more red pepper flakes, if desired. You can use the sauce as-is, or puree it. Refrigerate the sauce in a jar for up to 2 weeks.

2 To use, add ½ cup/120 ml water and 4 to 5 cups/800 g to 1 kg of mixed veggies and beans to the sauce in a large frying pan pan. Stir and cook, then cover and simmer on medium-low heat to cook the vegetables through. Harder veggies will take longer and may need more water.

¼ cup/15 g hulled
pumpkin seeds

¼ cup/35 g white sesame
seeds

2 small corn tortillas, torn
into pieces

5 medium scallions/
spring onions, chopped

2 cups/60 g cilantro/
fresh coriander

1 cup/190 g chopped
fresh tomatillos

3 small jalapeños, seeded

2 cups/480 ml Basic
Vegetable Stock (page 49)

¼ tsp salt

MAKES ABOUT
3½ CUPS / 840 ML

This lean, green sauce, known in Spanish as *pipian verde*, is quick and versatile. A puree of sesame and pumpkin seeds thickens a mix of cilantro and tomatillos, and it quickly simmers to a slightly spicy coating for tofu, seitan, tempeh, or beans and veggies. Just sauté the protein and when browned, pour in this sauce and simmer until thick.

Guatemalan Pumpkin Seed Simmer Sauce

1 In a small frying pan over high heat, dry-toast the pumpkin seeds until they start to pop and smell toasty. Transfer them to a food processor or blender. In the same pan, toast the sesame seeds, swirling over the heat until they darken just a shade. Transfer them to the processor, and grind the seeds to a fine mince. Add the tortillas, scallions/spring onions, cilantro/fresh coriander, tomatillos, and jalapeños and process until smooth. With the machine running, pour in the stock, then add the salt. Process to puree. The sauce will be thin, but it will reduce as you simmer it. Refrigerate the sauce in a jar for up to 2 weeks.

2 To use, sear 12 oz/340 g tofu, tempeh, or seitan in oil with a handful of chopped onion and a boiled, cubed potato and other veggies to make 4 cups/800 g of vegetables. Add the sauce and bring to a boil, then reduce it to a good simmer. Stir frequently until thick, and serve with tortillas or over rice, with lime wedges to squeeze over.

SAUCES AND CONDIMENTS

131

1 tsp extra-virgin olive oil

1 rib celery, chopped

1 medium onion, coarsely chopped

2 garlic cloves, sliced

25 oz/750 ml Chardonnay

½ cup/15 g fresh parsley stems

One 4-in/10-cm stem fresh rosemary

2 large bay leaves

1 tsp agave syrup

1¼ tsp cornstarch/cornflour

2 tbsp Earth Balance margarine

Salt

Freshly cracked black pepper

MAKES ABOUT

¾ CUP / 180 ML

Herbs and white wine are cooked down to make this velvety sauce, concentrating so much flavor into a small space that you might just swoon. Drizzle it on cooked vegetables or a plateful of soft rice. This is a vegan version of the classic *beurre blanc* or reduced pan sauce, but with even more intense wine flavor.

White Wine and Herb Reduction

1 In a 4-qt/4-L pot, heat the oil over medium heat, then add the celery, onion, and garlic. Sauté until the vegetables are soft and lightly golden. Add the wine, parsley, rosemary, and bay leaves and raise the heat to high. Bring to a boil, then reduce the sauce to a gentle simmer until the vegetables are limp, about 1 hour.

2 Strain the liquids into a clean pot, pressing on the solids. Discard the vegetables. Put the sauce over high heat and bring it to a boil. Reduce the heat to keep it at a vigorous simmer, and cook until the liquids are reduced to ¾ cup/180 ml, about 15 minutes. When the liquids are reduced, stir in the agave syrup. In a small cup, whisk the cornstarch/cornflour with 1 tbsp water and then whisk the paste into the simmering liquid. Cook, whisking for a couple of minutes until glossy and thick. Take it off the heat and whisk in the margarine. Taste and season with salt and pepper. Refrigerate in an airtight container for up to 2 weeks and reheat gently to keep from separating.

2 tsp extra-virgin olive oil

1 medium onion, coarsely chopped

1 rib celery, coarsely chopped

1 large carrot, chopped

4 garlic cloves, sliced

25 oz/750 ml light red wine (such as Beaujolais Nouveau)

2 cups/480 ml Basic Vegetable Stock (page 49)

½ oz/12 g dried mushrooms

2 tsp agave syrup (optional)

Salt (optional)

MAKES ½ TO ¾ CUP / 120 TO 180ML

(DEPENDING ON HOW MUCH YOU REDUCE IT)

If you want a concentrated, deeply flavorful, and very low-fat sauce, try this. The mushrooms and wine have so much umami and intensity that just a few spoonfuls will make your taste buds sing. Try it over bruschetta, roasted veggies, or beans. Drizzled over pasta or pizza, it instantly makes food red-wine compatible.

Red Wine and Mushroom Reduction

1 In a large pot, heat the oil for a minute over high heat, then add the onion, celery, carrot, and garlic. Stir until the veggies sizzle, then lower the heat and sauté over medium-low heat until the onion is nice and golden, about 10 minutes. If you have time, continue to cook to fully caramelize the onion. Add the wine, stock, and mushrooms and raise the heat to bring it all to a boil. Reduce the heat immediately to just a gentle simmer, but don't let it boil. Simmer for 1 hour, uncovered, until the vegetables are limp.

2 Strain the mixture into a large bowl, pressing gently on the solids to get the liquids out. Discard the vegetables. Transfer the wine mixture to a small saucepan, put it over high heat, and bring to a boil. Lower the heat to maintain a vigorous simmer and boil until the liquids are reduced by half, about 10 minutes. For a glace (glaze), keep simmering until the liquid is very thick. When the desired consistency is reached, taste it and season with the agave syrup and salt, if desired. Use immediately for drizzling over foods, or cool and refrigerate for up to 3 weeks, then rewarm over low heat.

5

Appetizers
and Snacks

Appetizers and snacks are generally attractive tidbits, something to whet the appetite before a meal or to nosh on when hunger strikes. Any time that you bring people together, you probably need some kind of snack. A platter of tasty food is very welcoming and serves to keep your guests from getting too tipsy or hungry as they enjoy your company. You might want to put out a bowl of tasty nuts or caramel corn for kids and adults to share, or you might want a platter of sushi or gyoza. Either way, they are a great way to enjoy a few bites of something really tasty before the main course or just because.

The great difference between vegan snacks and apps and those served in omnivorous circles is that these may be more nourishing. Instead of a high-fat dip or the empty calories of potato chips, these noshes feed you real food. A handful of nuts or roasted garbanzo beans is actually good for you as well as yummy. Spring rolls are packed with veggies, and there are a few tidbits with soy foods, all so appealingly packaged and seasoned that even your tofu-phobic friends will have to have some.

What good is it to have a party if everybody feels worse when it's over? Stick to these delightful finger foods, and you will have fun, inside and out.

½ cup/5 g popcorn
kernels

Vegetable oil spray

½ cup/120 ml brown rice
syrup

¼ cup/60 ml agave syrup

1 tbsp cold-press corn oil

½ to ¾ tsp salt

¾ cup/85 g pecans,
chopped

SERVES 8

You don't need butter to make a luscious caramel corn. The natural caramel taste of brown rice syrup saves the day, and a little buttery corn oil takes it over the top. Use a hot-air popper if you have one, or pop it on the stove.

Caramel-Nut Popcorn

1 Preheat the oven to 325°F/165°C/gas 3. Pop the popcorn and try to lift just the popped kernels into a large bowl, leaving the unpopped kernels behind. Coat two baking sheets/trays with sides with vegetable oil spray.

2 Mix both syrups, the oil, and salt (according to your taste) in a measuring cup. Pour them over the popcorn and add the nuts. Gently toss to mix, then spread everything on the baking sheets/trays.

3 Bake for 10 minutes, stir, and reverse the position of the pans. Bake until sticky and dried, 10 minutes more. Scrape immediately into a storage tub. Let it cool slightly before eating or cool thoroughly, uncovered, before storing tightly covered at room temperature for up to 1 week.

2 tsp cornstarch/
cornflour

½ cup/50 g powdered/
icing sugar

2 tbsp unsweetened
cocoa powder

1 tsp vanilla extract

½ tsp cayenne

½ tsp coarse salt

1 cup/115 g raw cashew
halves

2 cups/230 g whole
almonds

2 cups/100 g pumpkin
seeds, hulled and raw

SERVES 10

As long as you are snacking, have some health-ful nuts, loaded with good fats and minerals. Antioxidant-rich cocoa boosts the nutrition of a good-for-you treat, guaranteeing it won't last long at your next party.

Cocoa–Spicy Nut Mix

1 Preheat the oven to 250°F/120°C/gas 1. Line a baking sheet/tray with parchment/baking paper or a silicone baking sheet.

2 In a medium bowl, whisk together the cornstarch/cornflour and 2 tbsp water for a few seconds. Whisk in the powdered/icing sugar, cocoa, and vanilla. Whisk in the cayenne and salt, then toss the mixture with the nuts and seeds. Spread every-thing on the prepared pan in a single layer.

3 Bake, stirring every 20 minutes, until dry and crisp, about 1 hour. Remove from the oven and use a spatula to lift the mix off the pan and break up the clusters a bit. Let them cool completely on the pan before transferring them to an airtight storage container. These will keep for up to 1 week.

14 oz/400 g canned/
tinned chickpeas,
drained

2 tbsp extra-virgin olive oil

½ tsp salt

½ tsp ground chipotle
chile

½ tsp freshly cracked
black pepper

½ tsp ground coriander

½ cup/50 g pumpkin
seeds, hulled and raw

½ tsp dried oregano

SERVES 5

Italian delis sometimes sell deep-fried chickpeas,
which are a delicious snack. This baked version
has a spicy crunch, as well as the nutritional bonus
of pumpkin seeds.

Toasted Chickpeas and Pumpkin Seeds
with Chipotle

1 Preheat the oven to 400°F/200°C/gas 6.

2 In a large bowl, toss the chickpeas with the oil, salt,
chipotle, pepper, and ground coriander.

3 Spread the chickpeas on a rimmed baking sheet/tray and
bake for 20 minutes. Add the pumpkin seeds and oregano
and stir. Bake until the pumpkin seeds are toasted and popping, about 15 minutes more.

4 Let the chickpeas cool on the pan; don't transfer them to
a bowl while hot or they will not be crisp. Serve warm. Store
leftovers in the refrigerator, tightly covered, for up to 1 week.

2 tsp toasted sesame oil

14 oz/400 g raw whole almonds

2 tsp tamari or soy sauce

1 tsp sugar

½ tsp wasabi powder

1 pinch cayenne

1 tbsp finely chopped nori

SERVES 3

Looking for a nosh to put out with some sushi, or just to pack in your lunch box? These tempting almonds are coated with Japanese flavors and mineral-rich nori. Nori are the paper-like sheets of edible seaweed that are used to wrap sushi rolls, and are easily chopped or crumbled.

Nori-Wasabi Almonds

1 Line a baking sheet/tray with wax/greaseproof paper. Heat the oil in a large nonstick frying pan over low heat and add the almonds. Cook, stirring constantly, until the nuts begin to smell toasted, about 5 minutes.

2 Add the tamari, sugar, wasabi, and cayenne and cook until the liquid has become tacky and is sticking to the nuts.

3 Sprinkle the nori over the almonds and stir quickly.

4 Scrape the almonds onto the wax/greaseproof paper and spread them out to cool. When completely cooled, keep them in a tightly covered jar for up to 1 week.

½ cup/55 g shelled pistachios

½ cup/55 g hazelnuts

¼ cup/35 g sesame seeds

2 tbsp coriander seeds

2 tbsp cumin seeds

1 tbsp black peppercorns

½ tsp salt

8 large whole-wheat/wholemeal pita breads, cut into triangles and warmed, for serving

½ cup/120 ml extra-virgin olive oil, for serving

SERVES 8

Break free of the tired old concept of dip made from sour cream and powdered soup mix. This Egyptian spice mix is an ancient way to add some nuts, flavor, and fruity olive oil to your daily bread. If you don't have pita, feel free to use hunks of crusty whole-wheat baguette.

Dukkah Dip
with Pita Triangles

1 Preheat the oven to 375°F/190°C/gas 5.

2 On a baking sheet/tray with sides, spread the pistachios on one end and the hazelnuts on the other. Toast for 10 minutes, then remove the pistachios from the pan using a metal spatula. Transfer them to a bowl or large measuring cup. Continue to toast the hazelnuts until they are golden brown, 5 minutes more, then use a heavy kitchen towel to rub off the skins. Transfer the hazelnuts to the bowl with the pistachios.

3 Put the sesame seeds, coriander seeds, cumin seeds, and peppercorns on the baking sheet/tray and toast until they are fragrant, about 10 minutes. Transfer them to a spice grinder and pulse to grind them to a coarse powder (but don't make them into a paste!). Scrape the spice powder into a small bowl.

4 Grind half of the pistachios to a powder in the spice grinder and transfer them to the bowl with the spice powder. Grind half of the hazelnuts to small chunks and transfer them to the bowl. Coarsely chop the remaining nuts, add them and the salt to the bowl, and mix well.

5 Serve the dukkah with the pita triangles and a bowl of olive oil. Dip the bread in oil, then in the nut mixture.

2 cups/350 g shelled edamame

2 garlic cloves, peeled

½ cup/120 ml tahini paste

6 tbsp/90 ml freshly squeezed lemon juice

2 tbsp white miso

2 tbsp extra-virgin olive oil, plus extra for serving (optional)

⅛ tsp ground cayenne

SERVES 6

Regular chickpea hummus is great, but it gets old. Try this fresh take made with healthful edamame, the green soybeans. Edamame are available frozen, with the hulls removed, so it takes very little effort to put this spread together. Serve it with pitas or chips and crackers, or spread it on sandwiches.

Edamame Hummus

1 Thaw the edamame if they are frozen. You can just put them in a colander and run hot water over them. Drain the edamame well. Put the garlic in a food processor and process to mince. Scrape down the sides, then add the edamame and process until well minced. Scrape down the sides and add the tahini, lemon juice, miso, oil, and cayenne. Process until very smooth.

2 If desired, drizzle with olive oil at serving. Store in a tightly covered tub in the refrigerator for up to 1 week.

½ cup/100 g red lentils, sorted and rinsed

6 garlic cloves

3 tbsp extra-virgin olive oil, plus extra for serving (optional)

6 tbsp/90 ml freshly squeezed lemon juice

6 tbsp/90 ml tahini paste

1 tsp salt

1 pinch ground cayenne

SERVES 6

Explore the concept of hummus with a colorful and tasty version made with red lentils. Roasting gives the garlic a smoky, deep flavor that makes it absolutely craveable.

Red Lentil–Roasted Garlic Hummus

1 Put the lentils in a small pot with 1½ cups/360 ml water and bring them to a boil. Cook for about 30 minutes, keeping an eye on the water level and stirring occasionally. You want them to get very tender, with just enough water to keep them from sticking. Drain in a wire strainer, saving the cooking liquid. Don't rinse the lentils, just toss them to shake out the water and let them cool.

2 Preheat the oven to 350°F/180°C/gas 4. Peel the garlic and put it in an ovensafe ramekin. Drizzle with 1 tbsp of the oil and cover with a small plate or foil. Put the garlic in the oven for 20 minutes, give the ramekin a shake to toss the cloves, and bake for 10 minutes more, depending on the size of the cloves. Uncover and pierce a clove with a paring knife; they are done when they are butter soft. Let them cool.

3 Put the lentils in a food processor with the garlic and the oil from the ramekin. Puree thoroughly, scraping down the sides and repeating until smooth. Add the remaining 2 tbsp oil, the lemon juice, tahini, salt, and cayenne and process until very smooth. With the machine running, pour in about ¼ cup/60 ml of the reserved cooking liquid to make a good consistency for dipping. Remove the hummus to a bowl or platter and drizzle it with additional olive oil, if desired, for serving. Store leftovers in an airtight container in the refrigerator for up to 1 week.

1 cup/200 g dried black turtle beans

2 garlic cloves, peeled

2 medium chipotle chiles in adobo sauce

2 tbsp freshly squeezed lime juice

½ cup/15 g cilantro/fresh coriander, plus sprigs for garnish

¾ tsp salt

SERVES 4

Black beans are the highest in antioxidants in the bean family, thanks to that deeply pigmented black skin. The instant complexity that smoked chipotle chiles add makes this a go-to dip or filling for burritos.

Chipotle– Black Bean Dip

1 Soak the beans overnight in cool water to cover them generously. Drain the soaked beans, then put them in a 2-qt/2-L saucepan and add 5 cups/1.2 L water. Over high heat, bring the beans to a boil, then lower the heat to allow them to simmer gently. Cook, stirring occasionally, until the beans are very tender, about 1 hour. Take them off the heat and let them cool in their liquid for 10 minutes. Drain, reserving ½ cup/120 ml of the cooking water.

2 In a food processor, mince the garlic and chipotles. Add the beans and process to puree, adding the lime juice and reserved bean cooking water to make a creamy paste. Add the cilantro/fresh coriander and salt and process to mix. Scrape the dip into a bowl and garnish with cilantro/fresh coriander sprigs. Store in an airtight container in the refrigerator for up to 1 week.

1 lb/455 g fresh spinach

2 garlic cloves, peeled

2 tbsp extra-virgin olive oil

1 tbsp champagne vinegar

14 oz/400 g canned/tinned white beans, drained

½ tsp salt

½ cup/90 g chopped fresh tomato

½ tsp red pepper flakes

SERVES 4

A whole pound of spinach goes into this little bowl of bean dip, so you can feel good about getting all your leafy greens as you nosh. Canned beans make it convenient, but you can soak and cook your own, instead. Let the dip come to room temperature for the fullest flavor and serve it with crackers or bread, or in sandwiches.

Creamy Spinach and White Bean Dip

1 Put on a large pot of water to boil for the spinach. Drop the spinach into the boiling water and stir. When it comes back to a boil, cook for 1 minute and drain. Rinse with cold water, then squeeze out the leaves completely. Wrap them in a towel and put the package under a pot or cutting board to extract all the water.

2 Unwrap the spinach and chop it. In a food processor, combine the spinach and garlic, and process to chop them finely. Scrape down the sides and process again. Add the oil and vinegar and process until smooth. Add the beans and salt and process until smooth. Scrape the mixture into a medium bowl, and stir in the tomato and pepper flakes. Refrigerate the dip in an airtight container for up to 4 days.

1 cup/200 g dried kidney beans

½ oz/15 g dried ancho chiles, stemmed and seeded

8 large/15 g sun-dried tomato halves

4 garlic cloves, peeled

2 small/150 g roasted red bell peppers/capsicums, chopped

4 small scallions/spring onions, chopped

2 tbsp freshly squeezed lime juice

½ tsp salt

SERVES 6

Beans and chiles just go together. In this dip, the warm, deep flavor of ancho chiles is just barely hot, so don't fear the ancho. Pass hot sauce for the chile heads. This dip is great with corn chips or in Mexican dishes that call for refried beans.

Tomato–Ancho Chile Bean Dip

1 Soak the beans overnight in cool water to cover them generously. Drain the soaked beans, then put them in a large saucepan with fresh water to cover by 2 in/5 cm. Over high heat, bring the beans to a boil, then lower the heat to allow them to simmer gently. Cook, stirring occasionally, until the beans are very tender, 45 minutes to 1 hour. Take them off the heat and let them cool in their liquid for 10 minutes. Drain the beans.

2 In a small saucepan, cover the anchos and sun-dried tomatoes in water and bring them to a boil. Cover and take off the heat to let them soften, then drain, saving some of the cooking liquid to use to thin the dip later.

3 In a food processor, mince the garlic, then add the anchos and tomatoes. Process to puree. Add the beans and process until smooth. Transfer the puree to a medium bowl, then stir in the bell peppers/capsicums, scallions/spring onions, lime juice, and salt. Thin with the reserved cooking liquid as desired. Cover and refrigerate the dip for up to 1 week.

1 lb/455 g red or yellow potatoes

½ cup/120 ml extra-virgin olive oil

¼ cup/60 ml freshly squeezed lemon juice

3 tbsp red wine vinegar

1 cup/115 g pistachios

4 large garlic cloves, peeled

Salt

SERVES 6

The original Greek *makedonitiki* dip is made with walnuts, but for all the great flavor in it, the gray hue is off-putting. So using bright green pistachios instead makes it as appealing to look upon as to scoop on bread and devour.

Makedonitiki Skordalia

1 In a large pot of water over high heat, boil the potatoes until very tender, then drain and let them cool. Do not try to process the potatoes; they will turn gluey. Mash pieces of the warm potatoes very thoroughly with a ricer or fork, and as they are mashed, work in some of the oil, lemon juice, and vinegar.

2 Use a food processor to finely mince the pistachios and garlic. Add the remaining oil, lemon juice, and vinegar, a little at a time, while processing the nuts to a smooth paste. Stir the mixture into the potatoes and season with salt. Store in an airtight container in the refrigerator for up to 4 days.

1 oz/30 g dried porcini mushrooms

½ cup/240 ml boiling water

2 tbsp extra-virgin olive oil

12 oz/340 g fresh button mushrooms

2 small shallots, diced

2 garlic cloves, sliced

½ cup/55 g pecans

¼ cup/7 g chopped fresh parsley

2 tbsp chopped fresh tarragon

½ tsp freshly cracked black pepper

SERVES 6

Mushrooms are the "meat" of the vegan world, rich in protein, nutrients, and mouth-filling umami. This dense, nutty pâté will woo even the skeptic to the vegan end of the appetizer table. It's great smeared on crackers or bread or stuffed in sandwiches.

Porcini-Pecan Mushroom Pâté

1 Put the porcinis in a heat-safe cup and pour the boiling water over them. Let them soak for half an hour, then wring out the mushrooms and rinse them to get rid of any dirt. Strain the soaking water and save for another purpose, like cooking rice or soup.

2 In a large frying pan, heat the oil over medium heat. Add the button mushrooms, shallots, and garlic and sauté until juice comes out and then reduces, about 30 minutes, lowering the heat as the mixture gets drier.

3 In a food processor, puree the pecans with the parsley. Add the mushroom mixture, porcinis, tarragon, and pepper and process to mix thoroughly. Scrape the dip into a bowl and let it rest at room temperature for up to 2 hours or refrigerate overnight before serving. Store in an airtight container in the refrigerator for up to 1 week.

Salad Rolls

2 oz/55 g baby spinach, chopped

2 oz/55 g bean sprouts

1 cup/30 g fresh spearmint leaves

1 cup/140 g grated peeled green mango

1 small carrot, shredded

¼ cup/30 g roasted cashews, chopped

2 tbsp palm sugar or brown sugar

2 tbsp freshly squeezed lime juice

1 tsp toasted sesame oil

¼ tsp salt

Eight 12-in/30.5-cm rice-paper rounds

Dipping Sauce

½ cup/120 ml soy sauce

½ cup/120 ml freshly squeezed lime juice

2 tbsp palm sugar or brown sugar

1 tbsp fresh lime zest

1 pinch red pepper flakes

SERVES 8

On a hot day, transport your taste buds to the tropics with these tangy, light finger foods. Each ethereally light roll is about four bites worth of tangy, crunchy goodness. Buy the most rock-hard mango that you can find; tartness is essential to the dish.

Vietnamese Spinach–Green Mango Salad Rolls

1 TO MAKE THE SALAD ROLLS: In a large bowl, toss together the spinach, sprouts, spearmint, mango, carrot, and cashews.

2 In a small bowl, stir together the palm sugar, lime juice, oil, and salt, then toss them with the mango mixture.

3 Put 1 in/2.5 cm of hot water in a roasting pan/tray and lay out a thick kitchen towel next to it.

4 Soak a rice paper round in the water for a minute or so, just until softened. Take it out and place it flat on the towel. In the center of the wrap, place a small handful of filling, about ½ cup/100 g. Fold in the sides and roll up the wrapper to make a spring roll.

5 Put the roll on a plate, seam-side down, and continue wrapping the remaining rolls, positioning them so that they do not touch (or they'll stick together). As you work, cover the rolls with a damp towel. You can cover a single layer of finished rolls with a wet paper towel/absorbent paper and wrap them tightly for up to 4 hours. Serve them sliced in half on a diagonal.

6 TO MAKE THE DIPPING SAUCE: In a small bowl, whisk together the sauce ingredients. Serve the sauce alongside the rolls for dipping.

10 oz/280 g reduced-fat firm tofu, drained and pressed (see page 68)

½ oz/15 g dried shiitake mushrooms

¾ cup/180 ml boiling water

3 tbsp toasted sesame seeds

½ cup/15 g cilantro/fresh coriander leaves

1 tbsp chopped peeled fresh ginger

1 tbsp minced garlic

2 tsp soy sauce

2 tsp fresh lemon zest

1 tsp sugar

1 tsp cornstarch/cornflour, plus extra as needed

½ tsp salt

28 round eggless gyoza or wonton wrappers

1 tbsp canola oil

SERVES 6 TO 8

Potstickers are little bundles of joy—soft dumplings packed with tasty filling, their tender wrappers soft on top and crispy on the bottom. This is a great way to serve tofu to people who think they don't like it! The potstickers are delicious with Chinese Sesame Sauce (page 127) or a simple dip of soy sauce.

Sesame-Lemon-Shiitake Potstickers

1 Crumble the tofu into a large bowl.

2 In a heat-safe cup, submerge the dried shiitakes in the boiling water. Cover and let the mushrooms soften for about 20 minutes. When they are soft and cool enough to handle, squeeze out the excess water, trim off the stems, and mince the caps. Save the mushroom-soaking water.

3 In a spice grinder or coffee mill, grind the sesame seeds to meal, then add it to the tofu. Add the mushrooms, cilantro/fresh coriander, ginger, and garlic. Mix in the soy sauce, lemon zest, sugar, cornstarch/cornflour, and salt. Knead and mix the tofu-sesame mixture with your hands until it holds together when squeezed.

4 Sprinkle a bit of cornstarch/cornflour on a baking sheet/tray for the assembled potstickers. Get a pastry brush and a cup of cool water for sealing the potstickers.

5 On a cutting board, lay out several wrappers. Scoop a rounded tablespoon of tofu onto the center of each wrapper. Brush half of the exposed edge with the cool water. Fold over the other half to enclose the tofu filling. Press down on the filled potsticker to flatten and make a base, with the sealed edge pointing straight up. Pinch the edge with the thumb and forefinger of both hands to seal it and press each hand toward the other to create ridged pleats.

6 Set the finished potstickers on the prepared sheet/tray and cover them loosely with plastic wrap/cling film as you assemble the rest. When all are assembled, cover them well and refrigerate for up to 24 hours, or freeze for up to 1 month.

7 To cook, heat the oil in a large, wide frying pan with straight sides and a lid. (You can use two if you don't have one big enough.) When the oil is hot, quickly drop the potstickers in the oil, flat-sides down, putting them close together but not touching. Cook until the bottoms are well browned. Pick them up by the tops to check. When all the potstickers are browned, hold the lid over the pan as you carefully pour in the reserved shiitake-soaking water; it will sizzle and steam. Cover immediately and lower the heat to medium. Cook, shaking the pan occasionally to loosen the potstickers, until they are cooked through, about 8 minutes. Check to see if they are drying out or sticking; add a little water if they are. Remove the pan from the heat. Remove the potstickers with a metal spatula and serve them hot with a sauce.

1 cup/200 g short-grain brown rice

¼ piece/1.5g kombu (optional)

¼ tsp salt (optional)

12 spears fresh asparagus

1½ tsp umeboshi plum vinegar

1 tsp sugar

Six 7-by-7.8-in/17-by-20-cm sheets nori

3 baby carrots, cut lengthwise into slivers

12 sprigs/25 g watercress

1 tbsp wasabi paste

½ cup Vegenaise or Vegan "Mayonnaise" (page 113)

Soy sauce, for serving

Pickled ginger, for serving

SERVES 6

Hand rolls are the easiest rolled sushi, because they don't have to be perfect cylinders, just cone shapes. Umeboshi vinegar is the tangy liquid left over from making salted umeboshi plums, so it is pink, salty, sour, and full of umami. Asian grocers and natural foods stores should carry it. Kombu is an umami-rich sea vegetable used to make soup stock, and it can add subtle flavor to rice as well.

Brown Rice, Asparagus, and Carrot Hand Rolls

1 Wash the rice and drain it, then put it in a 1-qt/960-ml pot and add 2 cups/480 ml water, the kombu (if using), and the salt. Put it over high heat, bring to a boil, then reduce the heat to low. Cover tightly. Cook until all the water is absorbed, about 30 minutes. Remove the pot from the heat and let it stand for 10 minutes, covered, to steam.

2 In a large pot, boil 1 qt/960 ml water for blanching the asparagus.

3 Cut the asparagus tips 3 in/7.5 cm long and blanch by dropping them in the boiling water for 1 minute, then draining and cooling in ice water. Reserve the stalks for another use.

4 In a small bowl, stir together the vinegar and sugar. When the rice is tender, stir the vinegar mixture into it, scrape it onto a plate, and let it cool, covered with a wet kitchen towel.

5 Using scissors, cut the nori sheets in half. On each half sheet, mound about ¼ cup/50 g rice on the left half, forming a rough square. Angle an asparagus tip from the lower right corner to the upper left. Place a carrot sliver and a watercress sprig along that. Roll the bottom left corner up and over the filling, forming a cone whose point is in the center of the sheet. Set each hand roll, seam-side down, on a plate while you prepare the remaining hand rolls.

6 Wasabi pastes differ in strength, so if yours is very strong, start out with 1 tsp and add to taste. Stir the "mayo" and wasabi together in a small bowl, then serve it with the hand rolls along with little bowls of soy sauce and some pickled ginger.

1½ cups/150 g sushi rice

½ cup/100 g millet

2 tbsp brown rice vinegar

2 tsp agave syrup

2 medium, ripe avocados

8 tsp black sesame seeds

Seven 7-by-7.8-in/17-by-20-cm sheets nori

1 large carrot, cut into long strips

7 tbsp/56 g red pickled ginger strips (beni shoga), drained, plus extra for serving

7 scallions/spring onions

Soy sauce, for serving

Wasabi paste, for serving

SERVES 7

Green avocado, orange carrot, and distinctive red pickled ginger give these rolls their name and irresistible appeal. Red ginger is less sweet than pink pickled ginger and is cut into julienne slices; you can find it in Japanese markets. You need a 9.5-in/24-cm square bamboo rolling mat to make an inside-out roll, but it is not as tricky as it seems. The sticky rice stays put when you turn over the nori sheet, so don't worry. If you want to make a regular nori-side-out maki roll, just don't turn over the sheet.

Inside-Out Three-Color Vegetable Roll

1 In a 1-qt/960-ml saucepan with a tight-fitting lid, bring 3¼ cups/780 ml water, the rice, and millet to a boil over high heat. Cover and reduce the heat to low until all the water is absorbed, about 15 minutes. Let the rice stand, covered, for 10 minutes. Transfer the rice to a plate or large, low bowl and cover it with a damp cloth.

2 Whisk together the vinegar and agave syrup and fold them into the rice.

3 Cut the avocados in half, remove the pits, slice the flesh lengthwise in the shell, and use a spoon to scoop out the slices.

4 When the rice is cool, set up your assembly area. You will need a clean, dry cutting board; a towel; and a bowl of cool water with a dash of vinegar to moisten your fingers. The bamboo mat should be wrapped in plastic wrap/cling film. Sprinkle a large, flat plate with the sesame seeds (for the finished rolls).

5 To make the rolls, lay a sheet of nori on the cutting board. Scoop 1 cup/160 g of rice on top and crumble it evenly over the nori. Using moistened fingertips, pat the rice to cover the entire sheet in as even a layer as possible. Slide your fingers under both ends of the covered sheet and flip it over onto the plastic-covered mat, centering it evenly between the edges. Across the end of the nori closest to you, place a few avocado slices, distributing them evenly across the rice. Above the avocado, line up two or three carrot slices and then 1 tbsp pickled ginger to make an even row. Finish with one scallion/spring onion above the ginger. To roll, lift up the mat edge closest to you and hold it tightly to the nori with your thumbs, while holding the fillings in place with your fingers. Using the mat, roll the nori away from you into a cylinder, moving your fingers as you go to keep the fillings tight. When the nori is rolled up, move the roll closer to you on the mat, using the mat to roll it and shape it. If the roll is loose, try unrolling it and rerolling it tighter.

6 Roll each finished hand roll on the sesame seeds until coated. Let it stand for 2 to 5 minutes to set, then cut each roll into six or eight slices. Moisten and wipe the knife between cuts for the best results. Serve immediately with soy sauce, more pickled ginger, and wasabi. Don't make the rolls more than 10 minutes before serving, as the nori will get soft.

1 cup/115 g unbleached all-purpose/plain flour, plus extra for counter

2 tsp matcha tea powder

2½ tsp sugar

4 oz/115 g fresh spinach, finely chopped

½ tsp salt

8 oz/225 g shelled edamame, thawed if frozen

1 medium scallion/spring onion, chopped

1 tbsp minced peeled fresh ginger

2 tsp toasted sesame oil

1 tsp cornstarch/cornflour

¼ tsp ground white pepper

Sweet chile sauce, Thai Blackened Chile Sauce (page 129), or Chinese Sesame Sauce (page 127), for serving

SERVES 4

Green tea is a great ingredient to have on hand, for both its antioxidants and its bright green color. Powdered matcha tea is both sweet and slightly tannic, and it makes an enigmatic contribution to these tender dumplings.

Edamame Dumplings
in Handmade Green-Tea Wrappers

1 In a large bowl, combine the flour, matcha, and ½ tsp of the sugar. Pour 5 tbsp/75 ml hot water over the mixture and mix together. Add more water if needed to make a soft dough. Knead until smooth, then let the dough rest for 30 minutes, covered.

2 In a medium bowl, toss the spinach with the salt; let it sit and after 15 minutes, wring out the moisture with your hands.

3 In a food processor, mince the edamame, then add the scallion/spring onion, ginger, oil, the remaining 2 tsp sugar, the cornstarch/cornflour, and pepper. Pulse to mix well. Add the spinach and pulse to mix. Transfer the mixture to a medium bowl.

4 Divide the dough into twelve pieces. On a lightly floured counter, roll out each piece into a 4-in/10-cm oval. Put 2 tbsp of the filling in the center and pull up the edges around and over the filling. Pleat the top as you seal it closed and flatten the bottom so it will stand up. Place it on a baking sheet/tray and repeat with the remaining ingredients. Once they are all made, cover the dumplings with plastic wrap/cling film and refrigerate for 24 hours or freeze for up to 1 week.

5 To cook the dumplings, drop them into gently boiling water until hot through, about 8 minutes, or prepare them like potstickers: Heat 2 tbsp canola oil in a large pot with a tight-fitting lid, then add the dumplings, flat-sides down, to fry until brown. Add ¾ cup/180 ml water or stock and cover; lower the heat to medium-low once it starts steaming. Cook until the dumplings are hot through, about 8 minutes. Carefully remove the dumplings with a metal spatula, adding more water to the pan if they stick. Serve them with the sauce of your choice.

2 tbsp freshly squeezed lime juice

2 tbsp palm sugar

1 tbsp minced peeled fresh ginger

2 tsp dark miso

1 pinch salt

1 lb/455 g Granny Smith apples

3 oz/85 g rice vermicelli, cooked

1 medium carrot, shredded

2 scallions/spring onions, chopped

½ cup/15 g fresh Asian basil, torn

1 large red Fresno chile, chopped

½ cup/55 g cashews, toasted, chopped

Six 12-in/30.5-cm rice-paper rounds

SERVES 6

These spring rolls are made with familiar tart apples instead of tropical fruits. They are crazy good, with flavorful Asian basil. This means you can use Thai basil, holy basil, or any spicy basil that you can find. Serve with Thai Peanut Sauce (page 128) or Thai Blackened Chile Sauce (page 129).

Green Apple and Cashew Spring Rolls

1 In a large bowl, mix together the lime juice, palm sugar, ginger, miso, and salt.

2 Skin, core, and grate the apples, using a grater or food processor. Add them to the bowl.

3 Add the vermicelli, carrot, scallions/spring onions, basil, chile, and cashews. Toss to combine everything.

4 To make the rolls, put 1 in/2.5 cm of hot water in a roasting pan/tray. Lay out a thick kitchen towel next to it and get all your ingredients together.

5 Submerge two sheets of rice paper at a time, if your pan is long enough to do it without them sticking to each other (two fit in a lasagna pan), and when they start to soften, transfer them to the towel without touching. On each round, place a scant ½ cup/120 ml of filling. Fold up the bottom, then fold in the edges and roll up the wrapper to make a spring roll.

6 Move the finished rolls to a platter, seam-side down, positioning them so that they do not touch (or they'll stick together). As you work, cover the rolls with a damp towel. When all the rolls are made, serve immediately or cover the platter with the damp towel and plastic wrap/cling film and refrigerate for up to 4 hours.

12 diagonal slices
baguette

½ cup/25 g shelled
pumpkin seeds

½ cup/15 g chopped
fresh parsley

2 tsp flax oil

1 tsp freshly squeezed
lime juice

1 large avocado

Tabasco sauce, for
garnish

Salt, for garnish

SERVES 4

Creamy avocado and crunchy pumpkin seeds top this crostini—so who needs cheese? The amazing health benefits of avocado and pumpkin seed fats are boosted even more with buttery flax oil. Don't tell anyone it's good for them!

Avocado-Pepita Crostini

1 Preheat the oven to 350°F/180°C/gas 4. Place the baguette slices on an ungreased baking sheet/tray and toast them to the desired crispness, 5 to 10 minutes.

2 In a small frying pan over high heat, toast the pumpkin seeds. Shake often, until they start to pop, about 4 minutes. Let cool.

3 In a small bowl, combine the pumpkin seeds, parsley, flax oil, and lime juice. Cut the avocado in half, then use a paring knife to cut it into dice inside the shell. Scoop it out with a spoon into the bowl, and toss gently. Top each baguette slice with some avocado mixture and sprinkle with Tabasco and salt. Serve immediately.

1 lb/455 g Italian bread, thickly sliced

8 oz/225 g lacinato kale, stemmed

3 tbsp extra-virgin olive oil

1 garlic clove, chopped

1 pinch red pepper flakes

1 large Roma tomato, seeded and chopped

¼ cup/60 ml prepared olivada or Tapenade (page 121)

SERVES 6

This Tuscan classic is a great way to show off the sweet, hearty flavor of lacinato kale, sometimes called *cavolo nero*, black cabbage, or dinosaur kale. Whatever you call it, it's great with olives and garlic. Olivada is an Italian version of tapenade, and both are great in this dish.

Kale, Olivada, and Tomato Bruschetta

1 Preheat the oven to 350°F/180°C/gas 4. Cut the bread slices into quarters and lay them out on baking sheets/trays. Toast until golden brown, about 10 minutes.

2 In a large frying pan with a lid, steam the kale with 2 or 3 tbsp water until wilted and bright green, about 5 minutes. Drain and rinse with cool water and squeeze out the leaves.

3 In the same pan over medium heat, warm the oil and lightly cook the garlic and pepper flakes. Do not let the garlic brown! Add the kale, tomato, and olivada to the pan and toss to coat with the garlic oil. Heat through. Divide the mixture among the pieces of toasted bread and serve immediately. You can also make the topping ahead and keep it in the refrigerator for up to 2 days. Reheat at serving time.

- ⅛ tsp liquid smoke flavoring
- ½ batch Almond-Cashew "Chèvre" (page 44)
- 8 slices whole-wheat/wholemeal baguette
- 1 cup/185 g chopped ripe heirloom tomato
- ¼ cup/7 g chopped fresh basil
- 1 tbsp extra-virgin olive oil
- 1 garlic clove, crushed
- Salt

SERVES 4

Smoke, as we learned earlier, adds umami to foods, giving them that much more satisfying flavors. Here, just a few drops of liquid smoke give you that magic and make the creamy "chèvre" a perfect complement to the tangy tomatoes.

Smoky "Cheese" Bruschetta
with Heirloom Tomato

1 In a small bowl, stir the liquid smoke into the "chèvre." Preheat the oven to 350°F/180°C/gas 4.

2 Toast the baguette slices just to crisp the edges, about 5 minutes.

3 Spread the smoky "cheese" on each slice and put it on a platter as you go. In a medium bowl, combine the tomato, basil, oil, and garlic and toss to mix. Top the bruschetta with the tomato mixture, then sprinkle them all with salt. Serve immediately.

¾ cup/85 g pine nuts

2 garlic cloves, peeled

⅓ cup/15 g nutritional yeast

3 tbsp white miso

1 tsp salt

1½ cups/360 ml plain rice milk

½ cup/55 g cornstarch/cornflour

¼ cup/60 ml canola oil

2 tsp champagne vinegar

4 sun-dried tomato halves, chopped

1 large jalapeño, chopped

1 tsp ground cumin

¼ tsp ground annatto (optional)

6 oz/170 g baked tortilla chips

Salsa, for serving

SERVES 4

If you miss the nachos you used to make with dairy cheese, you will be pleasantly surprised by this version. For a crunchy Mexican snack, make any of the salsas on pages 118 and 119 to go with these.

Spicy Nachos

1 In a food processor or blender, grind the pine nuts and garlic to a paste. Add the yeast, miso, and salt. Process to mix thoroughly. Reserve.

2 Preheat the oven to 350°F/180°C/gas 4. In a 2-qt/2-L pot, whisk together the milk, cornstarch/cornflour, oil, and vinegar. Put the mixture over medium-high heat, whisking constantly until it comes to a boil. When the sauce boils, reduce the heat and simmer until thickened, another 2 minutes, then scrape it into the food processor with the pine nuts. Puree until mixed.

3 When the sauce is very smooth, return it to the saucepan, then whisk in the tomatoes, jalapeño, cumin, and annatto (if using). Stir over low heat until just warmed, then remove from the heat.

4 Spread the tortilla chips on an ovenproof platter or plates and bake for 10 minutes to warm them, then pour the warm nacho sauce over the chips. Serve with salsa.

2 cups/240 g masa harina
or masarepa

½ tsp salt

3 tbsp coconut oil,
melted

2 tsp extra-virgin olive oil

½ cup/60 g chopped
onion

1 large red Fresno chile,
chopped

1 garlic clove, minced

½ cup/150 g cooked
black beans, drained

1 tbsp fresh oregano

Canola oil

½ cup/75 g diced
avocado

1 large lime, quartered,
for serving

1 cup/240 ml salsa, for
serving

SERVES 8

South American cuisines make magic with ground corn. These *arepas* are a version of the Guatemalan fried rounds, which are stuffed with all sorts of savory fillings. The creamy filling and crispy corn shells will disappear as soon as they are served.

Arepas
Stuffed with Spicy Black Beans

1 In a large bowl, combine the masa and ¼ tsp of the salt. Add the coconut oil and 1½ cups/360 ml cold water and mix well. Knead until the dough is smooth, then wrap and let it stand at room temperature for 15 minutes.

2 In a medium frying pan, heat the olive oil over medium-high heat. Add the onion and cook until it is golden; add the chile and garlic and cook until fragrant. Add the beans and oregano, mash everything in the pan, and cook briefly. Let it cool.

3 Divide the dough into eight pieces and form each into a ball. Flatten each into a 3-in/7-cm disk, about ¼ in/6 mm thick. Cover the disks with plastic wrap/cling film until frying time.

4 Preheat the oven to 400°F/200°C/gas 6. Put some paper towels/absorbent paper on a baking sheet/tray to drain the arepas. In a large frying pan, heat ¼ in/6 mm of canola oil until shimmery. Test it by dropping in a nugget of bread; if it sizzles, it is ready. Fry the arepas for about 4 minutes per side, until they are golden brown and crisp on the outside. Drain them on paper towels/absorbent paper, then bake until they are firm, about 15 minutes. Take them out and let them cool until you can touch them.

5 Mix the avocado and the remaining ¼ tsp salt into the black bean filling. Use a paring knife to open up the arepas like a pita bread, slicing along the circumference but leaving most of the edge intact. Insert a spoon, scrape out a little of the soft interior, and stuff a spoonful of filling inside each. Serve warm with the lime and salsa.

1½ cups/170 g slivered/flaked almonds

¼ cup/60 ml boiling water

1 acidophilus capsule (see page 520; check to make sure it is dairy free)

½ cup/55 g pine nuts

2 garlic cloves, peeled

1 tbsp extra-virgin olive oil

1 tsp freshly squeezed lemon juice

¾ tsp salt

½ tsp vegan Worcestershire sauce

SERVES 8

The old-school appetizer table was not complete without a nut-studded ball of mixed cheeses—and a swath of crackers surrounding it for dipping. In this totally nut-based version, you can have all that festive feel with none of the dairy products. I like to use acidophilus because it is a beneficial microbe that will give the nut paste a little tang as it ferments.

Almond-Covered "Cheese" Ball

1 Put the 1 cup/115 g of almonds in a food processor and pour the boiling water over them. Put on the lid and let the almonds soften a little. Process the nuts to a smooth paste, scraping down the sides of the bowl several times. If needed, add a couple additional tablespoons of water for smoothness.

2 Add the contents of the acidophilus capsule and process to mix. Scrape the puree into a jar, cover loosely with a towel, and let stand at room temperature for 24 hours to ferment slightly. It should become bubbly and fluffy.

3 Preheat the oven to 250°F/120°C/gas ½.

4 In the food processor, puree the pine nuts and garlic. Add the oil, lemon juice, salt, Worcestershire, and almond mixture. Process until very smooth.

5 On a heat-safe serving plate, spread the remaining almonds. Scrape the almond mixture out of the blender, form it into a ball, and roll the ball in the almonds to coat.

6 Put the ball on top of the remaining almonds and tuck them around the ball. Bake the ball for 25 minutes, or until the almonds are golden and the ball is heated through. Serve warm, or refrigerate, tightly wrapped, for up to 1 week. Serve cold.

Filling

1 tbsp cold-press corn oil or coconut oil

2 tsp cumin seeds

1 jalapeño, minced

2 tsp lemon zest

½ tsp ground turmeric

2½ cups/250 g cauliflower florets

1½ cups/210 g cubed sweet potatoes

¼ cup/20 g toasted unsweetened coconut

¼ cup/7 g cilantro/ fresh coriander, chopped

½ tsp salt

Dough

2 cups/255 g unbleached all-purpose/plain flour, plus extra for counter

1 cup/130 g chickpea flour

½ tsp salt

¼ cup/60 ml cold-press corn oil, chilled

Ice water

Chutney

1 medium apple, peeled

¼ cup/7 g fresh mint, chopped

1 in/2.5 cm peeled fresh ginger, grated

2 tbsp agave syrup or sugar

1 tbsp freshly squeezed lemon juice

SERVES 8

Samosas usually contain butter. These are far more interesting, with sweet potatoes and cauliflower wrapped in a flaky vegan pastry.

Cauliflower-Coconut Puffs
with Apple Chutney

1 TO MAKE THE FILLING: In a large frying pan over high heat, warm the oil briefly and add the cumin seeds. When they start to sizzle, add the jalapeño, lemon zest, and turmeric and stir. Add the cauliflower and sweet potatoes and cook, stirring, until the cauliflower is coated with spices. Add ¼ cup/ 60 ml water and bring to a boil. Cover and cook over medium heat, until the sweet potatoes are very tender. Stir in the coconut, then remove the pan from the heat and let the filling cool to room temperature. Stir in the cilantro/fresh coriander and salt, mashing the sweet potatoes a bit.

2 TO MAKE THE DOUGH: In a large bowl, mix together both flours and the salt. Sprinkle in the oil while stirring, then add enough ice water just to make a firm dough. Divide it into eight pieces and form them into disks. Let the dough rest for 30 minutes, covered. Preheat the oven to 400°F/200°C/gas 6. Line a baking sheet/tray with parchment/baking paper.

3 On a lightly floured counter, roll out each disk to make a thin oval about 4 in/10 cm long. Scoop a heaping ¼ cup/ 60 ml of the filling into the middle of each oval. Lightly dampen the edge of the dough, then fold the dough over the filling and seal with a fork. Put the packets on the prepared pan and continue until all are filled. Poke the top crust with a fork to let steam escape. Bake until the puffs are golden and crisp, about 20 minutes.

4 TO MAKE THE CHUTNEY: Chop half of the apple and put it in a medium bowl. Finely mince the rest of the apple and add it to the bowl. Stir in the mint, ginger, agave syrup, and lemon juice. Serve the chutney at room temperature with the puffs.

165

1 cup/130 g chickpea flour

½ tsp salt

½ tsp ground cumin

1 cup/30 g chopped fresh spinach

3 garlic cloves, slivered

⅛ tsp baking soda/ bicarbonate of soda

¾ cup/225 g canned/ tinned chickpeas, drained

2 small scallions/spring onions, chopped

1 cup/240 ml extra-virgin olive oil

¾ cup/180 ml Romesco Sauce (page 122), for serving

SERVES 4

Spanish tapas are such a fun way to eat—bite-size morsels of tasty food that just happen to taste great with Spanish wines. These fritters are flecked with spinach, and when you dip them in a roasty romesco sauce, you can't go wrong.

Spanish Chickpea Fritters
with Romesco Sauce

1 Preheat the oven to 200°F/95°C/gas ¼ (for keeping the fritters warm if you will not be eating them immediately). Set out a large cast-iron frying pan and a baking sheet/tray lined with three layers of paper towels/absorbent paper for draining the fritters.

2 In a large bowl, whisk together the flour, salt, and cumin, then add ¾ cup/180 ml hot water a little at a time, and stir to make a smooth paste. It should be about as thick as pancake batter. Let stand for 1 hour to hydrate the flour.

3 Stir the spinach, garlic, and baking soda/bicarbonate of soda into the batter, then stir in the chickpeas and scallions/ spring onions.

4 Pour the oil into the frying pan and turn up the heat to medium-high. Heat until a drop of batter sizzles in it (about 350°F/176°C). When the oil is hot, stir the batter and ladle scant ¼-cup/60-ml portions into the hot oil. When the oil starts to sizzle again, lower the heat to medium. Cook until the fritters are bubbling and browned, about 3 minutes per side. Drain on the paper towels/absorbent paper. Serve hot with the romesco sauce for dipping.

1½ lb/680 g new (baby) potatoes

2 red Fresno chiles

2 garlic cloves, chopped

2 tbsp red wine vinegar

1 tsp smoked paprika (pimentón)

1 tsp sweet paprika

1 tsp ground cumin

3 tbsp extra-virgin olive oil

1 large green jalapeño, slivered

SERVES 6

Spicy tidbits with a Spanish accent, these potatoes require no special "bravery." They are not so hot that you need chile training; they're just delicious. Smoked paprika (pimentón) is sweet paprika with the umami and flavor boost of smoke. Once you get a can, you will want to put it in everything. Serve these potatoes with the Spanish Chickpea Fritters with Romesco Sauce (facing page), the Spanish Saffron Tortilla (page 423), and some crunchy Marcona almonds, and you have tapas!

Patatas Bravas

1 In a large pot, cover the potatoes with cold water. Put the pot over high heat and bring to a boil. Simmer vigorously; pierce the potatoes with a paring knife after 10 minutes to see if they are tender. When the potatoes are just tender, drain and let them cool. Cut the potatoes into halves or quarters, if large.

2 In a food processor or by hand, mince the chiles and garlic, then add the vinegar, both paprikas, and the cumin. Process until smooth or stir until combined.

3 Heat a large cast-iron frying pan over high heat until hot. Add the oil, then add the potatoes, cut-sides down. Fry them, undisturbed, until a nice crust is formed on the bottoms, about 5 minutes. Reduce the heat to medium-high if they are burning or sticking. Flip the potatoes and cook until they are crusty. When they're hot and browned, drizzle them with the chile mixture and toss to coat. Add the jalapeño and toss the potatoes until the jalapeño is just softened. Serve immediately.

Salads

A salad, in my experience, can be just about anything with a dressing on it. Warm, cold, cooked, or raw, it's really a pretty broad concept. As a plant-based eater, you will be looking for exciting ways to eat vegetables, just to keep things interesting. Exploring the concept of salad is one way to expand your repertoire of great vegan food. In this chapter, you will find grain-, bean-, and pasta-based salads; cooked veggie salads; warm salads; and wilted salads. Some are sides, while some can easily serve as a main course.

If there is one thing that makes it a salad, it seems to be the presence of something sour in the dressing. That touch of piquancy balances the assorted vegetal flavors in all the plants, makes the salad a nice counterpoint to a savory main course, and gives it zing. In many cases, it also has a nutritional bonus. In the case of a raw spinach salad, the leaves are rich with iron, but also with phytic acid, which inhibits your body's ability to absorb the iron. In nature's infinite wisdom, foods that contain vitamin C help to counteract this phenomenon. That means that dressing spinach with lemon juice or tossing it with oranges or other vitamin C–rich foods makes the spinach better for you. Good oils also make the nutrients in vegetables easier to absorb, so don't get too carried away with cutting fat. Antioxidants in vegetables, like the lutein in greens, carotenoids in greens and carrots, lycopene in tomatoes, and others are all better absorbed by the body with a little healthy fat in the mix.

Hopefully, these recipes will broaden your meal choices. Make them your own. A skill that vegans should definitely master is the art of building an improvised salad. I've put together a basic Pyramid Salad recipe (see page 171) to help you to prepare a meal with very little effort. Of course, you can't improvise very well without some basic ingredients in the fridge and pantry, so use this as a guide to what you should have on hand.

2 cups/60 g greens (dark leafy spinach, baby greens, romaine, or heartier greens like kale, chard, and collards; blanched, if desired)

½ cup/about 90 g red vegetables (tomatoes, red bell peppers/capsicums, red cabbage, grated raw or cooked beets/beetroot)

½ cup/about 90 g orange vegetables (carrots, orange or yellow bell peppers/capsicums, summer squash, cooked winter squash or sweet potatoes)

½ cup/about 75 g green vegetables (broccoli, zucchini/courgette, cabbage, Brussels sprouts, snow peas/mangetouts)

Sea vegetables (a sprinkling of shredded nori, a pinch of dried wakame soaked for 10 minutes, or some dry dulse, crumbled)

½ cup/100 g whole grain (leftover cooked quinoa or other grain; good low-fat bread, crackers, or baked corn chips)

2 tsp flax, walnut, or extra-virgin olive oil

1 tsp freshly squeezed lemon or lime juice, or 2 tsp freshly squeezed orange juice

1 clove of crushed garlic, a sprinkling of herbs, a dash of mustard or soy sauce (depending on your mood and pantry)

2 tbsp nuts, seeds, or dried fruit (optional, for a more substantial meal)

SERVES 1

This salad contains a pretty good variety of the foods you need to eat every day, according to the Vegan Food Guide Pyramid (see page 22). If you have already eaten a bunch of one of the categories that day—perhaps you had lots of nuts for lunch or a high-fat breakfast—you can leave that component out. The salad is a great "readjustment" meal, where you can detox, get back in the groove with your veggies, and eat a little leaner if you have gotten out of balance. Basically, if you are feeling fat, go with more veggies and less dressing, but don't cut it all; you need healthful fats—even to lose weight.

Pyramid Salad

Build your salad on a plate, piling each vegetable on top of the last, ending with the grain, or keeping the breads to the side. Stir the oil and citrus juice together in a small bowl with the optional seasoning and drizzle over the salad; toss and enjoy. Top with nuts, seeds, or dried fruit, if desired.

2 cups/310 g shelled edamame, thawed if frozen

8 spears asparagus, tough bases snapped off

1 cup/65 g snow peas/mangetouts

4 scallions/spring onions, diagonally sliced

4 small French breakfast radishes, sliced

2 cups/250 g fresh raspberries

1 tsp agave syrup or sugar

½ tsp Dijon mustard

¼ tsp salt

¼ cup/60 ml walnut oil

1 head/165 g butter/Boston lettuce, leaves separated

Freshly cracked black pepper

¼ cup/30 g chopped toasted walnuts

SERVES 4

This salad sings of spring with its fresh asparagus, crisp peppery radishes, and the year's first raspberries. Edamame is a crunchy foil to the bright red dressing, and it's all held gently by tender butter lettuce leaves.

Edamame and Spring Vegetables
in Raspberry Vinaigrette

1 If desired, blanch the asparagus and peas/mangetouts: Boil a large pot of water, drop them into the boiling water for 1 minute, then drain and plunge them into cold water.

2 In a large bowl, combine the edamame, asparagus, peas/mangetouts, scallions/spring onions, and radishes.

3 In a food processor or blender, puree ½ cup/62.5 g of the raspberries, then add the agave syrup, mustard, and salt and puree to mix. With the machine running, drizzle in the oil to make an emulsified dressing. Pour the dressing over the vegetables in the bowl and toss.

4 On individual plates or one large platter, spread out the lettuce leaves, then distribute the dressed salad over them. Crack pepper on top, sprinkle the walnuts and remaining raspberries over it all, and serve immediately.

14 oz/400 g canned/
tinned black soybeans,
rinsed and drained

2 medium carrots,
julienned

8 oz/225 g canned/
tinned sliced water
chestnuts, drained

2 large scallions/spring
onions, chopped

2 tbsp apricot jam

2 tbsp rice vinegar

2 tbsp canola oil

2 tbsp red miso

1 tbsp white miso

1 tbsp grated or minced
peeled fresh ginger

1 tbsp mirin

½ oz/15 g dulse, soaked,
picked over, and
squeezed dry

SERVES 4

This simple, fast salad is a great way to get dinner on the table and enjoy nutritious black soybeans and seaweed. Black soybeans look like black turtle beans, but they are slightly firmer. They also contain the magic of soy, with extra protein and phytochemicals. Using two kinds of miso adds complexity and umami, as well as fermented soy's health benefits.

Black Soy, Dulse, and Carrots
in Miso-Ginger Dressing

1 In a large bowl, combine the soybeans, carrots, water chestnuts, and scallions/spring onions.

2 In a small bowl, whisk together the jam, vinegar, oil, both misos, ginger, and mirin. Pour the dressing over the contents of the large bowl and toss to coat.

3 Fold in the dulse and serve, or cover and refrigerate for up to 3 days.

½ cup/100 g wheat berries, rinsed

1½ cups/230 g shelled edamame, thawed if frozen

4 oz/100 g firm tofu, drained, pressed (see page 68), and crumbled

½ medium cucumber, peeled, seeded, and sliced

1 small green bell pepper/capsicum, chopped

2 large scallions/spring onions, chopped

1 rib celery, chopped

1 small carrot, grated

½ cup/15 g minced fresh parsley

¼ cup/60 ml Vegan "Mayonnaise" (page 113) or Vegenaise

1 tbsp red wine vinegar

2 tsp sugar

1 tsp dried dill

½ tsp salt

½ tsp freshly cracked black pepper

SERVES 3

In the early '80s, a version of "protein salad" was almost a requirement at any vegetarian potluck, except that it was made with cottage cheese, chunks of Cheddar cheese, and lots of mayonnaise. It was tasty and filling and probably holds nostalgia for some people, so I made up this vegan version.

Crunchy Protein Salad

1 In a small saucepan, combine the wheat berries and 3 cups/720 ml water. Over high heat, bring them to a boil, then reduce the heat and simmer until the berries start to burst and are tender, about 1 hour. Drain and let them cool.

2 In a large bowl, combine the wheat berries, edamame, tofu, cucumber, bell pepper/capsicum, scallions/spring onions, celery, and carrot.

3 In a small bowl, combine the parsley, "mayonnaise," vinegar, sugar, dill, salt, and pepper, and pour them over the edamame mixture. Toss to coat and serve at room temperature or cover and refrigerate for up to 3 days.

1 tbsp cold-press corn oil, plus 1 tsp

1½ cups/240 g raw corn (about 2 medium ears)

4 oz/100 g zucchini/ courgette, cut into ½-in/12-mm dice

¼ cup/30 g chopped onion

14 oz/400 g canned/ tinned black beans, drained and rinsed

1 small ripe tomato, chopped

½ cup/15 g fresh basil, slivered

1 garlic clove, minced

1 tbsp champagne vinegar

1 tsp agave syrup

½ tsp salt

SERVES 6

Sweet corn is bursting with sugars, so when you pan-toast it, you will caramelize all that wonderful sweetness. Zucchini, tomatoes, and basil are usually booming in the garden at the same time as corn, so use them all in this easy salad.

Pan-Toasted Corn and Black Bean Salad
with Basil

1 Heat a large cast-iron frying pan over high heat. Drizzle in the 1 tbsp corn oil. Add the raw corn, zucchini/courgette, and onion and stir. Keep stirring until the corn is tender and the zucchini/courgette is seared. Transfer the vegetables to a large bowl. Add the beans, tomato, and basil.

2 In a cup or bowl, combine the garlic with the vinegar, agave syrup, the remaining 1 tsp corn oil, and the salt. Whisk to mix, then drizzle over the corn mixture.

3 Toss to mix and serve, or cover and refrigerate for up to 2 days.

¼ cup/7 g minced fresh rosemary

4 garlic cloves, sliced

¼ cup/60 ml extra-virgin olive oil

½ tsp red pepper flakes

2 tbsp freshly squeezed lemon juice

14 oz/400 g canned/tinned white beans, drained and rinsed

1 tsp salt

1 cup/30 g minced fresh parsley

SERVES 4

Sometimes the simple classics are the best. Plump beans bathed in flavorful olive oil, garlic, and lemon are a timeless side dish to go with pastas like Maltagliati with Swiss Chard and Sage (page 372) and pizzas like the Roasted Potato and Rosemary Pizza (page 335).

Lemony White Beans
with Fresh Rosemary Vinaigrette

1 In a small frying pan over medium-low heat, cook the rosemary and garlic in the oil just to soften them.

2 Add the pepper flakes and cook them for a few seconds, then remove the pan from the heat and add the lemon juice.

3 Pour the beans into a medium bowl and toss gently with the oil mixture and salt. Add the parsley just before serving. Serve warm or chilled.

1 head/610 g broccoli

1 large carrot, julienned

¼ cup/60 ml extra-virgin olive oil

2 tbsp freshly squeezed lemon juice

½ tsp salt

½ tsp freshly cracked black pepper

14 oz/400 g canned/tinned chickpeas, drained and rinsed

1 cup/30 g minced fresh parsley

SERVES 6

This easy, hearty salad starts with some steamed broccoli and a can of chickpeas and just gets better from there. Serve it alongside whole-wheat toast for a lunch or any Mediterranean dish you are having for dinner.

Broccoli, Carrot, and Chickpea Salad
with Lemon Vinaigrette

1 Pour 1 in/2.5 cm of water into a pan that will hold your vegetable steamer, and bring it to a boil.

2 Slice the broccoli into bite-size florets, then peel and thinly slice the stems. Put the broccoli and carrot into the steamer. Steam until crisp-tender, 2 to 3 minutes, and rinse with cold water to cool. Drain thoroughly, then spread on a towel to dry.

3 In a small bowl, whisk together the oil and lemon juice, and season with the salt and pepper.

4 Toss together the chickpeas, carrot, broccoli, parsley, and dressing. Refrigerate until ready to serve, up to 3 days.

3 oz/90 g dried, flat tofu skins

4 tbsp/60 ml soy sauce

1 tbsp cornstarch/cornflour

1 tsp dark sesame oil

2 tsp sugar, plus 2 tbsp

3 medium carrots, julienned

2 scallions/spring onions, diagonally sliced

2 tbsp rice vinegar

1 tbsp canola oil

¼ tsp red pepper flakes

SERVES 4

I ate a salad like this at a Chinese restaurant and just had to make one myself. Tofu skins (also called *yuba* or bean-curd skins) are made from the skin that forms on top of a pot of simmering soymilk and is lifted off and dried to make a chewy, thin sheet. Tofu skins are sold in Chinese grocery stores in various shapes. Make sure to purchase the flat, paperlike skins, not the bunched skins.

Chinese Tofu Skin and Carrot Salad

1 Unwrap the tofu skins, put them in a large roasting pan/tray, and cover with cold water to soak. They should get soft in under an hour. Drain and then blot them dry with a kitchen towel.

2 In a small cup, whisk together 2 tbsp of the soy sauce, the cornstarch/cornflour, sesame oil, and the 2 tsp sugar.

3 Lay the tofu skins on the counter, then use a pastry brush to paint each skin with the soy mixture. Roll up each skin as tightly as you can. Some of the pieces will undoubtedly be broken, so cobble them together to make ¾-in-/2-cm-thick rolls. Put them on a heat-safe plate or steamer top.

4 Set up a steamer: You can use a round cake cooling rack and put the rolls on a heat-safe plate, as long as it will all fit in your pan over boiling water. Bring water to a boil in the steamer, put the plate of rolls over the steam, and cover the steamer. Reduce the heat to medium, then steam the rolls until they are firm, about 15 minutes. Remove the plate, pour off any excess water from the tofu skins, and put the plate on a rack to cool.

5 Steam the carrots just until crisp-tender, and put them in a medium bowl. Slice the cooled tofu rolls, widthwise, into ¾-in/2-cm pieces and add them to the carrots, then add the scallions/spring onions.

6 In a small cup, whisk together the remaining 2 tbsp soy sauce, the vinegar, the remaining 2 tbsp sugar, the canola oil, and pepper flakes. Pour it over the contents of the bowl. Toss very gently, then let the salad marinate for 1 hour in the refrigerator. Serve chilled.

4 cups/120 g mixed salad greens

2 large oranges, peeled and sliced into rounds

1 large carrot, shredded

¼ cup/30 g sliced red onion

1 garlic clove, peeled

1 small, ripe avocado

1 oz/30 g silken tofu

2 tbsp Basic Vegetable Stock (page 49)

1 tbsp flax oil

1 tbsp rice vinegar

1 pinch salt

SERVES 4

Green goddess dressing takes many forms, and in this one, creamy avocados and tofu give you all the decadent smoothness with far less fat—and all good at that! A shot of flax oil makes this a brain booster, as well as a beauty on the plate!

Green Goddess Salad with Oranges

1 On a platter or four salad plates, spread the greens, then top with the oranges, carrot, and onion.

2 In a blender or food processor, finely mince the garlic. Add the avocado and tofu and puree. Add the stock, oil, vinegar, and salt and puree until smooth.

3 Pour the dressing over the salad and serve. The dressing should be served within 3 hours, or it will discolor.

8 oz/225 g Napa cabbage, slivered

3 cups/60 g baby mustard greens or spinach, chopped

4 oz/115 g snow peas/mangetouts, trimmed

1 large carrot, julienned

4 large scallions/spring onions, thinly sliced

2 tbsp tahini paste

1 tbsp rice wine vinegar

1 tbsp tamari or soy sauce

1 tbsp agave syrup or sugar

1 tbsp minced peeled fresh ginger

1 tbsp canola oil

1 tsp dark sesame oil

1 tsp Szechuan peppercorns, ground

½ tsp red pepper flakes

½ cup/55 g dry-roasted peanuts (optional)

SERVES 4

Napa cabbage is the tender, frilly variety that is perfect for salads. Sliver it into a great fluffy pile and then adorn it with a creamy, spicy dressing to make a filling, crunchy salad that is a great accompaniment to stir-fries.

Napa Cabbage and Mustard Green Salad

with Sesame Dressing

1 On a platter or in a large bowl, arrange the cabbage, greens, snow peas/mangetouts, carrot, and scallions/spring onions.

2 In a small bowl, stir together the tahini, vinegar, tamari, agave syrup, ginger, both oils, ground pepper, and pepper flakes.

3 Toss the dressing with the vegetables just before serving. Top with the peanuts, if desired.

½ cup/120 ml dry
Prosecco

1 garlic clove, peeled

6 tbsp/45 g smoked
almonds, chopped

2 tsp freshly squeezed
lemon juice

1 tsp Dijon mustard

¼ tsp salt

1 pinch sugar

½ cup/120 ml extra-virgin
olive oil

2 tbsp minced fresh basil

Freshly cracked black
pepper

4 oz/115 g baby arugula/
rocket leaves

1 large fennel bulb with
fronds

1 large orange, peeled
and sliced into rounds

SERVES 6

Wine experts often say that pairing wine with salads is perilous. Sour dressings accentuate the sweetness of wines, and the vegetables can bring out odd flavors in some wines. With this salad, the bubbly, simple Prosecco goes in the dressing, and you can serve the rest of the bottle with the salad with no wine worries.

Arugula, Fennel, and Smoked Almond Salad

with Prosecco Dressing

1 In a small saucepan over medium-high heat, reduce the Prosecco to ¼ cup/60 ml. Let it cool.

2 In a food processor, mince the garlic and 2 tbsp of the almonds, then add the lemon juice, mustard, salt, and sugar and process. With the machine running, gradually pour in the oil. When the dressing is emulsified, add the basil and process to mix. Season with pepper.

3 Arrange the arugula/rocket on a platter or individual plates.

4 Use a mandoline to finely slice the fennel. Save ½ cup/ 15 g of the fronds. Spread the fennel and fronds over the arugula/rocket, top with the orange slices, and drizzle everything with the dressing. Top with the remaining 4 tbsp/30 g smoked almonds and serve.

1 lb/455 g whole
beets/beetroot

5 oz/140 g firm tofu,
drained and pressed
(see page 68)

1 tbsp rice vinegar

1 tsp salt

2 large navel oranges

2 tbsp red wine vinegar

2 tbsp extra-virgin olive oil

3 garlic cloves, minced

¼ cup/30 g chopped
walnuts, toasted

SERVES 6

Tofu "feta" is the easiest mock cheese of all time. Just toss crumbled tofu with vinegar and salt and you have a stand-in for the Greek cheese. Beets tinge the tofu pink, so put the tofu on at the last minute. If you have any leftovers, toss it all together and embrace the color!

Greek Beet and Orange Salad
with Tofu "Feta" and Walnuts

1 Put the beets/beetroot in a large pot of water and bring them to a boil over high heat for 10 to 20 minutes, depending on size. When the vegetables are tender (pierce them with a paring knife), drain them, then run cold water over each as you rub off the skin. Trim the tops and bottoms and let them cool completely.

2 In a small bowl, crumble the tofu and mix it with the rice vinegar and ½ tsp of the salt. Leave at room temperature to marinate for at least 10 minutes.

3 Grate the zest from 1 orange and measure 2 tsp. Peel the oranges, removing as much of the white pith as possible. Holding the segments together, gently slice each orange into thin rounds, across the segments. Pop out any seeds.

4 In a medium bowl, whisk together the red wine vinegar, oil, garlic, zest, and remaining ½ tsp salt.

5 Thinly slice the beets/beetroot, add them to the dressing, and toss. Spread them on a serving platter or individual plates. Cover with the orange slices and drizzle everything with the dressing, then top it with the crumbled tofu and the walnuts. Serve at room temperature.

2 large carrots
½ cup/85 g dates, pitted and sliced
3 tbsp freshly squeezed lemon juice
½ tsp ground cumin
½ tsp ground cinnamon
½ tsp salt
1 pinch ground cayenne
2 tbsp extra-virgin olive oil
¼ cup/30 g slivered/ flaked almonds, toasted

SERVES 4

If you use a food processor to shred the carrots, this salad is nearly instant. Carrots and dates are so sweet that a toss with lemon juice and spices makes a riotously sweet-and-sour salad, spiked with flavor.

Moroccan Carrot Salad
with Dates and Almonds

1 Coarsely grate the carrots and put them in a bowl with the dates.

2 In a small bowl, whisk together the lemon juice, cumin, cinnamon, salt, and cayenne. Gradually whisk in the oil.

3 Pour the dressing over the carrots and dates and toss to mix. Serve immediately, topped with the almonds, or cover and refrigerate for up to 4 days.

1 oz/30 g dried wakame

3 tbsp rice vinegar

2 tbsp mirin

2 tbsp soy sauce

1 tbsp toasted white sesame seeds

2 tsp sugar

2 tsp grated peeled fresh ginger

1½ tsp toasted sesame oil

1 tsp red pepper flakes

¼ tsp salt

SERVES 6

One of the best things at many sushi bars is the seaweed salad, which is usually made with long strands of seaweed and agar. This version has all the taste but is made with easy-to-find wakame. If you want to buy some agar strips, soak them and add them to the salad—you just might enjoy that authentic touch.

Sushi-Bar Seaweed Salad

1 Soak the wakame in a large bowl of warm water until it is soft, about 20 minutes. Drain it, then wrap it in a large towel and dry well.

2 In a large bowl, mix together the vinegar, mirin, soy sauce, sesame seeds, sugar, ginger, oil, pepper flakes, and salt. Add the seaweed and toss to mix.

3 Let marinate for at least 1 hour at room temperature. Store in the refrigerator for up to 1 week.

8 oz/225 g green cabbage

4 oz/100 g red cabbage

1 small carrot

½ cup/120 ml Vegan "Mayonnaise" (page 113) or Vegenaise

1 tbsp agave syrup or other liquid sweetener

1 tbsp Dijon mustard

½ tsp salt

½ tsp freshly cracked black pepper

SERVES 4

Classic "sweet slaw" is common all over the American South, and it is usually dosed with too much mayo and corn syrup for me. This version captures the original's appeal in a much more healthful incarnation. It is delicious, crisp, and fresh but will soften a bit if you want to chill it for a couple of hours.

Sweet and Creamy Coleslaw

1 In a food processor fitted with a slicing disk (or by hand), slice the green and red cabbages very thinly.

2 Switch to the grating disk (or use a grater) and grate the carrot.

3 In a large bowl, combine the "mayonnaise," syrup, mustard, salt, and pepper and mix well. Add the cabbage and carrots and toss to coat. Cover and refrigerate for up to 2 days until serving.

2 cups/225 g shredded cabbage

½ large red bell pepper/ capsicum, thinly sliced

1 cup/110 g shredded carrot

4 large scallions/spring onions, slivered

¼ cup/7 g fresh mint, chopped

2 tbsp extra-virgin olive oil

2 tbsp freshly squeezed lemon juice

2 garlic cloves, minced

¼ tsp ground mustard

½ tsp salt

½ tsp freshly cracked black pepper

1 dash hot sauce

SERVES 4

Let's not forget that the much-beloved Mediterranean diet includes the cuisine of places like Syria. This is a nice change from the cucumber salad we are usually served with Middle Eastern food. Just pair it with your pita and hummus and dig in!

Syrian Vegetable Slaw

1 In a large bowl, combine the cabbage, bell pepper/ capsicum, carrot, and scallions/spring onions.

2 In a small bowl, whisk together the mint, oil, lemon juice, garlic, mustard, salt, pepper, and hot sauce.

3 Pour the dressing over the vegetables and toss to mix. Serve at room temperature. Refrigerate leftovers for up to 3 days.

1 medium/170 g raw beet/beetroot

2 medium Granny Smith apples

2 cups/225 g green cabbage

3 tbsp champagne vinegar

1 tbsp agave syrup

1 tbsp Dijon mustard

¼ tsp salt

¼ cup/60 ml extra-virgin olive oil

½ cup/15 g fresh parsley, chopped

SERVES 7

The early fall flavors of beets and apples give this cabbage salad a whole new dimension. Be sure to use Granny Smiths or some other very tart apple to keep the sweet beets in check.

Beet and Apple Slaw
with Champagne Vinaigrette

1 In a food processor fitted with a shredding disk, coarsely shred the beet/beetroot and apples. Put them in a large bowl.

2 Switch to the slicing disk and thinly slice the cabbage. (Alternatively, use a grater and slice the cabbage by hand.) Add it to the bowl.

3 In a small bowl, whisk together the vinegar, agave syrup, mustard, and salt. Whisk in the oil.

4 Pour the dressing over the cabbage mixture and toss to coat thoroughly. Transfer the salad to a serving bowl and sprinkle the parsley over it all. Cover and refrigerate for up to 2 days. Serve chilled.

2 lb/910 g Napa cabbage

3 tbsp kosher salt

5 oz/140 g scallions/
spring onions, cut into
1-in/2.5-cm pieces

½ cup/55 g grated
daikon

¼ cup/24 g minced
peeled fresh ginger

3 tbsp minced garlic

2 tsp red pepper flakes

Soy sauce (optional)

SERVES 8

Kim chee is a Korean culinary treasure in which vegetables are transformed by fermentation into a wildly tangy, spicy condiment/side dish. While it usually takes weeks to make, this quickie version is a good introductory kim chee for beginners, with a little fresher flavor and more crunch.

Instant Kim Chee

1 Wash and dry the cabbage, then slice it into 1-in/2.5-cm pieces. Put them in a large bowl, sprinkle with the salt, and mix well with your hands, massaging the salt into the leaves. Let stand for at least 3 hours or overnight.

2 Over the sink, take handfuls of the cabbage and wring out the water, then put the cabbage in a bowl. Toss it with the scallions/spring onions, daikon, ginger, garlic, and pepper flakes.

3 At this point, you can eat it, adding soy sauce if you think it needs it, or pack it in jars and let it age in the refrigerator for a day. Eat within 1 week, since this quicker process doesn't preserve it as well as fully fermented kim chee.

1 small cucumber

1 large tomato

½ small honeydew melon, peeled and seeded

1 small papaya/pawpaw, peeled

2 cups/330 g chopped fresh pineapple

½ small red onion, slivered

1 small jalapeño, chopped

½ cup/15 g cilantro/ fresh coriander sprigs

2 tbsp rice vinegar

1 tbsp canola oil

2 tsp agave syrup or sugar

¼ tsp salt

SERVES 6

Who says fruit salads and vegetable salads can't meet, or for that matter, that fruits are best with goopy sweet dressing? Toss up this vibrant mix of sweet, tart, and refreshing and you will be singing the praises of vegetable-fruit fusions.

Asian Tropical Fruit and Vegetable Salad

1 Cut the cucumber, tomato, melon, and papaya/pawpaw into bite-size pieces. Put them in a large bowl with the pineapple, onion, and jalapeño.

2 Reserve a few sprigs of cilantro/fresh coriander for garnish and chop the rest. Add it to the bowl.

3 In a small bowl, whisk together the vinegar, oil, agave syrup, and salt. Pour this over the fruit mixture and toss to mix. Cover and refrigerate until serving. Let the salad come to room temperature before serving, about 1 hour, garnished with the reserved cilantro/fresh coriander sprigs.

1 small mango, peeled and sliced

1 large red grapefruit, peeled and sectioned

2 cups/300 g green grapes

1 cup/120 g peeled, finely julienned jícama

3 tbsp freshly squeezed lime juice

2 tbsp palm sugar or brown sugar

1 large jalapeño, chopped

1 tbsp canola oil

¼ cup/30 g pine nuts, toasted

SERVES 4

If you are looking to fill out a Mexican-inspired meal, this refreshing and colorful salad is a great way to do it. Southwestern food is a natural fusion of north and south of the border, combining the best of both. Pile this next to a taco or burrito and you will delight both your eyes and taste buds.

Spicy Southwestern Fruit Salad
with Piñons

1 Combine the mango, grapefruit, grapes, and jícama in a large bowl.

2 In a cup, whisk together the lime juice and sugar to dissolve. If the sugar stays grainy, let the mixture sit for 10 minutes to soften, then whisk again. Whisk in the jalapeño and oil.

3 Pour the dressing over the fruit. Toss to mix, then serve topped with the pine nuts.

8 oz/225 g jícama

2 large mangoes, peeled

1 small red bell pepper/
capsicum, slivered

½ small red onion, thinly
sliced

1 large jalapeño,
chopped

½ cup/120 ml freshly
squeezed lime juice

2 tbsp sugar

2 tbsp extra-virgin olive oil

½ cup/30 g pumpkin
seeds

SERVES 4

Mangoes are so luscious and good for you, and with the addition of crunchy jícama and pumpkin seeds (*pepitas*), this salad will become a regular on your table.

Mango-Jícama Salad
with Lime Dressing and Pepitas

1 Peel and thinly slice the jícama, then stack the slices and slice them into ¼-in/6-mm sticks. Put them into a large bowl.

2 Slice the mango flesh across the grain and add it to the bowl, along with the bell pepper/capsicum, onion, and jalapeño.

3 In a small bowl, whisk together the lime juice, sugar, and oil. Pour the dressing over the mango mixture.

4 In a small frying pan over high heat, dry-toast the pumpkin seeds, swirling and tossing them in the pan. When the seeds start popping and are toasted and fragrant, pour them onto a plate to cool slightly.

5 Serve the salad topped with the crunchy seeds.

Mango-Jícama Salad
with Lime Dressing and Pepitas
FACING PAGE

Beautiful Papaya-Carrot Booster PAGE 58

Edamame Dumplings
in Handmade Green-Tea Wrappers
PAGE 156

Spanish Chickpea Fritters with Romesco Sauce PAGE 166

Wild Rice and Blueberry Salad PAGE 215

Chilled Minted Peach and Prosecco Soup PAGE 228

New Potato Rendang
with Green Beans
PAGE 280

Watermelon and
Tomato Salad with Basil
FACING PAGE

4 cups/435 g cubed seedless red watermelon

1 large yellow tomato

½ cup/15 g fresh basil

3 tbsp freshly squeezed lemon juice

3 tbsp sugar or agave syrup

1 pinch salt

Freshly cracked black pepper

SERVES 4

Tomatoes are technically a fruit, so why not toss them in with some sweet watermelon? The two are at their peak at the same time, and every bite will bring new appreciation for the flavors of both. This is a fast, effortless summer dish, perfect for a hot night.

Watermelon and Tomato Salad
with Basil

1 Put the watermelon into a large bowl.

2 Slice the tomato into thin wedges and add them to the watermelon.

3 Slice the basil into thin strips and add them to the bowl.

4 In a small bowl or cup, whisk together the lemon juice, sugar, and salt. Pour the mixture over the melon and tomato. Serve topped with generous amounts of cracked pepper.

- 1 tbsp sun-dried tomato paste/puree
- 1 tbsp extra-virgin olive oil
- 1 tbsp balsamic vinegar
- 1 tbsp freshly squeezed lemon juice
- 1 garlic clove, crushed
- ½ tsp sugar
- ¼ tsp salt
- 10 oz/280 g zucchini/courgette
- 1 large carrot
- 2 large scallions/spring onions, chopped

SERVES 3

If you are looking for a pretty salad and a change of pace from the usual lettuce, you have found your recipe. A simple kitchen peeler makes restaurant-style curls from these crunchy vegetables, with delicious results.

Zucchini-Carrot Ribbon Salad
in Tomato-Herb Dressing

1 In a small bowl or cup, whisk together the tomato paste/puree, oil, vinegar, lemon juice, garlic, sugar, and salt.

2 On a cutting board, peel the zucchini/courgette down to the seeds, turning it as you go to remove the flesh evenly. Discard or eat the core. Do the same with the carrot—down to the core.

3 Transfer the zucchini/courgette and carrot curls and the scallions/spring onions to a salad bowl and drizzle them with the dressing. Toss to coat and serve immediately.

4 thick slices peasant bread

1 cup/30 g fresh parsley

½ cup/15 g fresh basil

½ cup/15 g fresh mint

¼ cup/7 g fresh oregano

3 tbsp extra-virgin olive oil

2 tbsp freshly squeezed lemon juice

1 garlic clove, minced

½ tsp coarse salt

½ tsp freshly cracked black pepper

4 large tomatoes

SERVES 4

A salad like this is perfect for making use of the tail end of a great loaf of bread—and for giving you large quantities of nutritious, dark green parsley and herbs. Look for a crusty, artisan, whole-grain loaf, and when it gets a little old, use it for this salad. Why waste good bread when you can make an easy meal out of it?

Mediterranean Chopped Herb and Bread Salad

1 Toast the bread, either in the toaster or by putting the slices on a baking sheet/tray and toasting them in an oven at 350°F/180°C/gas 4 for 10 minutes. Cut or tear the toast into chunks.

2 Chop the herbs together finely.

3 In a small bowl, whisk together the oil, lemon juice, and garlic and season with the salt and pepper.

4 Cut the tomatoes into chunks and put them in a large bowl with the herbs. Add the bread and dressing and toss. Let stand for about 5 minutes before serving, topped with more cracked pepper.

1 small head romaine/
Cos or iceberg lettuce,
thinly sliced

¾ cup/90 g diced carrot

¾ cup/130 g diced
zucchini/courgette

¾ cup/140 g diced
tomato

¼ cup/30 g diced red
onion

12.5 oz/355 g extra-firm
silken tofu

Salt

Freshly cracked black
pepper

¼ cup/60 ml vegan
ketchup/tomato sauce

1 tbsp agave syrup

¼ tsp Tabasco sauce

2 tbsp sweet pickle relish

SERVES 4 TO 6

As long as you are making a salad, why not arrange the veggies in attractive rows across the top? A platter spread with a rainbow of chopped veggies and drizzled with a familiar pink dressing will appeal to everyone.

Chopped Salad
with Tofu Thousand-Island Dressing

1 Spread the lettuce on a large platter or on individual dinner plates.

2 Arrange the carrot, zucchini/courgette, tomato, and onion in rows across the greens, making a thinner row of the onion and leaving a space for a row of tofu.

3 Dice half of the block of tofu and sprinkle it with salt and pepper. Arrange a row of seasoned tofu on the salad along-side the veggies.

4 Put the remaining tofu in a food processor or blender and puree until smooth, scraping down the sides occasionally. Add the ketchup/tomato sauce, agave syrup, ½ tsp salt, and the Tabasco and puree. Add the relish and pulse to mix. Drizzle the dressing over the salad and serve.

1 garlic clove

¼ cup/60 ml red wine vinegar

1 tbsp freshly squeezed orange juice

1 tsp Dijon mustard

1 tsp vegan Worcestershire sauce

1 tsp agave syrup or sugar

½ tsp salt

½ cup/120 ml extra-virgin olive oil

½ head/300 g romaine/ Cos lettuce

1 ripe avocado, diced

1 cup/165 g corn, cooked

4 oz/115 g smoked tempeh, chopped

2 oz/55 g fresh button mushrooms, sliced

12 cherry tomatoes halved

1 small cucumber, peeled, seeded, and sliced

½ cup/55 g toasted walnuts, chopped

SERVES 4 TO 6

The original Cobb salad is a steakhouse standard, covered with bacon and blue cheese and a mayonnaise-based dressing. This version is just as fun, filling, and visually resplendent, but with only nutritious plant foods to feed your body right. Smoked tempeh, labeled as "bacon," is sold next to the fake meats, but it is just tempeh basted in a smoky marinade and a convenient way to serve tasty soy.

Cobb Salad
with Smoked Tempeh

1 In a food processor, mince the garlic, then add the vinegar, orange juice, mustard, Worcestershire, agave syrup, and salt. Process to mix. With the machine running, drizzle in the oil. Transfer the dressing to a cruet or a cup with a spout.

2 On a medium round platter or on four individual dinner plates, lay out the lettuce, tearing it into bite-size pieces as you go. Drizzle it with a little of the dressing just to moisten and toss gently to coat.

3 On top of the lettuce, compose the avocado, corn, tempeh, mushrooms, tomatoes, and cucumber in six wedges, like a pie, alternating the colors. Drizzle the remaining dressing over the salad and top with the walnuts.

2 lb/910 g Yukon gold or red waxy potatoes

15 oz/430 g canned/tinned artichoke bottoms, sliced

4 ribs celery, chopped

½ cup/15 g chopped fresh parsley

¼ cup/30 g chopped red onion

10 pitted green olives, halved

¼ cup/30 g capers, drained

½ cup/120 ml extra-virgin olive oil

¼ cup/60 ml freshly squeezed lemon juice

4 garlic cloves, minced

½ tsp freshly cracked black pepper

½ tsp salt

SERVES 6

I'm sure that the French invented mayonnaise-based potato salads, but they also came up with light, vinaigrette-drizzled wonders like this. Your *pommes de terre* (potatoes) never had it so good! Provence is in the south of France, where olive oil, garlic, capers, and the fruits of the vine rule the table.

Potato Salad Provençal

1 Put the whole potatoes in a 4-qt/3.8-L pot and add cold water to cover. Bring to a boil over high heat, then reduce to a vigorous simmer and cook until the potatoes are tender when pierced with a paring knife, about 20 minutes. Drain the potatoes and let them cool just enough so you can safely handle them.

2 Cube the potatoes and put them in a large bowl. Add the artichoke, celery, parsley, onion, olives, and capers.

3 In a small bowl, whisk together the oil, lemon juice, garlic, pepper, and salt.

4 Pour the dressing over the potato mixture and toss to mix. Cover and refrigerate for up to 4 days until serving time.

1½ lb/680 g Yukon gold
potatoes

2 tbsp canola oil

1 lb/455 g onions,
slivered (about
4 medium)

4 oz/115 g smoked
tempeh, chopped

3 oz/85 g green
cabbage, finely chopped
(1 cup)

¼ tsp caraway seeds

2 tbsp cider vinegar

1 tsp sugar

½ tsp freshly cracked
black pepper

½ tsp salt

SERVES 5

This warm potato salad, sweetened with luscious caramelized onions and spiked with smoky tempeh, gives the old bacon version a run for the money. Make sure you take time to fully caramelize the onions for the full flavor.

Smoky German Potato Salad

1 Put the whole potatoes in a 4-qt/3.8 L pot and add cold water to cover. Bring to a boil over high heat, then reduce to a vigourous simmer and cook until the potatoes are tender when pierced with a paring knife, about 20 minutes. Drain and cool the potatoes, then slice them into ¼-in/6-mm rounds.

2 Heat the oil in a large frying pan over high heat and sauté the onions. Reduce the heat to low when they start to soften, and cook until they're caramelized, stirring and scraping the pan often, about 45 minutes.

3 When the onions are golden brown and sweet, add the tempeh, cabbage, and caraway and stir over medium heat until the cabbage is softened. Stir in the vinegar, sugar, pepper, and salt, and remove from the heat.

4 Gently mix the onions with the potatoes, trying not to break up the slices. Serve warm or cold. May be refrigerated for up to 4 days.

- 1 cup/120 g very thinly sliced red onion
- ¼ cup/60 ml extra-virgin olive oil
- 2 tbsp red wine vinegar
- ¼ tsp salt
- ½ tsp freshly cracked black pepper
- 1 lb/455 g sweet potatoes, cut into 1½-in/4-cm cubes
- ½ cup/15 g fresh parsley, chopped
- 1 small jalapeño, minced

SERVES 4

Cooked vegetable salads are great transition foods in late summer, when sweet potatoes are ready to be eaten, and when you may not be ready to eat hot food. The tangy, spicy dressing will make you see the humble sweet potato in a whole new way.

South American Sweet Potato Salad

1 In a large bowl, mix together the onion, oil, vinegar, salt, and pepper.

2 Put the sweet potato cubes in a medium saucepan and add enough cold water to cover. Bring to a boil, turn down the heat, and simmer gently just until they are tender (not falling apart), about 10 minutes. Test with a paring knife.

3 Drain the potatoes, let them cool slightly, then toss them with the onion mixture, parsley, and jalapeño. Cover and refrigerate for up to 4 days. Serve cool or at room temperature.

¼ cup/60 ml coconut milk
¼ cup/60 ml Vegan "Mayonnaise" (page 113) or Vegenaise
½ cup/15 g cilantro/fresh coriander, minced
1 tbsp freshly squeezed lime juice
1 tbsp raw sugar
1 tsp Tabasco sauce
¼ tsp salt
2 large ripe mangoes, peeled
14 oz/400 g canned/tinned hearts of palm, drained
1 large, ripe avocado
¼ cup/60 g chopped scallion/spring onion
8 leaves butter/Boston lettuce
1 large red Fresno chile, slivered

SERVES 4

Hearts of palm, which are the tender centers cut from sprouts that grow on palm trees, add a touch of the exotic tropics to this salad. You can almost imagine you are in Brazil, where fruit is picked ripe and juicy, and avocados fall from the trees.

Avocado, Mango, and Hearts of Palm Salad

1 In a large bowl, whisk together the milk and "mayonnaise." Whisk in the cilantro/fresh coriander, lime juice, sugar, Tabasco, and salt.

2 Slice the mangoes into long spears, then add them to the bowl.

3 Slice the hearts of palm on the diagonal and the avocado into cubes. Add them and the scallion/spring onion to the bowl and toss gently.

4 Arrange two lettuce leaves on each of four small plates and portion the salad onto the leaves. Sprinkle the chile over the top and serve immediately.

1 tbsp toasted sesame oil

8 oz/225 g seitan, thinly sliced

½ tsp salt

4 pita breads, toasted

1 head romaine/Cos lettuce, torn into bite-size pieces

3 medium tomatoes, chopped

½ medium English/hothouse cucumber, quartered and sliced

14 oz/400 g canned/tinned chickpeas, drained and rinsed

½ cup/15 g fresh mint

½ cup/15 g fresh parsley

3 garlic cloves

3 tbsp freshly squeezed lemon juice

¼ cup/60 ml extra-virgin olive oil

SERVES 5

The frugal use of yesterday's bread is a universal practice, and this Mediterranean dish is a great way to finish off the last of the pita—especially if you made the Whole-Wheat Pita Bread (page 107), which is too delicious to waste! Seitan, often called mock duck, is made from wheat gluten and has a meaty texture and lots of protein (see page 38).

Minted Fettoush Salad
with Seitan

1 In a large frying pan, warm the sesame oil over medium heat, then add the seitan and salt. Stir-fry until the seitan is crisp. Put it on a plate to cool.

2 Cut the pita into strips ¾ in/7 cm wide.

3 On a large platter, build the salad with the lettuce, tomatoes, cucumber, and chickpeas.

4 In a blender or food processor, mince the mint, parsley, and garlic. When they're finely ground, add the lemon juice. With the motor running, add the olive oil gradually to make a dressing.

5 Arrange the seitan and pita pieces on top of the salad. Pour the dressing over it all and toss. Serve immediately.

1 tbsp sliced peeled fresh ginger

2 garlic cloves, peeled

¼ cup/50 g almond butter

2 tbsp tamari or soy sauce

2 tbsp canola oil

2 tbsp rice vinegar

1 tbsp all-fruit apricot jam

½ tsp red pepper flakes

8 oz/225 g whole-wheat/wholemeal dried linguine or udon noodles

14 oz/400 g canned/tinned baby corn, drained

8 oz/225 g canned/tinned sliced water chestnuts, drained

4 scallions/spring onions, diagonally sliced

½ cup/55 g sliced/flaked almonds, toasted

SERVES 4

Almonds and apricots sound more like dessert ingredients, but they make a lovely, creamy dressing together. Whole-wheat pasta is best here, for its flavor and chewiness, and the dressing has enough energy to hold its own against the hearty taste of wheat.

Creamy Almond-Noodle Salad
with Baby Corn and Water Chestnuts

1 Bring a large pot of salted water to a boil over high heat for cooking the pasta.

2 In a food processor or blender, mince the ginger and garlic, then add the almond butter, tamari, oil, vinegar, jam, and pepper flakes. Process until smooth.

3 Cook the noodles according to the package directions. Rinse with cold water and drain well.

4 Put the pasta in a large serving bowl and add the almond butter mixture, corn, and water chestnuts. Toss to mix. Serve topped with the scallions/spring onions and almonds.

8 oz/225g tempeh

3 tbsp extra-virgin olive oil

1 tbsp tamari or soy sauce

2 tbsp balsamic vinegar

2 garlic cloves, minced

½ cup/15 g fresh parsley

½ tsp dried thyme

½ tsp salt

½ tsp freshly cracked black pepper

6 oz/170 g dried spiral (rotini) pasta

4 medium Roma tomatoes, seeded and chopped

2 ribs celery, sliced

¼ cup/30 g slivered red onion

SERVES 4

Take this to a picnic and watch it disappear! No need to explain that your healthy lifestyle is vegan—people will devour the chewy tempeh and love it with the tangy tomatoes and curly pasta.

Tempeh and Tomato Pasta Salad

1 Bring a large pot of salted water to a boil for cooking the pasta. Set up a steamer and bring the water to a simmer. Cut the tempeh into bite-size pieces and steam them until they are moistened, about 5 minutes. Remove them to a plate to cool.

2 In a small bowl, whisk together 1 tbsp of the oil, the tamari, 1 tbsp of the vinegar, and half of the garlic. Pour the dressing over the tempeh. Marinate for 30 minutes or overnight in the refrigerator.

3 Preheat the oven to 400°F/200°C/gas 6. On a baking sheet/tray, spread out the tempeh and bake it for 10 minutes. Stir and bake until crisp, another 10 minutes. Remove the pan to a wire rack to cool.

4 In a food processor, mince the parsley. Add the remaining garlic and mince, then add the remaining 2 tbsp oil, 1 tbsp vinegar, and the thyme, salt, and pepper. Process until everything is pureed.

5 Cook the pasta according to the package directions. Drain and rinse with cold water. Combine the pasta with the herb mixture, tempeh, tomatoes, celery, and onion. Cover and refrigerate for up to 2 days until serving.

¼ cup/60 ml agave syrup

1 tbsp Sriracha or other hot sauce

1 tbsp dark miso

1 tbsp tamari or soy sauce

1 tbsp dark sesame oil

3 tbsp toasted white sesame seeds

7 oz/200 g dried soba noodles

1 medium cucumber, peeled, seeded, and julienned

1 medium Asian pear, julienned

6 oz/170 g extra-firm silken tofu, drained and cut into small cubes

SERVES 4

Soba is a hearty, nutritious, fat noodle made from varying amounts of buckwheat. Look for one with buckwheat listed first in the ingredients. It's usually associated with the Japanese, but Koreans love it, too, and use it with their spicy flavors and fresh herbs for a unique dish.

Korean Buckwheat Noodle Salad
with Asian Pears

1 Bring a large pot of salted water to a boil for cooking the soba noodles.

2 In a small bowl, whisk together the agave syrup, Sriracha, miso, tamari, sesame oil, and 2 tbsp of the sesame seeds.

3 Cook the soba noodles according to the package directions, then rinse with cold water. Drain well. Put the noodles in a large serving bowl or on a platter, drizzle with the Sriracha mixture, and toss to coat.

4 Pile the cucumber, pear, and tofu cubes on top of the salad. Sprinkle with the remaining 1 tbsp sesame seeds. Cover and refrigerate for 1 hour to chill. Serve cold. If making up to a day ahead, don't cut the pears until serving.

1 stalk lemon grass, thinly sliced

5 small shallots, thinly sliced

2 garlic cloves, thinly sliced

1 tbsp tamari or soy sauce

1 tsp sugar

1 tsp toasted sesame oil

1 tsp white sesame seeds

½ tsp ground white pepper

½ tsp red pepper flakes

8 oz/225 g seitan, thinly sliced

Sauce

2 small fresh jalapeño or serrano chiles, minced

1 tbsp canola oil

1 tbsp tamari or soy sauce

1 tbsp rice vinegar

1 tbsp white miso

1 tsp sugar

1 garlic clove, chopped

4 oz/100 g dried rice vermicelli

2 oz/55 g bean sprouts

1 cup/30 g fresh Asian basil, julienned

Vegetable oil

SERVES 4

This is a hot and cold salad, with slippery rice noodles and veggies forming the base for hot, just-crisped seitan. The lively tastes and textures combine into a fabulous hot-weather meal.

Vietnamese Noodle Salad

with Lemon Grass Seitan, Sprouts, and Basil

1 In batches in a coffee grinder or spice grinder (a food processor will not grind lemon grass), grind the lemon grass, shallots, and garlic to a paste. Scrape each batch out into a medium bowl, and mix together with the tamari, sugar, sesame oil, sesame seeds, pepper, and pepper flakes. Add the seitan and let it marinate in the refrigerator for at least 2 hours or overnight.

2 Set up a rack in the oven 6 in/15 cm from the broiler/grill, then preheat the broiler/grill.

3 Meanwhile, boil a large pot of salted water for cooking the rice vermicelli.

4 TO MAKE THE SAUCE: In a large bowl, whisk together the chiles, oil, tamari, vinegar, miso, sugar, and garlic.

5 Drop the vermicelli into the boiling water. Watch carefully: When the noodles are just cooked, drain and rinse them with cold water. Roll them in a towel to dry thoroughly. Add the noodles to the bowl with the sauce and toss to coat. Arrange the noodles on a platter, then cover them with the sprouts and basil.

6 Remove the seitan from the marinade, spread it on an oiled baking sheet/tray and broil for 1 minute on each side, until lightly browned. Scatter the seitan over the noodles and serve immediately.

1 cup/215 g wild rice

¼ tsp salt

¼ cup/60 ml canola oil

2 tbsp raspberry vinegar

2 tbsp maple syrup

1 cup/125 g fresh
raspberries

1 cup/155 g fresh
blueberries

2 ribs celery, chopped

3 scallions/spring onions,
chopped

SERVES 6

I live in Minnesota, land of the best hand-harvested wild rice. The real deal is completely different from the hard, shiny kernels of cultivated wild rice, which take much longer to cook. Check the rice package for instructions, and enjoy the nutty flavor and superb nutrition of the Native Americans' Mother Grain. When berries are at their best, toss their sweet-tart goodness with earthy wild rice for a true treat. This will elevate a simple sandwich to a gourmet meal, or go along well with a picnic.

Wild Rice and Blueberry Salad

1 In a medium saucepan, bring 2 cups/480 ml water to a boil. Add the rice and salt and simmer until the water is absorbed, 25 to 45 minutes. Remove the pan from the heat, cover, and let it stand for 10 minutes to steam. Remove the rice to a bowl and refrigerate it to cool.

2 In a small bowl, whisk together the oil, vinegar, and syrup.

3 To serve, add the berries, celery, and scallions/spring onions to the rice. Toss together. Add the dressing and mix.

14 oz/400 g extra-firm tofu, drained, pressed (see page 68), and cut into small dice

2 tbsp soy sauce

¼ cup/60 ml mirin

4 oz/115 g baby spinach

½ cup/120 g diagonally sliced scallions/spring onions

½ cup/60 g canned/tinned sliced water chestnuts, drained

½ carrot, julienned

3 tbsp rice vinegar

1 tbsp minced peeled fresh ginger

2 tbsp canola oil

1 garlic clove, minced

⅛ tsp salt

Freshly cracked black pepper

1 cup/215 g cooked sushi rice

SERVES 4

Easier and faster than a stir-fry, but warmer and more substantial than the usual spinach salad, this wilted salad is a great quick meal. Just keep some tofu, spinach, and carrots on hand and you can grab the rest from the pantry.

Warm Teriyaki Tofu and Wilted Spinach Salad

1 Put the diced tofu into a bowl, drizzle it with the soy sauce and mirin, and toss gently to coat.

2 Place the spinach in a large serving bowl with the scallions/spring onions, water chestnuts, and carrot.

3 In a small bowl, combine the vinegar and ginger.

4 In a large frying pan over medium heat, warm the oil. When it is hot, add the tofu and stir-fry until lightly browned. Add the garlic and sauté briefly, then add the vinegar and ginger and cook until the tofu is glazed.

5 Dump the spinach mixture into the frying pan, add the salt, and toss just until the spinach begins to wilt. Season with pepper and scrape everything into a serving bowl. Serve at once, with the sushi rice on the side.

1 lb/455 g broccoli, cut into florets, stems peeled and sliced

1 small red bell pepper/capsicum, sliced

8 oz/225 g canned/tinned sliced water chestnuts, drained

½ cup/120 ml rice vinegar

½ cup/100 g sugar

1 tbsp tamari or soy sauce

1 tsp red pepper flakes

1 tsp toasted sesame oil

SERVES 4

Just like hot-and-sour soup, this quick and easy salad tickles your taste buds in all the right ways. A whisper of toasted sesame oil is the only fat in this satisfying dish.

Hot-and-Sour Broccoli Salad

1 Set up a steamer with simmering water or a pot of boiling water. Steam the broccoli just until crisp and bright green or blanch (boil) it for 1 minute, then rinse with cold water until cool, and let drain. Pat it dry with a kitchen towel and transfer it to a large bowl. Add the bell pepper/capsicum and water chestnuts.

2 In a small saucepan, mix together the vinegar, sugar, tamari, and pepper flakes. Bring to a boil over high heat, stirring constantly. Reduce the heat to a steady simmer and stir until the sugar is dissolved.

3 Remove the pot from the heat and stir in the oil. Let the mixture cool slightly, then pour it over the broccoli and toss. Serve at room temperature, or cover and refrigerate for up to 2 days.

8 oz/225 g cauliflower
florets

1 cup/110 g julienned
carrots

1 large radish, diced

1 large jalapeño, minced

1 tsp cumin seeds

1 tsp brown mustard
seeds

1 tsp fennel seeds

1 tsp ground coriander

½ tsp ground turmeric

2 tbsp coconut milk

¼ cup/60 ml Vegan
"Mayonnaise" (page 113)
or Vegenaise

SERVES 4

What a perfect way to enjoy cauliflower, and how delicious it is to eat that radish you just pulled from the garden! The dressing has just enough coconut milk for a tropical flavor, and vegan "mayo" carries the spices with panache.

Curried Cauliflower, Carrot, and Radish Salad

1 Set up a steamer and bring the water to a simmer. Steam the cauliflower and carrots for 2 minutes, or just until crisp-tender. Let them cool, then put them in a large bowl with the radish and jalapeño.

2 In a small saucepan, dry-toast the cumin, mustard, and fennel seeds over medium-high heat until crackling and fragrant.

3 Add the ground coriander and turmeric, swirl for just a second, then take the pan off the heat and add the milk. Stir to mix, then transfer the mixture to a small bowl. Let it cool, then stir in the "mayonnaise." Pour this over the vegetable mixture and stir to coat. Serve immediately or cover and refrigerate.

½ cup/100 g wheat, farro, or kamut berries

½ cup/25 g packed fresh basil

2 tbsp chopped walnut pieces

2 tbsp pine nuts

1 garlic clove, peeled

2 tbsp extra-virgin olive oil

2 tbsp freshly squeezed lemon juice

1 tsp fresh lemon zest

¼ tsp salt

5 oz/130 g zucchini/courgette, cubed

2 cups/480 ml chopped fresh tomatoes, drained

2 tbsp sliced red onion

SERVES 5

Whole wheat doesn't get any more whole than a wheat berry. The fat grains take awhile to cook, but you will be rewarded with a crunchy delight filled with nutrients. Pesto is just a little zingier with lemon, and it complements the hearty wheat perfectly.

Hearty Wheat Berries
with Lemon Pesto

1 In a small, heavy saucepan over high heat, combine the wheat and 2 cups/480 ml water. When it comes to a boil, reduce the heat to low, and cover. Cook for about 1 hour, then check for tenderness. The grains should burst. Cook for 30 minutes more, if necessary. Drain the wheat, put it in a bowl, and let it cool to room temperature.

2 In a food processor or blender, puree the basil, walnuts, pine nuts, and garlic into a paste. With the motor running, drizzle in the oil and lemon juice, and then add the lemon zest and salt and pulse to mix.

3 Scrape out the pesto over the cooled wheat, then stir to mix. Add the zucchini/courgette, tomatoes, and onion. Toss everything together, then serve immediately.

NOTE: *You can keep this in the fridge for a few days, but drain the tomatoes well before adding so they don't make the salad soupy.*

1 cup/200 g medium-grind bulgur

½ tsp salt

1 garlic clove

½ cup/15 g fresh parsley

½ cup/15 g fresh mint

3 tbsp pomegranate molasses or juice concentrate

¼ tsp ground cinnamon

¼ cup/60 ml extra-virgin olive oil, plus extra if needed

½ tsp freshly cracked black pepper

1 cup/110 g shredded carrot

1 cup/120 g minced celery

¼ cup/30 g pistachios, toasted

Seeds from 1 large pomegranate

SERVES 4

Bored with the old lemony tabbouleh stand-by? Break out with a new taste sensation, and use pomegranate instead of lemon, and pistachios instead of chickpeas. Pomegranate provides a tart, sweet, complex flavor that also happens to pack an antioxidant punch.

Pomegranate Tabbouleh
with Pistachios

1 In a small saucepan, bring 1½ cups/360 ml water to a boil. Add the bulgur and salt, and return to a full boil for a few seconds, then cover, lower the heat, and simmer for 10 minutes. When all the water is absorbed, remove the pot from the heat. Let it stand for 10 minutes, then remove the bulgur and refrigerate it for 1 hour to chill.

2 In a food processor, process the garlic until it is finely chopped. Add the parsley and mint and process until they are finely minced, scraping down the sides a few times. Add the molasses and cinnamon and process until smooth. With the machine still running, pour in the oil to make a dressing. Taste for sourness; if the pomegranate seems strong to you, add more olive oil. Add the pepper.

3 Pour the dressing over the cooled bulgur, then add the carrot and celery. Toss together and refrigerate until ready to use and up to 3 days.

4 To serve, spread the bulgur mixture on a platter and sprinkle the pistachios and pomegranate seeds over it all.

½ cup/55 g whole almonds

1¼ cups/300 ml Basic Vegetable Stock (page 49)

1 pinch salt

1 cup/200 g whole-wheat/wholemeal couscous

½ tsp plus ¼ cup/60 ml extra-virgin olive oil

1 cup/30 g fresh parsley

½ cup/15 g fresh mint

2 tbsp agave syrup

¼ cup/60 ml freshly squeezed lemon juice

½ cup/60 g pitted dates, coarsely chopped

SERVES 4

Whole-wheat couscous is the fastest whole grain out there, and it lends itself to light, quick dishes like this one. With crunchy almonds, sweet dates, and the classic minty dressing, this pairs perfectly with hummus platters, Mediterranean Chopped Herb and Bread Salad (page 203), or Armenian Lentil-Apricot Stew (page 238).

Middle Eastern Couscous
with Mint, Dates, and Almonds

1 Preheat the oven to 350°F/180°C/gas 4. Toast the almonds on a rimmed baking sheet/tray until fragrant, about 10 minutes, then chop them very coarsely.

2 In a small saucepan, bring the stock and salt to a boil. Add the couscous and the ½ tsp oil, stir quickly, and just as bubbles start forming, cover and remove the pot from the heat. Let the couscous steam for 5 minutes.

3 In a food processor, mince the parsley and mint. Add the agave syrup and process. With the motor running, add the lemon juice and the remaining ¼ cup/60 ml of oil gradually to make a bright green dressing.

4 Toss the couscous with the dressing, then fold in the dates and almonds. Serve warm, or cover and refrigerate for up to 3 days.

Soups

Soups are a world unto themselves, from the hot to the cold, the brothy to the creamy, the light to the hearty. They can be as simple as boiled beans or a little more sophisticated, and as long as they are eaten with a spoon, they must be soup! Soups are always recommended as a way to keep your weight down, because they fill you up with both liquid and lots of vegetables. If you are trying to drop pounds, just add a bowl of a lean soup to the beginning of every meal, and your appetite will be satisfied before you get to dessert.

Don't think that soups are time consuming or require too much effort. To the contrary, many are quick and easy. Conveniences like veggie stock in a box, canned beans, and canned tomatoes make soup a realistic weeknight meal. Of course, you can use the recipes for Basic Vegetable Stock (page 49) and Mushroom Stock (page 51), and even then, veggie stock is not the production that animal stocks are. The vegetables give up their essences in a quick simmer instead of a long slow one, and vegan soups just don't need hours and hours.

Creamy soups are still on the menu, thanks to the judicious use of some great nondairy milks. You will notice that vegetable purees make up most of the base of creamy soups, adding more veggies to your meal. The comforting, rich feel of a pureed soup is just as satisfying in these plant-based wonders. They only *seem* decadent, and that is the best kind of decadent, isn't it?

3-in/7.5-cm white baguette, crust removed

½ cup/55 g slivered/flaked almonds

1 tbsp sherry vinegar

1 garlic clove, peeled

½ tsp salt

1 cup/240 ml ice water

¼ cup/60 ml extra-virgin olive oil

2 cups/300 g seedless green grapes, halved

1 cup/100 g finely diced cucumbers

SERVES 4

Tomato gazpacho is the great standard, but the word *gazpacho* refers to bread crusts used to thicken this type of soup, not tomatoes. This refreshing, non-tomato soup boasts smoothly pureed almonds and bread for a filling meal.

Almond Gazpacho
with Grapes

1 In a food processor, combine the baguette, almonds, vinegar, garlic, and salt. Process, adding the ice water gradually to make a smooth puree.

2 With the machine running, drizzle in the oil. Transfer the puree to a medium bowl or tureen, then stir in the grapes and cucumber. Refrigerate for up to 3 days until serving.

3 oz/85 g watercress

1 large leek

2 tbsp Earth Balance margarine or olive oil

1 lb/455 g Yukon gold potatoes, peeled and cubed

1 cup/240 ml plain vegan creamer

Salt

Freshly cracked black pepper

SERVES 4

The classic cold potato puree is even better with a deep green infusion provided by peppery watercress. Boost your nutrition while enjoying this simple, light soup.

Vichyssoise Verte

1 Trim the watercress, rinse it well, and spin or pat it dry.

2 Cut the root end from the leek and split it lengthwise to wash thoroughly. Chop it into chunks, including some of the tender greens.

3 In a medium pot over medium heat, sauté the leek in the margarine until very soft.

4 Add the potatoes and just enough water to cover. Cover the pot and bring to a boil. Cook until the potatoes are tender, about 10 minutes. Add the watercress and cook for 1 minute. Let cool.

5 In a blender or food processor, puree the vegetables, adding the cooking liquids to help puree smoothly. Put the lid on and hold it down with a folded kitchen towel so that no splatters will burn you. Add the creamer and season with salt and pepper. Add a little water if the soup is too thick. Cover and refrigerate up to 4 days. Serve cold.

3 lb/1.4 kg cantaloupe/
rockmelon

½ cup/120 ml plain soy
yogurt

2 tbsp agave syrup, plus
extra if needed

¼ tsp almond extract

1 pinch salt

1½ tsp lemon zest

6 tbsp/45 g sliced/flaked
almonds, toasted

SERVES 3

Cantaloupe soup is really, really good when it's hot outside and a smooth, cool soup is exactly what you need. Just adjust the sweetness of the soup to taste, as the natural wonder that is melon can vary in sweetness.

Chilled Cantaloupe Soup
with Toasted Almonds

1 Wash and halve the cantaloupe/rockmelon, then scoop out the seeds and cube the flesh. You should have about 4 cups/960 ml.

2 Put the cubes in a blender or food processor with the yogurt, agave syrup, and almond extract and puree until smooth. Add the salt and process, then taste. If the melon is not very sweet, add more agave to taste.

3 Refrigerate up to 4 days. Serve the soup in 1-cup/240-ml portions topped with ½ tsp of lemon zest and 2 tbsp of toasted almond.

2 lb/910 g fresh peaches, peeled and pitted

1½ cups/360 ml dry Prosecco

½ cup/15 g fresh mint, finely chopped

½ cup/120 ml coconut milk

2 tbsp agave syrup, plus extra if needed

1 tbsp freshly squeezed lemon juice, plus extra if needed

4 sprigs mint

SERVES 4

Use very ripe peaches for this recipe. The peels should strip off easily. If not, boil a pot of water, cut an X in the bottom of each peach, and drop them in the boiling water for a minute to loosen the skins. Plunge into ice water, then strip off the skins with a paring knife. Prosecco is the inexpensive Italian sparkling wine that gives you a champagne feeling for half the price. If you want to sub another sparkler, get a dry champagne, Cava, or other bubbly.

Chilled Minted Peach and Prosecco Soup

1 Chop the peaches and put them in a 4-qt/3.8-L saucepan with the Prosecco. Bring to a boil and reduce to a simmer. Cook until the peaches are breaking down, about 30 minutes. Remove from the heat, then stir in the mint and let cool.

2 In a blender or food processor, puree the peaches with the milk, agave syrup, and lemon juice.

3 Refrigerate the soup up to 4 days. Taste and adjust the seasoning: Does it need a little more lemon juice? Agave? Serve in bowls with mint sprigs.

2½ medium avocados

1 cup rice milk or other milk

¼ cup/60 ml freshly squeezed lime juice

1 tbsp white miso

1 tsp agave syrup

¼ tsp salt

¼ cup/30 g sliced scallions/spring onions

¼ tsp chili powder

4 oz/100 g corn chips, for serving

SERVES 3

Avocados are so lush and velvety in this puree, you need only a bit of the milk to make a soup of it. A hint of chili powder puts a zesty spin on the smooth soup, rich in essential fats to keep you going all summer long.

Creamy Chilled Avocado-Lime Soup

1 In a blender, combine the flesh of 2 avocados, reserving the remaining for garnish. Add the milk, lime juice, miso, agave syrup, and salt. Process until smooth, then transfer the soup to a pitcher or bowl and refrigerate, covered (press plastic wrap/cling film onto the surface of the soup to prevent browning).

2 To serve, portion ½ cup/120 ml soup into each bowl, garnish with the scallions/spring onions, and dice the remaining avocado to sprinkle in the center of each serving. Sprinkle each bowl with chili powder. Set on a small plate and surround with the corn chips.

3 large Granny Smith
apples, peeled and sliced

1 cup/240 ml apple juice

½ cup/120 ml white wine

¼ cup/60 ml agave syrup

1 in/2.5 cm fresh ginger,
peeled and sliced

¼ tsp ground cinnamon

1 cup/240 ml vanilla rice
milk or other milk

2 large Honeycrisp or
Golden Delicious apples

¼ cup/7 g fresh mint,
julienned

1 tbsp freshly squeezed
lemon juice

SERVES 4

An apple a day is easy to do with this sprightly
soup. The apple puree creates a smooth base and a
few crunchy apple bits floating on top makes a hit!

Crunchy Apple Soup

1 In a 2-qt/2-L pot, combine the Granny Smith apples, apple
juice, wine, agave syrup, ginger, and cinnamon. Bring to a
boil, then reduce the heat to a simmer. Cover, and cook until
the apples are very soft, about 5 minutes.

2 When the apples are very tender, carefully transfer the
solids from the pot to a blender with a slotted spoon. Cover
the lid of the blender with a folded kitchen towel and puree
the apples carefully—they are hot! Uncover and add the
liquids from the pot. Puree until very smooth. Add the milk,
puree, and then refrigerate the soup for up to 3 days.

3 When the soup is cold, finely chop the Honeycrisp apples
and toss them with the mint and lemon juice. Serve bowls of
the soup with a pile of chopped apple in the center.

2 lb/910 g ripe tomatoes, chopped

1 cup/120 g diced celery

1 cup/100 g diced cucumber

1 cup/180 g diced zucchini/courgette

½ cup/50 g chopped scallions/spring onions

1 cup/240 ml carrot juice

1 cup/30 g fresh basil or parsley, finely chopped

¾ cup/180 ml coconut milk or other milk

2 tbsp balsamic vinegar

½ tsp salt

SERVES 6

The secret ingredient in this soup is carrot juice, which sweetens the tomato and vegetable mélange. It also adds valuable carotenoids for your health.

Chunky Chilled Tomato and Summer Vegetable Soup

1 In a blender or food processor, puree the tomatoes, and then strain them through a fine-mesh strainer set over a bowl. Press on the solids, then discard what remains.

2 Stir the celery, cucumber, zucchini/courgette, and scallions/spring onions into the tomato puree. Add the carrot juice, basil, milk, vinegar, and salt. Refrigerate the soup for up to 3 days. Serve cold.

1 tbsp extra-virgin olive oil

2 cups/225 g chopped cabbage

1 cup/120 g diced onion

1 large carrot, chopped

2 ribs celery, sliced

1 tbsp ground cumin

1 garlic clove, chopped

½ tsp dried oregano

2 cups/480 ml Basic Vegetable Stock (page 49)

14 oz/400 g canned/tinned black beans, drained

14 oz/400 g canned/tinned diced tomatoes

½ tsp salt

½ tsp red pepper flakes

SERVES 4

Make this soup with canned beans, so you can put it together at the end of a long day. The lively spices and hearty cabbage make a great lunch or dinner soup. It's especially good the day after it is made.

Cuban Black Bean Soup
with Cabbage

1 In a large pot over medium heat, warm the oil. Add the cabbage, onion, carrot, and celery. Sauté, stirring, until the onion is golden, about 5 minutes.

2 Add the cumin, garlic, and oregano, stir for 1 minute, and then add the stock, beans, tomatoes, salt, and pepper flakes.

3 Simmer for 10 minutes, or until the vegetables are tender and the flavors are developed. Serve hot, or let it cool thoroughly and refrigerate and reheat the next day.

2 tsp canola oil

1 tsp black mustard seeds

2 tsp cumin seeds

2 cups/225 g chopped cabbage

1 cup/120 g chopped onions

2 tbsp minced peeled fresh ginger

1 large jalapeño, seeded and minced

1 tsp ground turmeric

1 cup/240 g tomato puree/sieved tomatoes

14 oz/400 g canned/tinned chickpeas, drained and rinsed

1 tbsp brown sugar

1 tbsp freshly squeezed lemon juice

½ tsp salt

1½ cups/275 g cooked brown basmati rice

½ cup/15 g cilantro/fresh coriander

SERVES 4

This thick and hearty stew is well spiced but not hot. If you want some heat, add an extra jalapeño. Turmeric is a potent anti-inflammatory and anti-oxidant spice, so keep eating lots of it to protect your brain and joints—all necessary in life!

Curried Chickpea Stew

1 In a large frying pan, heat the oil over medium-high heat. Add the mustard and cumin seeds and fry until the seeds are fragrant and begin to pop.

2 Add the cabbage, onion, ginger, and jalapeño. Stir and cook, reducing the heat to medium and sautéing until the vegetables have softened.

3 Add the turmeric and stir for 1 minute, then add the tomato puree/sieved tomatoes, chickpeas, brown sugar, lemon juice, and salt. Simmer for 5 minutes to blend the flavors and thicken the sauce.

4 Serve the stew over the cooked rice, with the cilantro/fresh coriander sprinkled over the top.

1 large red bell pepper/
capsicum, diced

1 bulb fennel, chopped

1 small zucchini/
courgette, chopped

2 large carrots, chopped

1 medium red onion,
diced

½ medium sweet potato,
cubed

2 oz/55 g fresh cremini/
brown mushrooms, sliced

6 large garlic cloves,
peeled

1 tbsp extra-virgin olive oil

1 qt/960 ml Roasted
Vegetable Stock
(page 50) or boxed stock

3 tbsp sun-dried tomato
paste/puree

14 oz/400 g canned/
tinned white beans,
drained and rinsed

2 cups/225 g chopped
savoy cabbage

½ tsp salt

8 slices whole-wheat/
wholemeal bread,
toasted

SERVES 8

Ribollita means "reboiled" and refers to this type
of reheated soup stretched with day-old bread. The
result is such a lovable concoction that we now
make this soup on purpose, instead of waiting for
the right leftovers. If you are going to make the
Roasted Vegetable Stock, roast all the vegetables
at once to save time.

Roasted Vegetable Ribollita

1 Preheat the oven to 425°F/220°C/gas 7.

2 In a deep roasting pan/tray, toss the bell pepper/capsicum,
fennel, zucchini/courgette, carrots, onion, sweet potato,
mushrooms, and garlic with the oil and cover with foil. Roast
for 20 minutes, then stir and roast for 20 minutes more.
Uncover and roast until slightly brown, 10 minutes more.

3 When the vegetables are roasted, pick out the garlic and
reserve. Scrape the veggies into a soup pot, add the stock
and tomato paste/puree, and heat until warm.

4 Puree or mash half of the beans with the roasted garlic.
Add the mashed and unmashed beans to the pot. Add the
cabbage and salt and simmer until softened, about 10 minutes. Serve the soup over a slice of toasted bread.

Stew

1 cup/200 g dried chickpeas

1 large carrot, chopped

2 medium Yukon gold potatoes, chopped

1 medium onion, chopped

2 ribs celery, chopped

1 medium red Fresno chile

2 stems fresh rosemary

3 tbsp tomato paste/puree

¼ tsp salt

Freshly cracked black pepper

Rice

1 cup/215 g long-grain white rice

1 tsp lemon zest

½ tsp salt

3 cups/90 g spinach leaves, chopped

2 tbsp extra-virgin olive oil

1 tbsp rosemary leaves

2 garlic cloves, minced

Kalamata olives, chopped, or pistachios, toasted, for garnish (optional)

SERVES 6

This is the rare moment when white rice seems like a better idea than brown—the delicate lemon and spinach really stand out with a pale rice in the background.

Greek Chickpea Stew with Rosemary
over Spinach-Lemon Rice

1 TO MAKE THE STEW: Soak the chickpeas overnight in cold water to cover, then drain. Put them in a large pot with 4 cups/960 ml fresh water and bring to a boil over high heat. Add the carrot, potatoes, onion, celery, chile, and rosemary stems and return to a boil, then reduce to medium for a good simmer. Simmer until the beans are tender, about 45 minutes, adding more water as necessary.

2 When the beans are tender, stir in the tomato paste/puree. Scoop out 1 cup/240 ml of the mixture and puree it in a blender, then return it to the soup. Season with the salt and pepper.

3 TO MAKE THE RICE: In a 1-qt/960-ml saucepan, bring 1½ cups/360 ml water to a boil, and add the rice, lemon zest, and salt. Resume the boil and cover, lowering the heat to the lowest setting. Simmer for 15 minutes. When all the water has been absorbed, remove the pan from the heat and let the rice steam, covered, for 5 minutes.

4 When the rice is cooked, stir in the spinach and cover. Let it stand for another 5 minutes.

5 Just before serving, warm the oil in a sauté pan and heat the rosemary leaves and garlic. Serve the stew with the rice, drizzled with the garlic oil. If desired, garnish each bowl with chopped olives or toasted pistachios.

2 tsp canola oil

4 garlic cloves, minced

14 oz/400 g canned/tinned fire-roasted tomato puree/sieved tomatoes

2 tsp chopped chipotle chile in adobo sauce

1 qt/960 ml Basic Vegetable Stock (page 49)

14 oz/400 g canned/tinned chickpeas, drained and rinsed

½ tsp freshly cracked black pepper

½ tsp salt

8 oz/225 g dried whole-wheat/wholemeal angel hair pasta

2 ears corn on the cob, kernels cut off (about 1 cup/90 g)

1 cup/180 g diced zucchini/courgette

Cilantro/fresh coriander, for garnish

SERVES 4

This is a "dry soup," in which the fine pasta soaks up the tasty broth, creating a cross between a soup and a plate of pasta. Whatever you call it, it's quick, spicy, and veggie-rich.

Sopa Seca de Fideos
with Chickpeas

1 In a soup pot, warm the oil over medium-high heat and sauté the garlic until fragrant and lightly golden. Add the tomato puree/sieved tomatoes and chipotle and cook the mixture until thick, about 5 minutes.

2 Add the stock, chickpeas, pepper, and salt. Simmer for a few minutes and adjust for salt. Add the pasta (breaking it up as you add it), corn, and zucchini/courgette. Simmer, stirring constantly, until the noodles are al dente, about 5 minutes. Add more stock if needed.

3 Transfer everything to a serving dish, then top with cilantro/fresh coriander.

1½ cups/375 g French lentils/Puy lentils, soaked and rinsed

2 ribs celery, chopped

1 large carrot, sliced

1 large Yukon gold potato, chopped

1 large bay leaf

1 tbsp extra-virgin olive oil

1 onion, chopped

2 garlic cloves, chopped

1 tbsp fresh thyme, chopped

½ cup/15 g fresh parsley, chopped

½ tsp freshly cracked black pepper

½ tsp salt

SERVES 6

French green lentils are a very different sort of legume than the regular brown lentils. With a deep flavor and a firmer skin, they stay separate in the soup even when tender, and people will think you are the best cook ever.

French Lentil–Potato Soup

1 Put the lentils in a soup pot with 6 cups/1.4 L water. Add the celery, carrot, potato, and bay leaf. Bring to a boil over high heat. Cover and simmer for about 20 minutes before testing a lentil for doneness. When the lentils are tender but not falling apart, turn the heat to low.

2 While the lentils cook, heat a small frying pan over medium heat and add the oil. Add the onion and sauté, lowering the heat as the onion softens. Cook until the onion is tender, golden, and sweet, stirring occasionally. Add the garlic and thyme and cook for another minute.

3 Scrape the onion and oil into the lentils, then add the parsley, pepper, and salt. Simmer for another 10 minutes or so to blend the flavors and serve warm.

1 cup/250 g red lentils, soaked and rinsed

1 medium onion, chopped

1 small Japanese eggplant/aubergine, peeled and diced

14 oz/400 g canned/tinned diced tomatoes

½ cup/85 g dried apricots, chopped

2 tsp paprika

½ tsp salt

¼ tsp ground cinnamon

⅛ tsp ground allspice

⅛ tsp cayenne

1 cup/30 g fresh parsley, chopped

½ cup/15 g fresh mint, chopped

Rice

3 large shallots, chopped

1 tbsp extra-virgin olive oil

¼ cup/35 g sesame seeds

1½ cups/320 g long-grain brown rice

½ tsp salt

3 tbsp tahini paste

2 tbsp freshly squeezed lemon juice

SERVES 6

Red lentils simmer into a creamy stew, piqued with bits of tangy apricot and tender eggplant. The warming spices make it even more delicious, perfect over the sesame-fortified brown rice. All you need is a salad and you have a complete meal.

Armenian Lentil-Apricot Stew
over Sesame Brown Rice

1 In a 4-qt/3.8-L pot, combine 1 qt/960 ml water, the lentils, and the onion. Bring to a boil over medium-high heat, then reduce the heat to a simmer. Cook for 10 minutes, stirring frequently.

2 Add the eggplant/aubergine, tomatoes, and apricots and simmer, covered, for about 20 minutes, stirring every 5 to 10 minutes.

3 When the lentils are falling-apart tender and the vegetables are also tender, add the paprika, salt, cinnamon, allspice, and cayenne and simmer for another 5 minutes to marry the flavors. Add the parsley and mint just before serving. Keep the soup warm while cooking the rice.

4 TO MAKE THE RICE: In a 2-qt/2-L pot over medium heat, sauté the shallots in the oil. When the shallots are clear and soft, add the sesame seeds and sauté for 5 minutes.

5 Add 3 cups/720 ml water, the rice, and salt. Bring to a boil, then cover and reduce the heat to a low simmer. Check after 35 minutes. When all the water has been absorbed, remove the pot from the heat and let it sit, covered, to finish steaming the rice, 5 to 10 minutes.

6 In a small cup, stir together the tahini and lemon juice, then fold them into the rice. Serve the rice hot with a ladleful of soup on top.

238

1 lb/455 g yucca
(cassava root)

1½ cups/375 g red lentils,
soaked and rinsed

1 large onion, chopped

4 ribs celery, chopped

1 red bell pepper/
capsicum, chopped

½ cup/15 g chopped
fresh parsley

¼ cup/60 ml freshly
squeezed orange juice

2 tbsp ground coriander

2 tbsp paprika

1 tbsp chopped peeled
fresh ginger

2 garlic cloves, chopped

1 tsp salt

¼ tsp red pepper flakes

¼ tsp ground cinnamon

SERVES 8

Yucca, or cassava root, is a big, brown-skinned tuber with creamy white flesh. It's starchy, like a potato, but has none of the mealy texture that potatoes can have. Try it in this spicy soup and see if you don't love it.

African Red Lentil–Yucca Soup

1 Peel and chop the yucca, discarding the hard cores. Add the lentils and yucca to a large pot with 1 qt/960 ml water. Bring to a boil over high heat. Reduce the heat and simmer, adding more water as it thickens.

2 After 10 minutes, add the onion, celery, and bell pepper/capsicum and simmer until they are tender. Add the parsley, orange juice, ground coriander, paprika, ginger, garlic, salt, pepper flakes, and cinnamon and simmer to blend the flavors. Serve the soup hot.

½ cup/100 g dried kidney beans

1 tsp canola oil

1 cup/120 g chopped onions

½ cup/45 g chopped green bell pepper/ capsicum

1 small jalapeño, chopped

1 garlic clove, chopped

½ tsp ground turmeric

½ tsp chili powder

1 medium tomato, chopped

1 cup/240 ml coconut milk

2 tsp sugar or agave syrup

½ tsp salt

SERVES 4

Plenty of meatless meals are eaten in Africa, and this is a prime example of the inventive uses of beans and vegetables that characterize the continental cuisine. The soup is just a little bit hot, but you can spice it up with more chile for a real metabolic boost.

Kenyan Kidney Bean and Coconut Soup

1 Soak the beans overnight in cold water to cover. Drain them and put them in a 2-qt/2-L pot. Add water to cover by 3 in/7.5 cm. Bring to a boil, then reduce the heat to a simmer. Cook until the beans are tender but not falling apart, about 40 minutes. Drain.

2 Set a 4-qt/3.8-L pot over high heat. When the pot is hot, add the oil, then add the onion, bell pepper/capsicum, and jalapeño. Stir and, when the vegetables are sizzling, reduce the heat to medium and stir until softened and golden, about 10 minutes.

3 Add the garlic, turmeric, and chili powder and stir for 1 minute. Add the tomato, cooked kidney beans, milk, sugar, and salt. Simmer until slightly thickened, about 10 minutes, adding water if it gets too thick. Serve the soup hot.

¼ cup/50 g wheat berries or farro

2 tbsp extra-virgin olive oil, plus extra for garnish

1 large carrot, coarsely chopped

1 small onion, coarsely chopped

½ rib celery, chopped

1 small fennel bulb, chopped

3 garlic cloves, minced

14 oz/400 g canned/tinned kidney beans, drained and rinsed

3 sprigs rosemary, plus extra for garnish

¼ cup/7 g chopped fresh sage

2 tbsp fresh thyme, chopped

½ tsp salt

Freshly cracked black pepper

SERVES 4

This traditional Tuscan stew has been made much quicker with canned beans. The slow sauté of fennel and vegetables melts into the creamy bean puree, which is studded with chewy wheat berries. This makes a great first course before your pizza or pasta or can be a meal on its own with a salad and whole-wheat bread.

Italian Kidney Bean and Wheat Berry Stew

1 Soak the wheat berries in cold water to cover overnight in the refrigerator.

2 Drain the wheat berries and put in a small saucepan with plenty of water. Bring to a boil, then reduce the heat and simmer until tender, about 1 hour. After the grains are splitting and plump, drain off any excess water.

3 In a large pot, warm the oil over medium heat and add the carrot, onion, celery, and fennel. Sauté until the vegetables are tender, about 10 minutes. Add the garlic and sauté for 2 minutes more, then add the drained beans.

4 Add 2 cups/480 ml water, the rosemary, sage, and thyme. Raise the heat and bring to a boil. Cover and cook for 10 minutes.

5 Remove the rosemary sprigs and transfer the bean mixture to a blender, being very careful not to burn yourself. Puree the bean mixture, in batches if necessary, holding a folded towel over the lid to keep it from spilling, then put the puree back into the pot.

6 Add the cooked grains and bring the soup to a simmer. Season with the salt and pepper. Ladle the soup into bowls, drizzle with oil, and garnish with rosemary sprigs.

1 tbsp extra-virgin olive oil

1 large onion, chopped

8 oz/225 g Mock Duck (page 38) or chicken-style seitan, chopped

2 garlic cloves, chopped

1 tsp ground cumin

1 pinch ground cloves

1 qt/960 ml Basic Vegetable Stock (page 49) or mock chicken stock

1 small sweet potato, cubed

¼ cup/45 g quinoa, rinsed

1 tbsp chopped chipotle chile in adobo sauce

1 tsp dried oregano

¾ tsp salt

Six 6-in/15-cm corn tortillas

1 tbsp canola oil

½ cup/15 g cilantro/fresh coriander

1 large lime, cut into wedges, for serving

SERVES 4

Tortilla soups are so fun—adding a handful of crisp tortilla chips just before serving is wa-a-a-y better than crackers. In this lighter version, you can bake fresh chips and skip several grams of fat from the usual fried chips.

Tortilla Soup
with Mock Duck and Chipotles

1 In a large pot, heat the olive oil over high heat. Add the onion and stir for 5 minutes or so, lowering the heat to medium. When the onion is soft, add the mock duck, garlic, cumin, and cloves. Stir for a few minutes.

2 Add the stock, sweet potato, quinoa, chipotle, and oregano and bring to a boil. Add ½ tsp of the salt. Reduce the soup to a simmer and cook for about 15 minutes. When the quinoa is throwing off its tiny white halos and the sweet potato is tender, reduce the heat to low.

3 Preheat the oven to 375°F/190°C/gas 5. Stack the tortillas and slice them into strips ¼ in/6 mm wide. Place them on a baking sheet/tray and drizzle with the canola oil and the remaining ¼ tsp salt. Bake, stirring every 5 minutes, until the strips are crisp, 20 to 25 minutes.

4 Serve the soup topped with the cilantro/fresh coriander and tortilla strips, with lime wedges for squeezing over the soup.

3 oz/75 g dried kombu (kelp)

4 large dried shiitake mushrooms

1 medium burdock root, peeled and chopped

1 large carrot, thinly sliced

2 cups/345 g shelled edamame, thawed if frozen

6 tbsp/90 ml barley miso or other dark miso

2 cups/60 g fresh spinach or watercress leaves

6 scallions/spring onions, diagonally sliced

SERVES 6

Miso soup is the magical health food of Japan. Studies show that people who eat miso soup every day have much lower risks of cancer and other ills. Good thing it's so tasty! It's easy to eat it often. Don't wash the kombu. The white dusting of sea salt is part of the seasoning for this seaweed.

Mushroom Dashi and Miso Vegetable Soup

1 In a large pot, combine 3 qt/2.8 L water, the kombu, and mushrooms over medium-low heat. Cook for about 10 minutes, or just to the boiling point. Remove from the heat; remove the kombu and let the mushrooms steep. Strain the broth through a coffee filter or cheesecloth/muslin into a soup pot. Discard the kombu and mushrooms.

2 Return the broth to the pot and heat over medium-low heat. Add the burdock and carrot and simmer until tender, about 10 minutes. Add the edamame and simmer gently for a few minutes. Ladle a bit of hot broth into a small bowl and mix well with the miso. Stir the miso into the soup, remove from the heat, and add the spinach. Serve the soup with scallions/spring onions on each serving.

2 tsp canola oil

12 oz/340 g firm tofu, drained and pressed (see page 68)

3 tbsp tamari or soy sauce

4 cups/960 ml Basic Vegetable Stock (page 49) or mock chicken stock

1½ tbsp cornstarch/cornflour

1¾ tsp freshly cracked black pepper

¼ cup/60 ml rice vinegar

1 tsp toasted sesame oil

1 large carrot, julienned

5 scallions/spring onions, diagonally sliced

SERVES 6

Most Chinese restaurants serve hot-and-sour soups that are heavy on MSG and so salty that they should have a heart-health warning. This delicious, easy soup is a better way to enjoy the lively black pepper kick of a good soup.

Hot-and-Sour Soup
with Tofu

1 Preheat the oven to 400°F/200°C/gas 6. Spread the canola oil on a baking sheet/tray.

2 Cube the tofu, spread it on the prepared pan, and sprinkle it with 1 tbsp of the tamari. Bake for 20 minutes, then flip the pieces and bake until firm and browned, 10 minutes more. Put the pan on a rack to cool.

3 Heat the stock in a medium saucepan over medium heat.

4 Combine the cornstarch/cornflour and pepper in a small bowl, then whisk in the vinegar, the remaining 2 tbsp tamari, and the sesame oil. Whisk the cornstarch/cornflour mixture into the hot stock and bring the mixture to a boil for 1 minute.

5 Add the carrot to the soup and simmer for about 3 minutes. Stir in the scallions/spring onions and baked tofu, and remove from the heat. Taste and adjust the seasoning before serving.

1 tsp canola oil

1 small dried Thai red chile

4 large dried mushrooms (any variety)

1 large stalk lemon grass, bruised with the back of a chef's knife

4 garlic cloves, coarsely chopped

6 kaffir lime leaves, or 1 lime, zest pared off in strips

4 slices fresh ginger

4 large shallots, sliced

1 large carrot, sliced

4 oz/100 g fresh straw or shiitake mushrooms, sliced

2 tbsp palm sugar or brown sugar

2 tbsp tamari or soy sauce

1 tbsp dark miso

12 oz/340 g firm tofu, drained and pressed (see page 68)

1 cup/30 g cilantro/fresh coriander

SERVES 5

The soups of Thailand are hot, sour, salty, and sweet, just like the rest of the cuisine, but you rarely find a vegan version in a restaurant. Take matters into your own hands and make it at home—it's better that way.

Tom Yum Soup
with Tofu

1 In a large pot over high heat, warm the oil. Add the chile. Stand back, turn on the fan, and cook until it is blackened. Remove the pan from the heat, take out the chile, and add 2 qt/2 L water, the dried mushrooms, lemon grass, garlic, lime leaves, and ginger.

2 Return the pot to high heat and bring to a boil. Lower the heat to a gentle simmer and cook until the stock is tinted and flavorful, about 45 minutes.

3 Strain the stock into a large bowl or pot and discard the solids. Taste the stock: If you want more heat, return the chile to the pot and cook it with the soup.

4 In a second large pot, combine the stock with the shallots, carrot, fresh mushrooms, palm sugar, tamari, and miso. Bring to a simmer, and cook until the mushrooms are tender. Taste and adjust the seasoning.

5 Cube the tofu. Gently stir it into the soup and heat through. Stir in the cilantro/fresh coriander and serve.

4 large dried shiitake or black mushrooms

3 oz/85 g daikon, peeled and sliced

½ medium onion, sliced

One 6-in/15-cm piece dried kombu

6 tbsp/90 ml dark miso

4 slices/11 g fresh ginger

4 garlic cloves, halved

1 tsp red pepper flakes

2 cups/360 g cubed zucchini/courgette

8 oz/225 g cubed red potato

4 oz/115 g fresh shiitake mushrooms, stemmed

12 oz/340 g silken tofu, cubed

1 large red Fresno chile, slivered, for garnish

2 large scallions/spring onions, diagonally sliced, for garnish

SERVES 4

Japan's miso soups are understated and minimalist compared to this Korean version. This winter stew has all the spice and flavor you would expect from the people who invented kim chee. Serve the stew with rice and Instant Kim Chee (page 189) or some Sushi-Bar Seaweed Salad (page 185) on the side for a great meal.

Korean Miso-Tofu Soup

(Doenjang Jigae)

1 Put 2 qt/2 L water in a large pot and add the dried mushrooms, daikon, onion, kombu, miso, ginger, garlic, and pepper flakes. Bring to a boil, then reduce the heat to a simmer for 20 minutes. Line a colander with a sturdy paper towel/absorbent paper and set it over a bowl. Strain the liquid through the paper, carefully shifting the vegetables to the sides to help it drain completely. Discard the solids.

2 Add the broth to a large pot and bring it to a simmer. Add the zucchini/courgette, potato, and shiitakes and cook for about 10 minutes, until the potatoes are cooked all the way through.

3 Add the tofu and simmer for about 5 minutes to heat through. Serve the soup in bowls garnished with the chile and scallions/spring onions.

6 ears corn, kernels reserved (keep cobs for stock)

2 tbsp extra-virgin olive oil

1 cup/120 g chopped onions

½ cup/60 g chopped celery

4 garlic cloves, roughly chopped

1 medium Yukon gold potato, chopped

1 cup/185 g seeded diced tomato

1 tbsp minced fresh dill

½ tsp salt

½ tsp freshly cracked black pepper

Cayenne

½ cup/85 g shelled edamame, chopped

SERVES 4

There comes a moment in summer when all that sweet corn on the cob is ripe and ready. That's the perfect time to make this light and lean soup. The corncobs help to flavor the stock, so don't throw them out.

Summer Corn Soup
with Edamame Garnish

1 Break the cobs in half and put them in a large pot with 6 cups/1.4 L water. Bring to a boil over high heat, then reduce the heat and simmer for 30 minutes. Strain the liquid and reserve it, discarding the cobs.

2 In the same pot, warm the oil over medium heat and add the onions, celery, and garlic. Sauté, stirring, until the onions are soft and clear, about 5 minutes. Add the potato and stir for a few minutes, then add the corncob water. Bring to a boil, then reduce the heat to medium and cover. Cook for 10 minutes.

3 Add the corn kernels to the pot and simmer for 5 minutes. Scoop out 1 cup of the vegetables and reserve.

4 Transfer the remainder of the pot to a food processor or blender in batches, and hold the lid on with a folded kitchen towel so that no splatters will burn you. Carefully puree; the liquid will be hot. Return the puree to the pot and stir in the reserved vegetables.

5 Stir in the tomato, dill, salt, and pepper. Season with cayenne. Serve each bowl of soup garnished with 2 tbsp chopped edamame.

1 tbsp canola oil

2 large onions, thinly sliced

3½ cups/840 ml Basic Vegetable Stock (page 49)

2 large carrots, chopped

1½ cups/360 ml apple cider

½ cup/100 g pearl barley

1 tsp dried thyme

¼ tsp dried marjoram

1 bay leaf

2 cups/250 g chopped unpeeled apples

¼ cup/7g chopped fresh parsley

1 tbsp freshly squeezed lemon juice

¼ tsp salt

SERVES 6

This is a very old Scottish soup, one that would have been made to keep body and soul together in the fall and winter months. Barley is a great source of cholesterol-lowering fiber, and apples have been shown to improve brain health. Those Scots were onto something!

Apple-Barley Soup

1 In a small soup pot, heat the oil over medium heat. Add the onions and sauté for 5 minutes, stirring constantly. Reduce the heat, cover, and cook until the onions are browned, stirring frequently, about 10 minutes.

2 Add the stock, carrots, cider, barley, thyme, marjoram, and bay leaf. Cover and cook for 1 hour, or until the barley is tender.

3 Add the apples, parsley, lemon juice, and salt. Cook for 5 minutes, or until the apples are slightly soft. Discard the bay leaf and serve.

¾ oz/20 g dried wild mushrooms

1 large bay leaf

1 stem fresh thyme

½ tsp whole black peppercorns

1 small onion

1 garlic clove

1 tbsp extra-virgin olive oil

¼ cup/50 g farro or wheat berries, soaked overnight

¼ cup/60 ml dry sherry

2 tbsp tamari or soy sauce

¼ tsp salt, plus extra if needed

8 oz/225 g fresh oyster and shiitake mushrooms, sliced

Freshly cracked black pepper

SERVES 5

Farro is an ancient form of wheat from Italy. If you can't find it, use wheat berries, kamut, spelt, or even barley. The plump grains stay a bit crunchy in the soup, and explode with wheaty flavor. "Wild mushroom" is a term that refers to any mushroom besides the button variety, even though many of the formerly wild mushrooms are now cultivated, making them more available.

Wild Mushroom and Farro Soup

1 In a large pot, combine 6 cups/1.4 L water, the dried mushrooms, bay leaf, thyme, and peppercorns. Bring to a boil over high heat.

2 While the water is heating, slice the onion. Set the onion slices aside and put the trimmings into the pot with the dried mushrooms. Peel and chop the garlic, and throw the peels in the pot. When the water boils, reduce the heat to a gentle simmer. Simmer for 40 minutes, then strain the liquids into a large bowl or pot. Discard the solids.

3 In a 3-qt/2.8-L pot, heat the oil. Add the onion and garlic and stir and sauté over medium heat until softened. Add the farro, 1 qt/960 ml of the stock you just made, the sherry, tamari, and salt. Bring to a boil.

4 Cover the pot and reduce the heat to a simmer. Cook until the farro is tender, about 1 hour.

5 When the grains are tender, add the fresh mushrooms and simmer until soft. Season with salt and pepper and serve.

¼ oz/10 g dried mushrooms

1 tbsp extra-virgin olive oil

½ cup/60 g chopped onion (save the trimmings)

8 oz/225 g fresh cremini/ brown or baby bella mushrooms, chopped (save the trimmings)

2 garlic cloves, chopped

½ cup/100 g arborio rice

1½ cups/360 ml plain soymilk or other milk

½ tsp dried sage

½ tsp salt

1 dash Tabasco sauce

SERVES 4

If you love mushrooms, you will love this super mushroom soup, intensified with both dried and fresh mushrooms and a hint of earthy sage to keep it tethered to the ground. It has all the creamy, luxurious texture of a dairy-based soup, thanks to pureed rice, mushrooms, and nondairy milk.

Cream of Cremini Mushroom Soup
with Sage

1 In a 2-qt/2-L pot over high heat, bring 3 cups/720 ml water and the dried mushrooms to a boil, then lower the heat to a simmer. (Add any onion and mushrooms trimmings to the pot.) Cook, simmering gently, until the liquid is golden and fragrant, about 40 minutes.

2 In a large pot, heat the oil and sauté the onion until golden. Add the fresh mushrooms and garlic and cook until tender.

3 Remove half the sautéed vegetables to a bowl and reserve. Strain the dried-mushroom water through a coffee filter, saving the rehydrated mushrooms if desired. There should be 2½ cups/600 ml of stock, so add water if needed.

4 Pour the stock into the pot with the sautéed vegetables. Chop the reserved rehydrated mushrooms (if using) and add to the bowl of sautéed vegetables. Add the rice to the pot, bring to a boil, and reduce the heat. Simmer until the rice is falling apart, about 30 minutes.

5 In a blender or food processor, puree the hot mushroom mixture in batches. Put the lid on and hold it down with a folded kitchen towel so that no splatters will burn you. Return the puree to the pot, add the soymilk and reserved vegetables. Season with the sage, salt, and Tabasco. Heat through before serving. If it's too thick for your taste, add water or soymilk.

1½ lb/680 g leeks

2 tsp extra-virgin olive oil

2 garlic cloves, chopped

1 tsp fresh thyme

2 lb/910 g yellow
potatoes, chopped

3 to 4 cups/720 to 960 ml
Basic Vegetable Stock
(page 49) or water

3 scallions/spring onions,
chopped

½ cup/15 g fresh parsley,
chopped

1 tsp salt

1 dash cayenne

1 cup/240 ml soymilk or
other milk

SERVES 6

One of the first meals my mother taught me to make was a creamy potato soup made with leftover mashed potatoes and milk. That was pretty spartan, really, but it had the potato's creamy appeal that keeps us coming back again and again. Now I make it with fragrant thyme, garlic, and nondairy milk for a lush bowl of potato goodness.

Potato-Leek Soup

1 Slice the white part of the leeks into rounds, then submerge them in water to get out any grit. Drain and pat dry.

2 In a large soup pot, heat the oil over medium heat. Add the leeks and sauté until they are golden and sweet, reducing the heat to low if they start to stick.

3 Add the garlic and thyme and sauté for 2 minutes. Add the potatoes and just enough stock to cover them. Raise the heat and bring to a simmer, then cover and cook until the potatoes are tender and disintegrating, about 20 minutes.

4 In a blender or food processor, puree or coarsely mash the soup in batches. Put the lid on and hold it down with a folded kitchen towel so that no splatters will burn you. Return the soup to the pot. Add the scallions/spring onions, parsley, salt, and cayenne. Gradually stir in the soymilk to reach the desired thickness. Heat gently to serve, but don't boil or it might separate or scorch.

4 cups/400 g cauliflower florets

4 tsp canola oil

1 cup/120 g chopped onions

2 garlic cloves, chopped

1 tbsp minced peeled fresh ginger

1 tsp ground turmeric

1 tsp ground cumin

½ tsp ground coriander

2 medium Yukon gold potatoes, chopped (2 cups)

1 large carrot, chopped

1 cup/240 ml unsweetened rice milk or coconut milk

1 tbsp lemon zest

½ tsp salt

SERVES 4

Golden turmeric burnishes this smooth soup to a healthful glow, whose tint tips you off to the presence of this health-promoting spice. Roasting the cauliflower deepens the nutty flavor of this underappreciated vegetable.

Curried Cauliflower Soup

1 Preheat the oven to 400°F/200°C/gas 6. In a large roasting pan/tray, toss the cauliflower with 2 tsp of the oil and roast for 20 minutes, or until it is soft and browned.

2 In a large soup pot, heat the remaining 2 tsp oil over high heat. Add the onions and cook, stirring constantly. Reduce the heat as the onions start to sizzle. Sauté until the onions are soft and golden. Add the garlic, ginger, turmeric, cumin, and ground coriander and stir over low heat for 1 minute, or until fragrant.

3 Add the potatoes, carrot, 1 cup/240 ml water, and half of the roasted cauliflower. (Reserve the remaining cauliflower to add to the finished soup.) Bring to a boil, then cover and cook for about 10 minutes, or until the potatoes are falling-apart tender.

4 When everything is butter soft, transfer the soup to a blender or food processor in batches. Put the lid on and hold it down with a folded kitchen towel so that no splatters will burn you. Puree the soup. Add the milk, lemon zest, and salt and pulse to mix, then return the soup to the pot. Add the reserved cauliflower. Heat through and adjust the seasonings before serving.

1½ lb/675 g broccoli

½ cup/60 g sliced onion

2 cups/475 ml Basic Vegetable Stock (page 49), plus 2 tbsp

¼ cup/50 g white rice

1 cup/120 ml plain vegan creamer or other milk (optional)

1 tsp salt

Freshly cracked black pepper

1 pinch cayenne

Pesto

½ cup/15 g fresh basil

½ cup/60 g frozen peas, thawed

1 garlic clove, peeled

1 tbsp pine nuts

2 tbsp extra-virgin olive oil

Plain vegan creamer or other milk, as needed

½ tsp salt

SERVES 6

I used to make cream of broccoli soup in a restaurant once a week, but it was to use up all the broccoli stems that we had saved from other recipes. Broccoli stems are full of sweet, juicy broccoli goodness, so be sure to save them to use in this soup.

Creamy Broccoli Soup
with Basil-Pea Pesto

1 Peel and chop the broccoli stems, reserving the florets. Put the stems and onion in a big pot and add the 2 cups/ 475 ml stock and the rice. Bring to a boil and then reduce the heat. Simmer until the vegetables and rice are very tender, about 20 minutes. While the soup cooks, set up a steamer and bring the water to a simmer. Steam the broccoli florets just until they are bright green.

2 In batches in a blender or food processor, puree the broccoli stem mixture with about one third of the florets. Put the lid on and hold it down with a folded kitchen towel so that no splatters will burn you. Puree it until smooth, adding creamer only as necessary. Return the puree to the pan and gently reheat it, whisking in just enough creamer to make a consistency you like. Stir in the remaining broccoli florets, the salt, pepper, and cayenne.

3 TO MAKE THE PESTO: In a food processor or blender, process the basil, peas, garlic, and pine nuts until finely chopped. With the motor running, add the oil and process until smooth. If the mixture is very chunky, drizzle in creamer, 2 tbsp at a time. Add the salt and process to mix.

4 Serve bowls of warm soup with a swirl of pesto on each.

Ingredients

1 tbsp extra-virgin olive oil

1 cup/120 g chopped onions

2 cups/230 g cubed butternut squash (about half of a small squash)

½ cup/100 g millet

3 cups/720 ml Basic Vegetable Stock (page 49)

1 cup/240 ml plain soymilk or other milk

½ tsp salt

½ tsp ground cumin

1 small chipotle chile in adobo sauce, minced

¼ cup/7 g cilantro/fresh coriander, chopped, for garnish

SERVES 4

Smoky chipotle complements sweet squash perfectly, and golden millet thickens the soup with a whole-grain boost. If you are not a chile-head, start with half a chipotle, and see how you like it.

Puree of Squash and Millet Soup
with Chipotle

1 Set a 2-qt/2-L saucepan over medium heat, and when hot, add the oil. Add the onions and sauté until softened, then lower the heat and cook slowly until the onions are golden, about 10 minutes.

2 Add the squash and millet and raise the heat, stirring until the millet is hot and the squash is lightly browned. Add the stock, bring to a boil, and lower the heat to the lowest setting. Cover and cook until the millet is completely broken apart and porridgey, about 40 minutes.

3 Working in batches, transfer the soup to a blender or food processor. Put the lid on and hold it down with a folded kitchen towel so that no splatters will burn you. Puree the mixture thoroughly, then gradually add the soymilk with the machine running. Add the salt and cumin and pulse to mix.

4 Scrape the soup back into the saucepan to reheat or hold it until serving time. Stir the chipotle into the soup. Heat gently for about 5 minutes to infuse the soup with smoky flavor.

5 Serve each bowl garnished with the cilantro/fresh coriander.

2 tbsp Earth Balance margarine or oil

1 cup/120 g chopped onions

2 tsp caraway seeds

8 oz/225 g cabbage, finely chopped

1 medium red or yellow potato, chopped

3 cups/720 ml Basic Vegetable Stock (page 49) or water

1 cup/240 ml plain soymilk or other milk

1 cup/30 g fresh parsley, chopped

½ tsp salt

Freshly cracked black pepper

SERVES 6

Cabbage with caraway is a classic flavor combination, the peppery little seeds giving a bit of snap to the butter-soft cabbage. This is peasant food, so have a hunk of crusty bread and keep warm.

Creamy Cabbage and Caraway Soup

1 In a large soup pot, melt the margarine over medium heat. Add the onions and caraway, and sauté until the onions are golden, at least 10 minutes, reducing the heat if the food starts to stick.

2 Add the cabbage and potato and sauté for 5 minutes. Add the stock and raise the heat. When the soup comes to a boil, lower the heat to a simmer, then cover and cook until the potatoes are falling apart and the cabbage is very soft, about 15 minutes.

3 Scoop about half of the cabbage mixture into a blender or food processor. Put the lid on and hold it down with a folded kitchen towel so that no splatters will burn you. When the mixture is smooth, add the soymilk, parsley, and salt. Puree until smooth.

4 Return the puree to the pot with the remaining cabbage and stir over low heat. Serve warm, and crack lots of black pepper over each bowl.

1 tbsp extra-virgin olive oil

1 cup/120 g chopped
onions

1 lb/455 g beets/
beetroot, peeled and
diced (reserve the
greens)

1½ cups/210 g chopped
Yukon gold potatoes

2 medium carrots,
chopped

2 ribs celery, chopped

1 tsp caraway seeds

1 tbsp red wine vinegar

1 tbsp agave syrup

1 tsp salt

1 tsp dried dill

Black bread, for serving
(optional)

Soy yogurt or soy sour
cream, for serving
(optional)

SERVES 6

Borscht is synonymous with Russia, where peasants survived the frigid winters by filling a root cellar with beets to make borscht until spring. A big bowl of crimson beets is such an elemental pleasure, with the sweet, earthy roots swimming in hot broth. Beets are a great souce of iron, vitamin C, folate, and magnesium, so eat two bowls.

Borscht

1 Set a large soup pot over high heat. When it is hot, add the oil. Add the onions and sauté, reducing the heat when the onions start to brown. Cook for as long as you have time (longer cooking brings out the sugars), but at least until the onions are translucent. Add the beets/beetroot, potatoes, carrots, and celery. Keep stirring for about 5 minutes.

2 Chop 2 cups/60 g of the reserved beet greens. Add to the pot along with 1 qt/960 ml water and the caraway. Bring to a boil.

3 Lower the heat to a simmer and cook until the beets/beetroot are very tender, about 10 minutes. Add the vinegar, agave syrup, salt, and dill. Simmer for another 5 minutes to bring the flavors together.

4 Serve the soup hot with black bread, or refrigerate it until cold and serve with a dollop of soy yogurt, if desired.

1 cup/250 g lentils, soaked and rinsed

4½ cups/1 L Basic Vegetable Stock (page 49) or water

1 medium carrot, chopped

½ cup/60 g chopped onion

1 bay leaf

2 green bell peppers/capsicums, chopped

1 large dried ancho pepper, dry-toasted and crumbled

14 oz/400 g canned/tinned fire-roasted crushed tomatoes

½ cup/100 g bulgur

2 garlic cloves, chopped

1 tbsp ground cumin

1 tbsp chili powder

1 tbsp dried oregano

½ tsp salt

SERVES 5

There are a million ways to make chili, and this is a great one. Bulgur has the chewy quality of ground beef, but it adds only fiber, antioxidants, and protein—no fat. Lentils cook quickly and melt into this lush stew, rich with dried ancho chile flavor.

Lentil Chili
with Bulgur and Anchos

1 Put the lentils in a soup pot. Add the stock, carrot, onion, and bay leaf. Over high heat, bring to a boil, then reduce to a simmer, cover, and cook for 20 minutes.

2 Add the bell peppers/capsicums and ancho to the pot. Simmer for 20 minutes, then check the lentils for doneness. They should be very soft. Add the tomatoes, bulgur, garlic, cumin, chili powder, oregano, and salt.

3 Simmer the chili for 15 minutes more to bring the flavors together and finish cooking the bulgur, adding more water or stock if needed. Taste and adjust the seasonings before serving.

12 oz/340 g extra-firm tofu, drained and pressed (see page 68) and cubed

1 tbsp freshly squeezed lime juice

2 tsp tamari or soy sauce

1 tbsp Earth Balance margarine or olive oil

½ cup/50 g chopped scallions/spring onions

2 large red Fresno chiles, chopped

1 tbsp fresh thyme, chopped

2 garlic cloves, chopped

1 lb/455 g sweet potatoes, cubed

1 small carrot, chopped

1 tbsp mild curry powder

2 large bay leaves

3 cups/720 ml Basic Vegetable Stock (page 49)

14 oz/400 g coconut milk

3 cups/105 g chopped collard greens

½ tsp salt

Cooked rice, for serving

SERVES 6

An African influence is definitely present in the home cooking of Jamaica, where spices grow in abundance and coconuts are everywhere. Rastafarians are vegetarian as part of their religion, and it is easy to find vegan food on the island. Get small, tender collards if you can find them. They are the closest thing to the callaloo greens that Jamaicans put in this stew.

Jamaican Tofu Chowder
with Collards

1 In a bowl, gently toss the tofu with the lime juice and tamari. Set aside.

2 In a large pot over medium heat, melt the margarine. Add the scallions/spring onions, chiles, thyme, and garlic and cook until fragrant.

3 Add the sweet potatoes, carrot, curry powder, and bay leaves and stir over medium heat until the curry scents the kitchen. Add the stock and milk and bring to a boil, then reduce to a good simmer. Cook, uncovered, until the sweet potatoes are tender, about 10 minutes.

4 Stir in the collards and reserved tofu and simmer until the leaves are soft and bright green, about 10 minutes. Season the soup with the salt and serve it with rice.

2 tsp extra-virgin olive oil

½ cup/60 g chopped onion

8 oz/225 g seitan, cut into bite-size pieces

1 medium parsnip, chopped

1 large carrot, chopped

2 bay leaves

2 tsp fresh thyme, chopped

2 garlic cloves, chopped

1 strip orange peel

Freshly cracked black pepper

1½ cups/360 ml Basic Vegetable Stock (page 49)

1 cup/240 ml dry red wine

1 tsp cold-press corn oil

2 tbsp unbleached all-purpose/plain flour

8 oz/225 g dried eggless noodles

2 tbsp/7 g chopped fresh parsley

SERVES 4

This deep, winey, herbed stew is a great way to make seitan taste really beefy. Parsnips and carrots are bathed in the classic flavors of a bourguignon stew, served over comforting noodles.

Seitan Burgundy Stew
with Parsnips

1 In a 2-qt/2-L saucepan, heat the olive oil. Add the onion and sauté until it is translucent, about 5 minutes. Add the seitan, parsnip, carrot, bay leaves, thyme, garlic, orange peel, and a generous grinding of pepper. Cook, stirring, for 15 minutes.

2 Add the stock and wine and bring the soup to a simmer. Lower the heat to keep it at a simmer and cook until slightly reduced, about 15 minutes. Discard the orange peel and bay leaves.

3 To thicken the stew, heat the corn oil in a small saucepan. Work in the flour with a heat-safe spatula to make a paste and cook over medium-low heat for 2 minutes, stirring and mashing. Pour some of the stew liquids into the flour mixture and mix well. Stir the paste into the stew, and simmer for 5 minutes, or until thickened slightly. If it becomes too thick, add some stock or water.

4 Meanwhile, bring a large pot of salted water to a boil. Cook the noodles according to the package directions. Serve the stew over the noodles, sprinkled with parsley.

CHAPTER

8

Side Dishes

Let's say that you are going to a potluck party. What do you bring? If your nonvegan friends are coming, you might volunteer to bring one of these sides. You might want to bring a main for yourself, but your thoughtfulness in bringing a lively grain or vegetable side will be appreciated. From hearty risottos and pilafs to a gamut of tasty plant-based dishes, the vegan sides will win your friends over.

When pairing a side with a meal, the first thing to think about is the cuisine, as in is it Indian or Italian? A batch of tasty Curry-Roasted New Potatoes with Date-Nut Chutney (page 279) will fit right in with a curry meal, and dishes like Wine-Roasted Mushrooms (page 293) and Cipollini Onions in Agrodolce (page 295) are a nice change from the standard Italian fare. If they are picking up sushi, bring Japanese Asparagus with Walnut Dressing (page 275). Mexican fare? Yucca with Chipotle–Red Pepper Drizzle (page 286) is a great companion.

Exploring the flavors of grains and vegetables is one of the great joys of the plant-based kitchen. Now that you are not overwhelming your palate with animal foods, you can really pick up the nuances in the quinoa pilaf. A barley pilaf explodes with texture and flavor. The simple veggies that too often sit in a limp, steamy pile next to the steak are now stars. Try out these dishes that explore roasting, stewing, poaching, steaming in wine, and every technique that brings flavor to the fore. Treat your veggies like the stars that they are, with their own special sauces and sprinklings of herb and spice.

The sides may well outshine the main course, and that could be a good thing.

1 tbsp peanut/groundnut oil or canola oil

1 cup/120 g chopped onions

4 large Roma tomatoes, peeled and chopped

1 large carrot, chopped

1 tbsp minced peeled fresh ginger

1 large bay leaf

1 cup/240 ml coconut milk

1 cup/215 g long-grain brown rice

4 oz/115 g sliced fresh button mushrooms

1 large jalapeño, chopped

½ tsp salt

SERVES 4

This simple rice dish is a staple in parts of Africa—but usually made with white rice. Enjoy the satisfying texture and healthful benefits of brown rice with a little African flair. If you want to make a meal of it, add some chopped peanuts.

African Jollof Rice

1 In a heavy-bottomed, 2-qt/2-L saucepan, heat the oil over medium-high heat. Add the onions and sauté for a few minutes. Add the tomatoes, carrot, ginger, and bay leaf, and stir until bubbling. Add the milk and bring to a boil, then add the rice, mushrooms, jalapeño, and salt. Bring back to a boil, then reduce the heat to low and cover tightly.

2 Simmer the rice for 40 minutes, then check to see if all the liquid is absorbed. Take the pan off the heat and let it stand for 5 minutes, covered, to finish steaming. Serve hot.

5 cups/1.2 L Basic Vegetable Stock (page 49)

1 cup/120 g diced onions

4 garlic cloves, minced

4 tbsp/60 ml extra-virgin olive oil

1½ cups/250 g pearl barley

½ cup/120 ml white wine

¾ tsp salt

4 cups/120 g arugula/rocket

2 cups/60 g fresh spinach

½ cup/150 g canned/tinned white beans, drained and rinsed

¼ cup/60 ml plain rice milk

½ tsp freshly cracked black pepper

SERVES 6

Barley makes a wonderful risotto—creamy and comforting, with whole-grain nuttiness. A swirl of bright green arugula and spinach makes for a beautiful presentation with tons of flavor.

Barley and Creamed Greens Risotto

1 Bring a large pot of water to a boil to cook the greens. Heat the stock in a medium pot and keep at a simmer.

2 In a large frying pan over medium heat, sauté the onions and garlic in 2 tbsp of the oil. When the onions are clear and soft, add the barley and stir to coat with oil. Add the wine and 3 cups/720 ml of the simmering stock. Cover, turn the heat to low, and cook for 30 minutes.

3 Uncover and start stirring in the remaining 2 cups/480 ml stock. Keep simmering vigorously. As the barley absorbs the liquid, add more and keep stirring. When the risotto is creamy and thick, add ½ tsp of the salt and keep warm.

4 Blanch the arugula/rocket and spinach by dropping them into the boiling water for about 3 minutes, then drain and squeeze out the water. Finely chop the greens and put them in a food processor with the beans, then add the milk, pepper, the remaining ¼ tsp salt, and the remaining 2 tbsp oil gradually to make a smooth puree. Transfer the risotto to a serving bowl or individual bowls, and swirl in the greens mixture. Serve hot.

3 cups/720 ml Basic
Vegetable Stock (page 49)

2 tsp extra-virgin olive oil

1 cup/120 g chopped
onions

1 cup/215 g arborio rice

1 cup/170 g diced beets/
beetroot

½ cup/120 ml fruity red
wine, such as a New
World Pinot Noir

½ tsp salt

¼ cup/30 g toasted
walnuts, broken, for
topping

SERVES 4

If you are planning a meal with lots of green in it,
put this crimson risotto alongside it and watch the
colors pop. Beets and red wine paint the rice and
infuse it with earthy flavors.

Red Beet Risotto
with Walnuts

1 In a 1-qt/960-ml saucepan, bring the stock to a simmer,
then turn the heat to low.

2 In a large frying pan, heat the oil over medium-high heat.
When it's hot, add the onions, and when they sizzle, reduce
the heat to medium. Stir, cooking until the onions are soft
and clear. Add the rice and beets/beetroot, stir until they are
hot, then add the wine. Raise the heat to medium-high and
add a couple of ladles of warm stock.

3 Stir the mixture constantly until all the liquid is absorbed.
Add more stock when the pan gets almost dry. The rice
should be tender in about 19 minutes. If you run out of stock,
just add water a little at a time until the rice is tender and
the sauce is creamy. Stir in the salt and adjust the seasoning.
Serve in wide bowls, topped with the walnuts.

1 qt/960 ml Basic
Vegetable Stock (page 49)

1 lb/450 g fresh
asparagus

1 tbsp extra-virgin olive oil

1 small onion, finely
diced

½ cup/85 g quinoa

½ cup/100 g arborio rice

½ cup/120 ml white wine

½ tsp salt

Freshly cracked black
pepper

SERVES 4

When the first asparagus of spring comes to a
market near you, make this risotto. The stems cook
to butter softness with the rice, and the tender tips
make an alluring garnish.

Asparagus-Quinoa Risotto

1 Pour the stock into a medium saucepan and bring it to a
boil. Cut off 3 in/7.5 cm of the tips of the asparagus. Drop
them into the simmering stock to blanch for 3 to 4 minutes.
Use tongs to remove the asparagus to a plate and cover to
keep warm. Keep the stock barely simmering.

2 Thinly slice the remaining asparagus stems, discarding
the tough bases. In a large, heavy-bottomed frying pan over
medium heat, warm the oil and sauté the onion and sliced
asparagus stems until soft. Add the quinoa and rice and
sauté, stirring to coat the grains with oil. Add the wine and
cook until dry. Add the salt and season with pepper.

3 Add ladlefuls of stock to the pan and cook until the liquid
is absorbed before adding more. Start testing the rice for
doneness about 20 minutes from when you added the wine.
When the quinoa has thrown off its haloes of germ and the
rice is just tender, remove the pan from the heat. Serve the
risotto topped with the blanched asparagus tips.

1 tbsp extra-virgin olive oil

½ cup/60 g diced onion

1 large carrot, chopped

1 tbsp fresh rosemary, chopped

½ cup/85 g quinoa

½ cup/100 g basmati rice

1½ cups/180 ml Basic Vegetable Stock (page 49) or water

2 tsp dark miso

½ tsp freshly cracked black pepper

½ cup/55 g toasted hazelnuts, chopped

SERVES 4

Quinoa is one of the best friends of the vegan community, providing ample protein, calcium, and minerals. In this dish, it brings its nutty crunch into play against the tenderness of white basmati.

Quinoa-Basmati Pilaf
with Rosemary

1 In a 4-qt/3.8-L pot over high heat, warm the oil and add the onion and carrot. As the veggies start to sizzle, reduce the heat to medium and sauté, stirring. Cook until the onion is clear and soft. Add the rosemary and stir for 1 minute. Add the quinoa and rice, stir to coat, and then stir in the stock, miso, and pepper. Bring to a boil, then reduce the heat to low and cover tightly. Simmer for 20 minutes.

2 When all the liquids are absorbed, take the pan off the heat and let it stand, covered, for about 5 minutes to finish steaming the rice. Serve the pilaf topped with the nuts.

Chutney

½ cup/85 g raisins

½ cup/120 ml tamarind pulp

½ cup/120 ml tomato sauce/puree

1 tbsp minced peeled fresh ginger

1 tbsp sugar

1 tbsp freshly squeezed lemon juice

½ tsp red pepper flakes

¼ tsp salt

Croquettes

1½ cups/250 g cubed butternut squash (about 9 oz)

1 cup/200 g millet

1 cup/240 ml Basic Vegetable Stock (page 49)

¼ cup/30 g finely chopped onion

1 tsp salt

¼ cup/7 g cilantro/fresh coriander, chopped

½ tsp ground cumin

¾ cup/95 g chickpea flour

4 tsp cornstarch/cornflour

¼ tsp baking powder

Canola oil, for frying

SERVES 4

If you want a special way to serve grains, these croquettes will wow your diners. Soft, chewy millet and squash as finger food, crisply fried and dipped in a tangy chutney, will wake up your taste buds.

Millet and Squash Croquettes
with Tamarind Chutney

1 TO MAKE THE CHUTNEY: Combine the raisins, tamarind, tomato sauce/puree, ginger, sugar, lemon juice, pepper flakes, and salt in a small saucepan. Put over high heat and bring to a boil, then reduce to a slow simmer for about 5 minutes. The mixture should get quite thick. Puree the chutney in a blender or food processor, then thin it with water to a dipping consistency.

2 TO MAKE THE CROQUETTES: In a 1-qt/960-ml saucepan with a tight-fitting lid, combine the squash, millet, stock, 1 cup/240 ml water, the onion, and salt. Put the pan over high heat and bring to a vigorous boil, making sure the mixture is boiling in the center. Cover tightly and reduce the heat to low. Check the progress at 25 minutes to see if the liquids are all absorbed. When they are, take the pan off the heat and let it stand, covered, for at least 10 minutes. Transfer the mixture to a large bowl and mash it coarsely with a potato masher or fork, just until it holds together to form clumps that hold their shape. Stir in the cilantro/fresh coriander and cumin.

3 In a medium bowl, whisk together the flour, cornstarch/cornflour, and baking powder. Gradually whisk in ¾ cup/180 ml water—it should resemble heavy cream in thickness. Preheat the oven to 200°F/95°C/gas ¼ to hold the finished croquettes, although the sooner you eat them, the better. Line a baking sheet/tray with paper towels/absorbent paper for draining. To finish, scoop 2 tbsp of the millet mixture and form a small patty, then place it on a plate or baking sheet/tray. Repeat to make about 35 croquettes.

4 In a large frying pan over high heat, pour the oil to ¼ in/6 mm deep. When the oil looks shimmery (about 350°F/176°C), dip one croquette in the flour mixture and slide it into the oil. If it sizzles and bubbles, the oil is ready. Dip more croquettes and add them to the pan, leaving 1 in/2.5 cm of space between them. Turn the croquettes with tongs after a couple of minutes, when they are golden brown. Adjust the heat as needed. Remove the croquettes to the prepared baking sheet/tray to drain and keep them in the oven as you finish frying the remaining croquettes. Serve them with the room-temperature chutney.

1 tsp canola oil

3 medium shallots, chopped

1¾ cups/420 ml Basic Vegetable Stock (page 49)

1 cup/215 g Chinese black rice

1 tbsp dark miso

½ cup/55 g roasted, unsalted cashews, coarsely chopped, for topping

SERVES 3

Black rice is a gorgeous purplish-black color, making it a dramatic counterpoint to a colorful stir-fry or even simple steamed veggies. Seek it out, and you will be rewarded with a sweet, deep flavor and loads of antioxidants.

Black Rice
with Cashews

In a medium saucepan, heat the oil over medium-high heat. Add the shallots and cook, stirring, until they are golden, about 5 minutes. Add the stock, rice, and miso and bring to a boil. Cover the pan, reduce the heat to low, and cook for 30 minutes, or according to the rice package directions. When it is done, it will have absorbed all the liquids and be very tender. Serve the rice topped with the cashews.

1 cup/215 g basmati rice, or 3 cups/450 g leftover rice or grains

¼ cup/60 ml Basic Vegetable Stock (page 49)

2 tsp cornstarch/cornflour

1 tbsp soy sauce

1 tbsp canola oil

½ large red bell pepper/capsicum, diced

1 small red Fresno chile, chopped

1 garlic clove, minced

2 tsp curry powder

4 medium scallions/spring onions, cut into ½-in/12-mm slices

½ cup/55 g roasted peanuts, chopped, for topping

2 tbsp minced cilantro/fresh coriander, for topping

SERVES 4

Finally, you can have fried rice without the eggs! This is a great way to use up leftover rice, so go ahead and use what you have. Brown rice, millet, or other grains can all be quite delicious prepared like this.

Indonesian Fried Rice

1 Bring 1½ cups/350 ml water to a boil in a medium pot, then add the rice. Return it to a boil, then cover and lower the heat to the lowest setting. Cook for 15 minutes, then check to make sure all the water is absorbed. Let stand, covered, for the rice to finish steaming, for 5 minutes. If using cold rice, sprinkle it with 1 tbsp water before starting. In a small cup, mix together the stock, cornstarch/cornflour, and soy sauce.

2 Heat a large wok or frying pan over high heat, then pour in the oil and swirl to cover the pan. Add the bell pepper/capsicum, chile, and garlic and stir for 2 minutes, until the pepper starts to soften slightly. Add the curry powder and toss until fragrant, just a few seconds, and then add the stock mixture and stir until thickened. Quickly stir in the rice. Stir to coat the rice with the seasoning and heat it through. Add the scallions/spring onions and toss to just wilt them. Serve the rice topped with the peanuts and cilantro/fresh coriander.

1 tsp canola oil

1 tsp brown mustard seeds

1 tsp cumin seeds

2 cups/280 g cherry tomatoes, halved

1 cup/120 g chopped onions

2 tbsp minced fresh turmeric or ½ tsp ground turmeric

1 tbsp minced peeled fresh ginger

½ tsp chili powder

½ tsp garam masala

½ tsp salt

1 cup/215 g long-grain brown rice

Chopped peanuts or toasted coconut, for garnish (optional)

SERVES 4

A hearty brown rice dish for Indian-food lovers, this can sidle up to a curry and chutney, or stand alone as a light lunch. Cherry tomatoes are dependably flavorful all year-round, but you can use whatever tomatoes are ripe and bursting with tasty tomato essence.

Indian Masala Brown Rice
with Tomatoes

1 In a 4-qt/3.8-L saucepan with a lid, heat the oil over high heat. Add the mustard and cumin seeds and cook until the mustard seeds start to pop. Add the tomatoes, onions, turmeric, and ginger and sauté, lowering the heat to medium. Cook until the onions are soft and the tomatoes are bursting. Add the chili powder, garam masala, and salt and stir, then add the rice and 2 cups/480 ml water and bring to a boil. Cover and reduce the heat to low.

2 Cook for 45 to 50 minutes, until all the water is absorbed and the rice is tender. Let the pan stand, covered and off the heat, for 5 or 10 minutes to finish steaming. Serve the rice garnished with the peanuts, if desired.

4 tbsp/60 ml olive oil

1½ cups/180 g chopped onions

2 garlic cloves, minced

1 cup/215 g short-grain brown rice

3 tbsp tomato paste/puree

1 tsp salt

1 tsp freshly cracked black pepper

½ tsp paprika

2 cups/480 ml Basic Vegetable Stock (page 49)

½ lemon

6 whole artichokes

1 medium red bell pepper/capsicum, chopped

1 cup/300 g cooked chickpeas, drained

½ cup/80 g frozen peas

SERVES 4

Inspired by the flavors in a traditional paella, this hearty brown rice dish is much easier to make than paella, and no seafood is involved. Fresh artichokes are worth the time to trim, as their subtle flavors lift the dish up to company-worthy fare.

Spanish Brown Rice
with Artichokes and Chickpeas

1 In a 4-qt/3.8-L pot over medium heat, heat 2 tbsp of the oil and sauté the onions. When they are soft and golden, add the garlic and stir for 1 minute. Add the rice, tomato paste/puree, salt, pepper, and paprika and stir to mix well. Add the stock and bring to a boil, then reduce the heat to the lowest setting. Cover tightly and cook for 45 minutes to 1 hour. When all the water is absorbed, if the rice is still crunchy, add ¼ cup/60 ml more water and keep cooking until it is tender. Take off the heat and let the rice steam, covered, for 5 minutes.

2 Fill a large bowl halfway with cool water and squeeze in 1 tbsp or so of lemon juice. Pull off the leaves of each artichoke, and discard. Pare out the hairy center choke, trim off the tough skin around the artichoke bottom, and peel the stem, leaving only edible flesh. Cut it into slices ½ in/12 mm thick. Drop them in the lemon water to prevent browning and reserve.

3 In a large frying pan, heat the remaining 2 tbsp oil. Drain and pat dry the artichoke slices, then add them to the oil. Add the bell pepper/capsicum and stir, cooking over medium heat until the artichokes are completely tender, about 5 minutes. Add the chickpeas and peas and cook just until they are heated through. When the rice is tender, stir in the vegetable sauté and serve.

SIDE DISHES

273

½ cup/120 ml Vegan "Mayonnaise" (page 113) or Vegenaise

¼ cup/7 g fresh chervil

1 tbsp freshly squeezed lemon juice

1 pinch cayenne

1 lb/450 g fresh asparagus

SERVES 4

Tender asparagus with a decadent, creamy dip is a French classic. You don't have to pass it by, with this vegan version. Serve it as a first course, and linger over the herb-kissed "mayonnaise." Go ahead and eat with your hands!

Asparagus
with Chervil "Mayonnaise"

1 In a small bowl, stir together the "mayonnaise," chervil, lemon juice, and cayenne.

2 Trim off the tough ends of the asparagus. Set up a steamer and bring the water to a simmer. Steam the asparagus until just crisp-tender, about 2 minutes, depending on the thickness of the spears. Serve it right away with the "mayonnaise" drizzled over the spears.

½ cup/55 g chopped walnuts

1 tsp soy sauce

1 tsp sugar

1 tsp sake

1 lb/450 g fresh asparagus

SERVES 4

The Japanese are masters of simple nut-based sauces like this. Take care in toasting the nuts slowly so they don't scorch, and you will reap the reward of a deep, toasty flavor.

Japanese Asparagus
with Walnut Dressing

1 Set up a steamer and bring the water to a simmer. In a frying pan over medium heat, toast the nuts, stirring, until they are golden, about 8 minutes.

2 In a food processor, grind 6 tbsp/40 g of the walnuts, leaving 2 tbsp for garnish. Add the soy sauce, sugar, and sake to the food processor and blend, then add just enough water to make a smooth dressing.

3 Trim off the tough ends of the asparagus and steam it just until crisp-tender, about 2 minutes, then rinse it with cold water and drain. Pat it dry with a towel, then toss the spears with the walnut dressing. Arrange the asparagus on plates and top with the reserved walnuts.

1 tbsp Earth Balance margarine

2 tbsp unbleached all-purpose/plain flour

1 cup/240 ml plain rice milk

¼ cup/10 g nutritional yeast

1½ tsp Dijon mustard

1 garlic clove, minced

½ tsp salt

1 pinch paprika

1 lb/455 g fresh broccoli, cut into longer spears including stems

SERVES 6

If you miss the dairy sauces that once adorned your broccoli, try this. Cheesy-tasting nutritional yeast makes a creamy, familiar yellow topper, just like Mom used to make. You can use the mock cheese sauce on other things, as well, like noodles, toast, or rice.

Broccoli
with "Cheese" Sauce

1 In a 1-qt/960-ml saucepan, melt the margarine over low heat. Whisk in the flour, and continue whisking for a couple of minutes, until the roux is thoroughly bubbly. In a cup, whisk together the milk, yeast, mustard, garlic, salt, and paprika.

2 Take the flour mixture off the heat and gradually whisk in the milk mixture, until a smooth paste is produced every time you add more liquid. Over medium heat, bring the sauce to a simmer, whisking constantly. When the liquids come to a boil, whisk until they thicken. Take the pan off the heat. The sauce will be thick, to keep it from getting too watery on the broccoli—if you want it a little thinner, whisk in 1 tbsp of milk.

3 Set up a steamer and bring the water to a simmer. Steam the broccoli just until it is crisp-tender, 2 to 3 minutes. Serve it topped with the sauce.

12 oz/340 g green beans
½ cup/120 ml dry white wine
½ cup/120 ml Basic Vegetable Stock (page 49)
1 small shallot, minced
1 pinch saffron threads
2 oz/55 g silken tofu, mashed
1 tbsp cold-press corn oil
1 tbsp minced fresh parsley
¼ tsp salt
Freshly cracked black pepper

SERVES 4

Beurre blanc means, literally, "white butter." Of course, there is no butter in this sauce, but vegans can still use the method to make a tangy, intensely flavorful sauce that awakens the palate to the joy of green beans, à la Française.

Steamed Green Beans
with Saffron-Parsley "Beurre Blanc"

1 Clean and trim the beans and cut them in half if desired. Place a kitchen towel on a plate for drying the beans later. Set up a steamer and bring the water to a simmer over high heat. Put the beans in the steamer and cover. Set a timer for 3 minutes for standard green beans, or 2 minutes for smaller haricots verts. After about 1 minute, lower the heat to medium-high.

2 When the timer goes off, check the beans for doneness by piercing one with a paring knife. Take the beans off the steam and transfer them to the towel-lined plate, to remove excess moisture. Cover to keep warm.

3 In a 2-qt/2-L saucepan, bring the wine, stock, shallot, and saffron to a boil. Boil the liquids down to ¼ cup/60 ml, 8 to 10 minutes. The mixture will be very thick.

4 In a blender, combine the tofu and oil, and pour in the hot liquids. Puree thoroughly, scraping down the sides and repeating as necessary. Add the parsley and salt and pulse to mix. Transfer the beans to a serving bowl. Pour the hot sauce over the beans and toss to coat, then top them with cracked pepper. Serve immediately.

1 tbsp canola oil

1 lb/455 g long beans or French green beans, sliced into 1-in/2-cm diagonals

3 scallions/spring onions, diagonally sliced

2 tbsp minced garlic

1 tbsp minced peeled fresh ginger

1 tbsp tamari or soy sauce

1 tbsp white sesame seeds

1 tsp red pepper flakes

1 tsp agave syrup or sugar

SERVES 4

One day I looked around and noticed that restaurants all around me were serving Szechuan green beans. The appeal of these tasty, dry-cooked green beans is no fad. Savory, sweet, and spicy, the high-heat cooking concentrates their green bean essence for a timeless classic.

Szechuan Green Beans

1 Heat a wok or deep, heavy frying pan over high heat until very hot. When it is almost smoking, add the oil, swirl quickly, then add the beans. Stir-fry them over high heat until the beans start to shrivel and look wrinkly, about 5 minutes.

2 Add the scallions/spring onions, garlic, ginger, tamari, sesame seeds, pepper flakes, and agave syrup and stir. Cook just until the sauce coats the beans. Transfer them to a serving bowl and serve immediately.

1 tbsp canola oil

1 tsp curry powder

½ tsp ground cumin

½ tsp salt

1 lb/455 g new (baby) potatoes, halved

½ cup/15 g cilantro/fresh coriander, chopped

Chutney

½ cup/85 g pitted dates

½ cup/120 ml pineapple juice

1 tbsp minced peeled fresh ginger

1 tsp garam masala

½ tsp salt

½ cup/55 g toasted pistachios

SERVES 4

Roasted potatoes have much of the appeal of French fries, but with none of the greasy drawbacks. A crisp, spiced crust on a tender baby potato makes these irresistible, and the simple chutney only adds to the appeal.

Curry-Roasted New Potatoes
with Date-Nut Chutney

1 Preheat the oven to 400°F/200°C/gas 6. In a small cup, mix together the oil, curry, cumin, and salt. In a large roasting pan/tray, toss the potatoes with the oil mixture. Roast them for 20 minutes, then stir the potatoes with a metal spatula. Roast for 10 minutes more if you are using very small potatoes, or 20 minutes for larger potatoes. When the edges are crisp and the centers are tender, they are ready. Transfer the potatoes to a serving bowl, and sprinkle with the cilantro/fresh coriander.

2 TO MAKE THE CHUTNEY: Combine the dates, pineapple juice, ginger, garam masala, and salt in a small saucepan. Place over high heat, bring to a boil, then reduce the heat to low and cover. Cook for about 5 minutes, just to soften the dates. In a food processor or blender, chop the pistachios, then add the date mixture and pulse to make a coarse puree. Thin the chutney with water if necessary to make a dippable consistency.

3 Serve the chutney with the hot potatoes.

1 large red Fresno chile, seeded

¼ cup/30 g minced shallot

1 tbsp minced peeled fresh ginger

2 garlic cloves, peeled

1 lemon, zested

1 lime, zested

1 tsp ground turmeric

⅛ tsp ground cloves

1 cup/240 ml coconut milk

1 lb/455 g fingerling or small new (baby) potatoes, halved

4 oz/115 g green beans, trimmed

1 medium carrot, julienned

1 tbsp tamari or soy sauce

½ tsp salt

SERVES 4

Add some Malaysian flavors to your life with this addictively spicy potato experience. *Rendang* is a special kind of curry, in which a main ingredient is slowly cooked in spicy coconut milk until the sauce is deeply reduced. Tender new potatoes absorb the spice-infused coconut sauce and cook down to lush, citrusy perfection.

New Potato Rendang
with Green Beans

1 In a coffee grinder or mini chopper, combine the chile, shallot, ginger, garlic, lemon and lime zests, turmeric, and cloves. Process to puree them to a smooth paste. If needed, add a little of the milk to help it puree.

2 Transfer the paste to a large frying pan, and stir in the milk. Add the potatoes and bring them to a simmer, stirring. Cover and check often, stirring and adding water as needed to keep the potatoes from sticking. When the potatoes are almost tender, about 10 minutes depending on size, add the green beans, carrot, tamari, and salt and keep stirring. Cook until the vegetables are tender and the sauce is completely thick and coats the vegetables, about 5 minutes. Squeeze half of the zested lime over the vegetables, taste, and add more as desired. Serve hot.

1½ lb/680 g Yukon gold potatoes

8 oz/225 g parsnips, sliced

3 cups/720 ml Basic Vegetable Stock (page 49) or water

10 oz/280 g extra-firm silken tofu, drained

1 tbsp prepared horseradish

½ tsp salt

2 tbsp nutritional yeast (optional)

SERVES 4

Everybody loves mashed potatoes, so adding sweet parsnips and warming horseradish just takes them over the top. Nobody will even know there is tofu in the mix, and you can enjoy a comfort food with pure plant energy.

Mashed Potatoes and Parsnips

with Horseradish

1 Peel the potatoes about a quarter of the way, leaving some skin on for texture. Cut them into ¾-in/2-cm slices. Put the potatoes in a 2-qt/2-L saucepan. Put the parsnips on top and add the stock; it should be just enough to come almost to the top of the vegetables. Bring to a boil over high heat and cover, reducing the heat to medium to keep it at a simmer. Check the vegetables with a paring knife; when they are tender, put the whole block of tofu on top of the pile, cover, and cook for 10 minutes.

2 Remove the pan from the heat. Carefully, using a metal spatula or slotted spoon, transfer the tofu and parsnips to a food processor. Puree them thoroughly. Holding the lid of the pan slightly ajar, pour the cooking liquids into a heat-safe cup, leaving the potatoes in the pan. Mash the potatoes with a masher, ricer, or large fork. Scrape the contents of the processor into the pan and mix it with the potatoes. Add the reserved cooking liquids to thin the mixture to your taste. Stir in the horseradish and salt. Add the yeast (if using). Taste and adjust the flavor to suit you; you may want more horseradish. Serve hot.

12 oz/340 g parsnips

12 oz/340 g carrots, peeled

6 garlic cloves, peeled

2 tbsp fresh thyme

3 large bay leaves, halved

1 tbsp extra-virgin olive oil

½ tsp salt

½ tsp freshly cracked black pepper

¼ cup/7 g fresh parsley, minced

SERVES 4

Deep roots pull up the energy of the earth, or at least that is what macrobiotic practitioners believe. You can revel in the earthy sweetness of the humble parsnip and sunny carrot and let the energy ground you.

Roasted Parsnips and Carrots
with Thyme

1 Preheat the oven to 400°F/200°C/gas 6. Cut the parsnips and carrots in half lengthwise if they are thick, then cut them into ½-in/12-mm slices. Put them in a large, heavy roasting pan/tray with the garlic, thyme, bay leaves, oil, salt, and pepper. Toss to coat all the vegetables well.

2 Cover the pan with foil and bake for 20 minutes. Take the pan out, uncover it, and turn the vegetables with a metal spatula. Cover again and roast for 20 minutes more. Uncover, stir, and continue to roast until the vegetables are browned, about 10 minutes. Toss them with the parsley in the pan, then transfer everything to a serving bowl. Serve warm.

12 oz/340 g garnet yams

12 oz/340 g beets/
beetroot

1 large Golden Delicious
apple

1 tbsp toasted hazelnut
or walnut oil

¼ medium yellow onion,
thinly sliced

1 tbsp fresh thyme,
chopped

½ tsp sea salt

2 tbsp thawed apple
juice concentrate

1 tbsp/7 g chopped
walnuts

SERVES 4

Why not make your vegetables into something beautiful? Layering the colorful veggies and apple in a baking dish makes a pretty presentation, and you will love the apple flavor baked into every bite. Most of the yams and sweet potatoes that we buy today are actually sweet potatoes, as the true yams are drier and not very sweet. Garnet yams are a deep-orange sweet potato variety that are packed with carotenoids.

Gratin of Apples, Sweet Potatoes, and Beets
with Walnuts

1 Slice the yams, beets/beetroot, and apple ⅓ in/8 mm thick. In a shallow baking dish about 8 by 12 in/20 by 30.5 cm, smear a little bit of the oil. Lay a row of sliced yams across one end of the pan, leaning them up against the rim so they slant. Begin arranging rows against this one, first of beets/beetroot, then apples, then yams again, until they are used up. Sprinkle the onion, thyme, and salt over the top, pour the juice concentrate into the dish, and drizzle the remaining oil over it all. Cover the pan with foil. (At this point, the dish may be refrigerated to bake the following day.)

2 Preheat the oven to 400°F/200°C/gas 6. Bake, covered, for 30 minutes. Uncover and test the yams with a knife; if they are not soft, re-cover and bake for 10 minutes more to soften them. Uncover, top the dish with the walnuts, and bake until the walnuts are toasted, about 15 minutes. Serve hot, cutting portions with a spatula or knife.

SIDE DISHES

283

1½ lb/675 g garnet yams

2 tbsp extra-virgin olive oil

2 tsp chopped chipotle chiles in adobo sauce

1 tsp lime zest

2 tsp freshly squeezed lime juice

Salt

Freshly cracked black pepper

Tofu "sour cream," for garnish (optional)

SERVES 3

Sweet potatoes and yams really sing when they're set off with tangy lime and smoky chipotle. Roasting them in fat spears makes them much more attractive to eat than just mashing them up—and you will love the taste!

Smoky Roasted Sweet Potato Spears

1 Preheat the oven to 425°F/220°C/gas 7. Slice the yams lengthwise to make spears 1 in/2.5 cm wide. If the slices are very long, cut them in half. Put them in a heavy roasting pan/tray or baking dish and toss with the oil, chipotles, and lime zest.

2 Cover the pan with foil and roast for 30 minutes, taking it out to shake midway. If some of the yams are sticking, gently loosen them with a spatula. At 30 minutes, uncover and roast until the yams are lightly browned, about 10 minutes more.

3 Season the yams with the lime juice, salt, and pepper. Serve with tofu "sour cream," if desired.

1 lb/455 g beets/
beetroot, peeled and
cubed

1 large carrot, thickly
sliced

1 medium turnip, peeled
and cubed

2 tbsp chopped fresh
rosemary

1 tbsp extra-virgin olive oil

¼ cup/7 g fresh parsley

2 garlic cloves

½ cup/120 ml Vegan
"Mayonnaise" (page 113)
or Vegenaise

SERVES 4

Chunks of meltingly soft root vegetables, dipped in a tangy garlic dip, will take the edge off a bad day, or improve an already good one. Wintery dishes should all have some garlic, to ward off colds!

Roasted Root Veg
with Aioli

1 Preheat the oven to 400°F/200°C/gas 6. In a large roasting pan/tray, combine the beets/beetroot, carrot, and turnip. Sprinkle them with the rosemary and oil and toss to mix. Cover the pan tightly with foil, then roast for 20 minutes. Uncover and roast until the vegetables are tender when pierced with a paring knife, about 10 minutes more.

2 While the veggies roast, put the parsley and garlic in a food processor and process to mince. Add the "mayonnaise" and process to mix well. Transfer the aioli to a small serving bowl.

3 Serve the roasted veggies drizzled with the sauce or serve the sauce separately for dipping.

1 yucca
(about 14 oz/400 g)

1 roasted red bell
pepper/capsicum

2 tbsp freshly squeezed
lime juice

2 tsp chopped chipotle
chiles in adobo sauce

2 tbsp extra-virgin olive oil

SERVES 4

Ever wonder what those giant, brown-skinned carroty-looking things are at the market? They are yucca—the starchy tuber that is eaten in most tropical cultures, the way we eat potatoes, as a cheap and tasty root veg. Look for medium-size, firm roots with no soft spots. The smooth, rich texture of the yucca gives potatoes a run for the money.

Yucca
with Chipotle–Red Pepper Drizzle

1 Peel the yucca and cut it into quarters lengthwise. Slice out the tough core portion and then slice the pieces into 1-in/2.5-cm chunks. Put the pieces in a large pot with cold water to cover, then bring to a boil over high heat. Adjust the heat to maintain a simmer and cook for about 10 minutes, until the pieces are tender when pierced with a paring knife. Drain and cover to keep warm.

2 In a blender, puree the bell pepper/capsicum, lime juice, and chipotles. With the machine running, drizzle in the oil. Transfer the yucca to a large bowl and drizzle it with the red pepper sauce before serving.

1½ lb/680 g heirloom
cherry tomatoes

8 small shallots, peeled

6 garlic cloves, peeled

2 tbsp extra-virgin olive oil

Salt

½ cup/120 ml balsamic
vinegar

2 tbsp agave syrup

1 stem fresh rosemary

½ cup/55 g dried
bread crumbs, toasted
(optional)

SERVES 4

When my tomato plants are laden with fabulous fruit, I make this. You can roast the tomatoes and freeze them for a winter's day, or enjoy them with a piquant balsamic syrup.

Slow-Roasted Heirloom Tomatoes
with Sweet Balsamic Syrup

1 Preheat the oven to 225°F/110°C/gas ¼. Line two baking sheets/trays with parchment/baking paper and place the tomatoes, cut-side up, on the pan. Sprinkle the shallots and garlic around the tomatoes. Drizzle them with the oil and sprinkle with a pinch of salt. Roast until the tomatoes are shrunken and sweet, about 2 hours, switching the pan positions after an hour. Transfer them and any juices on the pan to a medium bowl.

2 In a small saucepan, combine the vinegar, agave syrup, and rosemary and bring to a boil. Cook for about 5 minutes over medium heat, until the liquids reduce to ¼ cup/60 ml and form a thick syrup. Remove the rosemary with a fork and season the syrup with a pinch of salt.

3 Toss the tomatoes with the bread crumbs to soak up the juices, if desired. Drizzle the syrup over the tomatoes and serve.

4 ears corn, kernels cut off (about 2 cups/180g)

1 large jalapeño, minced

2 cups/370 g chopped fresh tomatoes

2 tbsp freshly squeezed lime juice

½ tsp salt

SERVES 4

When sweet corn is in season, you can barbecue it or boil it and eat it right off the cob, but for a special Mexican-inspired treat, try this. The sweet, crunchy kernels are perfectly delicious with the spike of jalapeño and hint of lime.

Toasted Sweet Corn
with Chile and Lime

Heat a large cast-iron frying pan over high heat until hot. Add the corn and jalapeño and stir constantly until they are browned, about 3 minutes. Add the tomatoes, lime juice, and salt and cook until almost dry. Serve hot.

- 2 tbsp extra-virgin olive oil
- 1 medium red onion, sliced
- ½ cup/85 g golden raisins/sultanas
- 4 garlic cloves, coarsely chopped
- 12 oz/340 g fresh spinach
- ½ tsp salt

SERVES 4

Vegans need to eat their greens to make sure they get enough iron and calcium, and this quick sauté makes it both easy and delicious. Swiss chard is also wonderful cooked in this classic Italian style—it may just take a moment longer to soften.

Italian Spinach
with Garlic and Raisins

1 Heat a large frying pan over high heat until hot. Add the oil and tilt to coat the pan. Add the onion, raisins, and garlic, and sauté until the onion is golden, about 3 minutes.

2 Add the spinach, toss until it is just wilted, then add the salt. Toss the mixture well and serve.

1 lb/455 g fresh kale

2 tbsp white sesame
seeds

1 tbsp toasted sesame oil

½ tsp salt

SERVES 4

If you have never tried roasting kale, you are in for a treat. The leaves shrink and become crisp, and it's almost like eating potato chips. Any variety of kale is great in this, but Tuscan lacinato kale is especially sweet and tasty.

Crispy Sesame Kale

Preheat the oven to 350°F/180°C/gas 4. Slice the kale leaves off the stems. Discard the stems. In a large bowl, mix the kale, sesame seeds, oil, and salt. Spread the kale on two large baking sheets/trays and roast until the kale is crisp, 12 to 15 minutes. Serve immediately.

1 lb/455 g globe eggplant/aubergine, peeled

1 small red bell pepper/capsicum, seeded

1 medium onion

1 small yellow squash

1 small zucchini/courgette

½ cup/120 ml extra-virgin olive oil

3 garlic cloves, minced

2 tbsp fresh thyme

2 tbsp red wine vinegar

2 tbsp sugar

½ cup/15 g fresh basil

¼ cup/30 g capers, rinsed

1 tsp salt

¼ tsp freshly cracked black pepper

SERVES 5

Caponata is credited to Jewish settlers in Sicily, who brought together their sweet-and-sour traditions with the vegetables of the region. Whoever thought it up, it's a great way to cook up a bunch of veggies and have them on hand in the fridge, to eat warm or cold. The tender caponata is wonderful spread on a sandwich, or just devoured with a spoon!

Roasted Caponata

1 Preheat the oven to 400°F/200°C/gas 6. Dice the vegetables into ¾-in/2-cm cubes. Toss them in a deep roasting pan/tray with the oil, garlic, and thyme. Roast, covered, for 20 minutes. Stir and continue to roast, uncovered, until the vegetables are tender, about 10 minutes more.

2 Transfer the vegetables to a large bowl and toss them with the vinegar and sugar; let them cool to room temperature. Add the basil, capers, salt, and pepper and let them marinate for at least 1 hour or refrigerate for up to 1 week.

3 Serve at room temperature or reheat on the stove or in the microwave.

Vegetable oil

2 lb/910 g kabocha squash, halved and seeded

2 tbsp minced peeled fresh ginger

½ cup/120 ml white miso

1 tbsp rice vinegar

Crumbled nori, toasted, for garnish

SERVES 4

Kabocha squash is a variety bred in Japan, with green-and-white-striped skin and a squat profile. It is dense and sweet and shines with simple Japanese flavors, but you can also use other winter squashes in this recipe.

Kabocha Squash Puree
with Miso and Ginger

1 Preheat the oven to 400°F/200°C/gas 6. Oil a large baking sheet/tray and put the squash halves, cavity-side down on the pan. Roast for about 20 minutes, until the squash is very tender when pierced with a paring knife. Let it cool.

2 When it is cool enough to handle, scoop the flesh of the squash into a bowl, mashing it as you go. In a food processor or blender, combine the squash and ginger and puree until smooth. Add the miso and vinegar and process to mix well. Serve garnished with nori.

8 oz/225 g fresh cremini/
brown or baby bella
mushrooms, halved

¼ cup/60 ml red or
white wine

1 tbsp extra-virgin olive oil

1 tbsp fresh thyme,
chopped

1 tsp minced shallot

Salt

Freshly cracked black
pepper

SERVES 4

Roasting mushrooms concentrates their flavors and shrinks them down to little nuggets of umami. You can use whatever wine complements the rest of the meal—white or red. These make a great side dish, appetizer, or ingredient to add to pastas, pizzas, sandwiches, or salads.

Wine-Roasted Mushrooms

Preheat the oven to 425°F/220°C/gas 7. In a 9-in/23-cm square baking pan, toss together the mushrooms, wine, oil, thyme, and shallot. Roast for 20 minutes, then stir and roast for about 20 minutes more, until the liquids are all gone and the mushrooms are shrunken. Season with salt and pepper. Serve hot or cover and refrigerate for up to 1 week.

½ cup/120 ml apple cider or juice

¼ cup/60 ml Basic Vegetable Stock (page 49)

1 tbsp cider vinegar

1 tbsp agave syrup

2 tbsp Earth Balance margarine

2 lb/910 g carrots, cut into sticks

¼ tsp salt

⅛ tsp cayenne

¼ cup/7 g fresh parsley, chopped, for garnish

SERVES 8

I make these carrots in the fall, when beautiful fresh cider comes to market. You can also buy bottled ciders all year long, though, or even make this with plain apple juice. Serve with Homemade Mock Turkey Roast with Stuffing (page 422) or Cashew–Brown Rice Loaf with Red Pepper Glaze (page 402).

Cider-Glazed Carrots

1 In a small cup, combine the cider, stock, vinegar, and agave syrup.

2 In a large frying pan with a lid, melt the margarine over medium-high heat, then add the carrots, salt, and cayenne, and toss to coat. Sauté the carrots for 5 minutes, shaking the pan so they don't stick. Carefully pour in the cider mixture and bring it to a boil. Cover, reduce the heat to medium-low, and cook for 5 minutes more. Remove the lid and cook, turning the carrots to coat with sauce, until the glaze is thick. Serve them sprinkled with the parsley.

1 lb/455 g cipollini or pearl onions or tiny shallots

Sea salt

½ cup/100 g sugar

¼ cup/60 ml balsamic vinegar

SERVES 4

In Tuscany, they serve a dish like this made with cipollini onions, as a *contorno*, or side dish. I've found that the appeal of a sweet-and-sour onion is just as great with any small allium, so use pearl onions or shallots if that is what you can get.

Cipollini Onions
in Agrodolce

1 Peel the onions and remove the root ends. Bring a large pot of water to a boil, and add a big pinch of salt. Pour the onions into the boiling water. Boil them for 5 minutes, then drain, rinsing them with cold water. Drain on towels and dry well.

2 Put the sugar, vinegar, and ½ cup/120 ml water in a large saucepan. Over medium heat, simmer until the sugar has dissolved and formed a syrup, about 5 minutes.

3 Stir the onions into the syrup and mix well. Simmer, stirring, for 10 minutes, to glaze the onions. Serve hot.

8 oz/225 g pearl onions

2 tbsp extra-virgin olive oil

8 oz/225 g fresh snap
peas, trimmed

SERVES 4

In the spirit of adding complexity to a simple pea, these slow-caramelized onions elevate snap peas to gourmet fare. The sweet softness of the tiny onions complements the snappy crispness of the peas and gives the dish all the richness you might expect from a creamed side. Excellent alongside the Homemade Mock Turkey Roast with Stuffing (page 422) or Roasted Vegetable Phyllo Purses with Creamy Gravy (page 427).

Snap Peas
with Caramelized Pearl Onions

1 Bring a 2-qt/2-L pot of water to a boil. Dump in the onions, boil for 3 minutes, then drain them. Under cool running water, use a paring knife to cut off the root end of the onions, then peel them. Cut off the tails.

2 In the empty pot, heat the oil over medium heat and add the onions. Stir until the onions are hot and the oil is sizzling. Reduce the heat to the lowest setting, then stir every 10 minutes, until the onions are golden and soft. Cook for at least 30 minutes, but they are best after 50 minutes.

3 Prepare a steamer and bring the water to a simmer. Steam the peas just until crisp-tender, 2 to 3 minutes. Blot them with a kitchen towel, then toss them with the onions. Serve hot.

1 large lemon, halved

1 lb/455 g baby artichokes

2 cups/480 ml white wine, plus more if needed

4 sprigs thyme

1 large shallot, minced

1 tbsp freshly squeezed lemon juice

1 tbsp agave syrup

Salt

SERVES 4

Baby artichokes are actually a small variety of artichoke, and are about 3 in/7.5 cm long. Steaming them in wine flavors both the artichokes and the wine, which then becomes an herbed sauce. You can use well-trimmed large artichokes, but adjust the time and add more wine because they may take longer to cook.

Steamed Baby Artichokes
in Wine and Thyme Sauce

1 Fill a large bowl with cold water, and squeeze half the lemon into the water. Trim the leaves off the artichokes down to just the edible parts, removing any choke if there is one. Cut each artichoke heart in half, then put the pieces in the lemon water to prevent browning until time to cook.

2 In the bottom of a steamer, bring the wine to a simmer. Cut the other lemon half into thin slices. Put the artichokes, the lemon slices, and the thyme in the top of the steamer. Steam over the wine until the artichokes are tender, checking every 5 minutes to make sure there is still wine; add more if needed. When the artichokes are tender, 15 to 20 minutes, take the steamer basket out and cover to keep the artichokes warm.

3 To the wine in the bottom of the steamer, add the shallot and bring to a boil. Add the lemon juice and agave syrup and, stirring constantly, cook to a syrupy consistency, 3 to 5 minutes. Season with salt, then toss the artichokes in the pan to coat them with the sauce. Serve hot.

1 lb/455 g fresh Brussels sprouts, trimmed and halved

2 small shallots, quartered

1 tbsp extra-virgin olive oil

1 tbsp maple syrup

1 tsp Dijon mustard

Salt

Freshly cracked black pepper

SERVES 6

If you think you don't like boiled Brussels sprouts, you must try this version. All the sweetness and tenderness is concentrated and amplified by maple and Dijon. This is a great holiday side dish.

Maple-Roasted Brussels Sprouts and Shallots

Preheat the oven to 400°F/200°C/gas 6. In a heavy roasting pan/tray or baking pan, toss together the Brussels sprouts, shallots, oil, maple syrup, and mustard. Roast, uncovered, for 20 minutes. Stir, and roast until the sprouts are tender, about 20 minutes more. Season with salt and pepper and serve hot.

- 1 tsp extra-virgin olive oil
- ½ cup/60 g chopped onions
- 1 medium Granny Smith apple, chopped
- 1 lb/455 g red cabbage, finely sliced
- 1 cup/100 g fresh or frozen cranberries
- ¼ cup/50 g turbinado sugar
- 1 tbsp red wine
- 1 tbsp red wine vinegar
- ⅛ tsp ground cinnamon
- 1 bay leaf
- 1 pinch ground cloves
- ¼ tsp cornstarch/ cornflour
- ½ tsp salt
- ½ tsp freshly cracked black pepper

SERVES 6

Red cabbage usually gets short shrift, appearing as a few colorful shreds in a mixed-green salad, then disappearing completely. It's a shame, since the antioxidant-rich red leaves are really healthful and inexpensive to use. Here we give it the royal treatment, with a touch of tart cranberry.

Braised Red Cabbage
with Cranberries

1 In a large frying pan with a lid, heat the oil over high heat. Add the onions and apple and sauté. When they begin to soften, reduce the heat to low and cook until the onions are golden. Add ½ cup/120 ml water, the cabbage, cranberries, sugar, wine, vinegar, cinnamon, bay leaf, and cloves. Bring to a boil over high heat, then cover and reduce the heat to medium-low and braise for 10 minutes. Uncover the cabbage and test it for doneness. It should be very tender; if not, cover and braise for 5 to 10 minutes more.

2 In a small cup, mix 1 tsp water with the cornstarch/cornflour and whisk them into the hot liquids in the pan. Stir, simmering, until the liquids are glossy and thickened. Season with the salt and pepper and serve hot.

Main Courses

Some chefs call the traditional plate a "three-point landing." The three points are meat, veg, and starch. Even nonvegans get bored by that construct, and there is no reason to limit your thinking to the triangle. If vegetarians have one thing in common with vegans, I'd say it is a presence of vegetables in just about every course but dessert—vegetables add texture, color, and flavor. Since we are plant-based eaters, there is no need to build a wall between the grains, beans, and veggies. It's all good. This is a whole chapter of dishes that you can serve as main courses, but you have probably noticed that many of the other chapters contain hearty recipes with added protein. Nothing is stopping you from enjoying a salad or a soup as your main course, so eat what feels right.

That said, vegans still want exciting main dishes. Peanut butter sandwiches are nice, but you can break out of your rut and have amazing, beautiful meals with just a bit of effort. There are all sorts of faux meats and cheeses, and you may find them convenient—but don't fall into the habit of eating processed foods all the time. I hope you will try these real-food options and stuff your sammie with things like kale, broccoli, and arugula or a dense mushroom and nut pâté. Make your own burgers, and enjoy plant flavors like sweet red lentils and herbs or chickpeas with garlic and sesame. Vegans often crave pizza, so there are lots of options for fabulous vegan pies—some with creamy nut "cheese" or even white beans. Pasta never gets old, so try some really tasty riffs on noodles and spaghetti and everything in between. And don't fear making gnocchi or ravioli—these recipes make it easy.

There is a special kind of entree I call a "centerpiece" main course. These are the ones we put out for company, special occasions, or just when we want to have as much visual pleasure as taste. Molded, wrapped in pastry, or otherwise set apart, these kinds of dishes take an extra step to be beautiful and special. Try the Harvest Vegetable Stew in Mini Pumpkins (page 429) or the Roasted Vegetable Phyllo Purses with Creamy Gravy (page 427) when you are cooking to impress. Make your own seitan "turkey" with stuffing (page 422). Wow 'em.

½ cup/85 g frozen corn, thawed

¾ cup/180 ml Spanish Salsa Verde (page 119), plus extra for garnish

1½ cups/400 g refried beans or bean dip

¼ cup/30 g chopped scallions/spring onions

1 tsp ground cumin

Eight 6-in/15-cm whole-wheat/wholemeal tortillas

SERVES 4

The typical quesadilla is glued together with cheese and then fried in lots of lard or oil. Not these, which are spread with healthful refried beans and cooked in a dry pan, for all the fun and none of the junk. Try them with the Chipotle–Black Bean Dip (page 144) or Tomato–Ancho Chile Bean Dip (page 146), or use easy canned refried beans.

Quick Refried-Bean Quesadillas
with Corny Salsa Verde

1 In a small bowl, mix together the corn and salsa. Reserve.

2 If you aren't eating immediately, preheat the oven to 200°F/95°C/gas ¼ to hold the finished quesadillas. In a medium bowl, mix together the refried beans, scallions/ spring onions, and cumin.

3 On a cutting board or counter, lay out four tortillas. On each, spread 5 tbsp of the bean mixture. Top each with another tortilla, pressing gently to adhere.

4 Preheat a large cast-iron frying pan over high heat for 30 seconds. Place one quesadilla in the pan and cook for 1 minute. Flip it with a spatula; the tortilla should have toasty dark spots here and there. Cook the second side until it develops some toasted brown spots, then slide it onto the cutting board. Start the next quesadilla, then use a chef's knife or pizza cutter to cut the finished one into six wedges. Transfer the wedges to a heat-safe plate and hold them in the warm oven, if desired. Continue until all the quesadillas are done.

5 Serve the quesadillas immediately with the salsa, or cover them with foil and hold for up to 1 hour in the oven.

MAIN COURSES

305

Salsa

2 cups/200 g fresh cranberries

½ cup/60 g chopped red onion

1 red jalapeño, seeded and minced

1 cup/120 g diced jícama

¼ cup/7 g cilantro/fresh coriander

¼ cup/7 g fresh mint

2 tsp sugar

1 tsp salt

½ tsp ground cumin

Quesadillas

1 tsp extra-virgin olive oil

½ cup/60 g chopped shallots

3 cups/720 g mashed roasted winter squash

¼ cup/30 g toasted hazelnuts, skinned and chopped

½ tsp chili powder

½ tsp salt

Eight 8-in/20-cm whole-wheat/wholemeal tortillas

SERVES 4

Winter squash and holiday cranberries take on a slightly south-of-the-border pose as they collaborate in this quesadilla. The crunchy cranberry is a completely different berry once you take away all that sugar and give it some room to salsa!

Squash Quesadillas
with Cranberry-Jícama Salsa

1 TO MAKE THE SALSA: In a food processor, chop the cranberries coarsely. Add the onion and jalapeño and pulse a couple of times to combine. Scrape out the mixture into a medium bowl, and stir in the jícama, cilantro/fresh coriander, mint, sugar, salt, and cumin. Cover and refrigerate if not using right away.

2 TO MAKE THE QUESADILLAS: In a medium frying pan over medium-high heat, warm the oil. Add the shallots and sauté until they are soft and golden, at least 5 minutes or longer if you have time. Take the pan off the heat and stir in the squash, hazelnuts, chili powder, and salt. Lay out four tortillas and scoop ¾ cup/180 ml of the squash mixture onto each one. Spread it evenly, then top with the remaining tortillas and press lightly to adhere.

3 Heat a large cast-iron frying pan over high heat. When it is hot, place a quesadilla in it and cook until the bottom is toasted, 3 to 4 minutes. Flip it, then cook the other side just until it is toasted. Transfer the quesadilla to a cutting board and use a chef's knife to cut it into six wedges. Continue cooking until all the quesadillas are done, then serve them with the salsa.

Nut "Cheese"

⅓ cup/40 g macadamia nuts

⅓ cup/40 g raw cashews

⅓ cup/40 g slivered/flaked almonds

1 acidophilus capsule (see page 520, check to make sure it is dairy free)

1 tbsp cold-press corn oil

1 tsp freshly squeezed lemon juice

½ tsp salt

Salsa

1 large mango, diced

1 large jalapeño, chopped

3 tbsp chopped red onion

3 tbsp freshly squeezed lime juice

2 tbsp chopped fresh mint or cilantro/fresh coriander

¼ tsp salt

2 scallions/spring onions, chopped

¼ cup/7 g cilantro/fresh coriander

½ tsp chili powder

Eight 6-in/15-cm whole-wheat/wholemeal tortillas

SERVES 4

Lightly fermented nuts provide the creamy filling for these toasty quesadillas, and a delectable mango salsa makes a complete meal of it.

Three-Nut "Cheese" Quesadillas
with Fresh Mango Salsa

1 TO MAKE THE NUT "CHEESE": Put the nuts in a bowl, cover them with cold water, and refrigerate overnight. The next day, drain the nuts, then puree them with ½ cup/120 ml fresh water in a blender or food processor. It may take some scraping down and repeating to get it smooth. Add the contents of the acidophilus capsule and puree to mix. Transfer the mixture to a glass or ceramic bowl, cover loosely with plastic wrap/cling film, and let stand at room temperature for 24 hours. It should form some bubbles and smell cheese-like.

2 The next day, stir in the oil, lemon juice, and salt, then refrigerate.

3 TO MAKE THE SALSA: Put the mango in a medium bowl and add the jalapeño, onion, lime juice, mint, and salt. Toss to mix and refrigerate until needed.

4 When the nut "cheese" is cold, mix in the scallions/spring onions, cilantro/fresh coriander, and chili powder. Divide the mixture among four of the tortillas and top them with the remaining tortillas.

5 To cook, preheat a large cast-iron frying pan on high heat. When it is hot, put one quesadilla in the pan, and cook it for about 2 minutes per side, until it is dappled with brown spots and the "cheese" is heated through. Transfer it to a cutting board and slice the quesadilla into six wedges. Repeat with the other quesadillas. Serve hot with the mango salsa.

4 oz/115 g tempeh

2 tbsp tamari or soy sauce

1 tbsp cider vinegar

1 tbsp agave syrup

2 tsp toasted sesame oil

Vegetable oil spray

2 cups/225 g shredded cabbage

1 medium carrot, shredded

4 oz/115 g canned/tinned sliced water chestnuts, drained and chopped

¼ cup/60 ml Vegan "Mayonnaise" (page 113) or Vegenaise

1 tbsp rice vinegar

2 tsp wasabi paste

1 tsp sugar or agave syrup

¼ tsp salt

Four 8-in/20-cm whole-wheat/wholemeal tortillas

SERVES 4

Shredded cabbage is a common filler for Mexican tacos, but this version stuffs a wrap with Japanese-style flavors, like wasabi and sesame oil. The nutty tempeh and the crunchy slaw combine for a lunch-time feast of fusion.

Tempeh-Slaw Wraps

1 Set up a steamer and bring the water to a simmer. Thinly slice the tempeh and steam to moisten it, about 10 minutes. Let it cool, then place it in a flat-bottomed storage tub. In a small cup, whisk together the tamari, cider vinegar, agave syrup, and sesame oil. Pour them over the tempeh and toss gently to coat. Cover and let the tempeh marinate in the refrigerator for at least 3 hours or overnight.

2 Preheat the oven to 400°F/200°C/gas 6 and spread the tempeh on a lightly oiled baking sheet/tray. Bake the tempeh until crisped, about 20 minutes, stirring it halfway through. Let it cool.

3 While the tempeh bakes, put the cabbage, carrot, and water chestnuts in a medium bowl. In a small cup, whisk together the "mayonnaise," rice vinegar, wasabi, sugar, and salt. Pour them over the cabbage mixture and toss to mix.

4 Place the tortillas on a cutting board, and divide the tempeh and slaw among them. Roll up each one and place it seam-side down. They can be wrapped in wax/greaseproof paper and refrigerated for tomorrow's lunch or eaten immediately.

4 slices Savory Tofu "Steaks" (page 41) or 8 oz/225 g prebaked tofu

2 oz/55 g baby spinach, coarsely chopped

1 cup/160 g cooked brown rice

2 scallions/spring onions, chopped

Four 8-in/20-cm whole-wheat/wholemeal tortillas

¼ cup/60 ml Chinese Sesame Sauce (page 127)

Hot sauce (optional)

SERVES 4

Once you set yourself up with basics like the Savory Tofu "Steaks" and Chinese Sesame Sauce, you can make fast meals like this wrap. Leftover brown rice is good, but whatever leftover grain you have will probably be great.

Sesame Tofu-Spinach Wraps

Slice the tofu into smaller strips and set aside. In a medium bowl, combine the spinach, rice, and scallions/spring onions. On each tortilla, place one fourth of the spinach mixture, then top with tofu strips and drizzle everything with the sesame sauce. (If you like spice, drizzle with extra hot sauce) Tuck in the ends and roll up the tortillas. These can be wrapped in foil and heated in a 375°F/190°C/gas 5 oven for 15 to 20 minutes, or in wax/greaseproof paper in the microwave on high for 4 minutes. Serve immediately.

2 tsp extra-virgin olive oil

½ cup/60 g chopped onion

1 medium Yukon gold potato, cubed

1 large jalapeño, chopped

2 garlic cloves, minced

1 tsp achiote powder

¾ cup/160 g short-grain brown rice

1½ cups/360 ml Basic Vegetable Stock (page 49) or water

¼ tsp salt

1 cup/115 g whole almonds, toasted, coarsely chopped

½ cup/15 g cilantro/fresh coriander

Eight 8-in/20-cm whole-wheat/wholemeal tortillas

4 small Roma tomatoes, chopped

SERVES 4

If you can find achiote powder, do try it. It's made from brilliant orange seeds that grow in South America, and it gives foods a vibrant color and earthy flavor. If you can't get it, put in a pinch of turmeric for a similar color.

Chunky Almond and Yellow Rice Burritos

1 In a 4-qt/3.8-L saucepan, heat the oil over medium heat. Add the onion and potato and sauté for 10 minutes. Add the jalapeño, garlic, and achiote and stir until fragrant. Add the rice and stir for a couple of minutes, then stir in the stock and salt. Cover, bring to a boil, then reduce the heat to low and simmer, covered, for 25 to 30 minutes, until all the liquids are absorbed. Take the pot off the heat and let it stand for 5 minutes to finish steaming the rice. (To use the next day, let the filling cool completely, then cover and refrigerate it.)

2 Stir the almonds and cilantro/fresh coriander into the rice. On each tortilla, put ½ cup/120 ml of the rice filling, then sprinkle half of a chopped tomato on top. Roll up each burrito and place it, seam-side down, on a plate. Eat immediately or wrap in wax/greaseproof paper and refrigerate for up to 4 days.

2 tsp extra-virgin olive oil

8 oz/225 g winter squash, peeled and cubed

1 small red bell pepper/capsicum, chopped

1 tsp ground cumin

½ cup/120 ml Basic Vegetable Stock (page 49)

2 garlic cloves, chopped

6 oz/170 g smoked tempeh Fakin Bacon or Smoky Maple-Tempeh "Bacon" (page 39)

½ tsp salt

Pesto

½ cup/15 g cilantro/fresh coriander

¼ cup/30 g pumpkin seeds, dry toasted

1 garlic clove, peeled

2 tsp freshly squeezed lime juice

2 tsp extra-virgin olive oil

½ tsp salt

Four 10-in/25-cm whole-wheat/wholemeal tortillas, warmed

Jalapeño Tabasco sauce, for garnish

SERVES 4

Pepitas, or hulled pumpkin seeds, are a bonanza of minerals, healthful fats, and protein, and they taste great. With a pesto like this, you may even have people ask what kind of cheese is in it.

Smoked Tempeh and Squash Burritos
with Pepita Pesto

1 Heat the oil in a large frying pan with a lid over medium-high heat. Add the squash, bell pepper/capsicum, and cumin and sauté for 3 minutes. Add the stock and garlic, bring to a boil, then cover and reduce to a simmer. Cook for 10 minutes. Pierce the squash with a paring knife to see if it is tender. If so, boil off any remaining liquid, stirring gently. Stir in the tempeh and salt. Remove from the heat and keep warm if serving right away.

2 TO MAKE THE PESTO: In a food processor or blender, pulse the cilantro/fresh coriander, pumpkin seeds, and garlic to mince. Add the lime juice, oil, and salt and process until smooth.

3 Lay out the tortillas on a cutting board or counter. Divide the pesto among them and smear it down the center of the rounds. Divide the tempeh and squash filling among the tortillas, then fold in the ends and roll them up. Put the burritos on plates, seam-side down, or wrap them in wax/greaseproof paper for eating later. Pass Tabasco at the table to season them.

14 oz/400 g canned/
tinned kidney beans,
drained and rinsed

Vegetable oil spray

2 tsp minced garlic

1 tbsp ground cumin

1 pinch ground cinnamon

¼ cup/60 ml green salsa
(salsa verde), plus extra
for garnish

2 tsp soy sauce

1 large avocado

3 tbsp jalapeño Tabasco
sauce, plus extra for
garnish

½ tsp salt

Four 8-in/20-cm whole-
wheat/wholemeal
tortillas

1 cup/30 g chopped
romaine/Cos lettuce

SERVES 4

Stock the pantry with canned beans and salsa and you are halfway to these satisfying and just mildly spicy wraps. Green salsa is a nice, piquant version of the usual tomato ones, made with tart tomatillos.

Kidney Bean, Avocado, and Green Salsa Wraps

1 Put the beans in a bowl and coarsely mash them. Heat a large frying pan over high heat and coat it with oil spray. Add the beans, garlic, cumin, and cinnamon and stir well, then quickly add the salsa and soy sauce. Keep stirring until the mixture becomes dry again, then remove it from the heat.

2 In a small bowl, mash the avocado and stir in the Tabasco and salt. On each tortilla, spread one fourth of the avocado mixture. Sprinkle on the bean mixture and top with ¼ cup/ 7 g lettuce. Roll the tortillas up jelly-/Swiss-roll style and pin them closed in the center with a toothpick. Serve the wraps with extra salsa verde and hot sauce.

3 cups/470 g broccoli florets

4 cups/270 g chopped fresh kale

6 tbsp/90 ml tahini paste

¼ cup/60 ml freshly squeezed lemon juice

½ tsp salt

4 whole-wheat/wholemeal sandwich rolls

1 cup/140 g cherry tomatoes, halved

SERVES 4

These calcium-rich sammies are a tasty way to eat your greens. Tahini and lemon bathe the hearty greens with a hint of Middle Eastern flair, all while creating nutritional synergy by helping you absorb iron because of the vitamin C.

Fast Broccoli-Kale Sandwiches
with Tahini Sauce

1 Prepare a steamer and bring the water to a simmer. Put the broccoli and kale in the steamer and cover. Cook for 3 minutes, until the vegetables are just tender. Drain and cool, then pat them dry with a towel.

2 In a medium bowl, stir together the tahini, lemon juice, and salt. Add the broccoli and kale and toss to mix. Split the sandwich rolls and toast them, then stuff them with the broccoli mixture and tomatoes. Serve warm or cool.

8 oz/225 g tempeh

¼ cup/60 ml Basic Vegetable Stock (page 49)

¼ cup/60 ml tamari or soy sauce

¼ cup/60 ml white wine

1 tbsp toasted sesame oil

2 tsp Dijon mustard

½ tsp dried dill

½ tsp smoked paprika (pimentón)

½ cup/70 g sauerkraut

½ cup/55 g shredded carrot

½ cup/55 g shredded red cabbage

8 slices light rye bread, toasted

¼ cup/60 ml Tofu Thousand-Island Dressing (page 204)

Sliced tomato, red onion, and lettuce, for garnish

SERVES 4

Tempeh gets a flavorful marinade and then it's baked and piled high with colorful sauerkraut. Mixing red cabbage in causes the pigments (which are also antioxidants) to tint the whole batch a vibrant fuchsia pink.

Rainbow Reubens

1 On a cutting board, hold the tempeh flat with your palm and, holding the knife parallel to the board, slice the tempeh into two thin sheets. Depending on the shape of the tempeh, you can either divide it into four bread-size squares, or slice it into 2-in-/5-cm-wide strips. In a rimmed baking sheet/tray just large enough to hold the tempeh without overlapping, mix together the stock, tamari, wine, oil, mustard, dill, and paprika. Place the tempeh in the pan and turn it to coat. Cover and let it marinate in the refrigerator for at least 1 hour.

2 In a medium bowl, combine the sauerkraut, carrot, and cabbage and let it stand for at least an hour or up to overnight.

3 Preheat the oven to 350°F/180°C/gas 4. Bake the tempeh, uncovered, until the marinade is very thick and almost evapo-rated, about 30 minutes. Transfer the tempeh to a plate, and cover to keep it warm.

4 Heat the sauerkraut mixture in a small frying pan on the stovetop, stirring. On four slices of toasted bread, spread the dressing, layer on the tempeh, then the warmed 'kraut, tomato, onion, and lettuce, and top with the last slices of bread. Use a toothpick to hold the sandwiches together and serve immediately.

8 oz/225 g seitan

¼ cup/60 g Earth Balance margarine

8 slices whole-wheat/wholemeal bread

8 tsp Dijon mustard

2 medium avocados, sliced

1 tsp jalapeño Tabasco sauce

SERVES 4

If you miss the ease and speed of a grilled cheese, try this. Simple and tasty, these crispy sandwiches rely on the creaminess of avocado in the role of a slice of cheese.

Pan-Toasted Avocado-Seitan Sandwiches

1 Thinly slice the seitan and squeeze out any excess moisture. Spread margarine on one side of each slice of bread and put four of the pieces, margarine-side down, on a cutting board. Spread each one with 2 tsp mustard, then top with seitan, avocado, and a few dashes of Tabasco. Put the last four slices of bread on top, margarine-side up.

2 Place a large cast-iron frying pan over high heat. When it is hot, put in the sandwiches that will fit. Toast them for about 4 minutes per side, until the bread is toasted and browned around the edges. Cook the remaining sandwiches if necessary. Cut in half and serve hot.

12 oz/340 g firm tofu, drained and pressed (see page 68)

1 tbsp extra-virgin olive oil, plus ¼ cup/60 ml

Salt

½ tsp celery seeds

½ tsp freshly cracked black pepper

½ cup/15 g fresh parsley

12 oz/340 g silken tofu

2 tsp cider vinegar

2 tbsp Dijon mustard

1 tsp dried basil

1 rib celery, finely chopped

2 large scallions/spring onions, chopped

1 medium carrot, grated

¼ cup/30 g toasted sunflower seeds

SERVES 8

This makes a big batch of tasty sandwich stuffing, with lots of crunch and zippy dressing. I find most tofu "egg" salads boring because they just use mashed tofu, so I made this one with baked crumbles.

Best-Ever Tofu "Egg" Salad
with Sunny Seeds

1 Preheat the oven to 400°F/200°C/gas 6. On a large baking sheet/tray, spread the 1 tbsp of oil. Crumble the firm tofu into a bowl and mix in ½ tsp salt, the celery seeds, and pepper, then sprinkle the tofu mixture over the oil on the pan. Bake for 10 minutes, then use a metal spatula to turn the tofu and bake until it is browned, about 10 minutes more. Let cool on a rack.

2 In a food processor or blender, mince the parsley. Add the silken tofu and process to puree, scraping down the sides and repeating until the tofu is smooth. Add the vinegar, mustard, basil, and a pinch of salt and process to mix well. With the machine running, drizzle in the remaining ¼ cup/60 ml oil to make a "mayonnaise."

3 In a large bowl, combine the cooled tofu, the contents of the processor bowl, and the celery, scallions/spring onions, carrot, and sunflower seeds. Cover and refrigerate for up to 3 days.

1 cup/180 g sliced
zucchini/courgette

1 cup/140 g sliced fresh
mushrooms

1 large jarred roasted
red pepper/capsicum,
drained and sliced

4 oz/115 g marinated
baked tofu, cubed

½ cup/15 g fresh basil,
chopped

8 large kalamata olives,
sliced

3 tbsp extra-virgin olive oil

2 tbsp freshly squeezed
lemon juice

1 garlic clove, crushed

½ tsp salt

12-in/30.5-cm whole-
wheat/wholemeal
baguette

SERVES 4

The *pan bagnat* is the French picnic sandwich, stuffed with marinated vegetables and vinaigrette, then packed under a weight to soak the crusty bread with tasty juices. You don't need to go on a picnic to pack this vegan version; you can just take it to work in your bag.

Tofu Pan Bagnat

1 In a large bowl, combine the zucchini/courgette, mushrooms, bell pepper/capsicum, tofu, basil, and olives. In a cup, whisk together the oil, lemon juice, garlic, and salt. Pour the mixture over the vegetables and toss. Slice open the baguette and leave one side attached, like a hinge. Tear out the middles of the bread to make room for more filling.

2 Stuff the bread with the filling. Wrap it tightly with foil and put it under a weight such as a griddle or the rest of your picnic fare or cook it on a panini grill to heat. Cut the sandwich into four sections to serve.

5 oz/140 g rapini

2 cups/60 g arugula/rocket

½ cup/55 g shelled pistachios

1 garlic clove, peeled

2 tbsp extra-virgin olive oil

¼ tsp salt

12-in/30.5-cm whole-wheat/wholemeal baguette

6 slices ripe tomato

SERVES 4

Rapini (also known as broccoli raab) is a great big chewy leaf, and you will benefit greatly by pureeing it a bit for this sandwich. Melded with pistachios, garlic, and arugula, it becomes a mouthful of goodness that is easy to pack.

Baguettes Stuffed with Arugula and Rapini Pesto

1 Put on a pot of water to boil for blanching the rapini. Stem and chop the leaves and drop them in the boiling water for 2 minutes, then drain and rinse with cold water. Wring out the rapini until it is dry. In a food processor, pulse the arugula/rocket, pistachios, and garlic until finely ground. Add the oil and salt and process until smooth. Add the drained rapini and pulse to mix.

2 Preheat the grill/barbecue on medium heat or an oven to 400°F/200°C/gas 6. Split the baguette and tear out a bit of the middles to make room for the greens. Spread the rapini pesto in the baguette, then close it up. Wrap the sandwich in foil. Grill or bake until it is hot through, about 15 minutes. Open the sandwich and insert the tomato slices. Cut it into four pieces and serve immediately.

1 tbsp extra-virgin olive oil

8 oz/225 g fresh button mushrooms, sliced

1 small onion, chopped

2 garlic cloves, sliced

½ cup/55 g walnuts

¼ cup/7 g fresh parsley, plus extra for garnish

1 tbsp dark miso

1 tsp dried thyme

½ tsp freshly cracked black pepper

16-in/40.5-cm whole-wheat/wholemeal baguette

8 sun-dried tomato halves, soaked, drained, and chopped

SERVES 6

For a totally different kind of packed lunch, pack a baguette with dense mushroom pâté. For a picnic, bring a sharp serrated knife to cut the sandwich just before serving, and put out the rounds on a platter.

Mushroom-Walnut Pâté–Stuffed Baguettes

1 In a large frying pan over medium heat, warm the oil. Add the mushrooms, onion, and garlic and sauté until the mushrooms soften and weep out their moisture, then keep cooking until they are dry again.

2 In a food processor, process the walnuts and parsley to mince, then add the miso and mushroom mixture and puree coarsely. Add the thyme and pepper and process.

3 Slice the baguette partially in half, leaving one side attached so that you can open up the bread. Tear out some of the middles to make room for the pâté. Spread the pâté in the baguette and sprinkle it with the tomatoes. Close the bread and press to seal. Wrap in foil and refrigerate it until set. To serve, slice it into twelve rounds with a sharp serrated knife and serve the rounds topped with more parsley.

4 whole-wheat/
wholemeal sandwich
rolls, split

1 tsp extra-virgin olive oil

2 cups/225 g sliced
zucchini/courgette

1 cup/120 g chopped
onions

1 cup/149 g slivered red
bell peppers/capsicums

1 garlic clove, chopped

2 cups/315 g broccoli
florets

½ tsp dried thyme

½ tsp salt

½ tsp freshly cracked
black pepper

¼ cup/60 ml Dijon
mustard

2 tbsp agave syrup

1 cup/100 g peeled,
sliced cucumber

1 large tomato, sliced

SERVES 4

On a summer night, a light sauté of vegetables stuffed in a roll is a fine meal. A drizzle of sweet Dijon sauce is all you need with all that plant energy bursting out.

Sautéed Summer Veg Sandwiches

1 Toast the rolls and reserve. Pour the oil into a large frying pan. Heat the pan over high heat for a few seconds, then add the zucchini/courgette, onions, bell peppers/capsicums, and garlic. Toss them in the pan and sauté for 5 minutes or so, until the vegetables are golden and soft. Add the broccoli, thyme, salt, and pepper and sauté for 1 minute more, until the broccoli is bright green. Take the pan off the heat.

2 Mix together the mustard and agave syrup in a small bowl. On each roll, drizzle 1 heaping tbsp of the mustard mixture, then divide the vegetable sauté among the rolls and top with the cucumber and tomato slices. Serve immediately.

2 scallions/spring onions, chopped

2 tbsp freshly squeezed lemon juice

2 tbsp soy sauce

4 tsp sugar

1 tbsp toasted sesame oil

1 tbsp minced peeled fresh ginger

1 tbsp white sesame seeds

2 garlic cloves, minced

2 tsp molasses/treacle

½ tsp freshly cracked black pepper

½ tsp cayenne

8 oz/225 g seitan

Vegetable oil spray

8 pre-fried taco shells

1 cup/140 g Instant Kim Chee (page 189) or prepared kim chee

½ large lemon, thinly sliced

SERVES 4

In the food-truck scene in Los Angeles, there has been a fusion of Korean and Mexican foods. This vegan version of the melding of those flavors is really tasty, with lots of crunch and the tangy heat of kim chee.

Korean "Tacos"

1 In a large bowl, whisk together the scallions/spring onions, lemon juice, soy sauce, sugar, sesame oil, ginger, sesame seeds, garlic, molasses/treacle, pepper, and cayenne. Thinly slice the seitan and chop it into strips, then into smaller pieces, about ½ in/12 mm long. Add them to the marinade in the bowl and toss to coat. Marinate for at least 30 minutes.

2 Preheat the oven to 400°F/200°C/gas 6 and spread the seitan and marinade on an oiled rimmed baking sheet/tray. Bake until crisped, about 15 minutes, stirring midway.

3 Wrap the taco shells in a stack in foil and heat them at the same time. Serve a heaping ¼ cup/60 g seitan in each taco shell, with the kim chee on top, and lemon slices alongside.

NOTE: *To cook this on the stovetop, place a large frying pan or wok over high heat. When it is hot, add 1 tsp canola oil and swirl to coat. Add the seitan and marinade and stir, cooking until the seitan is toasted and browned.*

Olive oil

½ cup/80 g rolled oats

½ cup/15 g fresh parsley

2 garlic cloves, peeled

1 small carrot, cut into chunks

½ cup/80 g broccoli florets

12 oz/340 g firm tofu, drained and pressed (see page 68)

¼ cup/60 ml white miso

3 tbsp tahini paste

6 whole-wheat/wholemeal hamburger buns

Dijon mustard and ketchup/tomato sauce, for garnish

SERVES 6

Tofu and veggies make a cloudlike burger that is fluffy and filled with crunchy bits. The seasonings are Japanese, so if mustard and ketchup are too pedestrian, have these burgers with wasabi Vegenaise and pickled ginger.

Miso-Broccoli Tofu Burgers

1 Spread oil on a large baking sheet/tray. Preheat the oven to 400°F/200°C/gas 6.

2 In a food processor, finely grind the oats, then put them in a large bowl. Process the parsley and garlic until minced. Add the carrot and broccoli and pulse to mince, then scrape the mixture into the bowl with the oats. Add the tofu, miso, and tahini to the bowl and crush and mix with your hands. Knead until the mixture holds together when squeezed.

3 Form the tofu mixture into four patties and place them on the prepared pan. Bake for 20 minutes, then flip and bake for 10 minutes more, until the burgers are firm and toasted.

4 Serve the tofu burgers on buns with mustard and ketchup/tomato sauce.

1 cup/250 g red lentils
½ cup/115 g mashed potatoes
½ cup/60 g chopped onion
½ cup/80 g rolled oats
¼ cup/30 g raw cashews
¼ cup/7 g cilantro/fresh coriander
1 tbsp minced peeled fresh ginger
1 garlic clove, peeled
2 tbsp gluten flour
2 tsp freshly squeezed lemon juice
1 tsp ground cumin
1 tsp brown mustard seeds
½ tsp ground turmeric
¼ tsp ground cinnamon
¼ tsp ground allspice
¼ tsp salt
Olive oil
4 whole-wheat/wholemeal hamburger buns
6 tbsp/90 ml vegan ketchup/tomato sauce
2 tsp hot curry powder
1 cup/30 g baby spinach

SERVES 4

Red lentils are a delicious, quick-cooking plant protein, with added visual pizzazz from their orange hue. Soaking the lentils softens them enough to grind in a food processor, then baking cooks them into a tasty patty.

Red Lentil Masala Burgers
with Curry Ketchup

1 In a medium bowl, soak the lentils overnight in cool water, then drain well.

2 Preheat the oven to 400°F/200°C/gas 6. In a food processor, grind the drained lentils and potatoes, scraping down the sides and regrinding to make a coarse paste. Add the onion, oats, cashews, cilantro/fresh coriander, ginger, and garlic and grind to a fine mince. Add the flour, lemon juice, cumin, mustard seeds, turmeric, cinnamon, allspice, and salt and pulse to mix.

3 Oil a baking sheet/tray and scoop ½-cup/120-ml portions of the lentil mixture onto the pan, leaving plenty of space between them. Wet your palm with a little oil and flatten each scoop of lentil mixture into a patty ¾ in/2 cm thick. Brush the patties with more oil for a crisp top. Bake until the outsides are slightly crusty but still give a little when pressed, 25 to 30 minutes. Transfer the pan to a rack to cool slightly.

4 Toast the buns, then stir together the ketchup/tomato sauce and curry powder in a small bowl. Place ¼ cup/7 g of the spinach on a bun, put a hot burger on top, pour a heaping tablespoon of ketchup/tomato sauce mixture on each burger, and top with a bun. Serve hot.

2 cups/400 g dried chickpeas

1 cup/120 g chopped onions

1 cup/30 g fresh parsley

½ cup/60 g whole-wheat/wholemeal flour

6 garlic cloves, minced

2 tsp salt

1 tsp ground coriander

1 tsp ground cumin

1 tsp freshly cracked black pepper

1 tsp baking soda/bicarbonate of soda

Olive oil

1 cup/100 g chopped cucumber

3 oz/85 g silken tofu

2 tbsp freshly squeezed lemon juice

1 tbsp fresh dill, or 1 tsp dried dill

½ tsp salt

6 whole-wheat/wholemeal hamburger buns

Sliced tomato and lettuce, for garnish

SERVES 6

Felafel are usually a deep-fried event, so it is a real treat to get all the tasty chickpea goodness in a baked burger. With way less fat and a familiar-tasting cucumber sauce, you will feel like you are at a felafel stand in your own kitchen.

Felafel Burgers
with Cucumber-Dill Sauce

1 Soak the chickpeas in cold water to cover overnight. Drain, then transfer them to a food processor. Grind the chickpeas to a coarse mince. Add the onions, parsley, flour, garlic, salt, ground coriander, cumin, pepper, and baking soda/bicarbonate of soda and process to make a thick paste.

2 Divide the felafel mixture into six portions and form them into patties. Refrigerate them, covered, until time to cook.

3 Preheat the oven to 425°F/220°C/gas 7. Brush a baking sheet/tray with oil, place the patties on the pan, and brush the patties with oil. Bake for 15 minutes, then flip the patties and bake until browned, about 10 minutes more.

4 Puree the cucumber and tofu together in a blender or food processor. When they are smooth, add the lemon juice and dill, and puree. Add the salt and process to mix. Transfer the sauce to a small bowl.

5 Serve the hot burgers on the buns with a drizzle of sauce and some sliced tomato and lettuce.

8 oz/225 g tempeh, cubed

2 cups/120 ml Basic Vegetable Stock (page 49)

½ cup/15 g fresh arugula/rocket, plus extra for garnish

1 garlic clove

½ cup/55 g raw cashews

2 tbsp gluten flour

1 tbsp cornstarch/cornflour

1 tbsp nutritional yeast

1 cup/120 g chopped onions

2 tbsp tomato paste/puree

2 tbsp tamari or soy sauce

Canola oil

4 whole-wheat/wholemeal hamburger buns

Sliced tomato, for garnish

SERVES 4

The benefits of tempeh, with all its fermented charms, are put to good use in this chewy, nutty burger. Arugula adds deep green nutrition and a nutty-herbal flavor that no packaged burger can match.

Cashew-Tempeh Burgers
with Arugula

1 Preheat the oven to 400°F/200°C/gas 6. Put the tempeh and stock in a large pot, and bring them to a simmer. Cook on low heat, covered, until the tempeh is well moistened, about 15 minutes. Drain the tempeh in a colander. Spread it on a towel to dry, then let it cool.

2 In a food processor, mince the arugula/rocket and garlic. Add the cashews and process to a paste. In a small cup, mix together the flour, cornstarch/cornflour, and yeast.

3 Add the tempeh and onions to the processor, then sprinkle the flour mixture over the tempeh in the processor bowl. Add the tomato paste/puree and tamari and pulse to coarsely grind the mixture. Pause, take off the lid, and squeeze some of the mixture to see if it holds together. It should still have a chunky texture but form a ball easily.

4 Oil a baking sheet/tray, and scoop ½-cup/120-ml portions of the tempeh mixture onto the sheet. Rinse your hands and use your damp palms to flatten the patties to ¾ in/2 cm thick. Brush the tops with oil, then bake them for 15 minutes. Flip the patties with a spatula and bake until firm and toasted, about 10 minutes more. Transfer the pan to a rack to cool slightly.

5 Serve the hot patties on the buns with sliced tomato and additional arugula/rocket.

½ cup/85 g quinoa

14 oz/400 g canned/ tinned black beans, drained and rinsed

2 scallions/spring onions, chopped

¼ cup/7 g cilantro/fresh coriander, chopped

2 tbsp gluten flour

1½ tsp ground cumin

½ tsp chili powder

¼ tsp salt

3 tbsp white sesame seeds

Vegetable oil spray

4 whole-wheat/wholemeal hamburger buns

Salsa, for garnish

SERVES 4

Using canned beans makes these burgers fast and easy. A hint of cumin and some piquant cilantro give them Southwestern flavor, which really tastes good with the quinoa.

Black Bean and Quinoa Burgers
with Cumin

1 Preheat the oven to 425°F/220°C/gas 7. In a small sauce-pan with a lid, dry-toast the quinoa over high heat, swirling the pan to move the grains over the heat. When the quinoa is crackling hot and toasty smelling, take it off the heat and carefully pour in ¾ cup/180 ml water. It will bubble up, so add the water gradually. Place the pan back on the heat and bring it to a boil, then cover and lower the heat to the lowest set-ting. Cook until all the water is absorbed, about 15 minutes, then take it off the heat and let stand for 5 minutes to finish steaming. Drain if there is any excess water. Put the quinoa in a large bowl.

2 Add the beans, scallions/spring onions, cilantro/fresh coriander, flour, cumin, chili powder, and salt and mash every-thing together with your hands or a potato masher; the mix-ture should hold together but still be a little chunky. Divide the mixture into four portions. Spread the sesame seeds on a plate. Form the bean mixture into patties and coat them with the seeds.

3 Coat a baking sheet/tray with oil spray and place the patties on it. Bake for 15 minutes, then flip the patties carefully and bake until they are browned and crusty, about 10 minutes more. Serve them hot, on the buns, with salsa.

4 cups/500 g unbleached all-purpose/plain flour, plus extra for counter

1 cup/130 g pastry/ soft-wheat flour

2½ tsp bread-machine yeast

2 tsp salt

Olive oil

MAKES
SIX 10-IN/25-CM
OR
FOUR 14-IN/35-CM
CRUSTS

While whole-grain breads and pizzas are best for your health, there are times when it's fun to have a tender white crust. This recipe is based on the kind they use in authentic pizzerias, and makes a stretchy dough that tastes great rolled out thin or thick. Cake flour stands in for the soft "00" flour used in Italy.

Neapolitan Pizza Dough

1 In the bowl of a stand mixer with the dough hook or a large bowl, combine 3 cups/385 g of the all-purpose/plain flour, the pastry/soft-wheat flour, yeast, and salt and mix well. Add 2 cups/480 ml warm water and stir to mix. Knead in more all-purpose/plain flour, ½ cup/60 g at a time, until you have a smooth and unsticky dough. This takes about 5 minutes in the mixer, longer by hand. Transfer the dough to an oiled bowl, turn to coat the dough, and cover with plastic wrap/ cling film. Let it rise in a warm, draft-free place until doubled in volume, about 1 hour.

2 Punch down the dough and divide it into six pieces for 10-in/25-cm pizzas, or four pieces for 14-in/35-cm pizzas, then form the pieces into balls. (At this point, the dough can be refrigerated in oiled zip-top bags for up to 3 days or frozen—if you double the yeast—for up to 4 weeks until needed. Let it come to warm room temperature before topping and baking it.)

3 Place a ball of dough on a lightly floured counter or baking sheet/tray and cover with a towel. Let it rise until almost doubled in volume, about 45 minutes. Roll out to the desired size for a pizza.

4 Use this dough to make the Thin-Crust Pesto Pizza (page 332) or top with your own favorite toppings and bake for about 15 minutes at 400°F/200°C/gas 6, until bubbly and browned.

MAIN COURSES

327

5 cups/640 g
white whole-wheat/
wholemeal flour, plus
more for counter

1 tbsp bread-machine
yeast

1 tsp salt

¼ cup/60 ml extra-virgin
olive oil, plus extra for
bowl

2 tbsp brown rice syrup

Cornmeal

MAKES
4 THICK, 9-IN/23-CM
OR
4 THIN, 14-IN/35-CM
CRUSTS

White whole-wheat flour is a delicious product, made from a variety of wheat with a pale outer layer, making the 100 percent whole flour lighter in color than regular brown. The resulting crust is chewy and rises like a dream.

White Wheat Pizza Crust

1 In a stand mixer fitted with the dough hook or a large bowl, mix 3 cups/385 g of the flour with the yeast and salt. Mix 2 cups/480 ml warm water with the oil and brown rice syrup, and stir in, kneading as it gets too thick to stir. Knead in the remaining 2 cups/255 g flour gradually, to make a soft, barely sticky dough. Transfer the dough to a floured counter and knead for 5 minutes, until it is smooth. Transfer it to an oiled bowl, turn to coat the dough, and cover it with plastic wrap/cling film. Let the dough rise in a warm, draft-free place until it doubles in volume, at least 30 minutes.

2 Punch down the dough and divide it into four pieces. (At this point, the dough can be stored in an oiled zip-top bag or storage container in the refrigerator for up to 3 days. Let the dough come to warm room temperature before shaping for a pizza. If you want to make the dough to freeze, double the amount of yeast and proceed, freezing instead of refrigerating.)

3 To prebake crusts to top later, preheat the oven to 375°F/ 190°C/gas 5. Form each piece of dough into a disk and let it rest for 10 minutes to relax the gluten. Sprinkle a large baking sheet/tray or pizza pan/tray with cornmeal. Roll and stretch the dough into a disk of the desired size. Place the dough on the pan, poke it all over with a fork, and cover with a damp cloth. Let the dough rise in a warm, draft-free place until almost doubled in volume, about 30 minutes.

4 Bake the dough, depending on its thickness, until baked through but not browned, 10 minutes. Let cool on a rack, and when completely cool, wrap or bag it for use later in the week. Store in the refrigerator.

5 To serve, preheat the oven to 400°F/200°C/gas 6, and top the prebaked crust with desired sauces and toppings. Place the crust right on the oven rack or a baking stone in the oven. Bake until the toppings are hot, 13 to 15 minutes.

½ batch White Wheat Pizza Crust (page 328)

Cornmeal

16 garlic cloves, peeled

3 tbsp extra-virgin olive oil

8 oz/225 g kale, stemmed

½ tsp salt

1 cup/300 g cooked white beans

1 tbsp tomato paste/puree

2 tsp fresh thyme, chopped

¼ tsp red pepper flakes

Flour

SERVES 2 TO 4

White beans and kale are an old Tuscan combination, one that is just as good today. Roasted garlic adds sweetness to the pie, and red pepper flakes give it a hint of heat.

Kale and White Bean Pizza
with Roasted Garlic

1 Make the dough and let it rise for about an hour or bring refrigerated dough to warm room temperature. Form two disks and let them rest, covered, for 10 minutes to relax the gluten.

2 Put on a pot of water and bring it to a boil. Preheat the oven to 400°F/200°C/gas 6. If you have a pizza stone, put it in the cold oven. Prep a pizza peel or two baking sheets/trays by spreading cornmeal on them. Put the garlic on a square of foil, drizzle with 1 tbsp of the oil, and wrap it up to make a packet. Put the garlic in the oven for about 10 minutes, then shake it to keep it from sticking and roast for another 15 minutes. When the garlic is tender when pierced with a paring knife, take it out to cool.

3 Chop the kale leaves and drop them in the boiling water for 1 minute, then drain and rinse with cold water. Wring out all the moisture. Put the kale in a small bowl and toss it with 1 tbsp of the oil and ¼ tsp of the salt.

4 Drain and rinse the beans, and pat them dry. Put them in a medium bowl and mash coarsely with the remaining 1 tbsp oil, the roasted garlic and its oil, tomato paste/puree, thyme, pepper flakes, and the remaining ¼ tsp salt.

5 Divide the pizza dough in half and roll out each on a floured counter to make 12-in/30-cm disks. Place each round on either a cornmeal-covered pizza peel (to bake on a stone) or a cornmeal-covered baking sheet/tray. On each pizza, sprinkle the white bean mixture and spread it gently, then top with the kale. Slide the pizzas onto the hot pizza stone or put the baking sheets/trays in the oven. Bake until the crust is crisp and the kale is browned, about 15 minutes. Remove the pizzas to a cutting board, cut into wedges, and serve.

½ batch Neapolitan Pizza Dough (page 327)

Cornmeal

½ cup/120 ml Basil Pesto (page 116)

1 cup/55 g sun-dried tomato halves, rehydrated and chopped

½ small onion, chopped

SERVES 4 TO 6

These single-serving pies are simple and quick to make, especially if you have dough and pesto already in the fridge. The pesto is so rich and delicious, you will never miss the cheese. It's worth the effort to really stretch the crusts to cracker thinness; you will be rewarded with crisp crustiness.

Thin-Crust Pesto Pizza

1 Make the pizza dough and let it rise for about an hour or bring refrigerated dough to warm room temperature. Preheat the oven to 425°F/220°C/gas 7. If you have a pizza stone, put it in the cold oven. Prep a pizza peel or two baking sheets/trays by spreading cornmeal on them.

2 Divide the dough into four pieces and shape each into a disk. Let the disks rest for 10 minutes, covered, to relax the gluten. Roll out two disks on an unfloured counter, stretching them as thinly as you can; keep the others covered. Each one should make a 14-in/35-cm cracker-thin crust. You may have to let it rest for a minute to get it to stretch more.

3 When each dough round is very thin, put them one at a time on the pizza peel and slide it onto the pizza stone, or put it on a prepared baking sheet/tray, and bake for 6 minutes. Take out the crust and spread it very quickly with 2 tbsp of the pesto, sprinkle it with ¼ cup/15 g of the tomatoes, and some onion, and return it to the oven. Bake until the crust is browned and the toppings are bubbly, about 4 minutes more. Take out the pizza and slice it into wedges. Serve immediately.

1 prebaked 9-in/23-cm White Wheat Pizza Crust (page 328) or other crust

2 cups/60 g fresh spinach, chopped

¼ cup/55 g tofu "cream cheese"

2 garlic cloves, chopped

1 pinch salt

12 small cherry tomatoes, halved

2 oz/55 g broccoli florets

2 large fresh mushrooms, sliced

SERVES 2

This pizza calls for a prebaked crust, so when you make the White Wheat Pizza Crust recipe, bake off one round, then save it for this pizza. You can also throw this one together with a purchased crust—it's really fast, easy, and tasty.

Quick Tomato-Veggie Pizza

1 Preheat the oven to 400°F/200°C/gas 6. Place the pizza crust on a baking sheet/tray.

2 In a medium bowl, mix together the spinach, "cream cheese," garlic, and salt. Spread the mixture on the crust. Sprinkle on the veggies and bake until the broccoli has some browned spots, about 15 minutes. Slice and serve hot.

½ batch White Wheat Pizza Crust (page 328)

2 tsp extra-virgin olive oil, plus extra for pan

2 tsp chickpea flour

1 tbsp unbleached all-purpose/plain flour

¾ cup/180 ml rice milk or other milk

¼ tsp salt

2 cups/60 g fresh spinach, chopped

¼ cup/35 g oil-cured olives, drained and chopped

24 small cherry tomatoes, halved

SERVES 4

The benefits of cooking in cast iron are many. In the case of this pizza, the crust is perfectly crisp on the outside, and delightfully chewy on the inside. Cast iron holds heat well, so you can serve the pizza in the pan and it will stay warm at the table. The pan also puts measurable amounts of iron into your food, so it is a win-win all around.

Cast-Iron Alfredo Pizza
with Spinach and Olives

1 Make the pizza dough and let it rise for about an hour or bring refrigerated dough to warm room temperature. Preheat the oven to 425°F/220°C/gas 7.

2 In a small saucepan, whisk together the oil with the chickpea and unbleached flours. Place the pan over medium heat and stir constantly as it comes to a bubble. Cook for about 1 minute, then take it off the heat and add the milk, a little at at time, whisking until smooth after each addition. Put the pan back on the heat and whisk, adding the salt. Bring it to a boil, then lower the heat and simmer until thickened, another couple of minutes. Take the sauce off the heat and let it cool.

3 In a medium bowl, toss together the spinach and olives, coating the spinach with olive juice.

4 Lightly oil a 12-in/30.5-cm cast-iron skillet. Pat out the crust to make a 12-in/30.5-cm round in the pan. Spread the sauce over the crust, sprinkle over the spinach mixture, and top with the tomato halves. Bake for 20 minutes, until the top is golden and the bottom is crisp. Let stand outside of the oven for at least 5 minutes before serving; it will be very hot and the fillings will be very wet at first.

Crust

1 cup/115 g unbleached all-purpose/plain flour

¼ cup/30 g chickpea flour

1 tsp bread-machine yeast

1 tsp sugar

½ tsp salt

Olive oil

Topping

1 lb/455 g yellow potatoes, thinly sliced

2 tbsp extra-virgin olive oil

1 tbsp chopped fresh rosemary

3 garlic cloves, thinly sliced

¼ tsp red pepper flakes

¾ tsp salt

½ cup/55 g raw cashews

¼ cup/60 ml plain almond milk

Freshly cracked black pepper

Cornmeal

16 small cherry tomatoes, halved

SERVES 4

Roasted potato pizza is an old-fashioned Italian idea. The creamy sauce, sparked with rosemary leaves, make this comfort food of the highest order. The chickpea flour–laced crust adds protein and eggy flavor to the potato extravaganza.

Roasted Potato and Rosemary Pizza

1 TO MAKE THE CRUST: In a large bowl or a stand mixer fitted with the dough hook, mix together both flours, the yeast, sugar, and salt. Add ⅔ cup/150 ml warm water and knead, adding a little unbleached flour gradually to make a soft but not sticky dough. Knead until the dough is supple and smooth, about 5 minutes. Oil a large bowl and transfer the dough to the bowl, turn it to coat with oil, and cover with plastic wrap/cling film. Let the dough rise in a warm, draft-free place until doubled in volume, about 1 hour.

2 TO MAKE THE TOPPING: Preheat the oven to 450°F/230°C/gas 8. If you have a pizza stone, put it in the cold oven. In a large bowl, toss together the potatoes, oil, rosemary, garlic, pepper flakes, and ½ tsp of the salt. Spread the potatoes on a baking sheet/tray and roast until they are tender when pierced with a paring knife, 15 to 20 minutes. Let cool. While the potatoes roast, put the cashews in a blender or food processor and grind them to a fine paste. Add the milk gradually, just to make a smooth sauce. Add the remaining ¼ tsp salt and season with pepper.

3 Divide the pizza dough into four portions, and form each into a ball. Let them rest, covered, for 10 minutes, then roll each one out to make a thin, 8-in/20-cm pizza. Spread cornmeal on a baking sheet/tray or pizza peel and place a dough round on the sheet or peel. Spread it with one fourth of the cashew mixture, then one fourth of the potatoes, and one fourth of the tomatoes. Slide it onto the pizza stone, or put the sheet in the oven and bake until the crust is crisp and browned around the edges, 12 to 14 minutes. Serve immediately.

MAIN COURSES

Crust

2 tbsp olive oil, plus extra for pan and bowl

1 cup/115 g whole-wheat/wholemeal flour

½ cup/60 g unbleached all-purpose/plain flour, plus extra for counter

¼ cup/30 g wheat germ

1 tsp bread-machine yeast

½ tsp salt

1 tbsp brown rice syrup or malt syrup

Filling

2 tsp extra-virgin olive oil

2 cups/240 g chopped onions

4 garlic cloves, chopped

8 oz/225 g fresh button mushrooms, chopped

6 oz/170 g firm tofu, drained, pressed (see page 68), and crumbled

5 oz/150 g fresh spinach

½ cup/15 g fresh parsley, chopped

½ cup/55 g dry bread crumbs

1 tsp dried thyme

½ tsp salt

½ tsp freshly cracked black pepper

½ cup/120 ml Basic Veggie Spaghetti or Pizza Sauce (page 120)

SERVES 2

The Chicago-style deep-dish pizza is a true American original, packed with so many goodies that it towers over other slices. This tasty whole wheat–crusted beauty is stuffed with spinach, mushrooms, and savory tofu, all wrapped into a classic package. The hearty crust is perfect with the fillings, but you could use white wheat flour in this recipe, or use a quarter batch of the White Wheat Pizza Crust (page 328).

Deep-Dish Mushroom-Spinach Pizza

1 TO MAKE THE CRUST: Prepare a 9-in/23-cm round cake pan/tin by oiling it lightly. In a stand mixer with the dough hook or in a large bowl, mix together both flours, the wheat germ, yeast, and salt. In a cup, whisk together 1 cup/240 ml warm water, the oil, and brown rice syrup. Add the liquids to the dry with the machine running (or a sturdy spoon). Mix until the dough is soft and pliable, but if it's really sticky, add more flour. Knead for 5 minutes. Oil a large bowl and transfer the dough to the bowl, turn it to coat with oil, and cover with plastic wrap/cling film. Let the dough rise in a warm, draft-free place until doubled in volume, about 1 hour.

2 TO MAKE THE FILLING: In a large frying pan, heat the oil over high heat. Add the onions and sauté until golden, lowering the heat as they soften, and cooking for as long as possible to caramelize them. Add the garlic and cook for 1 minute, then add the mushrooms and tofu. Stir and cook until the mushrooms are golden and the tofu is browned a bit. Add the spinach and continue to sauté until it is wilted. Remove from the heat and add the parsley, bread crumbs, thyme, salt, and pepper. Stir to mix, then let the filling cool to room temperature.

3 Divide the dough by cutting off one third for the top crust. On a lightly floured counter, roll out the larger piece to 12 in/30cm wide. Fit it into the prepared pan to cover the bottom and sides of the pan. Fill the dough with the tofu mixture and pat it down evenly, then dollop in ¼ cup/60 ml of the sauce. Roll out the top crust to 10 in/25 cm and cover the filling. Pinch the two crusts together to join.

4 Bake the pizza on the bottom rack of the oven for 20 minutes, then take it out and spread the remaining ¼ cup/60 ml sauce over the top crust. Return it to the oven on the top rack until sauce is browned and the crust is crisp, 20 minutes more. Let it stand outside the oven for 5 minutes before slicing and serving.

Filling

1 tbsp extra-virgin olive oil

1 cup/120 g chopped onions

12 oz/340 g firm tofu, drained, pressed (see page 68), and crumbled

2 cups/130 g chopped fresh kale

3 garlic cloves, minced

3 oz/85 g silken tofu

½ cup/30 g sun-dried tomatoes, rehydrated and chopped

½ cup/55 g dry whole-wheat/wholemeal bread crumbs

½ cup/15 g fresh basil, chopped

½ tsp salt

Crust

2½ to 3 cups/315 to 385 g white whole-wheat/wholemeal flour, plus extra for counter

2 tsp bread-machine yeast

½ tsp salt

3 tbsp extra-virgin olive oil, plus extra for bowl

1 tbsp brown rice syrup

SERVES 8

This meal-in-a-pie is a great easy-to-pack lunch. Lots of lusty Italian flavors come from sun-dried tomatoes, garlic, and kale.

Kale and Sun-Dried Tomato Calzones

1 TO MAKE THE FILLING: In a large nonstick frying pan over high heat, warm the oil. Add the onions and firm tofu and sauté until the onions are starting to brown. Add the kale and garlic and cook for 2 minutes, until the kale is soft. Take the pan off the heat and add the silken tofu, tomatoes, bread crumbs, basil, and salt and knead until it holds together. Let cool.

2 TO MAKE THE CRUST: In a stand mixer fitted with the dough hook or a large bowl, mix 2½ cups/315 g of the flour, the yeast, and salt. In a measuring cup, measure 1¼ cups/300 ml warm water and stir in the oil and brown rice syrup. Add the liquids to the dry and mix, then knead until smooth and elastic, about 5 minutes. Oil a large bowl and transfer the dough to the bowl, and cover with plastic wrap/cling film. Let the dough rise in a warm, draft-free place until doubled in volume, about 1 hour.

3 Preheat the oven to 400°F/200°C/gas 6. Divide the dough into eight pieces. On a lightly floured counter, roll out each dough piece to a 6-in/15-cm oval. Scoop ½ cup/60 g of the filling into the center of each. Dampen the edge of the dough and fold over. Seal and crimp the edges with a fork. Put the calzones on an oiled baking sheet/tray. Poke a vent in the tops with a fork. Cover and let them rise in a warm, draft-free place until puffy, about 30 minutes.

4 Uncover and bake the calzones until the bottoms are browned, 20 to 25 minutes. Serve hot, or let them cool completely before wrapping in foil and refrigerating for tomorrow.

¼ batch White Wheat Pizza Crust (page 328)

½ cup/15 g fresh parsley

¼ cup/30 g pecans

2 tbsp fresh oregano or thyme

1 garlic clove, peeled

½ tsp salt

1 tbsp extra-virgin olive oil, plus extra for pan

14 oz/400 g canned/tinned white beans, drained and rinsed

8 cherry tomatoes, halved

Flour

SERVES 4

Tender white beans, bathed in a nutty herbal pesto, make these hand-held pies a feast for the senses. They are great as lunch the next day, and they even freeze well.

White Bean and Pecan Pesto Calzones

1 Make the pizza dough and let it rise for about an hour or bring refrigerated dough to warm room temperature. Preheat the oven to 400°F/200°C/gas 6.

2 In a food processor, combine the parsley, pecans, oregano, garlic, and salt and grind them to a paste, scraping down the sides and regrinding until the mixture is smooth. Add the oil and process. Scrape the pesto out into a medium bowl. Add the beans and tomatoes and toss to mix.

3 Oil a baking sheet/tray. Divide the dough into four pieces. On a lightly floured counter, roll out each piece to a 6-in/15-cm oval. Scoop about ½ cup/60 g of the bean filling into the center of each oval. Dampen the edge of the dough and fold over. Seal and crimp the edges with a fork. Put the calzones on the prepared pan. Poke a vent in the tops with the fork. Cover and let them rise in a warm, draft-free place until puffy, about 30 minutes.

4 Uncover and bake the calzones until the bottoms are golden brown, about 20 minutes. Serve warm, or let cool completely before wrapping in foil and refrigerating for tomorrow.

8 oz/225 g tempeh

1 tbsp dried sage

1 tbsp fennel seeds

½ tsp dried thyme

½ tsp dried oregano

¼ tsp red pepper flakes

3 garlic cloves, minced

1 tbsp extra-virgin olive oil, plus extra for pan

2 large fresh portobello mushrooms, finely chopped

½ cup/60 g chopped onion

¼ cup/10 g nutritional yeast

½ tsp salt

¼ batch White Wheat Pizza Crust (page 328)

Flour

2½ cups/600 ml Basic Veggie Spaghetti or Pizza Sauce (page 120)

SERVES 4

Spicy, fennel-flecked tempeh makes a stand-in for sausage in this zesty calzone, which is packed with meaty mushrooms. One hefty calzone is a meal, as well as a handful of textures and tastes.

Tempeh "Sausage" and Mushroom Calzones

1 Set up a steamer and bring the water to a simmer. Slice the tempeh into 1-in/2.5-cm slices and steam it until moistened, about 5 minutes. Blot the tempeh dry with a towel. Let it cool.

2 Put the cooled tempeh in a food processor with the sage, fennel, thyme, oregano, pepper flakes, and garlic, then pulse to grind it coarsely (don't puree). Reserve the mock sausage.

3 In a medium frying pan, heat the oil over high heat. Add the mushrooms and onions and sauté until the onions are browned and soft, reducing the heat to medium as you go. The pan should be dry when you are done. Push the mushrooms over to one side, add the tempeh mixture, and stir. Mix and stir over medium heat until the tempeh is lightly browned, about 4 minutes. Scrape the contents of the pan into a medium bowl and let it cool. Stir in the yeast and salt.

4 Preheat the oven to 400°F/200°C/gas 6. Divide the dough into four pieces. On a lightly floured counter, roll out each dough piece to a 6-in/15-cm oval. Scoop ½ cup/60 g of the filling into the center of each. Scoop 2 tbsp of sauce over the filling. Dampen the edge of the dough, and fold over. Seal and crimp the edges with a fork. Put the calzones to an oiled baking sheet/tray. Poke a vent in the tops with the fork. Cover and let them rise in a warm, draft-free place until puffy, about 30 minutes.

5 Uncover and bake the calzones until the bottoms are golden brown, about 20 minutes. While the calzones bake, heat the remaining 2 cups/480 ml sauce to ladle over them at serving time. Serve the calzones hot with sauce, or let them cool completely before wrapping in foil and refrigerating for tomorrow.

Dough

2 cups/255 g white whole-wheat/wholemeal flour

2 tsp bread-machine yeast

½ tsp salt

1 cup/240 ml hazelnut milk or rice milk

1 tbsp agave syrup

1 tbsp nut oil or olive oil, plus extra for bowl

½ cup/60 g unbleached all-purpose/plain flour, plus extra for counter

¼ cup/30 g chopped skinned hazelnuts

Filling

1 tbsp extra-virgin olive oil, plus extra for pan

1 lb/455 g seitan, drained and chopped

1 cup/120 g chopped onions

8 oz/225 g fresh cremini/brown mushrooms, sliced

1 cup/240 ml Madeira wine

1 cup/240 ml coconut milk

2 tbsp tamari or soy sauce

4 tsp unbleached all-purpose/plain flour

½ tsp freshly cracked black pepper

SERVES 8

Madeira wine and mushrooms are a match made in heaven, so buy a bottle of Rainwater Madeira, a particular style of the Portuguese fortified wine, just for mushroom cuisine. The rich flavor of the Madeira sets off the earthy mushrooms in a way that will leave you craving it. These freeze well, so save a few for another day.

Creamy Cremini-Madeira Turnovers

1 TO MAKE THE DOUGH: In a stand mixer fitted with the dough hook or a large bowl, combine the whole-wheat/wholemeal flour, yeast, and salt. Warm the hazelnut milk to about 100°F/38°C, then stir in the agave syrup and oil. Mix the liquids into the flour mixture and knead to make a soft dough, adding all-purpose/plain flour as needed. Mix in the hazelnuts at the end. Oil a large bowl and transfer the dough to the bowl, turn it to coat with oil, and cover with plastic wrap/cling film. Let the dough rise in a warm, draft-free place until doubled in volume, about 1 hour.

2 TO MAKE THE FILLING: In a large frying pan, heat the oil over medium-high heat. Add the seitan, onions, and mushrooms and sauté, stirring constantly, until the mushrooms are seared and browned. Add the Madeira, ½ cup/120 ml of the coconut milk, and the tamari and cook until the liquids are absorbed. Sprinkle the flour over the mushroom mixture in the pan and stir, then stir in the remaining ½ cup/120 ml coconut milk. Cook until thickened, and stir in the pepper. Transfer the filling to a bowl to cool to room temperature.

3 Preheat the oven to 375°F/190°C/gas 5. Oil a large baking sheet/tray. Put some cool water in a cup and get a pastry brush. On a lightly floured counter, divide the dough into eight pieces. Roll out each piece to a 6-in/15-cm oval, then measure a scant ½ cup/60 ml of the filling into the lower half of each oval, leaving ½ in/12 mm bare to seal. Dab the edge of the dough with water, fold the dough over the filling, and use a fork to crimp the edge. Transfer the turnovers to the prepared pan, leaving 2 in/5 cm of space between each one. Use the fork to poke a vent in the top of each turnover. Cover the turnovers loosely with plastic wrap/cling film and let them rise in a warm, draft-free place until puffy, about 30 minutes.

4 Uncover the turnovers and bake them until the bottoms are golden brown, about 20 minutes. Transfer the pan to a cooling rack to cool slightly before serving.

Ingredients

2 tbsp extra-virgin olive oil, plus extra for pan

2 lb/910 g kabocha squash, peeled and cubed

2 medium/10 g fresh ancho chiles, chopped

1 cup/240 ml Basic Vegetable Stock (page 49)

4 cups/140 g chopped Swiss chard/silverbeet

4 garlic cloves, chopped

1 tsp dried oregano

½ cup/55 g whole almonds, toasted and chopped

1¾ tsp salt

1 lb/455 g yucca, peeled and chopped

2 cups/255 g unbleached all-purpose/plain flour, plus extra for counter

3 tbsp coconut oil

2 tbsp annatto paste or achiote powder

SERVES 6

These amazing little Mexican-style turnovers are filled with meltingly soft squash, crunchy almonds, and tender Swiss chard, so every bite is full of sensations. Seek out the annatto paste for the unique crust, which glows golden from the bright yellow seeds. If you can't find any, it will still be delicious.

Squash and Ancho Empanadas
with Achiote-Yucca Crust

1 Preheat the oven to 375°F/190°C/gas 5. Place a large frying pan over high heat, add the olive oil, and swirl to coat the pan. Add the squash and anchos and sauté, stirring, until the squash is lightly browned, about 3 minutes. Lower the heat to medium and add the stock, then cover the pan tightly. Adjust the heat if needed to steam the squash for about 10 minutes. Uncover the squash and test by piercing a piece with a paring knife. When it is tender, uncover it and add the chard/silverbeet, garlic, and oregano and stir until the greens are wilted and the pan is nearly dry. Take it off the heat and stir in the almonds and ¾ tsp of the salt.

2 Bring a large pot of water to a boil. Boil the yucca until tender, then drain. In a food processor, combine the yucca, flour, coconut oil, annatto paste, and the remaining 1 tsp salt. Pulse to mix well. If the mixture is crumbly, add water, 1 tsp at a time, until it makes a smooth dough. Divide the dough into four portions, then divide each quarter into three pieces for twelve pieces total.

3 On a lightly floured counter, roll out the dough portions to 6-in/15-cm ovals. Fill each one with a heaping ¼ cup/60 g of the filling, then dampen the edge of the dough with water and fold it over the filling. Press the edges together and use a fork to seal. Place the empanadas on an oiled baking sheet/tray and poke vents in the top with the fork.

4 Bake the empanadas until the edges of the pastry are crisp and the bottoms are browned, about 25 minutes. Transfer the pan to a rack to cool slightly before serving two per person.

Dough

2 to 3 cups/255 to 385 g white whole-wheat/wholemeal flour, plus extra for counter

2 tsp bread-machine yeast

½ tsp salt

2 tbsp extra-virgin olive oil, plus extra for bowl

1 tbsp agave syrup or other sweetener

Filling

8 oz/225 g fresh green beans, cut into ½-in/12-mm pieces

8 oz/225 g diced yellow potatoes

Salt

Freshly cracked black pepper

1½ cups/45 g fresh basil

½ cup/55 g pine nuts

¼ cup/30 g pistachios

2 garlic cloves, peeled

1 tbsp extra-virgin olive oil, plus extra for pan

Diced fresh tomato, for garnish

SERVES 8

Unlike individual servings of calzone, this is a loaf stuffed with goodies, to slice and share. Lop off a chunk of this warm, fragrant loaf and find a spiral of rich, nutty pesto; tender potatoes; and crisp green beans. You will want to share this with friends, to enjoy the pretty presentation and revel in the herby-nutty sensations.

Green Bean and Potato Stromboli

1 TO MAKE THE DOUGH: In a stand mixer fitted with the dough hook or a large bowl, combine 2 cups/255 g of the flour, the yeast, and salt. In a large cup, mix 1 cup/240 ml warm water, the oil, and agave syrup. With the machine running (or using a sturdy spoon), stir the liquids into the dry ingredients. When the dough is well combined and becomes sticky, start sprinkling in more flour, up to 1 cup/130 g, until you have a soft dough that is only slightly sticky. Knead for a few minutes to finish. Oil a large bowl and transfer the dough to the bowl, turn it to coat with oil, and cover with plastic wrap/cling film. Let the dough rise in a warm, draft-free place until doubled in volume, about 1 hour.

2 TO MAKE THE FILLING: Set up a steamer and bring the water to a simmer. Steam the green beans and potatoes until the potatoes are very tender, about 10 minutes. Let them cool to room temperature.

3 Mix the beans and potatoes well with your hands to mash the potatoes just a little, and season with ½ tsp each salt and pepper. In a food processor, combine the basil, pine nuts, pistachios, and garlic and process to chop finely. Add the oil and ½ tsp salt and process until smooth.

4 Preheat the oven to 375°F/190°C/gas 5. Oil a large baking sheet/tray. On a lightly floured counter, pat out the dough to make an 8½-by-13-in/22-by-33-cm rectangle. Spread the pesto over the dough, leaving a border bare at one side to seal the roll. Cover the pesto with the potato mixture and roll up the dough like a cinnamon roll. Pinch the seam closed, then put the stromboli, seam-side down, on the prepared pan. Cover loosely with plastic wrap/cling film and let it rise in a warm, draft-free place until doubled in volume, about 30 minutes.

5 Uncover and bake the roll until the outside is golden brown and the loaf sounds hollow when tapped on the bottom, 25 to 30 minutes. Let cool for at least 10 minutes on the pan on a rack. Slice the stromboli into eight pieces and serve them with a sprinkling of diced tomatoes.

Dough

¼ cup/30 g toasted, skinned hazelnuts

1 cup/115 g white whole-wheat/wholemeal flour

½ cup/60 g unbleached all-purpose/plain flour, plus extra for counter

½ tsp salt

3 tbsp cold-press corn oil, chilled

½ cup/120 ml ice water

Filling

1 tbsp extra-virgin olive oil

1 cup/120 g chopped onions

5 oz/125 g Asian eggplant/aubergine, peeled and cut into ½-in/12-mm cubes

4 oz/115 g yellow squash, cut into ½-in/12-mm cubes

4 oz/115 g zucchini/courgette, cut into ½-in/12-mm cubes

3 medium scallions/spring onions, chopped

1 tbsp chopped fresh rosemary

1 cup/185 g diced ripe tomatoes

2 garlic cloves, minced

½ tsp salt

½ tsp coarsely cracked black pepper

½ cup/15 g fresh basil, shredded, for garnish

SERVES 4

Each diner gets her own tart, which is a beautiful serving of rustic French flavors. The crunchy hazelnuts in the pastry make it far more interesting than the butter-laden kind. Soft, sautéed vegetables are piled on top, and fresh basil scents the air as you dive in.

Individual Provençal Vegetable Tarts

1 TO MAKE THE DOUGH: Preheat the oven to 400°F/200°C/gas 6. In a food processor, grind the hazelnuts to coarse bits. Add both flours and the salt and process to mix, then whirl in the oil. Add 7 tbsp/105 ml of the ice water and pulse just until the dough is lumpy looking. Scrape the dough out onto a floured counter, press it together, and divide it into four portions. Flatten them into disks. If the dough will not hold together well, break it apart and sprinkle it with the remaining 1 tbsp water, then press it together. Don't overwork the dough. On the floured counter, roll each disk out to a 7-in/17-cm round and transfer them carefully to a large, rimless baking sheet/tray covered with parchment/baking paper or a silicone baking sheet. Refrigerate.

2 TO MAKE THE FILLING: Heat a large frying pan over high heat. Add the oil and onions and stir, reducing the heat to medium as they start to sizzle. Add the eggplant/aubergine, squash, and zucchini/courgette. Sauté, stirring constantly, to soften the vegetables, about 5 minutes. Add the scallions/spring onions and rosemary. Cook, reducing the heat to medium-low if the vegetables stick to the pan, until the vegetables are browned and shrunken, about 5 minutes. Add the tomatoes, garlic, salt, and pepper to the pan, and stir for another couple of minutes, until the mixture is thick. Take the pan off the heat and let the filling cool to room temperature.

3 Remove the dough rounds from the refrigerator and mound one fourth of the vegetables in the center of each round, leaving a 1½-in/4-cm border. Fold the dough over the filling and loosely pleat it, being careful not to tear it.

4 Bake the tarts until the crusts are quite browned and crisp, about 20 minutes. Slide the tarts onto a serving platter or cutting board and let them stand for 5 minutes to firm up. Top the vegetables in the center with the basil and cut each tart into four wedges to serve one tart per plate.

Filling

1 tsp canola oil

1 cup/120 g chopped onions

1 small carrot, chopped

1 cup/215 g short-grain brown rice

4 small dried mushrooms

¼ cup/10 g dried hijiki or wakame, soaked

½ tsp toasted sesame oil

½ tsp salt

Dough

4 cups/500 g whole-wheat/wholemeal pastry/soft-wheat flour, plus extra for counter

½ tsp salt

6 tbsp/90 ml cold-press corn oil or canola oil

½ cup/120 ml ice water

SERVES 8

The pasty was invented by coal miners in England to make taking a lunch easy—just grab the pastry-wrapped food and go. In this delicious rendition, the filling is brown rice and sea veggies, a yummy and sustaining vegan meal.

Sea Veggie and Brown Rice Pasties

1 TO MAKE THE FILLING: In a medium saucepan, heat the canola oil over medium-high heat. Add the onions and carrot and sauté for about 10 minutes until the onions get some color. Add 3 cups/720 ml water, the rice, and mushrooms. Bring to a boil, then cover tightly and reduce the heat to low. Cook until the water is all absorbed, 35 to 45 minutes. Take the pan off the heat and let it stand, covered, for 5 minutes to finish steaming the rice. Dump the cooked rice into a large bowl. Pick out the mushrooms and discard them, and stir in the hijiki, sesame oil, and salt. Stirring it should make it kind of sticky, so it will hold together a bit.

2 TO MAKE THE DOUGH: Preheat the oven to 400°F/200°C/gas 6. Prepare a baking sheet/tray with parchment/baking paper or a light coating of oil. Mix together the flour and salt in a large bowl, then drizzle in the oil as you toss the flour with a fork. Add half of the ice water and stir just to mix, adding more water, 1 tbsp at a time, to make a soft dough. Divide the dough into eight portions and form each into an oval. On a lightly floured counter, roll out the dough pieces into 6-in/15-cm ovals. Scoop ½ cup/60 g of the filling into the center of each dough oval, then dampen the edge of the dough. Fold the dough over the filling, pressing the dough to seal, then use a fork to crimp the edge. Use the fork to poke a vent in the top of the pasties. Place them on the prepared baking sheet/tray.

3 Bake the pasties until browned and crisp, about 20 minutes. Refrigerate tightly covered for up to 5 days; reheat in microwave or bake at 375°F/190°C/gas 5.

1 tbsp extra-virgin olive oil

1 cup/120 g chopped onions

1 medium carrot, chopped

1 cup/140 g chopped sweet potatoes

½ cup/60 g chopped celery

½ cup/85 g edamame, thawed

½ cup/15 g fresh parsley, chopped

2 tbsp white wine

2 tsp chopped fresh sage

2 tbsp plus 2 cups/255 g unbleached all-purpose/plain flour, plus extra for counter

2 cups/480 ml unsweetened soymilk or rice milk

2 tbsp tamari or soy sauce

1 cup/115 g whole-wheat/wholemeal pastry/soft-wheat flour

½ tsp salt

¼ cup/60 ml coconut oil, frozen

2 tbsp cold-press corn oil

Ice water

SERVES 5

I grew up thinking that frozen pot pies were a treat, with their machine-made crust and gooey filling. Then I started making really good ones at home, like this one—with a tender, flaky crust and lots of veggies in the filling. Try it and you will love it.

Veggie-Edamame Pot Pies

1 Assemble five mini-pie pans/tins (4 in/10 cm). Preheat the oven to 400°F/200°C/gas 6. In a medium pot over medium heat, heat the olive oil. Add the onions and cook, stirring, until softened, about 5 minutes. Add the carrot, sweet potatoes, celery, and edamame and cook until they start to soften, stirring occasionally. Add the parsley, wine, and sage and bring to a boil. Cover tightly and steam until the vegetables are tender, about 5 minutes. Uncover and sprinkle on the 2 tbsp of all-purpose/plain flour, working it in with a heat-safe spatula. Stir for 2 minutes. Gradually stir in the milk and tamari and cook, stirring, until thickened. Take off the heat and cover to keep warm.

2 Mix the remaining 2 cups/255 g all-purpose/plain flour and the pastry/soft-wheat flour in a large bowl and stir in the salt. Grate in the coconut oil, then swirl in the corn oil while fluffing the flour with a fork. Gradually stir in enough ice water to make a firm but pliable dough. Divide the dough into five pieces and form each into a disk. On a lightly floured counter, roll each disk into a round ⅛ in/3 mm thick.

3 Meaure ½ cup/60 g of the filling into each of the pie pans/tins, then top with the dough rounds, letting the edges drape down the sides. Use a sharp paring knife to slash two vents in the top of each pie. Put the pans on a baking sheet/tray and bake until the filling is bubbling and the crusts are browned, about 20 minutes. Let them stand outside the oven for 5 minutes before serving.

2 tsp extra-virgin olive oil

2 cups/240 g chopped onions

1 tsp ground coriander

½ tsp ground cumin

½ tsp ground allspice

¼ tsp ground cayenne

14 oz/400 g canned/tinned chickpeas, drained and rinsed

1 cup/170 g pitted prunes, chopped

1 cup/170 g dried apricots, chopped

1 cup/240 ml coconut milk

1 tbsp freshly squeezed lemon juice

2 tsp lemon zest

½ tsp salt

½ cup/120 ml coconut oil or olive oil spray

10 sheets (about 12 by 17 in/30 by 42 cm) phyllo dough, thawed overnight in the refrigerator

½ cup/55 g whole almonds, toasted and coarsely chopped

SERVES 8

This flaky treasure chest of a pie is packed with sweet and tangy dried fruit, crunchy nuts, and a creamy sauce spiked with fragrant spices. It's sure to be a hit with anyone who likes lots going on in their food.

Moroccan Chickpea B'stilla

1 Preheat the oven to 400°F/200°C/gas 6. In a large frying pan, heat the olive oil over medium-high heat. Add the onions and sauté to caramelize them, reducing the heat to low once they soften, about 20 minutes total. When the onions are soft and golden, add the ground coriander, cumin, allspice, and cayenne and stir until fragrant, about 5 minutes over low heat. Add the chickpeas, prunes, apricots, milk, lemon juice, lemon zest, and salt and bring to a simmer. Cook until very thick, about 10 minutes. Remove the pan and let the filling cool to room temperature.

2 Oil a 9-in/23-cm round cake pan/tin. Place the phyllo on the counter, cover with a sheet of plastic wrap/cling film, and place a barely damp towel on top to hold it down. Place one sheet of phyllo on the pan. Brush or spray the dough with oil, pressing it into the pan. Place another sheet perpendicular to the first, and alternate, oiling each sheet as you go. When all are used, put the filling in the pan, top it with the almonds, and fold the phyllo over the top to cover. Use your fingertips to fluff and ruffle the top edges of the phyllo, and oil them generously. Cut a couple of slits in the top for steam.

3 Put the pan/tin on a baking sheet/tray and bake until the phyllo is golden brown and crisp, 35 to 40 minutes. Let the b'stilla cool for 5 to 10 minutes before slicing and serving.

6 oz/170 g firm tofu, drained and pressed (see page 68)

1 tsp white vinegar

1 tsp plus ⅓ cup/75 ml extra-virgin olive oil, plus more for brushing

½ tsp salt

2 lb/910 g fresh spinach, stemmed

½ cup/115 g tofu "cream cheese," at room temperature

2 tbsp dry bread crumbs

1 tsp dried oregano

½ tsp freshly cracked black pepper

4 sheets (about 12 by 17 in/30 by 42 cm) phyllo dough, thawed overnight in the refrigerator

SERVES 4

Spinach pie is such a classic Greek dish, and happily, one that is easily made vegan. Creamy tofu "cream cheese" and dense green spinach filling are topped with tangy tofu "feta," for a delicious phyllo pastry that is sure to satisfy. This would make a great starter for a meal of Greek Chickpea Stew with Rosemary over Spinach-Lemon Rice (page 235).

Spinach "Feta" Pies in Phyllo

1 Crumble the tofu into a small bowl and sprinkle it with the vinegar, 1 tsp of the oil, and the salt and toss to mix. Let it stand for 30 minutes.

2 Preheat the oven to 400°F/200°C/gas 6. Bring a big pot of water to a boil, then blanch the spinach leaves by boiling them for 2 minutes. Drain and run cool water over them, then wring them out until very dry. Wrap the spinach in a kitchen towel and place a heavy pan on top for about 30 minutes, to dry it completely.

3 Mince the spinach and put it in a medium bowl. Add the "cream cheese," bread crumbs, oregano, and pepper, and mix well.

4 Place the phyllo on the counter, cover with a sheet of plastic wrap/cling film, and place a barely damp towel on top to hold it down. Put the remaining ⅓ cup/75 ml oil in a cup with a pastry brush. Place one sheet of phyllo on the counter and brush it lightly with oil. Fold it in half lengthwise, and brush it with oil again. Form one fourth of the spinach mixture into a square in the center of the bottom of the sheet. Top it with one fourth of the "feta" and fold the sides in, then fold it up to make a neat square. Brush the packet with oil and place it on an oiled baking sheet/ tray. When all the pies are formed, bake them until the phyllo is deeply golden, about 20 minutes. Cut open and serve hot.

MAIN COURSES

353

1 lb/455 g globe eggplant/aubergine, peeled

1 large onion, diced

6 garlic cloves, peeled

2 tbsp extra-virgin olive oil

10 large sun-dried tomato halves, rehydrated

½ cup/15 g chopped arugula/rocket

3 tbsp chopped walnuts

¼ tsp salt

4 sheets (about 12 by 17 in/30 by 42 cm) phyllo dough, thawed overnight in the refrigerator

Olive oil spray

½ cup/55 g dry bread crumbs

SERVES 4

These savory strudels are crackling little packages of moist roasted eggplant and crunchy nuts. Arugula and sun-dried tomatoes perk up within the deep sweetness of the eggplant. Serve them with a green salad or the Mediterranean Chopped Herb and Bread Salad (page 203).

Savory Eggplant-Walnut Strudels

1 Preheat the oven to 400°F/200°C/gas 6. Cut the eggplant/aubergine into cubes ¾ in/2 cm wide. In a large roasting pan/tray, toss the eggplant/aubergine, onion, and garlic with the oil. Cover the pan with foil and roast for 20 minutes, then stir. Re-cover and roast until browned and soft, 20 minutes more. Scrape the roasted vegetables into a large bowl. Let them cool to room temperature, then add the tomatoes, arugula/rocket, walnuts, and salt. Stir to mix.

2 Place the phyllo on the counter, cover with a sheet of plastic wrap/cling film, and place a barely damp towel on top to hold it down. Take out one sheet of phyllo, spray it with oil, then top it with another sheet. Spray that sheet, then fold them in half. Spritz it again, then place half of the bread crumbs at one end to cover a third of the phyllo, leaving the ends bare to fold over. Put half of the eggplant mixture on top, then fold in the sides and pull the phyllo over the filling. Roll the whole thing up like a jelly/Swiss roll. Spray it with oil and place on an oiled baking sheet/tray, seam-side down. Form another strudel with the remaining filling and dough.

3 Cut three slashes across the tops of the strudels, then bake them until the phyllo is deep golden brown, about 20 minutes. Cut each strudel in half and serve hot.

1 tbsp coconut oil or
Earth Balance margarine

3 scallions/spring onions,
chopped

2 garlic cloves, minced

1 tbsp mild curry powder

¼ tsp ground allspice

1½ cups/100 g chopped
collards

1 cup/185 g chopped
fresh tomato

1 cup/110 g chopped
green beans

1 cup/170 g shelled
edamame, thawed

4 oz/115 g fresh button
mushrooms, sliced

1 medium serrano or
Scotch bonnet chile,
minced

1 cup/240 ml Basic
Vegetable Stock
(page 49)

¼ cup/60 ml coconut milk

2 tbsp tomato paste/
puree

8 oz/225 g dried whole-
wheat/wholemeal angel
hair pasta

½ tsp salt

SERVES 4

If you go to Jamaica, you will see Rasta Pasta on all the menus at tourist-oriented restaurants. It's Island-speak for a vegetarian pasta dish made with the native produce and spice. Rastafarians practice vegetarian cuisine as part of their religion, and make some amazingly delicious vegan food as a result. Coconut milk is so rich and delicious, the natives don't really eat much dairy, and spices grow abundantly.

Rasta Pasta

1 Bring a large pot of water to a boil. Set a large frying pan over high heat and let it warm for a minute, then add the coconut oil. Add the scallions/spring onions and sauté for 1 minute, then add the garlic and stir until fragrant. Add the curry powder and allspice and stir, then add the collards, tomato, green beans, edamame, mushrooms, and serrano. Stir-fry over medium-high heat until they are softened, about 3 minutes.

2 In a cup, stir together the stock, milk, and tomato paste/puree. Pour them over the vegetables in the pan and bring to a simmer. Cook, stirring until thickened.

3 Cook the pasta according to the package directions, and drain it well. Season the sauce with the salt and taste to adjust the seasoning. Add the pasta to the pan of sauce and toss well to coat the noodles. Remove from the heat and transfer the pasta to a serving bowl or platter. Serve hot.

½ cup/60 g semolina flour, plus extra as needed

1 cup/115 g unbleached all-purpose/plain flour, plus extra as needed

½ cup/65 g chickpea flour

¾ tsp salt

2 tsp extra-virgin olive oil, plus ¼ cup/60 ml

2 cups/60 g fresh arugula/rocket

½ cup/55 g pine nuts

1 garlic clove, peeled

2 large Roma tomatoes, diced

¼ cup/30 g Almond-Crumb "Parmesan" (page 46; optional)

SERVES 4

Making fresh pasta is a labor of love, but tender, tasty pasta is more than worth the effort. Making it without eggs is a snap, and a little chickpea flour adds an eggy flavor and color to the final dish. *Bellissimo!*

Fresh Linguine
with Arugula Pesto and Tomatoes

1 In a food processor or bowl, mix together the semolina, all-purpose/plain, and chickpea flours and ¼ tsp of the salt. Measure ½ cup/120 ml water and add the 2 tsp of oil. Add it to the flours and stir or pulse to mix. When the dough starts to come together, or when the processor is full of chunks that can be pressed together, take out the dough and knead it on a lightly floured surface. If it is too dry to form a dough, sprinkle in water by the teaspoon while kneading; you want a smooth, firm dough. Divide the dough into two portions and form each portion into a rectangle, then wrap them tightly. Let the dough stand for 1 hour at room temperature to absorb the water.

2 Use a pasta-rolling machine and plenty of unbleached flour to roll out each piece of dough. Roll it using the widest setting, then fold the dough into thirds, and roll it again. Repeat 10 times per piece on the widest setting to knead the pasta and develop the gluten, then reduce the roller numbers each time you pass the dough through the roller until it is ¹⁄₁₆ in/25 mm thick (not the very thinnest setting). If your roller has a linguine cutter, attach it and roll the dough through the cutter to make linguine noodles. Otherwise, dust the dough with semolina flour and roll it up, then slice it with a chef's knife into linguine noodles. Toss the cut noodles with semolina and pile them loosely on a baking sheet/tray. Let them stand at room temperature, uncovered, for up to 1 hour, tossing them with your fingers occasionally to make sure they are not sticking together.

3 Bring a big pot of salted water to a boil. In a food processor, grind the arugula/rocket, pine nuts, and garlic until finely minced. Add the remaining ¼ cup/60 ml oil and the remaining ½ tsp salt and puree until smooth.

4 Drop the pasta into the boiling water and cook just until it is tender and still al dente, 2 to 3 minutes. Drain and immediately toss it with the pesto and tomatoes. Serve the pasta topped with the Almond-Crumb "Parmesan," if desired.

2 tbsp extra-virgin olive oil, plus extra for garnish

1 lb/455 g chopped onions

1 cup/115 g unbleached all-purpose/plain flour

½ cup/55 g whole-wheat/wholemeal flour

½ cup/65 g chickpea flour

¾ tsp salt

¾ cup/180 ml plain rice milk or other milk

½ cup/15 g fresh parsley, finely chopped

SERVES 4

Making pasta and gnocchi can take a little time, but if you want to opt for the fastest possible fresh pasta, try spaetzle. Stir it up and grate it in, and you have a wonderfully springy, chewy kind of noodle. It's perfectly adorned with slow-caramelized onions and a sprinkling of parsley.

Handmade Spaetzle
with Caramelized Onions

1 In a large cast-iron frying pan, heat the oil over high heat. Add the onions and cook, stirring, until the onions begin to soften. Turn the heat to low, then stir occasionally for at least 45 minutes, until the onions shrink and turn caramel brown.

2 Bring a large pot of water to a boil over high heat. In a large bowl, combine all three flours and ½ tsp of the salt. Stir to mix, then stir in the milk. Knead in the bowl to make a soft, sticky dough.

3 Place a grater with large holes over the bowl you mixed the dough in. Cut the dough in half and grate one portion of the dough into the bowl. Drop the contents of the bowl into the boiling water. When the spaetzle float, scoop them out with a slotted spoon and put them in a colander. Repeat with the second portion of the dough. Toss the finished spaetzle with a drizzle of oil.

4 When the onions are butter soft, stir in the remaining ¼ tsp of salt and then add the onions to the spaetzle. Add the parsley and toss; serve hot.

2 tbsp extra-virgin olive oil

12 oz/340 g cubed sweet potato

1 cup/120 g chopped onions

2 tbsp chopped fresh sage

2 garlic cloves, chopped

¼ cup/30 g pecans, finely chopped

6 oz/170 g dried whole-wheat/wholemeal angel hair pasta

2 tsp salt

SERVES 4

This pasta is cooked using a low-water method that I read about in Harold McGee's column in the *New York Times*. Cooking the angel hair in a small amount of salted water, then adding some of the wheaty-tasting cooking water to the sauce is a scientist's way to make the pasta extra-delicious. The sauce is all mine, though, combining sweet potato and pecans in an unexpected but delectable way.

Braised Sweet Potato and Pecan Pasta

1 In a large frying pan over high heat, heat the oil. Add the sweet potato and onions and stir. Lower the heat to medium-low as the vegetables start to sizzle. Sauté slowly to cook the sweet potato thoroughly. When several pieces are tender (pierce with a paring knife to test), add the sage and garlic and raise the heat to medium-high for a couple of minutes. Add the pecans, take the pan off the heat, and hold until the pasta is ready.

2 While the vegetables are cooking, rinse the dried pasta in cold water, then put it in a wide frying pan with 2 qt/2 L cold water and the salt. You may have to break the pasta in half to fit it in the pan. Bring to a boil over high heat, stirring constantly. Set a colander over a large bowl, and when the pasta is al dente, after 8 to 10 minutes, drain the pasta into the bowl. Measure ¼ cup/60 ml of the pasta water and add it to the vegetables, and then add the drained pasta. Toss the mixture in the pan over medium heat until the pasta is well coated. Serve immediately.

Lemon-Thyme Oil

½ cup/120 ml extra-virgin
olive oil

2 oz/55 g thyme sprigs

4 garlic cloves, sliced

2 large lemons, zested

2 cups/280 g cherry
tomatoes

½ cup/15 g fresh parsley,
chopped

2 garlic cloves, chopped

½ tsp salt

8 oz/225 g dried whole-
wheat/wholemeal angel
hair pasta

Freshly cracked black
pepper

¼ cup/30 g Almond-
Crumb "Parmesan"
(page 46; optional)

SERVES 4

Make the flavored oil for this recipe a day in advance. It makes enough for two batches of the pasta—or you can use it in other dishes where vibrant lemon and herbal thyme would be a good accent. The pasta is simplicity itself; once you add the concentrated flavor of the oil, you hardly need anything else.

Angel Hair and Tomatoes
in Lemon-Thyme Oil

1 TO MAKE THE OIL: In a small saucepan, combine the oil, thyme, garlic, and lemon zest. Over low heat, slowly bring it to barely bubbling. This will take about 30 minutes. Remove the pan from the heat and let the oil cool completely. Transfer it to a jar and let it steep overnight. The next day, strain the oil into a clean jar, pressing on the thyme to extract all the oil. Discard the solids. The extra oil will keep for up to 1 month in the refrigerator, tightly covered.

2 Chop the tomatoes, then take small handfuls of them and squeeze out the pulp over a bowl. Discard the pulp. In a medium serving bowl, mix together the tomatoes, parsley, ¼ cup of the lemon-thyme oil, the garlic, and salt. Let the mixture stand for 15 minutes and up to 3 hours.

3 When ready to serve, bring a large pot of salted water to a boil. Cook the pasta according to the package direc-tions. Drain it and toss with the tomato mixture from the bowl. Crack pepper over it all. Serve hot, with the Almond-Crumb "Parmesan," if desired.

2 tbsp extra-virgin olive oil

3 cups/340 g finely chopped cabbage

1 cup/110 g shredded carrots

½ cup/60 g chopped onions

½ cup/55 g slivered/flaked almonds

2 tbsp fresh thyme, chopped

2 garlic cloves, minced

¼ cup/60 ml white wine

½ tsp salt

6 oz/170 g dried whole-wheat/wholemeal or spinach farfalle

SERVES 4

This is peasant food, with hearty cabbage and carrots providing delicious sustenance for pennies. A diet loaded with cruciferous vegetables like cabbage is high in anti-cancer compounds, so enjoy them in pasta as well as in your salads.

Almond-Cabbage Farfalle

1 Bring a large pot of salted water to a boil for the pasta. Set a large cast-iron frying pan over high heat, and when it is hot, add the oil. Quickly add the cabbage, carrots, and onion. Stir and cook over high heat.

2 When the cabbage starts to soften, lower the heat to medium-low. Stir for 5 minutes, then add the almonds, thyme, and garlic. Cook, stirring constantly, until the almonds and cabbage have golden spots and the vegetables are tender. Add the wine and salt and let the wine boil off (it will evaporate quickly).

3 While the cabbage is cooking, cook the pasta according to the package directions, until it is al dente. Drain the pasta well, then toss it with the cabbage in the pan. Stir to mix, and serve hot.

2½ lb/1.2 kg kabocha or other winter squash

1 cup/40 g sun-dried tomato halves

1 tbsp extra-virgin olive oil

2 cups/240 g chopped onions

¼ cup/7 g chopped fresh sage

4 garlic cloves, minced

1 tsp dried thyme

1 cup/240 ml dry white wine

½ cup/60 g plus 2 tbsp unbleached all-purpose/ plain flour

6 cups/1.4 L almond milk or other milk

1 tsp salt

12 no-cook dried lasagna noodles

SERVES 8

This dramatic lasagna is made possible with the invention of no-cook lasagna noodles, which soak up the juicy sauce and meld into a gorgeous stack of pasta goodness. I used Whole Foods brand noodles, which are about half as long as standard, dried lasagna noodles, and are also egg-free.

Winter Squash and Sun-Dried Tomato Lasagna

1 Preheat the oven to 400°F/200°C/gas 6. Peel and cut the squash into ½-in/12-mm cubes. Rehydrate the tomatoes in hot water, then drain and squeeze them out. Chop the tomatoes and reserve.

2 In a large frying pan with a lid, heat the oil over medium-high heat. Add the onions and sauté for about 5 minutes to soften. Add the squash cubes and sauté just enough to brown the edges a bit. Add the sage, garlic, and thyme and cook until fragrant, about 3 minutes. Add the wine, bring to a boil, and cover for about 5 minutes, or until the squash is just tender. Don't cook it until the squash is falling apart.

3 Sprinkle the flour over the squash in the pan and turn to coat it. Cook, stirring gently, until the flour is smooth and lightly toasted, about 3 minutes. Gradually stir in the milk, bringing it to a simmer. Add the salt and cook until the mixture is thick. Remove it from the heat.

4 Lightly oil a 9-by-13-by-3-in/23-by-33-by-7.5-cm baking pan, then cover the bottom of the pan with lasagna noodles. Four noodles should be enough; they expand as they bake. Add a layer of about one third of the squash mixture and half of the sun-dried tomatoes. Cover with another layer of noodles, pressing them down to make an even layer. Cover with half of the remaining squash sauce and the remaining tomatoes. Top with noodles to cover, press down, and cover with the remaining squash sauce.

5 Cover with foil and bake for 25 minutes, then uncover and bake until the lasagna is bubbly and golden on top, 20 minutes more. Remove it from the oven. Let stand for 10 minutes before serving.

Filling

18 oz/510 g firm tofu, drained and pressed (see page 68)

1 lb/455 g fresh spinach, stemmed

14 oz/400 g canned/tinned artichoke hearts, drained and rinsed

2 tbsp nutritional yeast

2 tbsp white miso

1 tbsp extra-virgin olive oil

1 tsp salt

Sauce

1 tbsp extra-virgin olive oil

1 cup/120 g chopped onions

1 medium carrot, diced

2 garlic cloves, minced

14 oz/400 g canned/tinned diced tomatoes

1⅓ cup/415 ml tomato sauce/puree

1 tbsp agave syrup or other sweetener

1 tsp dried oregano

1 tsp fennel seeds

½ tsp salt

8 no-boil dried lasagna noodles

1 cup/160 g broccoli florets

2 tbsp sliced/flaked almonds or pine nuts

SERVES 6

Lasagna is one of those dishes everyone loves, and this version is no exception. Canned artichokes and spinach puree with tofu give it a big flavor punch and ricotta-like texture. Crunchy almonds on top make the perfect finish. If you prefer, you can substitute Basic Veggie Spaghetti or Pizza Sauce (page 120) for the sauce here.

Artichoke and Spinach Lasagna

1 Preheat the oven to 400°F/200°C/gas 6.

2 TO MAKE THE FILLING: In a food processor or blender, process the tofu until smooth. Add the spinach, artichoke hearts, yeast, miso, oil, and salt and process until smooth. Reserve.

3 TO MAKE THE SAUCE: In a large pot, heat the oil over medium-high heat. Add the onions and carrot and sauté, reducing the heat to medium-low when the vegetables start to sizzle. Cook until the onions are soft and lightly golden, about 5 minutes. Add the garlic and sauté for 1 minute. Add the tomatoes and tomato sauce/puree, agave syrup, oregano, fennel, and salt and bring to a boil over medium-high heat. Lower the heat and simmer until thick, about 5 minutes.

4 Oil a 9-in/23-cm square baking dish. Spread ½ cup/120 ml of the sauce in the pan, and lay two lasagna noodles on top—it's okay if they are not touching, because they expand in the oven. Scoop up a heaping 1 cup/120 g of the tofu mixture and dollop it over the noodles, then spread it evenly and sprinkle with ⅓ cup/55 g of the broccoli. Drizzle ¼ cup/60 ml sauce over it all. Repeat with the noodles, filling, broccoli, and sauce, pressing down each layer to make it even. On the last layer, layer two noodles, 1 cup/120 g tofu mixture, and the remaining ⅓ cup/55 g of the broccoli. Don't top the tofu mixture with sauce, but put on the last 2 lasagna noodles. Spread the remaining sauce across the top, making sure all the pasta is covered. Finish by sprinkling the almonds on top.

5 Bake until the lasagna bubbles all around the edges of the pan and the nuts are browned, about 40 minutes. Let stand for 10 minutes before serving, if you can wait! This makes a great leftover. To reheat, cover and bake in an oven at 375°F/190°C/gas 5 for about 25 minutes.

Filling

8 oz/225 g Swiss chard/silverbeet, stemmed and chopped

4 oz/120 g fresh spinach, chopped

2 tbsp extra-virgin olive oil

1 cup/120 g chopped onions

1 tbsp minced garlic

1 tsp lemon zest

6 oz/170 g firm tofu, drained and pressed (see page 68)

1 tbsp cornstarch/cornflour

1 tsp salt

1½ tbsp freshly squeezed lemon juice

40 eggless round gyoza or wonton skins

Sauce

3 tbsp extra-virgin olive oil, plus extra for cooking ravioli

½ cup/55 g chopped walnuts

2 garlic cloves, peeled

¼ cup/7 g chopped fresh parsley

½ cup/120 ml Basic Vegetable Stock (page 49)

½ tsp salt

SERVES 4

Look for the round gyoza or wonton wraps without eggs; they are usually a little thicker than the square wonton skins. These are worth the work, I promise! You'll end up with pillowy ravioli stuffed with greens and lemon and coated with a savory walnut sauce that adorns but does not distract from the delicious filling.

Chard and Spinach Ravioli
with Parsley-Walnut Sauce

1 TO MAKE THE FILLING: Bring a big pot of water to a boil. Add the chard/silverbeet to the boiling water. After 3 minutes, add the spinach and cook for 2 minutes more. Drain, rinse with cool water, and wring out the leaves thoroughly. Spread the greens on a kitchen towel, then fold up the towel and put a heavy pot on top of it for about 10 minutes to squeeze out all the water.

2 In a small frying pan over high heat, warm the oil. Add the onions and sauté for 5 minutes, reducing the heat as the onions soften. When the onions are golden and sweet, add the garlic, sauté for 1 minute, then remove the pan from the heat. Add the zest and let the mixture cool.

3 In a small bowl, crush the tofu with the cornstarch/cornflour and salt, and add it to the onion mixture with the lemon juice. Finely mince the greens and add them to the bowl. Mix well.

4 Bring another big pot of water to a boil for cooking the ravioli. Get a cup of cool water (for sealing them) and a piece of parchment/baking paper, a silicone baking mat, or floured baking sheet/tray (to put the ravioli on as you assemble them). On a counter or cutting board, spread twenty of the wrappers. Using about 1 tbsp filling for each, form a ball and place it in the center of each wrap. Dampen the wrap's edges with a little water and top with another wrap, carefully pressing the edges together to seal. Transfer each of the ravioli to the prepared pan. If not cooking immediately, cover with plastic wrap/cling film for up to 5 hours.

5 TO MAKE THE SAUCE: In a large frying pan, heat the oil. Add the walnuts and stir over medium heat until the nuts are lightly toasted and fragrant. Add the garlic and stir for 1 minute, then remove the pan from the heat.

6 In a food processor or blender, mince the parsley. Add the walnuts and oil from the pan and finely grind them. Add the stock and salt and process to make a smooth puree. Return the sauce to the pan.

7 When the pasta water is boiling, salt it, then drop in the ravioli (about eight at a time). Don't crowd the pan. Drizzle in some oil to keep them from sticking together. When they float, cook for 4 minutes more (reduce the heat to a simmer so they don't boil to pieces). Remove each ravioli with a skimmer and put it in a strainer, then transfer it to the pan with the walnuts, tossing gently to coat. Cook all the ravioli, toss them with sauce, and serve.

1½ lb/680 g winter squash

4 tbsp/60 ml extra-virgin olive oil, plus extra for pan

½ cup/60 g chopped onion

2 garlic cloves, minced

4 oz/115 g firm tofu, drained, pressed (see page 68), and pureed

½ tsp salt

44 eggless wonton skins

½ cup/60 g Almond-Crumb "Parmesan" (page 46)

SERVES 4

Making homemade ravioli is much easier with wonton skins, which are usually eggless as well. Creamy winter squash and sweet sautéed onions make a filling that is rich and delicious enough to need almost no sauce.

Squash Ravioli
with Almond-Crumb Topping

1 Preheat the oven to 400°F/200°C/gas 6. Cut the squash in half lengthwise and scoop out the seeds. Place it, cavity-side down, on an oiled baking sheet/tray and bake until tender when pierced with a paring knife, 20 to 30 minutes. Let the squash cool, then scoop out the flesh and puree it.

2 In a medium sauté pan, heat 1 tbsp of the oil over medium-high heat. Add the onion and sauté until it softens, then reduce the heat to low and cook for 10 minutes to bring out its sweetness. Add the garlic and squash puree, and raise the heat to medium, stirring and scraping the pan to reduce the squash to two thirds of its original volume, or about 1 cup/235 ml. Let the mixture cool to room temperature. Stir in the tofu puree and salt.

3 Bring a big pot of water to a boil for cooking the ravioli. Get a cup of cool water (for sealing them) and a piece of parchment/baking paper, a silicone baking mat, or floured baking sheet/tray (to put the ravioli on as you assemble them). On a counter or cutting board, spread 22 of the wrappers. Using 1 tbsp filling for each, form a ball and place it in the center of each wrap. Dampen the wrap's edges with a little water and top with another wrap, carefully pressing the edges together to seal. Transfer each of the ravioli to the prepared pan. If not cooking immediately, cover with plastic wrap/cling film for up to 5 hours.

4 When the pasta water is boiling, salt it, then drop in the ravioli (about eight at a time). Don't crowd the pan. Drizzle a little oil in the water to keep them from sticking. When they float, cook for 4 minutes more (reduce the heat to a simmer so they don't boil to pieces). Remove each one with a skimmer and put it in a strainer, then transfer it to a serving platter and drizzle with the remaining 3 tbsp oil, tossing gently to coat. Don't pile up the ravioli or they may stick and tear. Cook all the ravioli, toss them with the Almond-Crumb "Parmesan," and serve.

2 tbsp plus 1 tsp extra-virgin olive oil, plus extra for pan

2 tbsp unbleached all-purpose/plain flour

1 tbsp chickpea flour

1½ cups/360 ml plain soymilk or other milk

½ cup/120 ml white wine

½ tsp salt

1 pinch cayenne

6 oz/170 g dried whole-wheat/wholemeal penne

14 oz/400 g canned/tinned artichoke hearts, quartered

3 oz/85 g kale or Swiss chard/silverbeet, stemmed and chopped

1 medium carrot, chopped

2 tbsp capers, rinsed

½ cup/55 g panko or other dry bread crumbs

SERVES 4

"Al Forno" is the Italian, romantic-sounding way of saying this is a baked pasta dish. It really evokes the bubbling sauce and crusty edges that develop when a dish of creamy pasta meets a hot oven. This is a great make-ahead dish; you can put it together a day or two ahead, and when you walk in the door on a busy night, slide it into a hot oven for a genuinely fabulous meal.

Creamy Artichoke Pasta al Forno

1 Bring a large pot of salted water to a boil for cooking the pasta. Lightly oil a 2-qt/2-L baking dish. If you are serving the dish today, preheat the oven to 400°F/200°C/gas 6.

2 In a 4-qt/3.8-L saucepan, whisk together 2 tbsp of the oil and both flours. Set the pan over medium heat and stir constantly until the mixture starts to bubble. Cook, stirring, until the mixture is thick and bubbly, about 3 minutes. Remove the pan from the heat and gradually whisk in the milk, a little at a time, until it makes a smooth paste. Whisk in the wine, salt, and cayenne and set the pan over medium heat, whisking until the mixture comes to a bubble. Don't let it boil—just simmer it gently until thickened. Remove the pan from the heat and let it stand until the pasta is ready.

3 Drop the penne into the boiling water and set a timer for 5 minutes (less than the package directions say). When the timer goes off, add the artichoke hearts, kale, and carrot and cook until the pasta is al dente. Drain thoroughly, shaking the colander to get all the water off the greens.

4 Transfer the pasta and vegetables to the baking dish, add the capers, and cover everything with the reserved sauce. Toss gently to coat.

5 In a small bowl, toss the panko with the remaining 1 tsp oil, then sprinkle it over the casserole. (You can cover and refrigerate the casserole overnight at this point.) Bake until the casserole is golden and bubbly, about 25 minutes. If the casserole has been refrigerated, cover for the first 25 minutes, then uncover and bake for 20 minutes longer. Serve hot.

6 oz/170 g dried lasagna noodles, broken into rough pieces

3 tbsp extra-virgin olive oil

2 tbsp coarsely chopped fresh sage

4 cups/140 g chopped, stemmed Swiss chard/silverbeet

1 cup/140 g cherry tomatoes, halved

3 garlic cloves, minced

½ cup/60 g Almond-Crumb "Parmesan" (page 46)

SERVES 4

This is a great way to use up broken lasagna noodles, which look like triangular maltagliati pasta and make an interestingly random and toothsome pasta when cooked. The chard and tomatoes cook quickly for a tasty sauce, taking just minutes in the pan.

Maltagliati
with Swiss Chard and Sage

1 Bring a large pot of salted water to a boil. When the water is boiling, add the noodles and stir well. Cook according to the package directions, until the noodles are al dente. Drain them, and if holding for more than a couple of minutes, toss with some oil to prevent sticking.

2 In a large frying pan, heat the oil over medium-high heat. Add the sage and sauté for 1 minute. Add the chard/silverbeet, tomatoes, and garlic and sauté until the greens have softened to taste.

3 Toss the pasta in the pan with the greens and serve topped with the Almond-Crumb "Parmesan."

2 tbsp extra-virgin olive oil

1 cup/120 g chopped onions

2 garlic cloves, minced

½ tsp red pepper flakes

7 oz/200 g bottled roasted red peppers/capsicums, drained and rinsed

¼ cup/35 g kalamata olives, halved and pitted

2 medium pepperoncini, drained and sliced

2 tbsp tomato paste/puree

2 tbsp capers, rinsed

½ tsp dried oregano

½ tsp dried basil

¼ tsp salt

6 oz/170 g dried linguine or other long pasta

Almond-Crumb "Parmesan" (page 46; optional)

SERVES 4

This version of the classic puttanesca sauce is a celebration of the various forms that a pepper can take, from roasted and pickled to dried hot flakes. It's a zingy-hot specialty that you can make from a well-stocked pantry, so keep the ingredients on hand and you are halfway to dinner!

Pasta Puttanesca
with Roasted Red Peppers

1 Bring a large pot of water to a boil. In a large saucepan over medium heat, warm the oil. Add the onions and sauté until soft and golden, about 10 minutes. Add the garlic and pepper flakes and cook for 3 minutes more. Squeeze the liquid from the peppers/capsicums and mince them, then add them to the pan with the olives, pepperoncini, tomato paste/puree, capers, oregano, basil, and salt. Reduce the heat to medium-low and simmer until thick.

2 Cook the pasta in the boiling water according to the package directions, then drain. Add it to the pan with the sauce and toss to coat. Serve hot, seasoning with Almond-Crumb "Parmesan," if desired.

¾ cup/110 g diced carrot

¼ cup/30 g chopped onion

3 oz/75 g silken tofu

3 tbsp cold-press corn oil

2 tbsp chickpea flour

2 tbsp unbleached all-purpose/plain flour

1½ cups/360 ml plain almond milk

6 tbsp/15 g nutritional yeast

1½ tsp salt

1 tsp rice vinegar

11 oz/315 g dried elbow macaroni

Vegetable oil spray

1½ cups/170 g dried whole-wheat/wholemeal bread crumbs

SERVES 6

If you grew up eating macaroni and cheese from a box, you can't help but have fond memories of eating yellow-sauced, tangy macaroni with a spoon. You will find this to be a pretty satisfying substitute, with buttery corn oil and cheesy nutritional yeast standing in for that powdered cheese.

Mac and "Cheese"

1 Bring a large pot of water to a boil. Preheat the oven to 400°F/200°C/gas 6. Prepare a steamer and bring the water to a simmer.

2 Steam the carrot and onion until very soft, about 10 minutes. Transfer them to a blender or food processor, add the tofu, and mince, scraping down the sides to chop everything as finely as possible.

3 In a small saucepan, heat 2 tbsp of the oil and stir in the chickpea flour. Stir over medium heat for 1 minute, then remove the pan from the heat. Sprinkle in the all-purpose/ plain flour and stir until smooth. Return the pan to the heat and cook for a couple of minutes. Remove it from the heat again, and gradually whisk in the milk, then cook over medium-low heat until thickened. Pour the sauce into the blender with the tofu mixture. Add ¼ cup/10 g of the yeast, the salt, and vinegar and process until smooth. Scrape down the sides frequently and puree again, until it is very creamy.

4 Cook the pasta in the boiling water according to the package directions. Drain it well. Coat a 2-qt/2-L baking dish with oil spray and add the macaroni, then pour on the sauce and fold it into the pasta. In a bowl, mix together the bread crumbs, the remaining 2 tbsp yeast, and the remaining 1 tbsp oil, then sprinkle them over the macaroni. Bake in the middle of the oven until the top is toasted and the sauce is bubbly, about 20 minutes. Serve warm.

¼ cup/60 ml extra-virgin olive oil

1 small zucchini/courgette, diced

1 small yellow squash, diced

1 medium onion, chopped

2 garlic cloves, minced

1 tsp paprika

¼ tsp crumbled saffron

¾ cup/180 ml Basic Vegetable Stock (page 49)

¾ cup/180 ml white wine

¼ tsp salt

8 oz/225 g dried orzo

½ cup/15 g fresh parsley, minced

1 large lemon, zested

SERVES 4

Orzo, sometimes called *riso*, is a rice-size pasta that cooks to a satiny mouthful of tiny, slippery noodles. In this dish, the saffron paints the whole plateful a gorgeous gold, and imparts that unmistakable scent. It's not too saucy, just coated with flavored oil and reduced wine, and studded with a lot of vegetables.

Saffron Orzo
with Yellow Squash and Zucchini

1 Bring a pot of water to a boil.

2 In a large frying pan set over medium-high heat, warm the oil. Add the zucchini/courgette, squash, and onion and sauté until the vegetables are softened and beginning to brown. Add the garlic, paprika, and saffron and stir for 1 minute. Add the stock and wine; bring everything to a rapid boil. Add the salt and boil until the liquid is reduced by half and syrupy, about 5 minutes.

3 Cook the pasta in the boiling water according to the package directions, then drain. If the sauce seems too dry, add a splash of wine. Toss the pasta in the pan with the vegetables. Serve it in wide, flat bowls, topped with the parsley and lemon zest.

1 tbsp extra-virgin olive oil

1½ cups/180 g chopped
onions

2 garlic cloves, chopped

4 oz/115 g fresh button
mushrooms, sliced

½ large green bell
pepper/capsicum,
chopped

1 Roma tomato, chopped

1 tsp paprika, preferably
smoked (pimentón)

1 pinch saffron

1½ cups/360 ml Basic
Vegetable Stock (page 49)

¼ cup/60 ml red wine

4 medium artichoke
hearts from a jar, drained
and quartered

6 oz/170 g dried whole-
wheat/wholemeal angel
hair pasta

½ tsp salt

1½ cups/335 g Tempeh
"Chorizo" (page 40), cut
into chunks

SERVES 6

Fideua is like paella, but it's a pasta dish that is
cooked with flavorful broth instead of water, making
the pasta extra tasty. As soon as the fine strands
are al dente, the mélange goes in a baking dish for
a quick bake, creating a crusty top that finishes the
dish beautifully. You will need a batch of Tempeh
"Chorizo," unless you have a good packaged version
that you like.

Spanish Fideua Pasta
with Saffron

1 Preheat the oven to 425°F/220°C/gas 7. Lightly oil a 2-qt/
2-L baking dish. In a large pot over high heat, warm the oil
briefly. Add the onions and sauté until softened, about 5 minutes. Add the garlic and stir for 1 minute, then add the mushrooms, bell pepper/capsicum, tomato, paprika, and saffron
and stir. Lower the heat if the food starts to stick. When the
pot is dry and the vegetables are tender, add the stock and
wine and bring to a boil.

2 Add the artichoke hearts. Break the dried pasta in half
and drop it into the pan with the salt. Stir to moisten all the
pasta. Cover and cook according to the package directions,
about 4 minutes. Uncover and stir a few times. When the
pasta is al dente, transfer the contents of the pan to the baking dish, cover with the "chorizo," and bake for 15 minutes.
When the top is crusty (but not too dried out), remove from
the oven and serve the casserole right away.

2 tsp extra-virgin olive oil

1 cup/120 g chopped onions

1 tbsp unbleached all-purpose/plain flour

½ cup/120 ml plain almond milk or other milk

¼ cup/60 ml dry white wine

2 cups/60 g fresh basil

1 garlic clove

2 medium avocados

8 oz/225 g dried whole-wheat/wholemeal spaghetti

1½ cups/280 g chopped fresh tomatoes

½ tsp salt

Almond-Crumb "Parmesan" (page 46; optional)

SERVES 4

Avocados provide an unctuous, creamy sauce for this pasta, flecked with fresh basil and chopped tomatoes. The fabulous but fleeting creamy green color will darken in about an hour's time, so you need to eat it right away.

Creamy Avocado Pasta
with Tomatoes and Basil

1 Bring a large pot of water to a boil. In a large frying pan, heat the oil over medium-high heat. Add the onions and stir, cooking until they start to soften, then reduce the heat to low and cook for about 10 minutes. When the onions are soft and golden, sprinkle them with the flour and stir, cooking over medium heat until smooth and toasty, about 4 minutes. In a cup, combine the milk and wine, then whisk them into the onion mixture. Cook until the sauce is thick, then remove the pan from the heat.

2 In a blender or food processor, pulse the basil and garlic to mince. Add the flesh of 1 avocado, and puree until smooth, then add the sauce mixture from the pan. Process until smooth, then return the sauce to the pan.

3 Cook the pasta in the boiling water according to the package directions, drain, rinse it with hot water, then drain well. Dice the remaining avocado. Add the pasta to the pan, along with the diced avocado and tomatoes. Add the salt and toss the pasta in the pan over medium heat until the pasta and sauce are heated through. Serve warm, seasoning with Almond-Crumb "Parmesan," if desired.

1 large avocado, cubed

½ cup/15 g fresh parsley, chopped

8 large sun-dried tomato halves, rehydrated and chopped

2 tbsp extra-virgin olive oil

8 oz/225 g dried whole-wheat/wholemeal spaghetti

2 cups/140 g snap peas or snow peas/mangetouts

½ tsp salt

½ tsp freshly cracked black pepper

¼ cup/30 g pistachios, finely chopped

SERVES 4

In the simple spirit of *pasta al aglio*, where good pasta is simply tossed with olive oil and garlic, this pasta is coated with oil instead of a sauce. It's loaded with goodies, too, including tender avocado cubes with a melting quality that might remind you of cheese.

Green and Red Spaghetti

1 Bring a large pot of water to a boil. In a serving bowl, combine the avocado, parsley, tomatoes, and oil.

2 Cook the pasta in the boiling water according to the package directions, adding the peas for the last 2 minutes. When the pasta is al dente, drain it well, and return it to the hot cooking pot. Dump in the avocado mixture. Over low heat, toss the pasta and sauce to heat them through and to let the oil absorb into the pasta. Add the salt and pepper.

3 Serve the pasta hot, topped with the pistachios.

2 tbsp Earth Balance margarine

2 tbsp unbleached all-purpose/plain flour

2 garlic cloves, minced

1½ cups/360 ml plain vegan creamer

¼ cup/60 ml white wine

½ cup/15 g fresh chervil or parsley

1 tsp lemon zest

¼ tsp thyme

¼ tsp salt

Freshly cracked black pepper

4 oz/115 g dried fusilli or fettuccine

8 asparagus spears, trimmed and sliced

1 cup/65 g snow peas/mangetouts, strings removed

1 cup/160 g broccoli florets

1 small carrot, julienned

Almond-Crumb "Parmesan" (page 46; optional)

SERVES 4

This rich, creamy pasta is a true expression of the primavera, or spring. Snow peas, asparagus, and crisp tender vegetables are bathed in a creamy, lemon-zest-brightened sauce. Go ahead and double it if you want to share.

Pasta Primavera
with Chervil

1 Bring a large pot of water to a boil. In a large frying pan over medium-high heat, melt the margarine. Add the flour and garlic, whisking to mix them thoroughly. Cook over medium heat until smooth and lightly toasted, 2 to 3 minutes. Remove the pan from the heat and gradually whisk in the creamer and wine, then return the pan to the heat. Continue whisking and cooking until the sauce is thickened, about 2 minutes. Whisk in the chervil, lemon zest, thyme, and salt and season with pepper. Cover the pan and keep warm off the heat.

2 Cook the pasta in the boiling water according to the package directions, adding the asparagus, peas, broccoli, and carrot for the last 2 minutes. Thoroughly drain the pasta and vegetables and return them to the pasta pot, then cover them with the sauce. Toss to mix. Serve the pasta hot, seasoning with the Almond-Crumb "Parmesan," if desired.

3 tbsp extra-virgin olive oil

1 medium shallot, finely chopped

2 large garlic cloves, minced

1 large lemon, zested

½ cup/120 ml white wine

¼ cup/60 g green olive paste

8 oz/225 g dried whole-wheat/wholemeal spaghetti

1 lb/450 g fresh asparagus, trimmed and sliced

1 large carrot, shredded

1 cup/30 g fresh chervil or parsley, finely chopped

½ tsp salt

Freshly cracked black pepper

SERVES 4

This springtime pasta is a celebration of green—with asparagus, green olives, and chervil—accented with shreds of orange carrot. Look for green olive paste (sometimes called pate olive verdi) at your grocery, but if you can't find it, just process some good-quality green olives to a paste. Parsley can stand in for chervil, a delicate herb that bolts at the first heat of summer. Serve any leftover olive paste on bread.

Asparagus Pasta
in Green Olive–Chervil Sauce

1 Bring a large pot of water to a boil. In a large frying pan over medium heat, warm the oil. Add the shallot and garlic and sauté until they are softened. Add the lemon zest and cook for a few seconds, stirring. Add the wine and raise the heat to high to reduce the sauce to a syrupy consistency. Add the olive paste and turn off the heat.

2 Cook the pasta in the boiling water according to the package directions. Add the asparagus and carrots for the last 4 minutes. Drain well but do not rinse; the starch will thicken the sauce a tiny bit.

3 Dump the hot pasta into the sauce, add the chervil and salt, season with pepper, and toss well. Serve hot.

¼ cup/60 ml extra-virgin olive oil
12 large garlic cloves, peeled
1 cup/120 g chopped onions
½ cup/75 g chopped carrots
1 tbsp chopped fresh rosemary
¾ cup/180 ml white wine
½ cup/65 g kalamata olives, pitted and halved
14 oz/400 g canned/ tinned diced tomatoes, with juice
2 cups/60 g arugula/ rocket, chopped
1 dash red pepper flakes
½ tsp salt
8 oz/225 g dried whole-wheat/wholemeal penne
Almond-Crumb "Parmesan" (page 46; optional)

SERVES 3

Roasting a few cloves of garlic for pasta is a great way to add caramelized flavor, but you don't have to turn on the oven to get it. In this sauce, cloves of garlic are pan-roasted in olive oil, flavoring the oil and producing butter-soft, sweet cloves. Have no fear of vampires or colds, because garlic is a potent germ-fighter.

Pan-Roasted Garlic, Kalamatas, and Tomato Sauce over Penne

1 In a large frying pan, heat the oil for a few seconds. Halve the garlic lengthwise and add to the oil. Add the onions, carrots, and rosemary. Stir, and when the oil is bubbling, reduce the heat to medium or medium-low, just to keep the oil bubbling slightly. Cook, stirring occasionally, for 7 minutes. The garlic should be nearly tender when pierced with a knife. Add the wine and olives, turn the heat to high, and boil for about 4 minutes, until the sauce is reduced to a syrup.

2 Add the tomatoes, arugula/rocket, and pepper flakes. Simmer until the sauce is thick and the greens wilted. Add the salt.

3 Bring a large pot of salted water to boil. Cook the pasta according to the package directions and drain well, then toss it with the sauce in the pan. Serve it hot, seasoning with the Almond-Crumb "Parmesan," if desired.

2 tbsp extra-virgin olive oil

1 cup/120 g chopped onions

1 rib celery, chopped

1 medium carrot, chopped

4 cups/600 g chopped broccoli florets and stems

1 medium tomato, chopped

1 cup/240 ml white wine

2 garlic cloves, sliced

¼ cup/50 g silken tofu

½ cup/55 g chopped walnuts

½ tsp salt

Soy creamer (optional)

8 oz/225 g dried whole-wheat/wholemeal rotini

SERVES 4

On the first night of a trip to Tuscany, our hotel presented a buffet of incredible traditional food. One dish was pasta tossed with minced, very soft broccoli; it was simple, delicious, and unforgettable. I am sure it didn't contain tofu, but this version borrows that soft broccoli sensation to great effect.

Roman Broccoli-Walnut Pasta

1 Bring a large pot of water to a boil. In a large frying pan over high heat, warm the oil and add the onions, celery, and carrot. Sauté to soften the vegetables, 5 minutes. Add the broccoli, tomato, wine, and garlic. Bring to a boil, then reduce the heat and simmer until the pan is almost dry.

2 While the sauce simmers, put the tofu in a food processor or blender and puree it until smooth. Carefully transfer the sauce to the food processor or blender and add the walnuts and salt. Put the lid on and hold it down with a folded kitchen towel so that no splatters will burn you. Puree the sauce, adding soy creamer if it is very thick.

3 Cook the pasta in the boiling water according to the package directions and drain. Return the sauce to the frying pan, add the hot pasta, and toss. Serve hot.

3 large jalapeños

6 oz/170 g dried orzo

2 tbsp extra-virgin olive oil

8 oz/225 g seitan, drained and sliced

1 large red bell pepper/capsicum, sliced

1 tsp dried oregano

1 pinch cayenne

1 cup/120 g chopped onions

¼ cup/30 g unbleached all-purpose/plain flour

2 cups/480 ml rice milk or other milk

2 tbsp reposado tequila

2 tsp lime zest

½ tsp salt

SERVES 4

Tequila does two things in this pasta—adds its own flavor and then performs the alchemy of bringing out flavors from the other ingredients. *Reposado* means the tequila is aged, giving it more flavor for cooking. This is modeled after a South American dish, and it is a nice one to serve alongside other foods from that area, like the South American Sweet Potato Salad (page 208).

Seitan Pasta
in Tequila Cream Sauce

1 Preheat the broiler/grill and bring a large pot of water to a boil. Put the jalapeños on a baking sheet/tray and broil/grill them until blackened all over, 1 to 2 minutes per side. Put them in a small saucepan and cover tightly to steam. After 10 minutes, uncover and let the jalapeños cool, then peel them and cut them into long strips. Reserve. Cook the orzo in the boiling water according to the package directions. Drain and rinse it.

2 In a large frying pan, heat 1 tbsp of the oil and sauté the seitan and bell pepper/capsicum until the pepper is tender and the seitan is browned. Add the oregano and cayenne and toss for 1 minute. Transfer to a plate and cover loosely to keep warm.

3 Add the remaining 1 tbsp oil and the onions to the pan. Sauté over medium heat until the onions are golden, then work in the flour with a heat-safe spatula. Stir until the flour is smooth and lightly toasted, a couple of minutes. Combine the milk, tequila, and lime zest in a cup and whisk them into the pan. Cook, whisking, until thickened. Add the salt along with the seitan mixture and simmer briefly to heat everything through. Serve the vegetables and sauce over the orzo with the jalapeño strips on top.

2 small dried mushrooms (any variety)
2 tbsp unbleached all-purpose/plain flour
1 tbsp extra-virgin olive oil
8 oz/225 g seitan, thinly sliced
3 oz/75 g fresh shiitake mushroom caps, thinly sliced
2 garlic cloves, minced
1½ cups/360 ml plain soymilk or other milk
¼ cup/60 ml white wine
1 tbsp tomato paste/puree
1 tbsp nutritional yeast
1 tsp white miso
1 pinch ground nutmeg
1 pinch cayenne
1 pinch ground turmeric
½ cup/15 g fresh parsley or basil
½ tsp salt
Olive oil spray
8 oz/225 g fresh portobello caps, thinly sliced
8 oz/225 g dried fettuccine
¼ cup/30 g chopped walnuts, toasted

SERVES 4

This pasta is an opportunity to amplify and showcase the umami of mushrooms, with layer after layer of intense mushroom flavor. For the fungus lovers among us, this creamy, meaty pasta is a plateful of heaven.

Creamy Triple-Mushroom Fettuccine
with Walnuts

1 Bring a large pot of water to a boil. In a spice or coffee grinder, grind the dried mushrooms to a fine powder. Put them in a small bowl and stir in the flour. Reserve.

2 Heat the oil in a large saucepan over medium-high heat. Add the seitan and shiitakes and stir until browned, then add the garlic. When the vegetables start to sizzle, sprinkle them with the flour mixture and stir to combine. Keep stirring and scraping until the flour is well moistened and the mushroom powder is very fragrant.

3 As the mushroom-seitan mixture cooks, whisk together the soymilk, wine, tomato paste/puree, yeast, miso, nutmeg, cayenne, and turmeric in a measuring cup. Remove the pan from the heat and use a heat-safe spatula to stir in about one fourth of the soymilk mixture until smooth. Continue to add the soymilk mixture in fourths, stirring after each addition until all is incorporated. Stir in the parsley and salt and keep warm.

4 Heat a cast-iron frying pan over high heat. When the pan is hot, coat it with oil spray and sear the portobello mushroom slices, stirring as they shrink and brown. Cook the fettuccine in the boiling water according to the package directions and drain well.

5 In a serving bowl, toss the pasta with the sauce. Top with the seared mushrooms, sprinkle with the toasted walnuts, and serve.

Creamy Triple-Mushroom Fettuccine with Walnuts FACING PAGE

Three-Nut "Cheese" Quesadillas with Fresh Mango Salsa PAGE 307

Moroccan Chickpea B'stilla
PAGE 352

Sweet Potato Gnocchi
with Creamy Almond-Sage Sauce
PAGE 400

Nutty Curry-Stuffed Squashes
PAGE 428

Chocolate Sandwich Os
PAGE 474

Cherry and Apricot
Kanten-Cube Fruit Salad
PAGE 508

Indonesian Rice Noodles with Long Beans and Seitan FACING PAGE

- 2 tbsp canola oil
- 8 oz/225 g seitan, chopped into bite-size pieces
- 8 oz/225 g fresh long beans, chopped into 1-in/2.5-cm pieces
- 1 large carrot, thinly sliced
- 4 large shallots, chopped
- 1 large fresh red Thai chile, chopped
- 3 garlic cloves, minced
- 1 in/2.5 cm peeled fresh ginger, finely chopped
- 2 medium limes; 1 zested and juiced, 1 quartered
- 1 tsp ground coriander
- ½ tsp ground turmeric
- 6 oz/170 g dried rice vermicelli
- ¾ cup/180 ml coconut milk
- 2 tbsp soy sauce
- 1 tsp dark miso
- 1 tsp molasses/treacle
- ½ cup/15 g fresh Thai basil, julienned
- ¼ cup/30 g dry-roasted peanuts, chopped

SERVES 6

Long beans, also called yard-long beans or asparagus beans, are thinner and obviously longer than the usual green bean, and they have a wonderful nutty taste. Seek them out at Asian markets for this great noodle dish, kissed with coconut and spice. You can also use green beans.

Indonesian Rice Noodles
with Long Beans and Seitan

1 Bring a big pot of water to a boil.

2 In a wok or large frying pan over high heat, warm the oil. Add the seitan, beans, carrot, shallots, half of the chile, the garlic, ginger, lime zest, ground coriander, and turmeric. Stir-fry until the vegetables are crisp-tender. Taste and add more chile, if desired.

3 Cook the noodles in the boiling water according to the package directions. Drain and rinse them.

4 In a cup or medium bowl, whisk together the milk, soy sauce, miso, and molasses/treacle. Add the mixture to the vegetables and bring everything to a boil. Stir in 1 tbsp of lime juice. Add the drained noodles and turn them in the pan, coating them well with sauce. Cook until the sauce is thick and clinging to the noodles. Add the basil and serve, topped with the peanuts and with lime wedges on the side.

6 oz/170 g dried rice noodles

¼ cup/60 ml coconut milk

1 cup/140 g cherry tomatoes, halved

4 large scallions/spring onions, diagonally sliced

4 oz/115 g broccoli florets

1 medium carrot, julienned

¼ cup/60 ml freshly squeezed lime juice

2 tbsp sugar or agave syrup

2 tbsp tamari or soy sauce

1 tbsp minced peeled fresh ginger

2 tsp lime zest

2 garlic cloves, minced

1 cup/30 g fresh Thai basil, slivered

½ cup/55 g roasted peanuts, finely chopped

SERVES 4

Zesty lime and the anise flavor of Thai basil make a simple noodle dish into a real pick-me-up. Rice noodles are the Thai way, but you can use whole-wheat angel hair for a whole-grain alternative.

Thai Rice Noodles
with Lime-Basil Sauce

1 Bring a pot of water to a boil. Separate the noodles as well as you can—don't worry if they are woven together, they will separate in the water. Put them in a colander so they are ready to cook.

2 In a large frying pan, heat the milk over medium-high heat, then add the tomatoes, scallions/spring onions, broccoli, and carrot and toss. Bring them to a simmer just to soften them slightly, then add the lime juice, sugar, tamari, ginger, lime zest, and garlic. Keep stirring the vegetables in the pan until they are just crisp-tender, about 3 minutes.

3 Cook the noodles in the boiling water according to the package directions. Drain the noodles and wrap them in a kitchen towel to dry completely, then toss them into the pan with the vegetables. Stir to coat with the sauce and heat through. Add the basil and peanuts and toss to mix. Serve immediately.

- 8 oz/225 g dried whole-wheat/wholemeal angel hair pasta
- 2 tbsp canola oil
- ½ lb/225 g Mock Beef (page 37) or seitan, drained and sliced into strips
- 1 cup/120 g sliced onions
- 2 tbsp minced peeled fresh ginger
- 3 garlic cloves, minced
- 2 ribs celery, diagonally sliced
- 1 large carrot, diagonally sliced
- 1 large ripe tomato, chopped
- 1 tsp garam masala
- 1 tsp curry powder
- 2 cups/60 g fresh spinach, chopped
- 2 tbsp soy sauce
- Sriracha sauce or other hot sauce

SERVES 4

Tibet is wedged between India and China and, because of that, Tibet's food is a natural blend of those cuisines. Hence, warming spices married to soy sauce and noodles in the wok. This would go well with an appetizer of Sesame-Lemon-Shiitake Potstickers (page 150) or Chinese Tofu Skin and Carrot Salad (page 178).

Tibetan "Beef" Fried Noodles

1 Bring a large pot of water to a boil. Cook the pasta according to the package directions. Rinse with warm water so the noodles will be warm for the wok and drain well.

2 Heat a well-seasoned wok over high heat until hot. Swirl in the oil. Sear the mock beef, stirring until well browned. Use a wok tool or slotted spoon to transfer to a plate, leaving the oil in the wok. Add the onions, ginger, and garlic. Stir, cooking until the onions are limp. Add the celery, carrot, tomato, garam masala, and curry and stir-fry until almost dry, about 2 minutes. Add the spinach, cooked pasta, seared mock beef, and soy sauce, and stir over high heat until the spinach is soft and all the ingredients are hot. Serve with hot sauce on the side.

3 tbsp tahini paste

2 tbsp toasted sesame oil

3 tbsp tamari or soy sauce

2 tbsp rice vinegar

1 tbsp sugar

1 tbsp minced peeled fresh ginger

3 garlic cloves, minced

1 tsp Sriracha sauce or other hot sauce

12 oz/340 g dried linguine or fettuccine

1 medium cucumber, seeded and sliced into half-moons

¼ cup/30 g roasted peanuts, chopped

SERVES 6

These are the classic cold noodles, the ones you eat from a white cardboard box with chopsticks, but made with simple, clean ingredients. Great warm or cold, they have a creamy sesame sauce spiked with just a touch of heat.

Simple Sesame Noodles
with Cucumber

1 Bring a large pot of water to a boil. In a medium bowl, combine the tahini with the sesame oil and stir to a paste, then stir in the tamari. Whisk in the vinegar, sugar, ginger, garlic, and hot sauce.

2 Cook the noodles in the boiling water according to the package directions, then drain them very well. It doesn't hurt to wrap them in a kitchen towel and gently roll them around to absorb excess water so the sauce is not diluted. Add the noodles to the bowl of sauce. Add the cucumber and toss to coat. Serve topped with the peanuts.

2 tbsp extra-virgin olive oil, plus extra for pan

2 cups/230 g dry bread crumbs

1 tbsp lemon zest

3 tbsp Earth Balance margarine or oil

5 tbsp/35 g unbleached all-purpose/plain flour

3 cups/720 ml plain rice milk or other milk

1 tbsp white miso

8 oz/225 g dried eggless noodles

8 oz/225 g cherry tomatoes, halved

1 cup/120 g frozen peas

1 oz/30 g dried dulse, rinsed

½ tsp seafood seasoning, such as Old Bay (optional)

2 tbsp chopped fresh parsley

SERVES 4

The familiar old-fashioned casserole is a vegan treat with dulse—a gorgeous purple sea vegetable. Dulse is harvested in British Columbia, and is an especially mild but very nutritious kind of seaweed. It adds just enough of a taste of the sea to remind you a little of tuna, and if you use the seafood seasoning, you'll get a little of the spice of a crab boil.

Not-Tuna Casserole
with Dulse

1 Preheat the oven to 375°F/190°C/gas 5. Bring a large pot of water to a boil.

2 In a small saucepan, heat the oil over medium-low heat. Add the bread crumbs and lemon zest and stir until hot and toasted. Spread the crumbs on a plate to cool.

3 In a medium saucepan, melt the margarine over low heat. Whisk in the flour off the heat, then place the pan over medium heat and stir until smooth and toasted, about 3 minutes. Take the pan off the heat and gradually work in the milk, whisking in a little at a time. Whisk the miso in with the last of the milk. Keep whisking over medium heat until the mixture comes to a boil. Reduce the heat and whisk for a couple of minutes more, until thick. Take the pan off the heat and cover to keep warm.

4 Lightly oil a 2 qt/2L baking dish. Cook the noodles in the boiling water according to the package directions. Drain the noodles and put them in a large bowl. Add the white sauce, tomatoes, and peas. Mix gently and transfer half to the prepared baking dish. Chop the dulse coarsely and mix it with the seafood seasoning (if using), then sprinkle it over the noodles. Top with the remaining noodles. Scatter the lemon crumbs and parsley over the surface and bake until the casserole is bubbly and toasted, about 30 minutes. Serve immediately.

1 lb/455 g Yukon gold potatoes, peeled

1 cup/115 g unbleached all-purpose/plain flour, plus extra for counter

½ tsp salt

⅛ tsp ground nutmeg

2 tbsp extra-virgin olive oil, plus extra for gnocchi

½ cup/120 ml Chianti or other red wine

½ oz/15 g dried porcini mushrooms

1 small onion, chopped

½ rib celery, chopped

4 oz/115 g fresh cremini/brown mushrooms, sliced

2 garlic cloves, minced

14 oz/400 g tomato puree/sieved tomatoes

1 large bay leaf

Salt

Freshly cracked black pepper

SERVES 6

If you want to feel warm all over on a winter's night, try this incredibly satisfying gnocchi. I like to use Yukon gold potatoes to give the gnocchi a buttery taste and a light yellow glow like you would get with yolk-based gnocchi. The porcini sauce is so good you will be glad that there is plenty of it.

Tuscan Potato Gnocchi
with Porcini Ragout

1 Steam or boil the potatoes until they are tender and put them through a ricer or mash them thoroughly while hot. Let them cool completely to room temperature—but do not refrigerate them.

2 When the potatoes are completely cool, move them to a lightly floured counter. Add the flour, salt, and nutmeg. Work it all together, kneading to make a pliable, soft dough. Bring a large pot of salted water to a boil. Reduce the heat just a little so the water is not at a full boil. Test the dough by pinching off a nugget, rolling it in flour, then dropping it into the simmering water. When it floats, fish it out and let it cool. If the gnocco fell apart, knead more flour into the remaining dough. You want to add the smallest amount of flour possible to get gnocchi that stays together. Too much flour makes them tough. Keep testing a gnocco as you add flour.

3 Divide the dough into four pieces. Roll each piece out on the counter into a snake ¾ in/2 cm thick, using plenty of flour on the counter. Cut each snake into ¾-in/2-cm bits and shape each by pressing it across the tines of a fork to make traditional grooves. Put them on a lightly floured baking sheet/tray. (At this point, you can cover the tray and refrigerate overnight.) Drop twelve gnocchi at a time into the water. Sweep a slotted spoon across the bottom of the pan after 1 minute, in case some are sticking. Remove the gnocchi with a slotted spoon as they rise to the surface. Drain the gnocchi in a colander, then toss them with some olive oil, gently shaking the colander back and forth to coat them. Repeat with each batch of gnocchi, tossing each batch with oil in the colander.

4 Bring the wine to a boil in a small saucepan and add the dried mushrooms. Cover, remove from the heat, and let the mushrooms soften. When the mushrooms are soft, wring them out and mince; reserve the wine. In a medium saucepan over medium heat, warm the oil. Add the onion and celery and sauté until soft. Add the fresh mushrooms and sauté. Add the reconstituted porcinis to the sauté with the garlic and cook until soft, a few minutes. Add any remaining wine from rehydrating the mushrooms, the tomato puree/sieved tomatoes, and the bay leaf. Bring the sauce to a simmer and cook until it is thick. Season with salt and pepper.

5 Sauce the gnocchi to taste and serve. If you like a lighter sauce, there will be some delicious leftover sauce for another meal. Cover and refrigerate for up to 4 days and reheat as needed.

Gnocchi

1 lb/455 g sweet
potatoes

1¼ cups/140 g unbleached
all-purpose/plain flour,
plus extra for counter

¼ cup/30 g chickpea
flour

½ tsp salt

1 pinch ground nutmeg

Sauce

½ cup/55 g slivered/
flaked almonds, soaked
in water overnight

1 tbsp extra-virgin olive
oil or Earth Balance
margarine

½ cup/60 g diced onion

2 tbsp chopped
fresh sage

3 garlic cloves, minced

½ cup/120 ml white wine

½ cup/120 ml vegan
creamer or other milk

¼ tsp salt

Freshly cracked black
pepper

Olive oil

SERVES 4

These deep orange gnocchi are like little pillows from heaven. Tender and comforting, the gnocchi are swimming in a creamy sage sauce, sending the classic sweet potato–sage combination into a whole new dimension.

Sweet Potato Gnocchi
with Creamy Almond-Sage Sauce

1 TO MAKE THE GNOCCHI: Preheat the oven to 400°F/ 200°C/gas 6. Roast the sweet potatoes until they are very soft, about 30 minutes, and let them cool to room temperature. Bring a large pot of salted water to a boil. Reduce the heat just a little so the water is not at a full boil.

2 In a food processor, puree the sweet potatoes until very smooth, then scrape the puree onto a lightly floured counter. Add both flours, the salt, and nutmeg and mix together with your hands. When all the ingredients are well incorporated, the dough should be soft but not so sticky that you can't handle it.

3 Pinch off a small blob and roll it in flour. Drop it into the simmering water and wait for it to bob to the surface. When it floats, cook it for 30 seconds, and then fish it out with a slotted spoon and drop it into a colander to cool slightly. Test the gnocco. If it fell apart in the pot or is falling apart or melt-ing after it has cooked, knead more flour into the remaining dough. You want to add the smallest amount of flour possible to get gnocchi that stays together. Too much flour makes them tough. Keep testing a gnocco as you add flour.

4 When you have it right, divide the dough into four portions and roll each out into a snake ¾ in/2 cm thick, using plenty of flour on the counter. Use a bench knife or metal spatula to cut the snakes into ¾-in/2-cm bits. If desired, shape each gnocco across the back of the tines of a fork to make traditional grooves. Flour a baking sheet/tray and move the gnocchi to it as they are done, leaving room between the pieces. Let them sit to dry for up to 1 hour, or cover tightly and refrigerate for up to 1 day.

5 TO MAKE THE SAUCE: Drain the almonds and pat them dry, then transfer them to a blender. In a small saucepan over medium heat, warm the oil. Add the onion and sauté until the onion is golden, at least 10 minutes, and longer if you have time. When the onion is soft and golden, add the sage and garlic and cook until fragrant. Add the wine and bring to a boil.

6 Pour the sauce into the blender with the almonds and puree the mixture until smooth. Add the creamer gradually until the mixture is smooth. Season with the salt and pepper. Return the sauce to the saucepan over low heat and hold until the gnocchi are done.

7 Set up a colander over a bowl for the finished gnocchi. Drop about twelve gnocchi at a time into the simmering water. Sweep a slotted spoon across the bottom of the pan after 1 minute, in case some are sticking. When the gnocchi float, let them bob for 30 seconds and then scoop them out and into the colander. Drizzle the gnocchi with oil, gently shaking the colander back and forth to coat them. Repeat with each batch of gnocchi, tossing each batch with oil in the colander.

8 Transfer each finished batch of gnocchi to a large serving bowl. When all the gnocchi are cooked, heat the sauce gently, stirring constantly. Pour it over the gnocchi and toss to coat. Serve them immediately, or let them cool, refrigerate, and reheat in a 400°F/200°C/gas 6 oven.

1 tbsp extra-virgin olive oil, plus extra for pan

½ cup/100 g short-grain brown rice

1 tbsp vegetable bouillon/stock paste (optional)

1 tbsp dark miso

1 large onion, chopped

1 medium carrot, quartered and chopped

1 cup/115 g raw cashews

1 cup/30 g fresh parsley

½ cup/65 g chickpea flour

¼ cup/50 g cashew butter or almond butter

½ tsp salt

½ tsp freshly cracked black pepper

3 large roasted red peppers/capsicums from a jar, drained

2 tbsp tomato paste/puree

1 tbsp balsamic vinegar

SERVES 8

A zesty glaze tops this chewy loaf, packed with nutritious brown rice, cashews, and nut butter for a filling meal. Try a slab in a sandwich with a few more roasted peppers the next day.

Cashew–Brown Rice Loaf
with Red Pepper Glaze

1 Preheat the oven to 375°F/190°C/gas 5. Oil a 4-by-10-in/ 10-by-25-cm loaf pan/tin. In a small saucepan with a good lid, combine the rice, 1 cup/240 ml water, the bouillon/stock (if using), and the miso. Place the pan over high heat and bring it to a boil, then reduce the heat to low and cover. Simmer until the water is absorbed, 40 to 45 minutes. Take the pan off the heat and let it stand, covered, for 5 minutes to finish steaming the rice. Open and let the rice cool to room temperature.

2 In a large frying pan over high heat, warm the oil. Add the onion and carrot and sauté, reducing the heat to low, until the onion is soft and golden, about 10 minutes. In a food processor, grind the cashews to a fine mince, but not a paste. Scrape the cashews into the pan with the onions. Keep stirring and sautéeing until the nuts are lightly colored. In the processor, mince the parsley. Add the contents of the frying pan to the processor along with the flour, cashew butter, salt, and pepper. Pulse to mix. Add the rice and pulse to mix, but don't puree it. Scrape the mixture into the prepared pan, smooth the top, and bake for 30 minutes.

3 While the loaf bakes, puree the peppers/capsicums with the tomato paste/puree and vinegar. When the timer goes off, pour the puree on top of the loaf, spread it evenly, and bake until the topping is thick and browned and the loaf is firm, about 30 minutes more. Let the loaf cool for 5 minutes before slicing.

Olive oil

3 cups/750 g French lentils/Puy lentils, soaked and rinsed

1 lb/455 g Yukon gold or red potatoes, cubed

1 stem fresh rosemary

4 slices whole-wheat/wholemeal bread

4 garlic cloves, peeled

1 cup/15 g fresh parsley

¼ cup/50 g almond butter

3 tbsp gluten flour

2 tbsp fresh thyme, chopped

2 tbsp plus ½ cup/150 ml Dijon mustard

1 tsp freshly cracked black pepper

1 tsp dried tarragon

½ tsp salt

SERVES 12

The French love their lentils, usually using them as a bed or side, but always adding plenty of fresh herbs and garlic. This flavorful feast is great as is, or in sandwiches the next day. This makes a big, tall loaf, so if you want to make it in a smaller pan, halve the recipe and bake it for thirty minutes less.

Provençal Herbed Lentil Loaf

1 Preheat the oven to 400°F/200°C/gas 6. Oil a 4-by-10-in/10-by-25-cm loaf pan/tin.

2 Place the lentils in a large pot with a lid and add the potatoes, rosemary, and 10 cups/2.4 L water. Bring to a boil over high heat, then reduce the heat and cook, covered, until the lentils are falling apart, 40 to 50 minutes. Drain in a colander. Do not rinse, but gently turn the lentils to drain them well, and let them cool to room temperature.

3 In a food processor, pulse the bread to fine crumbs, then scrape them out into a large bowl. Grind the garlic in the food processor. Put half of the lentil mixture into the processor with the garlic and add the parsley, almond butter, flour, thyme, 2 tbsp of the mustard, the pepper, tarragon, and salt and process until smooth and well mixed. Transfer the puree to the bowl with the crumbs and add the remaining lentil mixture. Use your hands to mix well, squeezing to mash it all together.

4 Transfer the lentil mixture to the prepared pan and smooth the top. Bake for 1 hour, then spread the remaining ½ cup/120 ml mustard on top of the loaf and bake until firm and browned, about 20 minutes more. Let the loaf cool for 10 minutes before serving. It will slice best if stored overnight in the refrigerator.

½ cup/120 ml Basic
Vegetable Stock
(page 49)

¼ cup/20 g quinoa

½ cup/55 g pumpkin
seeds, finely chopped

2 tsp extra-virgin olive oil

4 large tomatoes, sliced

1 cup/90 g corn, 2 ears,
kernels cut off

¼ cup/7 g fresh basil,
shredded

½ tsp salt

Freshly cracked black
pepper

SERVES 4

Quinoa is so tasty, it makes a simple bake of tomatoes and basil into something really interesting.
This is a good way to celebrate the best heirloom
tomatoes as summer progresses.

Tomato-Quinoa Gratin
with Pumpkin Seeds

1 Preheat the oven to 400°F/200°C/gas 6. In a 1-qt/1-L saucepan, bring the stock to a boil. Add the quinoa, cover tightly,
reduce the heat to low, and cook until the liquid is absorbed,
about 15 minutes. Take it off the heat and fluff the quinoa
with a fork; transfer it to a plate to cool. When the quinoa is
cool, mix in the pumpkin seeds and reserve.

2 In a shallow 2-qt/2-L baking dish, spread a little of the oil,
then layer the tomatoes, and sprinkle the corn over the tomatoes. Cover with the basil, then the quinoa mixture and season
with the salt and pepper. Drizzle over the remaining oil.

3 Bake until the pumpkin seeds are toasted and the gratin
are bubbling, 25 to 30 minutes. Serve hot.

1 tbsp canola oil or Earth Balance margarine, plus extra for pan

1½ lb/680 g sweet potatoes

1½ cups/360 ml rice milk or other milk

1 tbsp dark miso

2 cups/240 g chopped onions

2 cups/285 g fresh cremini/brown or button mushrooms, sliced

2 large carrots, chopped

2 ribs celery, chopped

½ cup/120 ml white wine

2 tbsp chickpea flour

¼ tsp salt

2 cups/130 g chopped mustard greens or kale

1 cup/170 g shelled edamame, thawed

SERVES 6

The shepherd must have found a soybean plant in this fun version of his pie. Sweet potatoes boost the orange antioxidants and carotenoids, and greens and edamame meld with mushrooms in the creamy sauce.

Sweet Potato and Edamame Shepherd's Pie

1 Preheat the oven to 400°F/200°C/gas 6. Lightly oil a 2-qt/2-L baking dish.

2 Bake the sweet potatoes until they are very tender. Let them cool until you can handle them. Strip off the skins, drop the flesh into a food processor, and puree until smooth, scraping down the sides to get it all. Add ½ cup/120 ml of the milk and the miso and puree to mix well. Reserve.

3 In a large pot, heat the oil over medium-high heat. Sauté the onions, mushrooms, carrots, and celery, stirring frequently, until the carrots are crisp-tender and the mushrooms are softened. Add the wine and bring to a boil, stirring until the pan is dry. Sprinkle the flour over the contents of the pan and stir to coat the vegetables evenly. Drizzle in the remaining 1 cup/240 ml milk, add the salt, and stir constantly to mix well. Cook until the sauce is thickened, about 5 minutes. Stir in the greens and edamame and transfer the contents to the prepared pan. Dollop the sweet potato mixture over the filling and spread it to make an even topping.

4 Bake uncovered, until it is bubbling around the edges and browned on top, 30 to 40 minutes. Serve hot, or let cool and refrigerate; reheat slices in a toaster oven or microwave.

MAIN COURSES

Filling

1 tbsp Earth Balance margarine or oil, plus extra for baking dish

2 cups/240 g chopped onions

1 medium carrot, chopped

3 tbsp unbleached all-purpose/plain flour

2 tbsp chopped fresh sage

2 cups/70 g chopped collard greens

1 cup/240 ml plain soymilk or other milk

1 cup/240 ml Basic Vegetable Stock (page 49)

½ tsp salt

½ tsp freshly cracked black pepper

Dumplings

½ cup/55 g unbleached all-purpose/plain flour

½ cup/55 g whole-wheat/wholemeal pastry/soft-wheat flour

½ cup/70 g cornmeal

1 tsp dried thyme

½ tsp baking powder

½ tsp salt

2 tbsp Earth Balance margarine or coconut oil, chilled

½ cup/120 ml plain soymilk or other milk

SERVES 4

A homey casserole, topped with tender dumplings, is just the thing for a wintery day. Those cornmeal-flecked biscuit gems draw you in, and hearty collard greens provide leafy support from below.

Creamy Collards
with Cornmeal Dumplings

1 Preheat the oven to 400°F/200°C/gas 6. Lightly grease an 8-in/20-cm square baking dish.

2 TO MAKE THE FILLING: In a large frying pan over medium-high heat, melt the margarine. Add the onions and carrot and sauté, lowering the heat as they start to sizzle. Cook until the onions are golden and the carrot is tender, about 5 minutes. Add the flour and sage and stir to coat the vegetables. Cook for a few minutes to toast the flour, then add the collards and stir until they are bright green and slightly softened, about 2 minutes. Stir in the milk and stock and stir constantly over medium heat until the liquids bubble and thicken. Stir in the salt and pepper and transfer the mixture to the baking dish. Cover to keep warm.

3 TO MAKE THE DUMPLINGS: In a large bowl, mix together both flours, the cornmeal, thyme, baking powder, and salt. Grate or cut in the margarine. Quickly stir in the milk just to mix.

4 Distribute tablespoon-size pieces of dough over the surface of the collard mixture in the pan. There should be about eighteen dumplings. Bake until the sauce is bubbly and the dumplings are puffed and golden, about 25 minutes. Serve hot.

¼ cup/60 ml Basic
Vegetable Stock (page 49)

¼ cup/60 ml freshly
squeezed lime juice

¼ cup/60 ml tamari or
soy sauce

2 tbsp sugar

2 tsp cornstarch/
cornflour

2 tbsp canola oil

12 oz/340 g firm tofu,
drained and pressed (see
page 68)

1 tsp red pepper flakes

1 tbsp minced peeled
fresh ginger

2 garlic cloves, minced

8 oz/225 g dried wide
rice noodles (*banh pho*)

4 large scallions/
spring onions, cut into
1-in/2.5-cm pieces

4 oz/115 g bean sprouts

½ cup/55 g roasted
peanuts, chopped

½ cup/15 g cilantro/
fresh coriander

SERVES 4

The national dish of Thailand must surely be pad thai, in all its variations. This mélange of soft rice noodles, chiles, lime, and crunchy peanuts is so tasty you may find yourself eating it cold out of the refrigerator the next morning—I have!

Tofu Pad Thai

1 Bring a large pot of water to a boil. In a cup, mix together the stock, lime juice, tamari, sugar, and cornstarch/cornflour.

2 In a wok, heat the oil over high heat, and crumble the tofu into the pan. Add the pepper flakes and fry until the tofu is browned, stirring constantly. Add the ginger and garlic and stir for 1 minute.

3 Meanwhile, cook the noodles in the boiling water for 5 minutes, or until al dente. Drain them. Stir and add the stock mixture to the pan with the tofu. Stir and quickly add the noodles, scallions/spring onions, and sprouts. Stir-fry gently until the liquids are thickened and the noodles are coated, 1 to 2 minutes. Serve immediately, topped with the peanuts and cilantro/fresh coriander.

8 oz/225 g tempeh

1½ cups/360 ml white wine

¾ tsp salt

¼ tsp freshly cracked black pepper

1 tbsp extra-virgin olive oil

8 oz/225 g fresh button mushrooms, sliced

¼ cup/30 g chopped onion

2 garlic cloves, minced

2 tsp chopped fresh rosemary

1 tsp Dijon mustard

½ cup/120 ml Basic Vegetable Stock (page 49)

1 tsp cornstarch/cornflour

¼ cup/7 g chopped fresh parsley

SERVES 4

Searing the tempeh and reducing the wine for a pan sauce are the techniques that amp up this classic sauté. Herbs and mushrooms adorn the chewy tempeh "steaks."

Tempeh "Steaks"
with Mushroom–White Wine Sauce

1 Slice the tempeh carefully by holding it flat on a cutting board and using a chef's knife to cut parallel to the board to make two thin sheets of tempeh. Set up a steamer using 1 cup/240 ml of the wine instead of water, and bring the wine to a simmer. Put the tempeh in the steamer and steam until it's moistened, 5 minutes, then take it out to cool. Sprinkle with ¼ tsp each of the salt and pepper. Measure the remaining wine in the pot to use for the sauce. You should have ½ cup/120 ml. Add more wine to the cup if necessary.

2 Heat the oil in two large nonstick or cast-iron frying pans. Add the tempeh and cook until quite golden, about 1½ minutes on each side. Take the tempeh out with a slotted spatula and put it on a plate; cover to keep warm.

3 To the same pan, add the mushrooms, onion, garlic, and rosemary and sauté until softened and lightly browned. In a cup, whisk together the wine and mustard, then add them to the pan. Add the remaining ½ tsp salt and stir over medium-high heat until bubbly. In the same cup, whisk together the stock and cornstarch/cornflour, then pour them into the pan. Whisk and stir until the sauce is thickened.

4 Divide the tempeh among plates and cover it with sauce. Sprinkle the parsley over each plate and serve.

1 lb/455 g kale, leaves stripped from the stems

1 tbsp extra-virgin olive oil

1 cup/170 g shelled edamame, thawed

1 large carrot, quartered lengthwise and sliced

2 tbsp chopped fresh rosemary

2 garlic cloves, sliced

1 tbsp balsamic vinegar

¼ tsp salt

Freshly cracked black pepper

SERVES 4

Throw some deep green leaves, bright orange carrots, and snappy edamame into a hot pan with rosemary and olive oil, and you have a fast panful of Mediterranean goodness. This is a fast way to get some vegetables and protein on the table, and a side of whole-wheat bread or brown rice would complete an easy meal.

Mediterranean-Style Kale, Carrot, and Edamame Sauté

Chop the kale leaves and cut the stems into small slices. Place a large frying pan over high heat and, when hot, add the oil. Swirl the pan to coat, then add the edamame, kale stems, and carrots. Sauté for about 3 minutes to soften them. Add the rosemary and stir for another minute. Add the kale leaves and garlic and keep stirring, turning the kale until it is softened and deep green. Add the vinegar and salt and stir; the vinegar will cook off almost instantly. Take the pan off the heat, season with pepper and taste for salt. Serve hot.

1 lb/455 g French green beans, haricots verts, or green beans

1 tbsp extra-virgin olive oil

1 small onion, slivered

2 garlic cloves, minced

1 cup/185 g diced tomatoes, fresh or canned

½ cup/120 ml white wine

½ cup/90 g pitted green olives, halved

½ tsp dried tarragon

½ tsp dried thyme

1 tsp champagne vinegar

1 tsp sugar or agave syrup

½ cup/15 g fresh basil

½ cup/55 g walnut halves, toasted

SERVES 4

Crisp, fresh green beans get the French treatment here, with flavors and textures that will transport you to warm, breezy Provence. Serve this with Tofu Pan Bagnat (page 317) or Provençal Herbed Lentil Loaf (page 403) and a crisp white wine.

Provençal Green Bean Sauté
with Olives and Walnuts

1 Trim the green beans and leave them whole if they are small, or cut in half if larger; reserve. In a large frying pan, heat the oil over medium-high heat. Add the onion and garlic and sauté until they are soft and golden, about 5 minutes. Add the green beans and toss in the pan for 5 minutes. Add the tomatoes, wine, olives, tarragon, and thyme and stir, then bring to a boil. Reduce the heat to low and simmer until the beans are tender, about 5 minutes for thin beans, 7 minutes for larger beans.

2 Add the vinegar and sugar and stir well. Just before serving, stir in the basil. Serve the sauté topped with the walnuts.

12 oz/340 g extra-firm tofu, drained and pressed (see page 68)

1 tsp coarsely cracked black pepper

1 tsp paprika

1 tsp salt

½ tsp ground cumin

¼ tsp ground allspice

1 cup/240 ml Basic Vegetable Stock (page 49)

1 medium carrot, chopped

½ cup/60 g frozen peas, thawed

1 tsp extra-virgin olive oil

¾ cup/130 g whole-wheat/wholemeal couscous

2 tbsp canola oil

¼ cup/60 ml agave syrup

SERVES 4

Moroccan spices are warm and subtle, and when they combine with agave, as in this dish, it feels like a mouthful of North African adventure. Simmering tofu in the sauce on the stovetop is a fast way to marinate without having to plan ahead. This would go great with Moroccan Carrot Salad with Dates and Almonds (page 184) or Mediterranean Chopped Herb and Bread Salad (page 203).

Sweet Moroccan-Glazed Tofu
with Couscous

1 Slice the tofu into ½-in/1.25-cm strips and place them on a large plate. In a small bowl, mix together the pepper, paprika, ½ tsp of the salt, the cumin, and allspice. Cover the tofu slices with the spice mixture and pat to adhere it. Set aside.

2 In a small saucepan, bring the stock, carrot, peas, olive oil, and the remaining ½ tsp of salt to a boil, covered. Add the couscous, stir, and put a lid on the pan. Immediately remove it from the heat to steam for 5 minutes.

3 In a small frying pan, heat the canola oil and agave syrup until they start to bubble. Carefully lay the tofu in the bubbling pan, spiced-side down. Cook over medium-high heat for 3 minutes, then flip the tofu and cook until it has a sweet glaze, about 3 minutes more. As the syrup thickens in the pan, spoon it over the tofu.

4 Fluff the couscous and top with the tofu just before serving.

1 cup/215 g medium-grain brown rice, rinsed

8 oz/225 g Mock Beef (page 37) or seitan, drained

½ cup/120 ml Basic Vegetable Stock (page 49)

¼ cup/60 ml shao xing rice wine

3 tbsp hoisin sauce

2 tbsp soy sauce

2 tsp sugar

2 tsp cornstarch/cornflour

1 tsp toasted sesame oil

1 tsp Sriracha sauce (optional)

2 tsp canola oil

1½ cups/180 g julienned onions

1 medium carrot, julienned

1½ cups/235 g broccoli spears

3 garlic cloves, minced

1 tbsp minced peeled fresh ginger

½ cup/55 g unsalted roasted peanuts, chopped (optional)

SERVES 4

The classic beef and broccoli stir-fry is usually an eye-catching burst of green in a sea of brown-sauced main courses. This mock version has a more flavorful sauce, with hoisin and rice wine and chewy mock beef. Start the meal with Sesame-Lemon-Shiitake Potstickers (page 150) or Asian Tropical Fruit and Vegetable Salad (page 190).

Chinese "Beef" and Broccoli

1 In a 1-qt/1-L pot, bring 1¾ cups/420 ml water to a boil. Add the rice and return it to a boil, then cover tightly and reduce the heat to low. Simmer, covered, until the water is absorbed, 40 to 45 minutes. Let the rice stand, covered, for at least 5 minutes off the heat, to finish steaming.

2 Squeeze out the excess marinade from the mock beef, then slice it into strips ¼ in/6 mm wide.

3 In a small bowl, whisk together the stock, rice wine, hoisin, soy sauce, sugar, cornstarch/cornflour, sesame oil, and Sriracha (if using) and reserve.

4 Put a wok or cast-iron frying pan over high heat until it is very hot. Add the canola oil and swirl to coat. Toss in the mock beef and stir, scraping the pan, until it is well browned. Add the onions and carrot and stir for about 3 minutes. Add the broccoli, garlic, and ginger and stir for 2 minutes, just until the broccoli is bright green. Stir the sauce mixture and pour it into the center of the pan. Stir and toss the vegetables to coat with the sauce, cooking until the sauce is glossy. Serve over the rice, topped with the peanuts, if desired.

28-oz/800-g Mock Duck
(page 38) or canned/
tinned mock duck

1 cup/240 ml freshly
squeezed tangerine juice

¼ cup/50 g palm sugar
or brown sugar

2 tbsp tamari or soy
sauce

2 tbsp rice vinegar

4 tsp cornstarch/
cornflour

1 tbsp canola oil

2 large leeks, white parts
thinly sliced

3 tbsp minced peeled
fresh ginger

12 kumquats, thinly sliced

SERVES 6

A very creative Chinese chef named Tammy Wong makes a dish like this, with beef, for Chinese New Year at her famous Rainbow Chinese Restaurant in Minneapolis. The kumquats and tangerines symbolize money and add fabulous sweet-tart flavors. Serve this over steamed rice for an authentic presentation.

Chinese Tangerine Mock Duck
with Kumquats

1 Drain and squeeze the excess marinade from the mock duck and slice it into strips ½ in/12 mm wide.

2 In a medium bowl, mix together the tangerine juice, sugar, tamari, vinegar, and cornstarch/cornflour.

3 Heat a wok over high heat. When the wok is very hot, add the oil and swirl to coat. Add the mock duck and quickly stir. Keep stirring until the mock duck is lightly browned. Add the leeks and ginger and keep stirring until the leeks are softened, about 3 minutes. Stir the juice mixture and pour it into the pan, and keep stirring to coat everything with sauce. Stir until the sauce is thick and glossy. Add the kumquats and stir just to mix them in. Serve immediately.

1 cup/240 ml Basic Vegetable Stock (page 49)

2 tbsp soy sauce

1 tbsp cornstarch/cornflour

1 tsp red rice vinegar or red wine vinegar

2 tsp sugar

1 lb/455 g eggplant/aubergine, peeled

2 tbsp plus 2 tsp canola oil

6 oz/170 g extra-firm tofu, drained, pressed (see page 68), and crumbled

4 large scallions/spring onions, diagonally sliced

2 garlic cloves, minced

2 tsp red chile paste

½ tsp toasted sesame oil

¼ cup/30 g chopped roasted peanuts

SERVES 4

This is meltingly soft eggplant with tender tidbits of tofu, all glazed in a sweet, sour, and spicy sauce. It's just a bit hot, but if you are a fan of hot stuff, add another spoonful of chile paste.

Szechuan Eggplant
with Peanuts

1 In a cup or small bowl, combine the stock, soy sauce, cornstarch/cornflour, vinegar, and sugar; reserve.

2 Cut the eggplant/aubergine into slices ½ in/12 mm thick, then stack them and cut them into sticks ½ in/12 mm wide.

3 Heat a wok over high heat. Add the 2 tbsp canola oil and swirl to coat the pan. Add the eggplant/aubergine. It will soak up the oil; just keep stirring until it is all limp and soft. Transfer the eggplant/aubergine to a plate.

4 In the same wok, heat the remaining 2 tsp canola oil. Add the tofu and stir-fry until it is browned, about 3 minutes. When the tofu is ready, add the eggplant/aubergine, scallions/spring onions, and garlic and stir well. Make a well in the center and pour in the reserved stock mixture, then add the chile paste. Stir constantly until the sauce is glossy and thick. Add the sesame oil and toss to mix. Serve immediately, topped with the peanuts.

2 tbsp soy sauce

2 tbsp creamy unsalted peanut butter

1 tbsp rice vinegar

1 tbsp brown sugar

1 tbsp canola oil

2 cups/330 g corn

1 cup/100 g cauliflower florets

1 small yellow squash, sliced

4 scallions/spring onions, diagonally sliced

1 tbsp minced peeled fresh ginger

2 garlic cloves, minced

½ tsp red pepper flakes

6 oz/170 g dried whole-wheat/wholemeal angel hair pasta

¾ cup/85 g chopped roasted peanuts

SERVES 4

Sweet corn is not traditionally Chinese, but its sweet flavor and crisp texture lend themselves to stir-fries beautifully. This quick, peanutty noodle dish is a quick way to cook fresh sweet corn when it is available, or frozen corn the rest of the year.

Corn and Cauliflower Stir-Fried Noodles
with Peanuts

1 Bring a large pot of salted water to a boil. In a small cup, stir together the soy sauce, peanut butter, vinegar, and brown sugar.

2 Heat a wok over high heat. When it's very hot, add the oil and swirl to coat. Toss in the corn, cauliflower, and squash and stir-fry. When the vegetables are lightly browned and crisp-tender, add the scallions/spring onions, ginger, garlic, and pepper flakes, and stir briefly.

3 Cook the pasta in the boiling water according to the package directions; drain. Add the soy sauce mixture to the pan with the vegetables and stir to coat. Add the pasta and peanuts and toss to mix well. Serve immediately.

3 tbsp Basic Vegetable Stock (page 49)

2 tbsp creamy peanut butter

1 tbsp sugar

1 tbsp black bean paste

1 tbsp soy sauce

1 tbsp rice vinegar

½ tsp chile-infused sesame oil

1 tsp canola oil

1 cup/160 g broccoli florets

4 oz/115 g chopped cabbage

1 medium carrot, julienned

1 medium onion, julienned

2 tbsp minced peeled fresh ginger

2 garlic cloves, minced

14 oz/400 g canned/tinned black soybeans, drained and rinsed

2 cups/320 g cooked brown rice

SERVES 4

This dish calls for cooked brown rice, so plan to cook extra the day before, and you are set up for a great stir-fry. The classic Chinese black bean sauce is made from fermented black soybeans, which give it complexity and umami. Adding additional cooked black soybeans, available in convenient cans, just seemed like a good way to harmonize the dish, and it works.

Veggie Fried Rice
with Black Soy

1 In a small bowl, stir together the stock, peanut butter, sugar, black bean paste, soy sauce, vinegar, and sesame oil.

2 Place a wok over high heat and let it get hot for a couple of minutes. Add the canola oil and swirl to coat the pan. Add the broccoli, cabbage, carrot, and onion and stir-fry over high heat until the cabbage is wilted and the broccoli is bright green, about 3 minutes. Add the ginger and garlic and stir for 1 minute. Add the soybeans and rice and stir until they are heated through, about 3 minutes.

3 Stir the peanut butter mixture and pour it into the center of the pan, then immediately stir and toss to coat the rice and veggies. Keep stirring and tossing until the mixture is hot and the sauce is thick. Serve hot.

1 cup/240 ml coconut milk

1 cup/215 g long-grain brown rice

¼ cup/60 ml freshly squeezed lime juice

3 tbsp soy sauce

4 tsp brown sugar or palm sugar

4 tsp cornstarch/cornflour

1 tbsp dark miso

2 tbsp canola oil

4 large shallots, sliced

½ tsp red pepper flakes

12 oz/340 g firm tofu, drained and pressed (see page 68)

2 cups/170 g long beans or French green beans, trimmed and sliced

1 tbsp minced peeled fresh ginger

3 garlic cloves, minced

3 large scallions/spring onions, cut into 1-in/2.5-cm pieces

½ cup/15 g cilantro/fresh coriander, chopped

½ cup/15 g fresh Thai or other basil, chopped

½ cup/55 g roasted peanuts, chopped

SERVES 4

Fried rice can be a great way to use up leftover rice, but in this recipe, you cook a coconut-infused rice just to add to the spicy stir-fry, for an unforgettable coconut flavor. Long beans, also called asparagus beans or yard-long beans, are thin, nutty-tasting green beans that are worth seeking out at your Asian market. If you want to use regular green beans, that will be great, too.

Thai Fried Rice
with Tofu and Long Beans

1 In a small saucepan with a tight-fitting lid, bring the milk and 1 cup/240 ml water to a boil. Add the rice, return it to a boil, then reduce the heat to a low simmer. Cover tightly, and cook until all the liquids are absorbed, 40 to 50 minutes. Take the pan off the heat and let it stand, covered, for 5 minutes to finish steaming the rice.

2 In a cup, mix together the lime juice, soy sauce, brown sugar, cornstarch/cornflour, and miso and reserve.

3 Heat a large wok over high heat until very hot. Add the oil, swirling to coat the pan. Add the shallots and pepper flakes and fry over high heat until the shallots are golden, 2 minutes. Crumble the tofu in and fry it, scraping often, until golden and crisp. Add the beans and stir for 2 minutes. Add the ginger and garlic and cook for 1 minute. Pour in the liquid mixture and add the cooked rice, then start stirring and turning the mixture. Cook over high heat until the mixture is dry and well mixed. Add the scallions/spring onions, cilantro/fresh coriander, and basil and toss quickly, then scrape the mixture out into a serving bowl and top with the peanuts. Serve hot.

1 tbsp minced peeled fresh ginger

2 garlic cloves, peeled

1 medium onion, chopped

1 cup/240 ml coconut milk

1 tsp chili powder

½ tsp ground cinnamon

½ tsp ground turmeric

⅛ tsp ground cloves

⅛ tsp cayenne

2 cups/200 g cauliflower florets

14 oz/400 g canned/ tinned kidney beans, drained and rinsed

1 cup/185 g canned/ tinned diced fire-roasted tomatoes

½ tsp salt

SERVES 4

This simple curry packs a creamy flavor punch, with a sauce made up of onion puree, coconut milk, and spices. A simple simmer and some canned beans, and you have a feast fit for a rajah. Serve this with Cucumber Raita with Coconut Milk (page 114) and the Date-Nut Chutney from the Curry-Roasted New Potatoes (page 279). Quick Indian Flatbreads (page 106) would be perfect for scooping up the luscious sauce.

Bengali Curry of Cauliflower and Kidney Beans

1 In a food processor or blender, finely mince the ginger and garlic, then add the onion and puree. Pour in the milk and process. Add the chili powder, cinnamon, turmeric, cloves, and cayenne and process to mix. Transfer the sauce to a large frying pan over medium-high heat. Stir the mixture until it starts to bubble, then add the cauliflower and stir to coat it with sauce. Cover the pan and cook until the cauliflower is tender, 8 to 10 minutes.

2 Add the beans, tomatoes, and salt and cook, stirring with the lid off, until the sauce is thick and the beans are heated through. Serve hot.

½ cup/125 g green split peas, sorted, rinsed, and soaked overnight

½ cup/125 g yellow split peas, sorted, rinsed, and soaked overnight

1 lb/455 g sweet potatoes, chopped

1 tbsp canola oil

3 cups/360 g chopped onions

2 tsp black mustard seeds

2 tsp cumin seeds

1 large red jalapeño, chopped

1 tsp ground coriander

1 tsp ground turmeric

¼ tsp ground cinnamon

1 tbsp tamarind pulp

1 tbsp palm sugar or brown sugar

½ tsp salt

3 cups/480 g cooked brown basmati rice

SERVES 6

Thick and comforting, this curry balances the sweetness of the potatoes with a shot of acidic tamarind. The dish is high in flavor but not too hot. If you are a chile head, add a couple more jalapeños or use hotter chiles. Be sure to soak the split peas the day before, so they will cook quickly.

Curried Split Peas and Sweet Potatoes

1 Drain the split peas and put them in a medium pot with 3 cups/720 ml fresh water and the sweet potatoes. Over high heat, bring them to a boil, then reduce the heat, cover, and simmer until the peas are falling apart tender, about 1 hour, stirring a few times to keep them from sticking. You may need to add more water, but you want the mixture to be thick.

2 In a large pot over high heat, warm the oil briefly. Add the onions and stir until they start to sizzle and soften, then reduce the heat. Stir occasionally, and cook until the onions are brown and caramelized, about 45 minutes.

3 Add the mustard and cumin seeds to the onions, and raise the heat to medium-high. When the seeds start to crackle and toast, add the jalapeño, ground coriander, turmeric, and cinnamon and stir for 2 minutes. Add the cooked split peas and potatoes, tamarind, palm sugar, and salt and bring to a simmer. Cook until the split peas and sweet potatoes are falling apart, about 10 minutes, stirring occasionally. Add more water if needed.

4 If desired, you can puree the soup for a very smooth texture. Serve a scoop of rice in a bowl, with a ladle of the curry over it.

1 cup/215 g brown
basmati rice, rinsed

12 oz/340 g firm tofu,
drained and pressed (see
page 68)

1 tbsp canola oil,
plus 2 tsp

2 tsp freshly squeezed
lemon juice

1½ tsp salt

¼ tsp ground turmeric

¼ tsp paprika

1½ lb/680 g fresh spinach

1 tsp brown mustard
seeds

1 jalapeño, chopped

1 tsp ground cumin

½ tsp ground coriander

¼ tsp cayenne

2 tbsp unbleached
all-purpose/plain flour

2 cups/480 ml plain
soymilk or other milk

1 cup/235 ml tomato
sauce/puree

½ cup/15 g cilantro/fresh
coriander, chopped

SERVES 4

One of my favorite Indian dishes of all time is this
one, with creamy spinach sauce bathing cubes of
firm tofu. Paneer is the cheese that tastes like tofu
anyway, so it just seems right to do a completely
vegan and super-tasty tofu version.

Saag "Paneer"

1 In a 1-qt/1-L pot, bring 1¾ cups/420 ml water to a boil.
Add the rice and return it to a boil, then cover tightly and
reduce the heat to low. Simmer, covered, until the water is
absorbed, 40 to 45 minutes. Let the rice stand, covered, for
at least 5 minutes off the heat, to finish steaming.

2 Preheat the oven to 400°F/200°C/gas 6. Cut the tofu into
½-in/12-mm cubes. In a medium bowl, mix together the 1 tbsp
oil, lemon juice, ½ tsp of the salt, the turmeric, and paprika.
Put the tofu in the bowl, toss gently, and let it marinate at
room temperature for 30 minutes.

3 Spread the tofu on a baking sheet/tray and bake 20 minutes. Turn the cubes with a metal spatula and bake until firm
and toasted, 10 minutes more. Remove the pan and let the
tofu cool.

4 Wash the spinach and put the damp leaves in a large
pot over high heat and cover. After 2 minutes, uncover and
stir. When the spinach is wilted and shrunken but still bright
green, drain it in a colander. Rinse it with cold water and
wring it out very thoroughly.

5 In a small pot, heat the remaining 2 tsp oil over high heat. Add the mustard seeds and stir for 1 minute, until they start to pop. Add the jalapeño, cumin, ground coriander, and cayenne and sauté until fragrant. Take off the heat and whisk in the flour. Put the pan over medium heat and cook, stirring constantly, until the mixture is thick and lightly toasted, about 5 minutes. Whisk in the soymilk gradually and bring it to a simmer to thicken.

6 In a blender or food processor, mince the spinach. Add the soymilk mixture and puree to make a smooth sauce. Add the tomato sauce/puree, cilantro/fresh coriander, and the remaining 1 tsp salt and puree. Transfer the sauce to a large frying pan and stir in the baked tofu. Heat gently over low heat and serve over the rice.

Mock Turkey

2 tbsp extra-virgin olive oil, plus extra for bowl

½ cup/60 g minced onion

2 garlic cloves, minced

2 cups/255 g gluten flour

1 cup/130 g chickpea flour

½ cup/25 g nutritional yeast

1 tsp salt

6 oz/170 g firm tofu, drained and pressed (see page 68)

1 cup/240 ml Basic Vegetable Stock (page 49)

¼ cup/60 ml tamari

½ tsp ground sage

Stuffing

1 tsp extra-virgin olive oil

½ cup/60 g chopped onion

1 cup/55 g cubed bread

¼ cup/60 ml Basic Vegetable Stock (page 49)

½ tsp ground sage

½ tsp dried thyme

½ tsp salt

2 tbsp chopped walnuts

SERVES 8

For those of you who miss the turkey on holidays, this is a good way to mock up a bird. It's really not much trouble now that we can use gluten flour. Serve it with Basic Mushroom Gravy with Herbs (page 124) and all the traditional trimmings.

Homemade Mock Turkey Roast
with Stuffing

1 Preheat the oven to 350°F/180°C/gas 4. Oil a 3- to 4-cup/ 720- to 960-ml metal bowl or a small loaf pan/tin. Put a teapot of water on to simmer for the bain marie (water bath) later.

2 TO MAKE THE MOCK TURKEY: In a small frying pan over medium heat, warm the oil. Add the onion and garlic and sauté until soft and sweet, 5 to 10 minutes. In a medium bowl, mix together both flours, the yeast, and salt. In a blender or food processor, puree the tofu until very smooth. Add the stock, tamari, and sage to the tofu and blend. Add the onion, garlic, and oil from the pan and puree. Stir the contents of the blender into the flour mixture until smooth. Scoop about two thirds of the dough into the oiled bowl.

3 TO MAKE THE STUFFING: Heat the oil in a small frying pan over medium heat. Add the onion and sauté until soft and clear. Add the bread, stock, sage, thyme, and salt and stir until the bread is soft. Stir in the nuts.

4 Press the stuffing into a ball (or if you are using a loaf pan/ tin, into an oblong) and press it into the center of the mock turkey dough, then cover it with the remaining dough. Flatten the top, brush it with oil, and cover with foil. Put the bowl in a baking dish and pour in boiling water to make a bain marie. Carefully transfer to the oven and bake for 2 hours. When the "turkey" is quite firm, take it out of the water bath, then put the bowl on a rack to cool. Run a paring knife around the edge to loosen it, then invert it onto a cutting board or platter. Slice the "turkey" and serve.

2 tsp extra-virgin olive oil, plus extra for pan

8 oz/225 g yellow potatoes

12 oz/340 g Japanese-style tofu, drained and pressed (see page 68)

2 tbsp cornstarch/cornflour

1 medium zucchini/courgette, sliced

1 cup/120 g chopped onions

½ red bell pepper/capsicum, sliced

2 garlic cloves, chopped

1 pinch saffron, crushed

1½ tsp ground coriander

1 tsp salt

½ tsp paprika

½ tsp freshly cracked black pepper

SERVES 6

Golden saffron is a key ingredient in this pretty tortilla, which is the Spanish version of a frittata rather than the Latin American flatbread. The saffron adds its potent pigment and its haunting flavor and scent. Serve this with a glass of Spanish wine, and perhaps some Romesco Sauce (page 122), and you have a classic Spanish flavor combination, without the eggs. Japanese-style tofu has a texture between firm and silken, although you could use Chinese style and just puree it really well.

Spanish Saffron Tortilla

1 Preheat the oven to 400°F/200°C/gas 6. Lightly oil a 9-in/ 23-cm pie pan/tin.

2 In a large pot with just enough cold water to cover them, bring the whole potatoes to a boil and cook until tender. Drain them, then slice into rounds ⅓ in/8 mm thick. Puree the tofu in a food processor. Add the cornstarch/cornflour and process to mix it in.

3 In a large frying pan, heat the oil over high heat. Add the zucchini/courgette, onions, bell pepper/capsicum, garlic, and saffron and sauté, reducing the heat as they start to soften. When the onions are limp and golden, add the ground coriander, salt, paprika, and pepper and stir them in. Remove the pan from the heat. Stir the tofu mixture into the vegetables. Fold in the potato slices, and transfer the mixture to the prepared pie pan/tin.

4 Bake until the tortilla is firm and crusty on top, 30 to 40 minutes. Run a knife around the edges of the pan and invert it onto a serving plate. It's good served warm or cold.

MAIN COURSES

1 cup/240 ml dry white wine

1 cup/240 ml Basic Vegetable Stock (page 49)

2 tbsp agar flakes

2 lb/900 g fresh asparagus

2 tbsp extra-virgin olive oil

2 large leeks, white part only, sliced

4 oz/115 g fresh spinach

12 oz/340 g silken tofu, drained

1 tbsp chopped fresh dill, plus 6 sprigs

1 tsp salt

Olive oil, for the ramekins

SERVES 6

When asparagus is really good, and the first fresh, baby spinach comes on the scene, make this cool variation of charlottes, with gorgeous asparagus stems surrounding a creamy middle. You can show off your vegetable treasures in a pretty presentation, held together with a touch of agar for a sculpted main course.

Savory Asparagus Charlottes

1 In a small saucepan, whisk together the wine, stock, and agar, and let them stand to soak for 30 minutes to 1 hour. Place the pan over low heat and bring it to a simmer, whisking occasionally. Cook until the agar is dissolved, about 15 minutes. Remove it from the heat.

2 Set up a steamer and bring the water to a simmer. Prep the asparagus by holding an asparagus spear, tip down, in a 1-cup/240-ml ramekin to gauge the depth. Cut the tip to just below the depth of the ramekin, so it will not protrude above the rim. Cut all the tips to this length, and then the next section of the stems to the same length. Trim the remaining stems and peel them, if necessary, to make 10 oz/280 g. Steam the lowest part of the stems for 4 minutes. Add the middle sections of the stems and steam for 1 minute more, then add the tips and steam just until they are bright green, about 2 minutes more. Remove all the asparagus and rinse with cold water. Drain well and dry on towels.

3 In a frying pan, warm the oil over medium-low heat. Add the leeks and sauté, lowering the heat as they cook, to gently bring out the sweetness. When they are limp, add the spinach and turn it in the pan until it is shrunken and soft.

4 In a food processor, puree the tofu, scrape down the sides, and reprocess a couple of times. Add the lowest parts of the asparagus stems and the sautéed leeks and spinach, and puree. When the mixture is very smooth, pour in the agar mixture and puree. Add the chopped dill and salt and process to mix.

5 Generously oil the six 1-cup/240-ml ramekins. In each, place a sprig of dill, then a heaping tablespoon or so of the tofu-asparagus puree. Arrange the asparagus tips and middle sections of stems, alternating them, around the wall of each ramekin, tips down, adding more puree as needed to hold them up. Fill the asparagus-lined cup with puree just to the top of the asparagus, until all the cups are filled. Cover with plastic wrap/cling film and refrigerate, or let stand at room temperature until the filling is set, about 1 hour.

6 Run a paring knife around each charlotte to loosen it. Unmold by placing a plate over the ramekin and holding the ramekin tightly to the plate as you flip it. Tap it on the counter to knock out the charlotte and serve.

Tomato Sauce

2 tbsp tomato paste/
puree

2 tsp tamari or soy sauce

1 tbsp mirin

½ tsp Dijon mustard

Wasabi "Mayo"

2 tsp wasabi paste

3 tbsp Vegan
"Mayonnaise" (page 113)
or Vegenaise

Garnish

1 sheet (about ⅟₁₆ oz/
2.5 g) dried nori seaweed

3 tbsp black sesame
seeds

Pancake

2 cups/225 g shredded
cabbage

½ cup/55 g shredded
carrot

¼ cup/30 g chopped
onion

½ oz/15 g dried shiitake
mushroom, rehydrated
and sliced

12 oz/340 g silken tofu

3 tbsp cornstarch/
cornflour

2 tbsp nutritional yeast

1 tbsp white miso

1 tbsp mirin

½ tsp salt

1 tbsp toasted sesame oil

SERVES 4

It only takes a few minutes to make the multiple garnishes that make this veggie-packed wedge so special. In Japan, eggy versions of these are made tableside on griddles, but this fab tofu version is an easy bake-and-slice pie.

Japanese Okinomiyaki Veggie Pancake

1 TO MAKE THE SAUCE, "MAYO," AND GARNISH: In a small bowl, stir together the tomato paste/puree, tamari, mirin, and mustard; reserve. In another small bowl, stir the wasabi into the vegan "mayonnaise." Toast the nori over an open flame on a gas stove until it crisps, then crumble or chop it into pieces and put them in a bowl. Toast the sesame seeds in a small frying pan until they are fragrant and shiny with oil, and mix them with the nori.

2 TO MAKE THE PANCAKE: Preheat the oven to 400°F/200°C/ gas 6. In a large bowl, mix together the cabbage, carrot, onion, and shiitakes. In a food processor, puree the tofu and scrape down the sides, repeating until smooth. Add the cornstarch/ cornflour, yeast, miso, mirin, and salt and process to mix well. Stir the puree into the vegetable mixture.

3 Coat a 10-in/25-cm springform pan with half of the oil, then spread the tofu mixture in it. Press to make a flat, thin pancake, then drizzle the remaining oil on top. Bake until the pancake is golden and firm in the middle, about 30 minutes. Take it out, remove the pan sides, and carefully run a spatula between the cake and the springform bottom. Slide the pan-cake onto a platter or serving board and drizzle it with the sauce and wasabi "mayo." Cut it into four wedges, sprinkle with the nori garnish, and serve.

8 oz/230 g pearl onions

1 lb/455 g fennel, diced

2 medium yellow potatoes, cubed

2 tbsp extra-virgin olive oil

¼ cup/7 g chopped fresh parsley

½ cup/55 g raw cashews

1 cup/240 ml plain rice milk or other milk

2 tbsp red miso

2 tbsp nutritional yeast

6 tbsp/90 ml coconut oil

6 sheets (about 12 by 17 in/30 by 42 cm) phyllo dough, thawed overnight in the refrigerator

SERVES 6

Serve these gorgeous phyllo purses and crack into the crisp pastry to discover sweet pearl onions and fennel in a creamy cashew gravy.

Roasted Vegetable Phyllo Purses
with Creamy Gravy

1 Bring a medium pot of water to a boil, then drop in the onions for 5 minutes. Drain them, rinse with cold water, and use a paring knife to remove the root ends and peel. Reserve.

2 Preheat the oven to 400°F/200°C/gas 6. In a 9-by-13-in/ 23-by-33-cm pan, toss the fennel, potatoes, and onions with the olive oil. Cover with foil and roast for 30 minutes. Uncover, stir, and roast, 10 minutes more. Let cool. Measure ½ cup/60 g of the vegetable mixture for the sauce. Mix the parsley into the remaining vegetable mixture.

3 In a blender or food processor, grind the cashews to a paste. Add the reserved vegetables, the milk, miso, and yeast. Process until smooth and thick. Measure ½ cup/120 ml of the sauce and mix it into the vegetables in the pan. Transfer the rest of the sauce to a small saucepan to reheat later.

4 Melt the coconut oil. Lightly oil a baking sheet/tray. Place the phyllo on the counter, cover with a sheet of plastic wrap/ cling film, and place a barely damp towel on top to hold it down. Working with one at a time, brush each phyllo sheet with coconut oil, then fold it in half lengthwise. Place about ½ cup/60 g of the vegetable mixture in the center of each phyllo, then pull the dough up around it. Transfer the phyllo to the baking sheet/tray and decoratively bunch the phyllo into a purse on top. Brush the tops and out-sides lightly with oil. Bake until the phyllo is crisp and browned, about 20 minutes.

5 To serve, gently heat the remaining sauce, and place each purse on a plate. Drizzle some of the sauce around each purse.

3 small sweet dumpling squashes or mini pumpkins (about 13 oz/ 370 g each)

1 tsp canola oil, plus extra for pans

½ cup/60 g chopped onion

1 tbsp minced peeled fresh ginger

1 tsp black mustard seeds

1 medium jalapeño, chopped

1 tsp whole cumin seeds

1 tsp ground coriander

¼ tsp ground turmeric

¼ tsp ground cinnamon

¼ cup/50 g millet

½ cup/120 ml coconut milk

½ tsp salt

½ cup/55 g raw cashews

½ cup/55 g whole almonds, toasted

2 tbsp shredded/ desiccated unsweetened coconut

SERVES 6

These colorful, single-serving squash halves are speckled with golden millet, green jalapeño, and crunchy nuts. Redolent of spice and a touch of coconut, they will draw your guests to the table by scent alone.

Nutty Curry-Stuffed Squashes

1 Preheat the oven to 400°F/200°C/gas 6. Cut the squashes in half from the stem to the tip. Scoop out the seeds and place them, cut-side down, on oiled baking sheets/trays. Bake for 10 minutes (they will not be completely cooked). Take the pans out and flip the squash halves over. When they have cooled slightly, use a spoon to cut into the flesh, loosening it in spots but leaving it in the shell so that the sauce will permeate the whole squash. Reduce the oven temperature to 375°F/190°C/ gas 5.

2 In a 2-qt/2-L saucepan, heat the oil. Add the onion, ginger, and mustard seeds and sauté over medium-high heat until the onion is golden, about 5 minutes. Add the jalapeño, cumin, ground coriander, turmeric, and cinnamon and stir until they are fragrant. Add the millet and stir to coat, then add ¼ cup/ 60 ml water, the milk, and salt and bring to a boil. When it boils, cover the pan and turn the heat to low. Cook until the millet is tender, about 20 minutes. Take the pan off the heat and stir in the nuts, then stuff the mixture into the squashes. Sprinkle each with 1 tsp coconut.

3 Bake the squashes until the filling is set and bubbling and the squashes are easily pierced with a knife, about 20 minutes. Let them cool slightly before serving.

Four 6-in/15-cm mini pumpkins or small squashes

1 tbsp extra-virgin olive oil or Earth Balance margarine, plus extra for pan

2 cups/300 g finely chopped parsnips

2 cups/225 g chopped cabbage

3 ribs celery, finely chopped

1 cup/120 g chopped onions

1 large carrot, diced

¼ cup/7 g chopped fresh sage

2 garlic cloves, minced

½ cup/120 ml white wine

1½ cups/360 ml plain vegan creamer

¼ cup/60 ml tomato paste/puree

¾ tsp salt

½ cup/55 g pecans, chopped

SERVES 4

Whole baby pumpkins act as edible tureens for this impressive main course. Your guests can take the lids off their piping-hot gourds and release the sage-infused aroma, just before they dig into the creamy, pecan-studded stew. The size of the pumpkins will vary; you may have some extra stew left over if they are small.

Harvest Vegetable Stew
in Mini Pumpkins

1 Preheat the oven to 400°F/200°C/gas 6. Carefully slice off the top of each pumpkin to make a small lid. Scoop out the seeds, then place the pumpkins and lids upside down on an oiled baking sheet/tray. Bake until a paring knife can easily pierce the shells, 30 to 40 minutes. Take out the pumpkins, carefully turn them over, and let them cool.

2 In a large frying pan, heat the oil over medium-high heat. Add the parsnips, cabbage, celery, onions, and carrot. Stir and cook until the onions start to brown, then lower the heat to medium-low, cover, and cook for about 10 minutes. When the parsnips are tender, add the sage and garlic and cook for about 5 minutes. Add the wine and raise the heat to boil it off until almost dry. In a cup, whisk together the creamer and tomato paste/puree until smooth, then add them to the pan with the salt and bring to a simmer. Stir until the sauce thickens, then take the pan off the heat, mash some of the vegetables coarsely, and stir in the pecans.

3 Use a spoon to scoop some of the pumpkin flesh into bite-size chunks, so that it will mix with the stew. Fill the pumpkins with the vegetable mixture, then place the lids on top. Keep any leftover stew warm to serve in a bowl. Put the filled pumpkins in a baking dish, preferably with a lid, or cover them with foil. Bake until the pumpkins and stew are piping hot, about 30 minutes. Serve warm.

MAIN COURSES

429

1½ cups/360 ml coconut milk or plain vegan creamer

½ cup/65 g chickpea flour

½ cup/60 g unbleached all-purpose/plain flour, plus extra for filling

1 tbsp ground flax seeds

¾ tsp salt

Canola oil or Earth Balance margarine

2 tsp extra-virgin olive oil

7 oz/200 g fresh shiitake mushrooms, sliced

1 cup/120 g chopped onions

2 ribs celery, finely chopped

2 garlic cloves, chopped

1 cup/240 ml Marsala wine

2 cups/60 g fresh spinach, chopped

Freshly cracked black pepper

Herb Drizzle

1 cup/30 g fresh basil

½ cup/15 g fresh parsley

2 tbsp chopped fresh oregano

3 tbsp freshly squeezed orange juice

2 tbsp tomato paste/puree

3 tbsp extra-virgin olive oil

SERVES 4

Crêpes are always special, tender little pancakes stuffed with something good. In this case, a rich mushroom filling, fortified with deep marsala flavor, is cradled in the crêpes, then drizzled with a sprightly herb sauce.

Marsala-Mushroom Crêpes
with Herb Drizzle

1 In a blender, combine 1 cup/240 ml of the milk, ½ cup/120 ml water, both flours, the flax seeds, and ½ tsp of the salt. Blend until smooth, scraping down the sides as necessary. The mixture should have the consistency of heavy cream. Refrigerate the mixture for 1 hour; you can just leave it in the blender jar.

2 Blend the batter again and if it is thicker than desired, add a little water. Heat an 8-in/20-cm crêpe or frying pan over high heat. When the pan is hot, brush it lightly with canola oil. Measure ¼ cup/60 ml of the batter into the hot pan and swirl to coat the pan. Cook for about 2 minutes before running a spatula around the edge of the crêpe to loosen and then flip it. Cook for just a few seconds and then invert the crêpe pan over a cutting board or plate to drop the crêpe out of the pan. Continue until all the crêpes are cooked, stacking them once they are completely cool. (This makes about nine crêpes, but you can mess up the first one, because you only need eight!)

430

3 Preheat the oven to 375°F/190°C/gas 5. In a large frying pan, heat the olive oil. Add the mushrooms, onions, and celery. Stir and cook over medium-high heat until the mushrooms are very soft and shrunken and the onions are golden brown, about 5 minutes. Add the garlic and stir for 1 minute. Add the wine and cook until the pan is almost dry. Sprinkle on about 1 tsp flour and stir to incorporate, then cook for 1 minute. Add the remaining ½ cup/120 ml milk and the spinach and cook just until the spinach is wilted and the sauce is thick. Take the pan off the heat and stir in the remaining ¼ tsp salt and season with pepper.

4 Oil a shallow 1-qt/1-L baking dish for the finished crêpes. Divide the mushroom mixture among the crêpes, placing ¼ cup/30 g of the filling down the center of each, then roll up the crêpe. Place them, seam-side down, in the prepared dish. Bake for 15 minutes. The filling should still be warm, so it won't take long to just crisp the edges of the crêpes.

5 TO MAKE THE HERB DRIZZLE: In a food processor or blender, mince the basil, parsley, and oregano. Add the orange juice and tomato paste/puree and process to mix well. With the motor running, drizzle in the oil to make an emulsion.

6 Drizzle the sauce over the hot crêpes in the pan or after placing them on individual plates. Serve immediately.

14 oz/400 g
beets/beetroot

12 oz/340 g extra-firm
tofu, drained and
pressed (see page 68)

2 large Bosc pears

1 large onion, diced

3 tbsp extra-virgin olive oil

3 tbsp champagne
vinegar

½ tsp salt

½ tsp coarsely cracked
pepper

½ cup/15 g fresh basil
or parsley, chopped,
for garnish

SERVES 4

Since both beets and tofu are great roasted, why
not do them together? The beet and pear juices kiss
the tofu with both color and sweetness, and a tangy
vinaigrette balances out the whole thing in a way
that will wake up your taste buds. This is great
alongside savory foods such as Cream of Cremini
Mushroom Soup with Sage (page 250) or Snap
Peas with Caramelized Pearl Onions (page 296).

Tofu, Beet, and Pear Roast
with Vinaigrette

1 Preheat the oven to 400°F/200°C/gas 6. Cube the beets/
beetroot, tofu, and pears into ¾-in/2-cm pieces. Put them with
the onion in a large, deep roasting pan/tray, like a lasagna pan.
In a cup, whisk together the oil, vinegar, salt, and pepper and
pour over the tofu mixture in the pan. Toss to coat.

2 Cover with foil and roast for 25 minutes. Uncover, stir, and
roast until the beets/beetroot are very tender and the liquids
are reduced, about 25 minutes more. Transfer the mixture to
a serving bowl. Garnish with the basil and serve.

20 large sun-dried tomato halves

2 tbsp chopped fresh rosemary

4 tsp black peppercorns

4 tsp sugar

1 tsp salt

8 oz/225 g tempeh, cut into thin strips

1 lb/455 g broccoli, cut into large spears

2 large carrots, sliced

2 tbsp extra-virgin olive oil

SERVES 4

In a quick simmer on the stovetop, the tempeh in this dish absorbs an infusion of tomato and herb flavors, before being crisped in the oven. Bright broccoli and carrots balance the intensity of sun-dried tomatoes, all in an easy roast.

Mediterranean Tempeh and Broccoli Roast

1 Preheat the oven to 400°F/200°C/gas 6. In a large pot, combine 1½ cups/360 ml water, the tomatoes, rosemary, peppercorns, sugar, and salt. Bring to a simmer and cook uncovered, until the tomatoes are starting to soften, about 5 minutes. Add the tempeh and submerge it as much as possible. Simmer until the liquids are absorbed. Take out the tempeh and let it cool to room temperature. Pat it dry. Take out the tomatoes and chop them; reserve.

2 In a heavy roasting pan/tray, combine the tempeh, broccoli, carrots, and oil. Roast, uncovered, until the tempeh is browned and crispy, about 20 minutes. Add the tomatoes and toss, then roast for 5 minutes more to heat through. Serve hot.

2 medium onions, chopped

8 oz/225 g seitan, sliced

2 medium red jalapeños, slivered

2 tsp extra-virgin olive oil

8 oz/120 g Swiss chard/silverbeet, leaves chopped

2 garlic cloves, minced

1 tsp lemon zest

1 tsp freshly squeezed lemon juice

½ tsp salt

SERVES 4

The searing heat of the oven crisps chewy seitan and sweetens leafy chard, for a lightly spiced quick meal. A squeeze of lemon lifts the deep flavors with just the right amount of zing. It's great with a chunk of bread and Cider-Glazed Carrots (page 294).

Seitan and Swiss Chard Roast
with Lemon

1 Preheat the oven to 425°F/220°C/gas 7. Put the onions, seitan, and jalapeños in a deep, heavy roasting pan/tray. Add the oil and toss to coat. Roast for 20 minutes, shaking the pan halfway through.

2 Add the chard/silverbeet, garlic, and lemon zest and toss to mix. Roast until the greens are wilted, 10 minutes more, stirring at 5 minutes. Transfer everything to a serving bowl and add the lemon juice and salt; toss to coat and serve immediately.

1 lb/455 g winter squash, peeled and cubed

12 oz/340 g firm tofu, drained, pressed (see page 68), and diced

8 oz/225 g red onion, diced

1 tbsp canola oil

¼ cup/60 ml tamari

3 tbsp agave syrup

2 tbsp minced peeled fresh ginger

1 tbsp rice vinegar

1 garlic clove, minced

½ tsp toasted sesame oil

SERVES 5

Deep orange squash and red onions caramelize in the oven while the tofu soaks up the sweetness. A simple sauce heightens the sweet-and-sour flavor of it all, and gives it that magical tamari umami. Serve with Asian Tropical Fruit and Vegetable Salad (page 190).

Squash, Tofu, and Red Onion Roast

with Sweet Soy Glaze

1 Preheat the oven to 400°F/200°C/gas 6. Put the squash, tofu, and onion in a large roasting pan/tray. Drizzle them with the canola oil and toss to coat. Cover with foil, then roast for 20 minutes. Shake the pan to turn the cubes. If it feels like they are not moving, open the foil and turn them with a metal spatula. Cover and roast until tender when pierced with a paring knife, about 20 minutes more.

2 In a small cup, stir together the tamari, agave syrup, ginger, vinegar, garlic, and sesame oil. Pour them over the contents of the pan, and mix to coat. Roast, uncovered, until the liquids are absorbed and the pan is nearly dry, 5 to 7 minutes. Serve hot.

12 oz/340 g extra-firm tofu, drained, pressed (see page 68), and cubed

6 oz/170 g cauliflower, cut into florets

1 medium turnip, cubed

1 large carrot, thickly sliced

1 small parsnip, thickly sliced

½ cup/120 ml coconut milk

4 garlic cloves, sliced

1 tsp curry powder

1 tsp brown mustard seeds

1 tsp cumin seeds

¼ tsp salt

1 tbsp brown sugar

½ cup/15 g cilantro/fresh coriander, chopped, for garnish

SERVES 4

This one-pan meal makes its own sauce, as the veggies absorb the coconut milk and give off their juices to the bubbling glaze. If you like your curry hot, throw in a chile or two. Serve with any cooked grain, to soak up the sauce.

Roasted Tofu and Veggie Curry
in Garlicky Coconut Gravy

1 Preheat the oven to 400°F/200°C/gas 6. In a large roasting pan/tray, combine the tofu, cauliflower, turnip, carrot, parsnip, milk, garlic, curry powder, mustard seeds, cumin seeds, and salt. Toss to coat. Cover with foil and roast for 20 minutes. Uncover, stir, and pierce a parsnip to check for tenderness. If it is soft, put the pan back, uncovered, until the vegetables are browned, 10 minutes more. (If the parsnip is still hard, roast it for 10 minutes more, covered, before uncovering.)

2 Stir; the sauce should be thick. Take out the pan, sprinkle the vegetables with the brown sugar, and toss to mix. Transfer everything to a serving bowl and sprinkle with the cilantro/fresh coriander to serve.

12 oz/340 g firm tofu, drained, pressed (see page 68), and cubed

1 cup/215 g medium-grain brown rice

1 cup/80 g dulse, crumbled

1 cup/240 ml coconut milk

4 medium scallions/spring onions, chopped

1 medium carrot, chopped

2 garlic cloves, chopped

½ tsp salt

1 cup/30 g fresh parsley, chopped

Tamari, for garnish

SERVES 4

Dulse is a purplish sea vegetable with a delicate, salty taste that complements brown rice perfectly. It is also loaded with iodine and minerals, and has been a traditional food of Scotland and British Columbia for hundreds of years.

Tofu and Dulse Brown Rice and Veggies

In a heavy, large pot or rice cooker, combine 1 cup/240 ml water with the tofu, rice, dulse, milk, scallions/spring onions, carrot, garlic, and salt and bring to a boil. Cover tightly, reduce to a simmer, and cook until all the liquid is absorbed, 30 to 40 minutes. If cooking on the stovetop, let the pan stand, off the heat, for 5 minutes, covered, to finish steaming the rice. Serve hot, topped with the parsley and season with tamari as desired.

1 tbsp canola oil

1 tbsp brown mustard seeds

1 large jalapeño, minced

2 medium carrots, chopped

1 cup/215 g long-grain brown rice

1⅓ cups/415 ml light coconut milk

12 oz/340 g extra-firm tofu, drained, pressed (see page 68), and cubed

¾ cup/180 ml Basic Vegetable Stock (page 49)

¾ tsp salt

1 cup/30 g cilantro/fresh coriander, chopped

½ cup/55 g toasted, unsalted cashews

¼ cup/30 g shredded/desiccated unsweetened coconut, toasted

SERVES 4

Kerala is a coastal state in the tropical part of southern India, and it has a vibrant vegetarian cuisine. Coconut figures prominently, and this lightly spiced rice will make your taste buds sing. Serve this with your favorite chutneys.

Kerala Coconut Rice
with Tofu, Carrots, and Cashews

1 Preheat the oven to 375°F/190°C/gas 5. In a Dutch oven or other heavy ovenproof pot with a lid, heat the oil. Add the mustard seeds and jalapeño, and cook until the mustard seeds start to pop. Add the carrots and rice and stir, coating the grains with oil.

2 Add the milk, tofu, stock, and salt. Bring to a boil. Cover, then put the pot in the oven to bake for 55 minutes. Test the rice; if it is not tender, cover again and bake for 5 to 10 minutes more. Let the dish stand, covered, for 5 minutes after taking it out of the oven to finish steaming the rice.

3 Stir in the cilantro/fresh coriander while the rice is hot. Top with the cashews and coconut and serve.

1 tbsp extra-virgin olive oil

1 medium red bell pepper/capsicum, chopped

1 medium green bell pepper/capsicum, chopped

6 large scallions/spring onions, white and green parts chopped separately

2 ribs celery, chopped

1 large jalapeño, chopped

1 large bay leaf

3 garlic cloves, minced

½ tsp dried thyme

½ tsp dried oregano

½ tsp dried basil

2 cups/480 ml Basic Vegetable Stock (page 49)

1 cup/215 g long-grain brown rice

½ tsp salt

6 oz/170 g smoked tempeh Fakin' Bacon, sliced

½ cup/90 g canned/tinned diced tomatoes

SERVES 4

New Orleans is synonymous with spicy food, and lots of rice. Here, all the spices of the Crescent City give a pot of brown rice and peppers a touch of Zydeco spirit.

New Orleans Jambalaya
with Smoked Tempeh and Brown Rice

1 Heat the oil in a large pot with a tight-fitting lid over medium-high heat. Add both bell peppers/capsicums, the chopped whites of the scallions/spring onions, the celery, jalapeño, and bay leaf. Sauté until the vegetables are softened. Add the garlic, thyme, oregano, and basil and stir briefly, then add the stock and bring it to a boil. Add the rice and salt and bring to a simmer, then cover tightly and cook on very low heat until all the liquids are absorbed and the rice is tender, 35 to 45 minutes.

2 Fold in the tempeh and tomatoes and let stand, covered, to steam the rice and warm the tempeh and tomatoes through, about 5 minutes. Serve topped with the remaining chopped scallions/spring onion greens.

2 cups/280 g cubed sweet potatoes

2 cups/225 g chopped cabbage

1 cup/215 g short-grain brown rice

1 cup/110 g chopped green beans

½ cup/85 g raisins

5 garlic cloves, halved

2 in/5 cm fresh ginger, peeled and slivered

1 tbsp curry powder

½ lime

½ tsp salt

½ cup/55 g unsalted roasted peanuts, chopped

SERVES 4

Pile it all in the pot and let the magic begin, as sweet potatoes and cabbage become one with brown rice, curry powder, and raisins. This sustaining meal can keep in the refrigerator for a few days for easy lunches or dinners.

Simple Rice and Veggie Curry One-Pot

1 In a rice cooker, combine 3 cups/720 ml water with the sweet potatoes, cabbage, rice, green beans, raisins, garlic, ginger, curry powder, lime, and salt. Stir to combine, cover, and turn on the cooker. In about 45 minutes, open the lid and spoon out a few grains of rice to see if the rice is completely cooked. The veggies will be tender before the rice. If the rice is not done, and the water is all absorbed, add ¼ cup/60 ml more water and cook until the rice is tender, 5 to 10 minutes more. Alternatively, put the ingredients in a large pot on the stovetop over high heat and bring to a boil, then cover tightly and reduce the heat to low. Cook for about 45 minutes, or until the liquids are all absorbed. Let the pot stand, covered, for at least 5 minutes to finish steaming the rice before serving.

2 Remove and discard the lime half. Serve the rice mixture topped with the peanuts.

1 tsp canola oil

2 large carrots, sliced

1 cup/200 g millet

4 large scallions/spring onions, chopped

2 tbsp minced peeled fresh ginger

1 garlic clove, minced

1 large orange, zested and juiced

1½ cups/260 g edamame, thawed

2 tsp tamari or soy sauce

One 8¼-by-7¾-in/ 21-by-20-cm sheet nori, toasted and shredded

SERVES 4

Millet and orange give this yellow one-pot a sunny glow and a citrusy scent. It's an easy, fast meal that makes good use of the mild-tasting whole grain that is far too often wasted on birds. Any steamed veggie or simple salad would be a fine accompaniment.

Millet, Ginger, and Edamame One-Pot

with Orange

1 In a large saucepan with a lid, heat the oil briefly over high heat. Add the carrots and stir for 1 minute. Add the millet, scallions/spring onions, ginger, and garlic and stir until all the ingredients are hot and the millet is lightly toasted. Add the orange zest. Combine the orange juice with water to make 2½ cups/600 ml. Add the liquid to the pan with the edamame and tamari and bring to a boil. Cover tightly and reduce the heat to low. Cook, covered, for 25 minutes.

2 Uncover the pan. The millet should have absorbed all the liquids and be fluffy. Serve it topped with the shredded nori.

Grilling

Grilling, or barbecuing, food outdoors is the summer pastime of countless weekend warriors. If you are vegan, you may have let your barbecue rust, as it seems that the grill is all about cooking burgers. I know I had kind of fallen away from it for a time, especially because it seemed silly to me to light a big pile of coals for a few strips of zucchini/courgette. I was only cheating myself, though, and after trying out a friend's gas rig, I realized that I was missing out. I prefer gas, although I know there are purists who like charcoal. Once I discovered smoking chips, too, and started using wood to give the food all the flavor of smoke, I was back to grilling in a big way.

You see, your barbecue is more than just a place to sear things. If you learn a few tricks, it is a full-on food smoker, where you can infuse that smoky, umami-amping flavor into your food. It's an outdoor pizza and panini grill, one that doesn't heat up the kitchen. It's a roasting oven, where piles of summer bell peppers/capsicums and eggplant/aubergine can be softened and sweetened, all while you sip a cool drink and contemplate the blue sky between food flips. It's a social hub and a place where you can make flexi-vegan meals for your friends, throwing a few burgers on the other side from your vegan goodies—and burn away the evidence before the next use.

Grilling Guidelines

OIL: The most frustrating thing is to have your food stick to the grate and fall apart. Each time you cook, pour some canola oil in a small cup and wad up a paper towel/absorbent paper to apply it. Use a pair of tongs to quickly swab oil on the hot grate just before putting the food on.

WATER: Get a cheap spray bottle and use it only for water. When you are barbecuing and smoking, you can spray the wood chips if they start burning too fast and also spray any flare-ups in the coals below. When marinade or oil hits the coals, the flames that flare up can coat your food in icky-tasting carbon, so keep the sprayer handy.

SMOKER CHIPS: Buy some wood chips that are just for smoking food. Bags of mesquite, cherry, and other flavorful wood chips are easy to find in summer. If you are feeling experimental, try using herb stems, like rosemary or thyme, for part or all of the smoke. Put a couple handfuls of chips in a medium bowl, cover with cold water, and soak for at least 2 hours. For a gas barbecue, you can buy a special smoker box, which is a metal box that you set in the bottom of the grill right over the flames. You can also fashion one out of foil. Just fold a double layer of heavy foil into a rectangle and fold up some walls on the edges to hold in the chips. It will only last for one or two uses. Just before grilling, drain the chips well and either put them in the smoker box of the gas grill or sprinkle them over the coals in a charcoal grill.

GAS: To preheat a gas barbecue, remove the grill grate and turn the burners to high. In about 15 minutes, the grill will be hot. Prepare a smoker pan as described above. In the pan, put the drained wood chips. Put the pan on the hot burners, then put the grill grate back on and oil it. Keep an eye on the grill until you smell and see some smoke. Turn off the burner on the other side of the grill and turn the one under the smoking wood to low. To get maximum smoky flavor, keep the lid closed as much as possible while still keeping an eye on the food. Spray the chips with water occasionally to cool them off and keep the smoke coming.

CHARCOAL: If using a charcoal barbecue, build the fire on just one side of the bottom of the grill. Light the coals and let burn until they are white. Sprinkle some or all of the soaked, drained wood chips over the coals and then place the grate back on. Let the grate get hot and the chips start to smoke, then open the lid, oil the grate, and put the food on. If you are doing a longer smoke, like the Smoked Tofu or Tempeh (page 446), keep sprinkling on more soaked chips as you go.

¼ cup/60 ml tamari

¼ cup/60 ml toasted sesame oil

2 tbsp rice vinegar

½ tsp red pepper flakes

1½ lb/680 g firm tofu or tempeh

Canola oil

SERVES 6

This recipe makes a nice big batch, so you can either take it to a party or dole it out all week. I've served this with the Thai Peanut Sauce (page 128) and Chinese Sesame Sauce (page 127) for dipping, to rave reviews.

Smoked Tofu or Tempeh

1 In a square tub large enough to hold all of the tofu or tempeh, mix together the tamari, sesame oil, vinegar, and pepper flakes. Drain the water from the tofu and wrap the tofu in clean towels; press carefully to soak up water without breaking the tofu. Unwrap the tofu and slice it across the rectangle into five thick slices per block. Or, slice the tempeh into strips, then steam it for 5 minutes to moisten it, and pat dry. Place the slices in the marinade, turn them over to coat, and cover. Refrigerate for at least 24 hours or up to 3 days, turning occasionally to coat.

2 Prepare the grill/barbecue for smoking (see page 444) over high heat, with a cool zone on one side.

GAS: Drain the tofu or tempeh and place it on the oiled grate over the smoker pan; shut the lid. Keep an eye on the grill until you smell and see some smoke. Turn off the burner on the other side of the grill and turn the one under the smoking wood to low. Leave the grill closed, opening every 10 minutes to quickly turn the tofu. Smoke the tofu until firm and smoky, about 40 minutes; tempeh for 20 to 30 minutes. If it is drying out, take it off and put it back in the marinade for a few minutes, then let cool. Remove the tofu or tempeh to a platter and let it cool; serve or refrigerate until needed.

CHARCOAL: Place the tofu or tempeh on the cold side of the grill, then close and smoke the tofu until firm and smoky, about 40 minutes for tofu, or 20 to 30 minutes for the tempeh, checking and turning every 10 minutes. Remove the tofu or tempeh to a platter and let it cool; serve or refrigerate until needed.

½ large globe eggplant/
aubergine

1½ tbsp extra-virgin
olive oil

1 head garlic, cloves
peeled

¼ cup/60 ml tahini paste

¼ cup/60 ml freshly
squeezed lemon juice

½ tsp salt

¼ tsp smoked paprika
(pimentón) or ground
chipotle

Pita bread for dipping

SERVES 3

Eggplant soaks up the smoke of the grill, and gives it back in a garlicky dip that will knock your socks off. Slather it on pita or even in a sandwich, and savor all that umami.

Smoky Baba Ghanouj

1 Prepare the grill/barbecue for smoking (see page 444) over medium heat, with a cool zone on one side.

2 Brush the cut side of the eggplant/aubergine with some of the oil. Put the garlic on a square of foil, drizzle it with the remaining oil, and crimp the edges of the foil just to keep it from spilling (but leave it open so smoke can enter). Put the eggplant/aubergine on the grill, over the smoker chips, cut-side down, and the garlic packet on a shelf above that, or on the cool side of the grill. Close the grill and let it smoke for 10 minutes. Open the lid, turn the eggplant/aubergine over, and shake the garlic cloves in their packet. Close the grill again for about 10 minutes. The eggplant/aubergine should be very soft and collapsed, and the garlic should be soft when pierced with a paring knife. Transfer the eggplant/aubergine to a bowl and let it cool just until you can handle it without burning yourself; scoop the flesh out of the skin and discard the skin.

3 In a food processor or blender, puree the garlic and eggplant/aubergine. Add the tahini, lemon juice, salt, paprika, and any oil from the garlic and puree. Serve at room temperature with the pita bread. Cover and refrigerate any leftovers.

1 lb/455 g tempeh

¾ cup/180 ml coconut milk

1 tbsp grated peeled fresh ginger

1 tbsp minced garlic

1 tbsp molasses/treacle

1 tbsp soy sauce

½ tsp salt

½ tsp ground turmeric

½ tsp black pepper

½ tsp ground coriander

Salsa

8 oz/225 g cherry tomatoes

2 large jalapeños

2 small shallots, peeled

2 garlic cloves, peeled

Vegetable oil spray

8 oz/225 g round Thai eggplant/aubergine

½ cup/15 g cilantro/ fresh coriander, coarsely chopped

2 tbsp freshly squeezed lime juice

1 tbsp white miso

1 tbsp tamari

1 tsp chile-infused sesame oil

Canola oil

SERVES 4

Tempeh takes a bath in its ancestral flavors, all harking from the land of Indonesian spice. The little round Thai eggplants are a great treat, with no bitterness and a sweet, rich flavor on the grill, but if you can't find them, use the other kinds. The sauce is a great way to cook veggies on the grill, and melds them into an Indo-inspired dip that you will want to slather on everything.

Indonesian Tempeh
with Asian Salsa

1 Set up a steamer and bring the water to a simmer. Cut the tempeh into eight squares, and steam them until moistened, about 10 minutes; let them cool. Carefully split each square horizontally into two thin squares, holding each flat on the cutting board while slicing parallel to the board.

2 In a large frying pan, mix together the milk, ginger, garlic, molasses/treacle, soy sauce, salt, turmeric, pepper, and ground coriander. Add the tempeh and bring to a simmer, scooping some of the liquids over the tops of the slices. Simmer gently to infuse the flavors, until slightly thickened, about 15 minutes. Transfer the tempeh and marinade to a storage tub and let cool, then refrigerate overnight.

3 TO MAKE THE SALSA: Preheat the grill/barbecue on medium heat, with a charcoal grill set up for indirect cooking. Make a packet from a piece of foil 1 ft/30 cm wide. Lay the foil on the counter and put the tomatoes, jalapeños, shallots, and garlic in the center. Coat them lightly with oil spray and pull up the foil, crimping to make a closed packet. Put the packet on the grill over indirect heat. Grill the eggplants/aubergines whole over direct heat, turning every few minutes. Grill for about 5 minutes. When the eggplants are blistered and soft, and the garlic and shallots are tender when pierced with a knife, remove everything to a plate. Leave them to cool.

4 In a food processor, puree the eggplant/aubergine and the contents of the packet, removing the stems from the jalapeños. Stir in the cilantro/fresh coriander, lime juice, miso, tamari, and sesame oil.

5 Use a wadded paper towel/absorbent paper to rub oil on the grill grate. Over direct heat, grill the tempeh until marked, about 3 minutes per side, basting with any extra marinade.

6 Serve the salsa with the tempeh.

14 oz/400 g ripe tomatoes, halved

1 small red bell pepper/capsicum, halved and seeded

2 large jalapeños, halved and seeded

½ medium red onion, quartered

1 tsp extra-virgin olive oil

½ cup/15 g cilantro/fresh coriander

2 garlic cloves, peeled

2 tbsp freshly squeezed lime juice

1 tbsp chopped chipotle chile, in adobo sauce

½ tsp salt

SERVES 4

Fire up the grill and make a salsa with a real kick! If you have room in the freezer, you might want to pick up veggies at the farmer's market when they are cheap, make a few batches of this, end enjoy the smoky sensations of summer all winter long.

Smoky Chipotle Salsa

1 Prepare the grill/barbecue for smoking (see page 444) over medium heat. In a large bowl, combine the tomatoes, bell pepper/capsicum, jalapeños, and onion and drizzle them with the oil. Gently roll to coat. Place the tomatoes, cut-side up, and the other vegetables, cut-side down, on the hot grate and reduce the heat to low on a gas grill (or use indirect heat on a charcoal grill). Cover the grill and cook for about 5 minutes, then turn the onion, pepper/capsicum, and jalapeños. Cook until the vegetables are limp, about 5 minutes more. Carefully transfer the vegetables back to the bowl.

2 In a blender or food processor, puree the cilantro/fresh coriander and garlic to mince. Add the tomatoes and onion and pulse to coarsely chop. Peel and chop the bell pepper/capsicum and jalapeños into small pieces. Add them to the blender with the lime juice, chipotle, and salt and pulse just to mix. Serve immediately or cover and refrigerate for up to 5 days or freeze for up to 2 months.

½ cup/70 g polenta
(coarse cornmeal)

½ cup/100 g amaranth

¾ tsp salt

½ tsp dried oregano

Canola oil

2 small yellow squashes,
halved lengthwise

1 medium red bell
pepper/capsicum, halved
lengthwise

½ small red onion,
quartered

1 ear corn on the cob,
shucked

3 tbsp barbecue sauce

SERVES 4

Amaranth is a miracle grain. The tiny seeds contain concentrated minerals and protein and have an exotic flavor. Mixed with coarse cornmeal, they make a toothsome polenta. Just be sure to start the polenta at least three hours before you want to serve.

Amaranth Polenta
with Barbecued Veggies

1 In a large heavy saucepan, whisk together the polenta and amaranth, then slowly whisk in 2 cups/480 ml water. Add the salt and bring to a boil, stirring often. Reduce the heat to low and cook, stirring often, until the mixture is very thick, about 20 minutes. Stir in the oregano and take the pan off the heat. Let it stand, covered, for about 10 minutes to finish steaming. Oil a 4-by-10-in/10-by-25-cm loaf pan/tin. Scrape the polenta into the pan and spread it evenly. Oil your hands and pat the mixture until it is completely smooth. Refrigerate for at least 3 hours, covering it if leaving it overnight.

2 Preheat the grill/barbecue on high heat, with a charcoal grill set up for indirect cooking. Put the squashes, bell pepper/capsicum, and onion in a large bowl and toss them with 1 tsp of oil. Put the oiled veggies and corn on the grill and reduce the heat to low, or put them over indirect heat on the charcoal grill. Cover and cook for about 5 minutes, then turn the veggies. Keep turning until they all are tender and browned, about 5 minutes more. Transfer them back to the bowl. Let the veggies cool enough to handle them, then chop them into bite-size pieces, and cut the corn off the cob. Mix the veggies with the barbecue sauce and reserve. (Reheat them when it is time to serve.)

3 Cut the polenta into four squares, and oil both sides generously. Re-oil the grill grate, then put the polenta on the grill. Let it sit undisturbed for about 3 minutes, then carefully use a metal spatula to flip each slice. Grill until well-marked and heated through, another 3 to 5 minutes. Serve hot, topped with the warm veggies in sauce.

2 lb/910 g butternut squash

2 tsp extra-virgin olive oil

¾ cup/180 ml apple cider

2 tbsp red wine vinegar

2 tbsp agave syrup

1 tsp coarsely cracked black pepper

½ tsp salt

SERVES 4

At the end of summer, beautiful sweet squashes start appearing at the farmers' market, so why not grill them? The firm, sweet butternut squash grills to tender perfection, and a tangy glaze sets off the smoky char of the grill.

Butternut Squash Wedges
with Sweet-and-Sour Glaze

1 Preheat the grill/barbecue on high heat, with a charcoal grill set up for indirect cooking. Peel the squash, scoop out the seeds, and slice it into long slices no more than ¾ in/ 2 cm thick at the widest part. Put the slices in a large bowl and drizzle them with the oil. Prepare the glaze by combining the cider, vinegar, agave syrup, pepper, and salt in a small saucepan. Bring to a boil, then reduce the heat to a strong simmer and cook until the mixture is reduced by half, about 5 minutes. Let cool slightly.

2 Place the squash slices on the oiled grate, then turn down the heat to low, or use the cool side of the charcoal grill. Close the lid for about 4 minutes. Open, turn the slices, and cook again until marked, another 4 minutes. Test a slice with a paring knife. You want it to be tender but not to fall apart. Carefully transfer the squash to a flat plate and pour over the glaze. Let cool to room temperature before serving, since the flavor gets better as they sit.

1 lb/455 g carrots,
quartered lengthwise

1 tsp ground turmeric

1¼ tsp salt

1 tbsp canola oil

Freshly cracked black
pepper

2 tbsp maple syrup

2 tbsp apple juice

1 tbsp freshly squeezed
lemon juice

¼ tsp smoked paprika
(pimentón)

SERVES 4

Even the humble carrot can make the leap to the grill, for a summer version of the kind of glazed carrots we love in winter. These are much flashier, flaunting their grill marks from under a sweet and tangy glaze with a little smoked paprika to emphasize the grill flavor.

Carrots
with Smoky Maple-Apple Glaze

1 Preheat the grill/barbecue on medium heat, with a charcoal grill set up for indirect cooking. Put 6 cups/1.4 L water in a large pot. Put the carrots, turmeric, and 1 tsp of the salt in the pot and bring to a boil. Reduce the heat to a simmer and cook until the carrots are crisp-tender, about 4 minutes. Drain well and pat them dry. Put them in a bowl and toss with the oil, the remaining ¼ tsp salt, and the pepper.

2 In a small pot, combine the maple syrup, apple and lemon juices, and paprika. Place the pot over high heat and bring to a boil, stirring constantly, until thick. Take it off the heat.

3 Place the carrots on the oiled grate, then turn down the heat to low, or use the cool side of the charcoal grill. Close the lid. Check on them in 5 minutes and continue to turn until they are evenly marked by the grill. Transfer the hot carrots to a bowl and toss them with the sauce before serving.

1 large red bell pepper/
capsicum, halved

1 medium red onion,
quartered

1 medium zucchini/
courgette, quartered

½ medium eggplant/
aubergine, peeled and
sliced

8 oz/225 g ripe
tomatoes, halved

1 jalapeño

3 garlic cloves, halved

3 tbsp extra-virgin olive oil

½ cup/15 g cilantro/fresh
coriander or parsley

½ cup/120 ml plain vegan
creamer or coconut milk

¾ tsp salt

1 lb/455 g dried penne
pasta

SERVES 6

Use the grill to smoke a big pile of summer veggies, then puree them for an intense, flavorful
sauce. The sauce is flecked with charred bits of
veggie and coats the pasta like a dream.

Smoky Vegetable Sauce
with Penne

1 Preheat the grill/barbecue on medium-high heat, with a
charcoal grill set up for indirect cooking. Put the vegetables
in a large bowl and drizzle them with the oil. Bring a large pot
of water to a boil.

2 Place the vegetables on the oiled grate, cut-sides up,
stuffing the garlic cloves into the tomato halves, then turn
down the heat to low, or use the cool side of the charcoal grill.
Close the lid. On the gas grill, when the smoke is leaking out
the sides of the grill, lower the heat under the smoker box
side. Open the lid occasionally to spray the chips with water
if they are burning too fast. Smoke the vegetables, checking
every 5 minutes and turning them as they soften. Everything
will take different amounts of time, so when each one is tender, black in spots, and smoky, transfer it back to the bowl.

3 When all the vegetables are done, peel the jalapeño
and bell pepper/capsicum. In a food processor, puree the
cilantro/fresh coriander and the garlic first. Add the remaining vegetables and puree. Transfer the puree to a large
frying pan and stir in the creamer and salt over low heat.

4 Cook the penne in the boiling water according to the
package directions, or until it is al dente. Drain and toss the
pasta with the sauce in the pan. Serve hot.

1 lb/455 g spinach leaves
2 garlic cloves, peeled
3 tbsp extra-virgin olive oil
1 tbsp champagne vinegar
14 oz/400 g canned/ tinned white beans, drained and rinsed
Salt
½ cup/90 g chopped fresh tomato
½ tsp red pepper flakes
4 medium portobello mushrooms

SERVES 4

These beautiful little edible mushroom bowls are stuffed with creamy bean dip and an amazing amount of spinach in a small space. The meaty mushrooms are like steaks, and everyone likes creamed spinach with those.

Portobellos
Stuffed with Creamy Spinach

1 Bring a large pot of water to a boil. Drop in the spinach and stir. When it comes back to a boil, cook for 1 minute and drain. Rinse with cold water, then squeeze out the leaves completely. Wrap them in a towel and put under a pot or cutting board for 20 minutes or so to extract all the water.

2 Unwrap the spinach and chop it. In a food processor, process the spinach and garlic to chop finely. Scrape down the sides and process again. Add 2 tbsp of the oil and the vinegar and process until smooth. Add the beans and ½ tsp salt and process until smooth. Scrape the mixture into a medium bowl, and stir in the tomato and pepper flakes. (The filling can be made the day ahead and refrigerated.)

3 Prepare the portobellos by carefully scraping out the gills with a spoon while supporting the rims with your fingers. (You can skip this, but they will be much nicer this way.) Sprinkle the scraped surfaces with salt, and let the mushrooms drain on a kitchen towel for an hour. Preheat the grill/barbecue on high heat, with a charcoal grill set up for indirect cooking. Before grilling, wipe off any moisture from the mushrooms and rub them with the remaining 1 tbsp oil.

4 Turn one side of the gas grill to low. Place the mushrooms, gill-side down, on the hot side of the grate and close the lid to soften and cook them about 2 minutes. Open the grill and move the mushrooms to a plate, then fill them with the bean mixture. Put them back on the grill on the cooler side and cover the grill for 5 minutes, or until the bean mixture is hot and the mushrooms are browned. Serve immediately.

1½ lb/680 g new (baby) yellow or red potatoes

1 lb/455 g fresh asparagus, trimmed

5 tbsp/75 ml extra-virgin olive oil

2 tbsp champagne vinegar

½ tsp salt

½ tsp freshly cracked black pepper

½ cup/15 g fresh basil

SERVES 4

Start your grilling season off right, and celebrate the first asparagus and tender new potatoes with a fabulous salad. The grill roasts and shrinks the asparagus, giving it an intense and smoky flavor, and potatoes are always good with a hint of char.

Asparagus and New Potato Salad

1 Add the potatoes to a large pot of water and bring them to a boil. Boil them until tender but not falling apart, about 10 minutes. Drain them and refrigerate to chill them completely, then cut them in half. Put the potatoes and asparagus in a large bowl and toss them with 1 tbsp of the oil.

2 Preheat the grill/barbecue on medium heat. Put the asparagus on one side of the grill, and arrange the potatoes, cut-side down, on the other side of the well-oiled grate. Close the lid for a couple of minutes. Open the lid and roll the asparagus to turn; as they brown and curl slightly, they are done. Move the grilled asparagus back to the bowl. Use tongs to lift up the potatoes to check for grill marks. When they are marked and crispy around the edges, move them to the bowl.

3 In a cup, whisk together the remaining 4 tbsp/60 ml oil, the vinegar, salt, and pepper. Pour the dressing over the potatoes and asparagus and toss. Let them cool to room temperature. Chop the basil and add it to the cooled vegetables. Serve immediately.

12 ears corn, husks on

1 large, ripe avocado

1 tbsp freshly squeezed lemon juice

½ tsp salt

SERVES 6

Your companions may think that they need butter for their corn, but once they try it this way, they will change their minds. Rich, buttery avocado accents the sweetness of the corn, and if you get a little browning on the kernels from grilling, the better it is. The smooth green "butter" looks lovely on the bright yellow corn.

Grill-Roasted Corn
with Avocado "Butter"

1 Preheat the grill/barbecue on medium heat, with a charcoal grill set up for indirect cooking. Strip off all but one layer of husks and soak the corn in cold water for 15 minutes so the husks will help steam the corn.

2 Take them out and shake the water off, then drain the corn on a towel. At this stage, you can peel back the remaining husks and remove the silks if you want (and even oil the kernels and sprinkle them with spices or herbs). Replace the husks and tie them into a little package at the top with twine or a strip of husk, if desired.

3 Mash or puree the avocado with the lemon juice and salt. (If you want to add herbs or chiles, go ahead.)

4 Put the corn on the hot grate and turn frequently, until the husks are marked, about 5 minutes. Turn down the heat to low or move the ears to the cooler, indirect side of a charcoal grill. Cook, covered, until the husks are dry and burnt and the corn is tender and marked in spots, 10 minutes or so, turning every 3 minutes. Use tongs to take the corn off the grill, and wearing heavy gloves, peel back the husks. Serve the corn with 1 tbsp of avocado butter smeared all over each ear.

1 large zucchini/
courgette, sliced

1 tsp extra-virgin olive oil

4 sandwich rolls

½ cup/120 ml pesto, such
as Basil Pesto (page 116)

1 large, ripe avocado,
sliced and scooped out
of the skin

4 slices red onion

2 roasted red peppers/
capsicums from a jar,
drained and chopped

SERVES 4

You need some bricks for this recipe—not to eat, but to press the sandwiches like a panini press. They are cheap, so pick up a few at the local builder's supply store and wrap them in foil. Then your grill can be a panini grill all summer long!

Stuffed Sandwiches

with Summer Veggies and Pesto

1 Wrap four bricks with foil and place them by the grill. Preheat the grill/barbecue on high heat. In a large bowl, toss the zucchini/courgette with the oil, then place the slices on the grill and turn frequently until they are seared, marked, and soft. Transfer them back to the bowl as they are done.

2 Halve the rolls, then spread each with 2 tbsp of the pesto, and divide the zucchini/courgette, avocado, onion, and bell peppers/capsicums among the sandwiches. Wrap each in foil.

3 Place the sandwiches on the grill and put a brick on top of each one. Mash it flat. Cook for about 4 minutes, then take off the brick and turn the sandwiches over. Put the brick back on until the sandwiches are hot through, about 3 minutes. Take all the sandwiches off the grill, unwrap, and serve.

½ batch White Wheat Pizza Crust (page 328) or Neapolitan Pizza Dough (page 327)

Flour

6 oz/170 g seitan, chopped and wrung out

½ cup/120 ml barbecue sauce

2 large, ripe avocados

¼ tsp salt

Cornmeal, for dough

1½ cups/245 g chopped fresh pineapple

SERVES 3

These tropical-themed pizzas come together fast—just make sure you have all your ingredients assembled and ready to eat. Creamy avocado takes the place of cheese, and the combination of barbecue sauce and sweet-tangy pineapple is an easy instant party. The avocado turns a little dark over the heat, but it still tastes great.

Barbecued Seitan Pizza
with Pineapple and Avocado

1 Make the dough and let it rise for about an hour or bring refrigerated dough to warm room temperature. On a lightly floured counter, divide the dough into three rounds and let rest for 10 minutes. Put the seitan in a medium bowl, pour over the barbecue sauce, and mix. In a small bowl, mash the avocados with the salt.

2 Preheat the grill/barbecue on medium heat. Roll out the dough rounds very thinly, to about ⅛ in/3 mm in diameter. Transfer the rounds to a cormeal-sprinkled baking sheet/tray or large cutting board. Carefully place the rounds of dough on the well-oiled grill grate by picking up one edge and laying each one across the grid like a tablecloth (grilling in batches if necessary). Cover and cook the dough for 5 minutes, then uncover and flip the dough over. Quickly spread one third of the seitan mixture over each of the crusts, top with the pineapple, and dollop on the avocado mixture. Cover the grill again and cook until hot, about 5 minutes more. Slide the pizzas onto a cutting board or baking sheet and cut; serve immediately.

Dough

1 tbsp agave syrup

2 tsp bread-machine yeast

3 cups/385 g unbleached all-purpose/plain flour, plus extra for counter

¾ cup/85 g wheat germ

1 tsp salt

Canola oil

Pesto

2 oz/55 g fresh arugula/rocket

¼ cup/30 g pistachio nuts or pine nuts

2 garlic cloves

¼ tsp salt

6 tbsp/80 ml extra-virgin olive oil

1 medium zucchini/courgette

1 medium red bell pepper/capsicum

2 tsp extra-virgin olive oil

1 tsp balsamic vinegar

Cornmeal, for dough

1¼ cups/300 ml Almond-Cashew "Chèvre" (page 44; optional)

SERVES 4

If you have a hungry mob, these pizzas will fill them up. Creamy and spicy arugula pesto enriches the wheat germ–flecked crust, and if you add the "chèvre" on top, it is a real pizza experience. Don't worry that your dough will flop into the grate—just throw it on there and watch the magic happen.

Arugula Pesto Pizza
with Grill-Roasted Veggies

1 TO MAKE THE DOUGH: In a large mixing bowl or the bowl of a stand mixer fitted with the dough hook, mix 1½ cups/360 ml warm water with the agave syrup and yeast and let them stand for 10 minutes to proof. When the yeast is foamy, stir in the flour, wheat germ, and salt, kneading to make a soft, but not sticky dough. Transfer it to an oiled bowl, turn to coat the dough, and cover it with plastic wrap/cling film. Let the dough rise in a warm, draft-free place until it doubles in volume, about 1 hour.

2 TO MAKE THE PESTO: Wash and dry the arugula/rocket, and pull off the stems. In a blender or food processor, combine the arugula/rocket, pistachios, garlic, and salt and process to grind as finely as possible. With the motor running, gradually drizzle in the oil and process to make a smooth paste.

3 Preheat the grill/barbecue on medium heat. Slice the zucchini/courgette and bell pepper/capsicum into pieces large enough to not fall through the grill grate. Toss the veggies with the oil and vinegar. Put the veggies on the grill and cook until they are marked and soft, about 5 minutes. If desired, chop them into smaller pieces.

4 On a lightly floured counter, divide the dough into two pieces, form them into disks, and let them rest for 10 minutes to relax the gluten. Roll each out to a 12-in/30-cm circle, then transfer to a cornmeal-lined baking sheet/tray or large cutting board. Carefully place a round of dough on the well-oiled grill grate—you can slide it off the cornmeal-lined pan or just pick up one edge and lay it on like a tablecloth. Cover and cook the dough for 5 minutes, then uncover and flip the dough over. Quickly spread half of the pesto on the dough, top with half of the veggies, and half of the "chèvre" (if using). Close the lid again and cook until the toppings are warmed, about 5 minutes more. Slide the pizza onto a cutting board or baking sheet/tray and cut; serve immediately. Repeat for the second pizza.

1¼ cups/175 g cornmeal

1½ cups/360 ml plain almond milk

½ cup/100 g brown sugar

2 tbsp ground flax seeds

2 tbsp Earth Balance margarine, melted

1 tbsp orange zest

¼ tsp salt

Canola oil

1 tsp ground cinnamon

2 large, ripe but not too soft peaches, halved and pitted, skins intact

Nondairy ice cream (optional)

SERVES 4

A whiff of smoke gives a hunk of sweet polenta a nice crispy edge, and it pairs well with the exploding juices of summer peaches. It's a neat trick to grill peach halves this way. Be sure to make the polenta at least three hours ahead of grilling time, so it will have time to chill and solidify.

Sweet Polenta
with Cinnamon Peaches

1 In a large heavy saucepan, whisk together ⅓ cup/75 ml water and the cornmeal. Then gradually whisk in ⅔ cup/165 ml water, the milk, ¼ cup/50 g of the sugar, the flax, margarine, orange zest, and salt. Over medium-high heat, bring the mixture to a boil, stirring often. Reduce the heat to low and continue stirring, until the mixture is very thick, about 10 minutes. Oil an 8-in/20-cm square baking pan and scrape the polenta into the pan. Spread it with the spatula, then place wax/greaseproof paper on top and press to smooth it flat. Uncover and refrigerate until set, at least 3 hours.

2 Preheat the grill/barbecue on high heat, with a charcoal grill set up for indirect cooking. Cut the polenta into four squares and put them on a plate. Mix together the remaining ¼ cup/50 g sugar and the cinnamon in a small bowl. Place the peaches, cut-side down, on the grill, then turn down the heat to low, or use the cool side of the charcoal grill. Put the polenta on the grate over the higher heat. Turn the peaches every 2 minutes for about 6 minutes, until soft but not falling apart. Finish with the cut-sides up, so they can bubble up with their juices. Turn the polenta every 2 minutes until it has nice grill marks and is heated through, about 8 minutes total. When the peaches are bubbling and tender throughout, sprinkle each half with one fourth of the cinnamon-sugar mix-ture. Close the lid for 1 minute more to melt the sugar a bit. Slice the polenta squares in half, corner to corner, to make triangles. Serve two triangles with half a peach on top and, if desired, a scoop of nondairy ice cream.

1 medium pineapple, peeled
½ tsp ground cinnamon
½ cup/120 ml mango juice or other tropical juice
2 tsp cornstarch/cornflour
1 tbsp raw sugar
1 tsp vanilla extract
2 tbsp maple syrup
2 tsp canola oil or Earth Balance margarine, melted
1 pt/480 ml Coconut Sorbet (page 514)

SERVES 6

Grilled fruit is a perfect ending for a hot summer day, especially topped with a cooling sorbet. Pineapple is sturdy enough to take the heat of the grill, and caramelizes beautifully. Try the Coconut Sorbet with this, or branch out and have it with the Avocado-Lime Sorbet (page 515).

Pineapple Sundaes
with Sorbet

1 Cut the pineapple into six rounds ¾ in/2 cm thick. Cut the cores out of the center with the tip of a paring knife or an apple corer, leaving the rounds intact. Put the slices on a plate, sprinkle the cinnamon over both sides, and rub to distribute it. Core and trim the remaining pineapple for the sauce. Mince it and place it in a medium saucepan. Whisk in the mango juice, cornstarch/cornflour, sugar, and vanilla and bring them to a simmer, stirring until thickened and clear, about 2 minutes.

2 Preheat the grill/barbecue on medium heat. In a small cup, mix together the maple syrup and oil; brush the pineapple slices with the oil mixture and place them on the grill. Turn and grill until the slices are marked and soft. Put them on plates and top with a scoop of sorbet and some of the sauce and serve.

CHAPTER

11

Desserts

As much as people need their three squares of balanced nutrition, they need desserts, too. Maybe not every day, but the allure of a bite of something sweet is undeniable. In fact, in all my experiences with vegan cooking and baking for sale to the public, the thing people looked for most was desserts. They could figure out the savory food, but getting their plant-based sweets to rock like the ones they were used to posed more of a dilemma. Special-occasion desserts, like holiday pies or birthday cakes, were big sellers. Everyday sweets, like cookies/biscuits and cupcakes/fairy cakes, also kept us busy. A freezer case stocked with nondairy ice creams was a bustling spot, too.

So vegans have a sweet tooth, and we might as well plan for some well-deserved indulgences to feed the soul.

Of course, desserts are classified as cookies/biscuits, pies, ice creams, and such. But they are subdivided into the categories of chocolate, nuts, fruit, and crunchy or creamy. I've always been able to rationalize that a dessert with nuts was packed with protein, so why not call it part of the meal? And apple pie is mostly apples, so it counts toward your fruit servings, even with the crazy-good streusel in my recipe. Now that chocolate has emerged as the antioxidant darling that triggers love chemicals in your brain, why on earth not have some? Crunchiness is good exercise for your mouth, so a few sheets of crispy phyllo can engage you in mild exercise. Creamy, and its cousin, tender, are all about comfort. Pudding says: "Relax, be still; the universe is paying you back." Tender cakes and melting cookies/biscuits give your palate a little joyride, taking you away from your daily cares. And ice cream is necessary for a good life, so if you have been waiting for some dairy-free recipes to make at home, here they are.

Baking vegan is fun; it just takes some adjustments. The chemistry of many baked goods is dependent on eggs for lift, butter for richness, and white sugar for sweetness. To bake vegan, eggs are replaced with ground flax seeds, egg replacer powder made from starch and leavening, and purees made from fruit, vegetables, or tofu. Vegetable oils add the fats that keep baked goods from being dry, and coconut oil has a special ability to stay solid like butter in certain recipes. Earth Balance or other vegan margarines are quite handy for times when you really want something buttery. Vegan sweeteners run the gamut from unbleached cane sugars to agave syrup, brown rice syrup, and other more whole sources of sweetness.

You will find an assortment of treats here, with a variety of sweeteners, oils, and levels of whole-graininess. For an afternoon snack, cookies/biscuits like the Almond Butter–Quinoa Cookies with Apricots (page 471) or the Tropical Dried Mango Bars with Cashew Crumble (page 479) are full of healthful grains and fruit, and almost qualify as dessert-like meals. On the other end of the spectrum, Banana Cream Pie (page 482) and Peanut Butter Tart with "Ganache" (page 485) will put the perfect decadent ending on a special meal. In between are puddings, sorbets, ice creams, and pies galore.

Now you can enjoy your vegan desserts as well, and enjoy life.

CHAPTER

1½ cups/170 g pastry/
soft-wheat flour

¼ cup/20 g unsweetened
cocoa powder

1 cup/100 g powdered/
icing sugar

⅛ tsp salt

6 tbsp/90 ml coconut oil

3 tbsp cold-press corn oil

1 tsp vanilla extract

2 tsp bottled raspberry
juice

MAKES 16 COOKIES

Shortbreads are usually a paean to butter. These meltingly tender morsels may just fool you, though. Cake flour and powdered sugar combine with coconut oil and buttery tasting corn oil to make a cookie that you will be proud to serve to family and friends.

Chocolate Shortbreads
with Raspberry Glaze

1 In a large bowl, sift together the flour, cocoa, ½ cup/50 g of the sugar, and the salt. Melt the coconut oil and corn oil together in a small pan or in the microwave. Stir in the vanilla and mix the oils into the dry mixture.

2 Form the dough into a cylinder 2½ in/6 cm across and about 8 in/20 cm long. Wrap it in a piece of plastic wrap/cling film about 10 in/25 cm long and refrigerate until fully chilled, 1 hour or longer.

3 Preheat the oven to 350°F/180°C/gas 4. Take the dough out and let it come to room temperature for about 10 minutes. It is very delicate and will crumble if you slice it while it is really cold. To cut, hold the dough on either side of the knife and go slowly. Using a sharp chef's knife, slice the dough into four segments, then divide each of those into four slices. Place the disks on an ungreased baking sheet/tray, and bake for 9 minutes, then turn the pan and bake until a few cracks form in the cookies/biscuits, about 9 minute more. Let cool on the pan for 5 minutes, then transfer them to cooling racks to cool completely.

4 Put the remaining ½ cup/50 g sugar in a cup and stir in the juice to make a thick paste. Drizzle the tops of the cookies/biscuits with the glaze and let it dry before storing in an air-tight container at room temperature for up to 1 week.

½ cup/80 g rolled oats

½ cup/55 g pistachios

1 cup/115 g unbleached all-purpose/plain flour, plus extra for counter

½ cup/60 g whole-wheat/wholemeal pastry/soft-wheat flour

1 tsp baking powder

¼ tsp salt

½ cup/120 ml maple syrup

¼ cup/60 ml coconut oil

1 tsp vanilla extract

15 tsp/75 ml all-fruit jam

MAKES ABOUT 30 COOKIES

Come holiday time, these tender little nuggets are a great addition to the cookie platter—especially if you put red jam in to complement the green pistachio-flecked cookies. Pistachios taste so buttery, they really make your mouth sing.

Pistachio Thumbprints
with Jam

1 In a food processor, grind the oats and pistachios to a fine powder. Add both flours, baking powder, and salt and pulse to mix. Add the maple syrup, oil, and vanilla to the flour mixture and pulse until the dough comes together. Don't process it any more after the dough forms. Scrape out the dough onto a lightly floured counter and knead it to incorporate any loose flour.

2 Preheat the oven to 350°F/180°C/gas 4. Roll tablespoon-size portions of the dough into balls. Place them on parchment/baking paper–lined baking sheets/trays and press a wet fingertip into the middle of each dough ball, using your fingers to press any cracks in the dough back together. Scoop ½ tsp jam into each indentation, then refrigerate the cookies/biscuits on the pans for 30 minutes to prevent too much spreading.

3 Bake for 7 minutes, then reverse the position of the pans in the oven and bake until the edges are golden, about 8 minutes more. Let them cool on a rack on the pan for 5 minutes, then remove the cookies/biscuits to the rack with a metal spatula. Let cool completely and then store for up to 1 week in an airtight container at room temperature.

1 tbsp ground flax seeds

2 tbsp rice milk or other milk

6 tbsp/90 ml agave syrup

¼ cup/60 ml coconut oil

½ tsp vanilla extract

½ tsp almond extract

¼ cup/30 g slivered/flaked almonds

1 cup/115 g unbleached all-purpose/plain flour

¼ cup/30 g whole-wheat/wholemeal pastry/soft-wheat flour

2 tbsp finely ground coffee

½ tsp baking soda/bicarbonate of soda

¼ tsp salt

MAKES ABOUT 22 COOKIES

These are cookies for grown-ups, with a healthy dose of finely ground coffee laced through the dough. The chocolatey taste of coffee is emphasized in a cookie, and you will get a bit of a lift as you munch.

Espresso-Almond Cookies

1 Preheat the oven to 325°F/165°C/gas 3. In a large bowl, stir together the flax and milk, then beat for a few strokes to thicken. Stir in the agave syrup, oil, vanilla, and almond extract.

2 In a blender or food processor, grind the almonds to a powder, then add both flours, the coffee, baking soda/bicarbonate of soda, and salt. Pulse to mix well, then transfer everything to the bowl with the wet ingredients. Stir them in and mix well. Form rounded tablespoon-size balls of dough and place them on an ungreased baking sheet/tray. Flatten them with your palms to ½ in/12 mm thick.

3 Bake until the edges are golden and the tops are a little cracked, 12 to 14 minutes. Transfer them to racks and let cool completely, then store in an airtight container at room temperature for up to 1 week.

Vegetable oil spray

½ cup/120 ml canola oil

½ cup/100 g almond butter

½ cup/120 ml agave syrup

½ tsp almond extract

¾ cup/85 g whole-wheat/wholemeal pastry/soft-wheat flour

2 tbsp vegan protein powder or chickpea flour

1 tsp ground cinnamon

¼ tsp baking soda/bicarbonate of soda

¼ tsp salt

1 cup/95 g rolled quinoa flakes

½ cup/85 g dried apricots, chopped

½ cup/55 g almonds, coarsely chopped

MAKES 8 BIG COOKIES

Rolled quinoa is kind of like rolled oats, but made from tiny quinoa. The light flakes bake into these hearty cookies with that nutty quinoa taste and chewy texture. These are the healthiest cookies you will find—packed with nuts, fruit, and grain—but they still have all the charms you expect from a cookie.

Almond Butter–Quinoa Cookies
with Apricots

1 Preheat the oven to 350°F/180°C/gas 4. Coat a baking sheet/tray with oil spray and reserve. In a large bowl, stir together the canola oil, almond butter, agave syrup, and almond extract. In a small bowl, mix together the flour, protein powder, cinnamon, baking soda/bicarbonate of soda, and salt. Stir the flour mixture into the wet mixture until well combined. Stir in the quinoa, apricots, and almonds.

2 Use a ¼-cup/60-ml measure to form eight balls of dough, placing each on the prepared pan with 3 in/7.5 cm between them. Wet your palm under running water and use it to flatten the balls to ½ to ¾ in/12 mm to 2 cm thick.

3 Bake for 8 minutes on the bottom rack, then move the pan to the top rack. Bake until the tops are golden brown, but slightly soft when pushed in the center, about 8 minutes more. Let cool on the pan for 5 minutes, then transfer the cookies/biscuits to racks to cool completely. Store them in an airtight container or zip-top bag at room temperature for up to 1 week, or freeze for up to 2 months.

2 tbsp flax seeds

1 cup/200 g sugar

½ cup/120 ml cold-press corn oil or canola oil

1 tsp vanilla extract

1 cup/115 g whole-wheat/wholemeal pastry/soft-wheat flour

½ tsp baking soda/bicarbonate of soda

½ tsp salt

1 cup/155 g rolled oats

1 cup/170 g vegan chocolate chips

1 cup/170 g raisins

½ cup/55 g chopped walnuts

MAKES 12 BIG COOKIES

Big fat cookies, studded with chips, nuts, and raisins, can be just as satisfyingly chewy and good when made vegan. Try these and don't tell anyone they are plant-based, and watch them disappear!

Monster Chocolate Chip– Oat Cookies

1 Preheat the oven to 375°F/190°C/gas 5. Line two heavy baking sheets/trays with parchment/baking paper. In a spice grinder or clean coffee grinder, grind the flax to a fine powder. If your grinder can handle liquids, add ¼ cup/60 ml water and process until a thick paste forms. If not, put the ground flax in a small bowl and stir in the water, and beat for a couple of minutes. Let stand for 5 minutes.

2 In a stand mixer or large bowl, combine the flax mixture, sugar, oil, and vanilla. Beat until smooth. In a bowl, mix together the flour, baking soda/bicarbonate of soda, and salt and add to the sugar mixture. Beat until well mixed. Stir in the oats, then add the chocolate chips, raisins, and nuts and mix just to combine. You may have some chips and nuts in the bottom of the bowl. Scoop ¼-cup/60-ml portions of dough to make twelve cookies/biscuits, and place them 2 in/5 cm apart on the baking sheets/trays. Flatten the dough to ¾ in/2 cm thick, and press any leftover chips into the tops of the cookies/biscuits.

3 Bake for 8 minutes, then reverse the pans and bake until the edges are golden brown and the centers are puffed, about 8 minutes more. Let them cool on the pans on racks for about 5 minutes, then transfer the cookies/biscuits to the racks to cool. When cooled, store them in an airtight container at room temperature for up to 1 week.

Vegetable oil spray

1½ cups/300 g sugar

¾ cup/180 ml coconut oil
or ¾ cup/170 g Earth
Balance margarine

4 oz/115 g prune-oat
baby food from a jar

1 tsp vanilla extract

1¼ cups/150 g whole-
wheat/wholemeal pastry/
soft-wheat flour

¾ cup/75 g unsweetened
cocoa powder

3 tbsp ground flax seeds

1 tsp baking soda/
bicarbonate of soda

½ tsp salt

1½ cups/255 g vegan
chocolate chips

MAKES 14 COOKIES

If you love deep, dark chocolate, these are the
cookies for you. Small children may even find these
a little too chocolatey—leaving more for the lucky
adults! Prune baby food is a great secret ingredient, adding richness, fruity sweetness, and some
nutrients as well.

Double Chocolate Chip Cookies

1 Preheat the oven to 375°F/190°C/gas 5. Lightly coat two
airbake baking sheets/trays with oil spray.

2 In a stand mixer fitted with the paddle or a bowl, beat
together the sugar and oil. Beat in the baby food and vanilla.
In a small bowl, mix together the flour, cocoa powder, flax,
baking soda/bicarbonate of soda, and salt. Mix them into the
oil mixture until well combined. Stir in the chocolate chips.

3 Form 14 balls from ¼-cup/60-ml portions of dough, and
flatten them to ¾ in/2 cm thick. Bake for 6 minutes, then
turn the pans and bake until puffed and dry looking, about
6 minutes more. They will be too soft and gooey to take off
the pans, but they will firm as they cool. Let the cookies/
biscuits cool on the pans on racks for 10 minutes, or until
firm enough to remove with a metal spatula. Transfer the
cookies/biscuits to the rack to finish cooling completely.
Store in an airtight container at room temperature for up
to 1 week.

Dough

½ cup/115 g Earth Balance margarine

1 cup/200 g sugar

3 to 4 tbsp/45 to 60 ml rice milk or other milk

½ tsp vanilla extract

1½ cups/170 g unbleached all-purpose/plain flour

¾ cup/75 g unsweetened cocoa powder

½ tsp salt

Filling

2½ cups/250 g powdered/icing sugar

½ cup/120 ml coconut oil

1 tsp vanilla extract

MAKES 16
FAT SANDWICH COOKIES

If you miss those familiar packaged cookies—the ones we used to dunk in cold milk—these will make you very happy. The crisp, dark, jumbo cookies are double-stuffed with creamy sweet filling, so prepare for a cookie buzz.

Chocolate Sandwich Os

1 TO MAKE THE DOUGH: Preheat the oven to 325°F/165°C/gas 3. Line two baking sheets/trays with parchment/baking paper or silicone baking mats.

2 In a stand mixer or bowl, beat the margarine with the sugar until fluffy. Beat in 3 tbsp of the milk and the vanilla. In a medium bowl, whisk together the flour, cocoa powder, and salt. Mix them into the wet mixture; it will make a stiff dough. Add the remaining 1 tbsp milk only if the dough is too crumbly to hold together. Scoop 2-tbsp portions and form them into disks to make thirty-two cookies, then use a metal spatula to flatten them to ¼ in/6 mm thick. Dip the spatula in flour to keep it from sticking. Put the disks on the prepared pans 2 in/5cm apart.

3 Bake for 8 minutes, turn the pans, then bake until the edges look darkened, about 8 minutes (check at 5 minutes for scorching). Let them cool on racks.

4 TO MAKE THE FILLING: Put the sugar, oil, and vanilla in a stand mixer fitted with the paddle or a medium bowl and beat to combine. It will be stiff. Roll the filling into a cylinder and slice it into 16 portions, then flatten each one to fit in the cookies/biscuits.

5 Put each portion of filling between two cooled cookies/biscuits; press lightly to adhere. Store in a tightly covered container in the refrigerator for up to 1 week; let them come to room temperature before serving.

Brownies

Vegetable oil spray

1 cup/170 g pitted dates

¾ cup/180 ml coconut milk

1½ cups/170 g unbleached all-purpose/plain flour

½ cup/50 g unsweetened cocoa powder

½ tsp salt

¼ tsp baking powder

¼ tsp baking soda/bicarbonate of soda

2 oz/55 g unsweetened/cooking chocolate, chopped

½ cup/120 ml cold-press corn oil or canola oil

1 cup/200 g sugar

2 tsp egg replacer powder

2 tsp vanilla extract

½ tsp rice vinegar

Frosting

2 cups/200 g powdered/icing sugar

¼ cup/25 g unsweetened cocoa powder

¼ cup/60 ml coconut oil, melted

2 tbsp coconut milk

2 tsp vanilla extract

MAKES 16 BROWNIES

These rich, fudgy squares will ring all your brownie bells. Date puree adds creaminess, and the combination of cocoa and melted chocolate gives them a deep, dark, chocolate taste.

Frosted Chocolate Bomb Brownies

1 TO MAKE THE BROWNIES: Preheat the oven to 350°F/180°C/gas 4. Coat a 9-in/23-cm square baking dish with oil spray.

2 In a small saucepan, bring the dates and ¼ cup/60 ml water to a boil; cover tightly and simmer over the lowest heat until the dates are soft, about 4 minutes. Let them cool, drain off the water, then puree the dates. Scrape down the sides and add ½ cup/120 ml of the milk, gradually, with the motor running, to make a smooth puree. In a large bowl, whisk together the flour, cocoa, salt, baking powder, and baking soda/bicarbonate of soda. In the top of a double boiler, melt the chocolate with the corn oil, stirring until smooth. Take off the heat and stir in the date puree and sugar.

3 In a small bowl, stir together the remaining ¼ cup/60 ml milk, the egg replacer, vanilla, and vinegar and stir them into the chocolate mixture. Stir the chocolate mixture into the flour mixture just until combined, then scrape the batter into the prepared pan.

4 Bake until a toothpick inserted 2 in/5 cm from the side of the pan comes out dry, but the middle is still undercooked, 20 to 25 minutes. Let the pan cool on a rack.

5 TO MAKE THE FROSTING: Mix the sugar and cocoa in a food processor, pulsing until well combined. Add the coconut oil, milk, and vanilla and process until smooth.

6 Spread the frosting over the cooled brownies, patting out the stiff spread with your hands. Refrigerate. Slice the brownies 4 by 4 in the pan and keep in the refrigerator, tightly covered for up to 1 week.

½ cup/115 g Earth Balance margarine, melted, plus extra for pans

1 cup/240 ml brown rice syrup

1 tsp vanilla extract

1 cup/115 g unbleached all-purpose/plain flour

½ cup/60 g whole-wheat/wholemeal pastry/soft-wheat flour

½ tsp baking soda/ bicarbonate of soda

¼ tsp salt

¾ cup/95 g malt-sweetened chocolate chips

MAKES ABOUT 12 BARS

The caramel flavor of brown rice syrup is used to its unctuous best in these chewy bars. Topping them with grain-sweetened, luscious chocolate means the bars are only sweetened by the subtle sugars contained in the grains.

Chocolate Toffee Bars

1 Preheat the oven to 350°F/180°C/gas 4. Grease a 9-in/ 23-cm square baking dish. In a bowl, combine the margarine, brown rice syrup, and vanilla and stir to mix well. In a medium bowl, mix together both flours, the baking soda/bicarbonate of soda, and salt. Stir the flour mixture into the margarine mixture and mix well.

2 Spread the batter in the prepared pan. Bake until the top is golden and the center does not wiggle when shaken lightly, 25 to 30 minutes. Take out the pan and sprinkle the chocolate chips evenly over the surface of the bars. Return the pan to the oven for 2 to 3 minutes, then spread the chips gently with a spatula. When they are evenly spread, let the bars cool, then refrigerate them. When they are completely cold, slice the bars 3 by 4 and let them come to room temperature to serve. Store them, covered, in the refrigerator for up to 1 week.

Vegetable oil spray

2 cups/310 g rolled oats

1½ cups/170 g whole-wheat/wholemeal pastry/soft-wheat flour

1½ cups/250 g turbinado sugar

1 tsp baking powder

1 tsp baking soda/bicarbonate of soda

½ tsp salt

6 tbsp/90 g Earth Balance margarine

¾ cup/180 ml rice milk or other milk

2 tsp vanilla extract

1 cup/240 ml apricot preserves

1 cup/170 g dried apricots

2 tsp almond extract

MAKES 18 BARS

Jammed with fruit and chewy with oats, these bars are a real treat to pack for a lunch, or to serve at a gathering. Dried fruit and fruit-sweet preserves combine to make a tangy filling that provides more nutrition than anyone needs to think about at dessert.

Apricot-Filled Oat Bars

1 Preheat the oven to 350°F/180°C/gas 4. Coat a 9-by-13-in/23-by-33-cm baking dish with 2-in/5-cm sides with oil spray.

2 In a large bowl, combine the oats, flour, sugar, baking powder, baking soda/bicarbonate of soda, and salt. Mix well. Cut in the margarine with two knives or a pastry blender and work it in until the fat is the size of rice grains. In a medium bowl, whisk together the milk and vanilla. Reserve. In a food processor, combine the preserves, apricots, and almond extract and process to mix well.

3 Mix the milk mixture into the oats mixture and stir to combine. Spread a little more than half of the batter in the prepared pan; use wet hands to flatten it without sticking. Spread the apricot mixture over the batter, then dollop the remaining batter over the filling. Bake until the edges are deep golden brown and the center of the bars wiggles only slightly when shaken, about 35 minutes. Let the bars cool completely, then cut 3 by 6 to make 18 bars. Store in the refrigerator for up to 1 week.

Vegetable oil spray

2 cups/31 g rolled oats

2 cups/255 g unbleached all-purpose/plain flour

1 cup/200 g brown sugar

½ tsp salt

½ cup/120 ml coconut oil, melted

¼ cup/60 ml vanilla soymilk or other milk, plus 3 tbsp

1 lb/455 g rhubarb, chopped (4 cups)

1¼ cups/250 g granulated sugar

½ cup/85 g crystallized ginger, chopped

3 tbsp cornstarch/cornflour

1 tsp vanilla extract

MAKES 18 BARS

I planted two rhubarb plants in my garden, because I love the tangy taste of the stalks. The plants grow like weeds and provide me with ruby red, tart vegetables that you would swear were fruit. You can use frozen rhubarb for these and enjoy them all year long.

Rhubarb Streusel Bars

1 Preheat the oven to 350°F/180°C/gas 4. Coat a 9-by-13-in/23-by-33-cm baking dish with oil spray. In a large bowl, mix together the oats, flour, brown sugar, and salt. Drizzle in the oil, tossing to mix, then drizzle in ¼ cup/60 ml of the soymilk. Mix, compressing it with your hands to make crumbly chunks.

2 Measure out 2 cups/480 g of the chunkiest bits and put them in a small bowl. If the remaining mixture still has loose flour, drizzle in another tablespoon of milk, to make a dough that will hold together. Sprinkle the dough in the prepared pan and press it in to make a crust, covering just the bottom.

3 In a 4-qt/3.8-L saucepan, combine the rhubarb and granulated sugar and stir over high heat. When the mixture starts to bubble, reduce the heat and cook, stirring, until the rhubarb is tender and the mixture is juicy, 5 to 10 minutes. Stir in the ginger. In a small cup, stir the remaining 3 tbsp soymilk with the cornstarch/cornflour and vanilla. Pour them into the rhubarb mixture and cook, stirring, until thickened and glossy. Let the mixture cool slightly, then pour it over the bottom crust. Sprinkle on the reserved crumbles.

4 Bake until the top is golden brown and the rhubarb bubbles thickly around the edges, about 40 minutes. Let the pan cool on a rack and cut the bars 3 by 6. Store in the refrigerator for up to 1 week.

Bars

12 oz/340 g dried mango, chopped (4 cups)

½ cup/120 ml dark rum

1 tbsp lemon zest

½ cup/120 ml agave syrup

5 tbsp/40 g unbleached all-purpose/plain flour

Vegetable oil spray

1½ cups/170 g whole-wheat/wholemeal pastry/soft-wheat flour

6 tbsp/75 g sugar

⅛ tsp salt

6 tbsp/90 ml coconut oil, frozen

3 tbsp almond milk

Crumble

1 cup/115 g whole-wheat/wholemeal pastry/soft-wheat flour

1 cup/155 g rolled oats

½ cup/60 g raw cashews, chopped

½ cup/100 g sugar

⅛ tsp salt

½ cup/120 ml coconut oil, melted

3 tbsp almond milk

MAKES 9 BARS

On a sunny afternoon in San Francisco, we stopped for a snack at a coffee shop in Haight Ashbury. I had a vegan bar that had a filling made from dried mango, and I just had to go home and make one like it. I guess the home of the hippies is still a source for tasty munchies, all these years later.

Tropical Dried Mango Bars
with Cashew Crumble

1 TO MAKE THE BARS: In a small saucepan, combine the mango, rum, ½ cup/120 ml water, and the lemon zest. Over high heat, bring the mixture to a boil, then reduce the heat to the lowest setting and cover. Simmer until softened, about 5 minutes, then take the pan off the heat and let it stand for 10 minutes. Uncover and stir in the agave syrup and unbleached flour. Reserve.

2 Preheat the oven to 350°F/180°C/gas 4. Coat a 9-in/23-cm square baking dish with oil spray. In a medium bowl, mix together the pastry/soft-wheat flour, sugar, and salt, then cut in the coconut oil until it is the size of rice. Stir in the milk until it holds together when squeezed. If crumbly, toss in a little more milk. Press the dough into the pan and bake until dry looking, 5 minutes. Let the crust cool slightly.

3 TO MAKE THE CRUMBLE: In a medium bowl, mix together the pastry/soft-wheat flour, oats, cashews, sugar, and salt. Stir in the coconut oil to mix well. Sprinkle in the milk and stir, squeezing the mixture to form clumps.

Spread the mango mixture over the crust, then top with the cashew mixture and flatten it slightly. Bake until the top is toasted golden brown and the mangoes are bubbling thickly, 40 to 45 minutes. Let the pan cool on a rack and slice it 3 by 3 or smaller. Store in the refrigerator for up to 1 week.

Vegetable oil spray

2 cups/60g cocoa-rice crisp cereal or other vegan cocoa cereal

2 cups/60 g peanut butter puff cereal or other vegan cereal

1 tbsp coconut oil or Earth Balance margarine

½ cup/100 g sugar (use a smaller, lighter granulated one that will dissolve)

½ cup/120 ml brown rice syrup

1 tsp vanilla extract

½ tsp almond extract

MAKES 12 BARS

Crunchy cocoa-rice crisps and peanut butter crunch cereal combine in the classic krispie treat here, making this a triple threat. Check labels, and use vegan cereals. It feels like you are eating decadent candy, but it is really mostly healthful cereal.

Crispy Cocoa–Peanut Butter Cereal Bars

1 Coat an 8-in/20-cm square pan at least 2 in/5 cm deep with oil spray. In a large bowl, mix together the cereals. In a small saucepan, melt the coconut oil. Add the sugar, brown rice syrup, vanilla and almond extracts and bring to a simmer. Boil until the sugar is dissolved, lowering the heat to keep it from boiling over, about 3 minutes. Pour the liquids over the cereals and mix with a wooden spoon; be careful, it is hot. Spread the mixture in the prepared pan and use a piece of wax/greaseproof paper to press it flat.

2 When the pan is cooled to room temperature, cut the bars 4 by 3. Wrap tightly and refrigerate for up to 1 week, but let the bars come to room temperature to serve.

Vegetable oil spray

6 cups/180 g brown-rice cereal

1 cup/240 ml brown rice syrup

½ cup/100 g sugar (use a smaller, lighter granulated one that will dissolve)

2 tbsp Earth Balance margarine

1 tsp vanilla extract

1 pinch salt

MAKES 36 SMALL BARS

The Rice Krispies bar is a nostalgic comfort food for many of us—a bar we made with our moms or ate at Scouts. Since the usual kind contains gelatin in the marshmallows, we skip those here and use more natural stuff, like brown-rice cereal and syrup. The final bar is just as sweet and crunchy.

Brown-Rice Krispie Treats

1 Coat a 9-in/23-cm square pan with vegetable oil spray. Measure the rice cereal into a large bowl. In a small saucepan over medium heat, stir together the brown rice syrup, sugar, and margarine. When the mixture starts to boil, reduce the heat to keep it from boiling over. Stir as the mixture boils rapidly, about 1 minute. Add the vanilla and salt.

2 Pour the hot syrup mixture over the cereal and stir with a large, sturdy spoon. When all the cereal is coated, scrape the mixture into the prepared pan. Using a piece of wax/greaseproof paper to cover the cereal, pat it down firmly to pack it in the pan, being careful if it is very hot. Refrigerate the pan.

3 The bars will be hard right out of the refrigerator, so let them sit at room temperature for 1 hour before slicing 6 by 6 to make 36 squares. They're best served at room temperature, but store them in the refrigerator for up to 1 week.

1½ cups/360 ml coconut milk

1 cup/240 ml soy or coconut creamer

½ cup/100 g palm sugar or brown sugar

5 tbsp/40 g cornstarch/cornflour

3 tbsp carrot baby food from a jar

1 tsp vanilla extract

½ tsp almond extract

Salt

1 cup/115 g whole-wheat/wholemeal pastry/soft-wheat flour, plus extra for counter

4 tbsp/60 ml coconut oil or ¼ cup/55 g Earth Balance margarine, frozen

5 tbsp/75 ml ice water

2 large, just-ripe bananas

2 tsp freshly squeezed lemon juice

Vegan whipped topping (optional)

8 large, fresh strawberries, for garnish (optional)

SERVES 8

Rich, creamy pudding and bananas—how can you go wrong? The pie is so delicious that it is just as fun without vegan whipped topping, but if you go that route, it's a festival of happy memories.

Banana Cream Pie

1 In a medium saucepan, whisk together the milk, creamer, sugar, cornstarch/cornflour, and baby food. Put the pan over medium heat and whisk until the mixture is very thick. Take it off the heat and whisk in the vanilla, almond extract, and a pinch of salt. Scrape the pudding into a medium bowl and cover with plastic wrap/cling film, pressing onto the surface of the pudding to prevent a skin from forming. Refrigerate to chill the pudding completely.

2 In a large bowl, mix together the flour and ⅛ tsp salt. Grate or cut in the oil until the fat looks like grains of rice. Drizzle in 1 tbsp of the ice water while tossing the flour mixture with a fork. Gently gather the dough, pressing the pieces together and adding more water, 1 tbsp at a time, to moisten any loose flour. When the dough can be pressed together into a ball, form a disk, wrap it in plastic wrap/cling film, and refrigerate for 20 minutes.

3 Preheat the oven to 400°F/200°C/gas 6. On a lightly floured counter, roll out the dough to a round 12 in/30 cm in diameter. Fit it into a 9-in/23-cm pie pan/tin, fold under the edges, and flute the edge of the crust. Place a sheet of foil over the pie crust and press it lightly to touch the bottom, making sure it covers the crust completely. Fill the foil with pie weights and bake for 20 minutes. Take off the foil and weights and bake until the crust is fully baked and crisp, about 5 minutes more. Let it cool completely, then refrigerate.

4 Slice the bananas and toss with the lemon juice to prevent browning. Distribute them in a single layer in the bottom of the pie crust. Spread the pudding over the bananas and level the top. Cover and refrigerate the pie. If desired, top it with vegan whip and garnish with the strawberries just before serving.

½ cup/60 g whole-wheat/wholemeal pastry/soft-wheat flour

¾ cup/85 g unbleached all-purpose/plain flour, plus extra for counter

½ tsp salt

¼ cup/60 ml coconut oil, frozen

1 tbsp cold-press corn oil

4 tbsp/60 ml ice water

2 cups/245 g sliced rhubarb

1 cup/125 g fresh raspberries

½ cup/100 g sugar

½ tsp almond extract

2 tbsp cornstarch/cornflour

4 cups/450 g fresh strawberries, hulled and sliced

Edible flowers, for garnish (optional)

SERVES 8

Strawberries, raspberries, and rhubarb are perfect partners for pie—tart, red, and in season at the same time of year. In this easy version, the filling is cooked on the stovetop, so that the tangy rhubarb forms a base to enclose the uncooked berries. This is a great way to fully appreciate good local berries when they are at their sweet peak.

Fresh Strawberry-Rhubarb Pie

1 In a large bowl, mix together both flours and the salt with a fork. Use the coarse holes of a grater to grate the coconut oil into the flour, tossing to coat the shreds. Still tossing with the fork, drizzle in the corn oil. Drizzle in the ice water, 1 tbsp at a time, tossing and turning with the fork. As soon as the dough holds together when pressed, form a disk, wrap it in plastic wrap/cling film, and refrigerate for 30 minutes.

2 Preheat the oven to 400°F/200°C/gas 6. On a lightly floured counter, roll out the dough to a round 12 in/30 cm in diameter. Fit it into a 9-in/23-cm pie pan/tin, fold under the edges, and flute the edge of the crust. Cover the whole pan with foil and put pie weights in the bottom of the shell. Bake for 20 minutes, then take off the foil and weights, and bake until the crust is fully baked and crisp, about 5 minutes more. Let it cool completely.

3 In a medium pot, combine the rhubarb, raspberries, sugar, and almond extract and bring them to a simmer. Lower the heat to medium and simmer until the mixture is as thick as jam, about 15 minutes. In a cup, whisk together 2 tbsp water and the cornstarch/cornflour. Stir the mixture into the rhubarb, stirring constantly until it comes to a boil. Reduce the heat and simmer until the sauce is very thick. Take it off the heat and quickly fold in the strawberries. Scrape the filling into the baked pie shell. Refrigerate the pie until fully cool. If desired, garnish it with edible flowers before serving.

¾ cup/90 g unbleached all-purpose/plain flour, plus 2 tbsp and extra for counter

½ cup/60 g whole-wheat/wholemeal pastry/soft-wheat flour

½ tsp salt

¼ cup/60 ml coconut oil, frozen

1 tbsp cold-press corn oil

4 tbsp/60 ml ice water

2 lb/910 g Granny Smith apples (about 2 qt/2 L sliced)

1 cup/200 g sugar

2 tbsp cornstarch/cornflour

1 tbsp freshly squeezed lemon juice

1 tsp vanilla extract

Streusel

½ cup/60 g whole-wheat/wholemeal pastry/soft-wheat flour

½ cup/100 g sugar

½ cup/80 g rolled oats

1 tsp ground cinnamon

1 pinch salt

¼ cup/60 ml coconut oil, at room temperature

SERVES 8

It's apple pie, in all its vegan glory. In this rendition of the classic, the tart Granny Smiths bathe in just a touch of vanilla and lemon, and the cinnamon is all in the jumble of scattered streusel.

Apple Streusel Pie

1 In a medium bowl, combine the ¾ cup/90 g unbleached flour, pastry/soft-wheat flour, and salt. Use the coarse holes of a grater to grate the coconut oil into the flour, tossing to coat the shreds. Swirl in the corn oil, then add the ice water, 1 tbsp at a time, and stir. Fluff the mixture with a fork, adding water just until the flour is all moistened. When the dough can be pressed into a ball, form a disk, wrap it in plastic wrap/cling film, and refrigerate for 30 minutes.

2 Preheat the oven to 400°F/200°C/gas 6. On a lightly floured counter, roll out the dough to a round 12 in/30 cm in diameter. Fit it into a 9-in/23-cm pie pan/tin, fold under the edges, and flute the edge of the crust. Refrigerate it.

3 Peel and slice the apples into a large bowl, then add the sugar, 2 tbsp unbleached flour, cornstarch/cornflour, lemon juice, and vanilla and toss to coat the apples. Let stand for 10 minutes for the juices to start flowing.

4 TO MAKE THE STREUSEL: In a medium bowl, stir together the flour, sugar, oats, cinnamon, and salt, then stir in the oil to make a chunky mixture.

5 Transfer the apples to the chilled crust; they will form a tall mound in the dish. Cover the top with the streusel, then cover that loosely with foil. Place the pie on the bottom rack of the oven for 20 minutes.

6 After 20 minutes, slip a baking sheet/tray under the pie to catch any juices and reduce the heat to 350°F/180°C/gas 4. Bake for 30 minutes more, then uncover the pie and bake until the juices are bubbling thickly around the edges and the streusel is browned, 30 to 40 minutes more. Let the pie cool on a rack for at least 40 minutes before cutting.

Vegetable oil spray

¾ cup/85 g unbleached all-purpose/plain flour, plus extra for counter

¼ cup/30 g whole-wheat/wholemeal pastry/soft-wheat flour

¼ cup/50 g granulated sugar

⅜ tsp salt

¼ cup/60 ml coconut oil, frozen

6 tbsp/90 ml ice water

¾ cup/150 g brown sugar

¾ cup/180 ml vegan creamer, plus 1 tbsp

2 tbsp cornstarch/cornflour

¾ cup/150 g creamy peanut butter

6 oz/170 g vegan chocolate chips

½ cup/120 ml coconut milk or vegan creamer

¾ cup/85 g roasted unsalted peanuts, coarsely chopped

SERVES 12

Peanut butter and chocolate get the luxe treatment here, in a tart fit for a fine restaurant. The crisp crust cradles a peanut butter cream, and the topping of deep dark "ganache" is as decadent as any you have tried.

Peanut Butter Tart
with "Ganache"

1 Coat a 10-in/25-cm round tart pan/flan tin with a removable bottom with oil spray. In a large bowl, combine both flours, granulated sugar, and ⅛ tsp of the salt. Use the coarse holes of a grater to grate the coconut oil into the flour, tossing to coat the shreds. Use a fork to lightly mix in the ice water, 1 tbsp at a time, just until the dough forms clumps and holds together. Form a disk, wrap it in plastic wrap/cling film, and refrigerate for 1 hour.

2 Preheat the oven to 350°F/180°C/gas 4. On a lightly floured counter, roll out the dough to a round 12 in/30 cm in diameter, then fit it into the prepared pan. Cut off excess dough to make a clean edge. Cover the whole pan with foil and put pie weights in the bottom of the shell. Bake for 20 minutes, then take the foil and weights off the crust. Let it cool.

3 In a medium saucepan, whisk together the brown sugar and ¾ cup/180 ml of the creamer, then place the pan over medium heat. Cook, whisking, until the sugar is dissolved. In a small cup, stir together the cornstarch/cornflour and the remaining 1 tbsp creamer and then whisk them into the simmering mixture. Simmer until slightly thickened, 3 to 5 minutes. Take the pan off the heat and whisk in the peanut butter and the remaining ¼ tsp salt. Pour the filling into the crust and bake until set, about 15 minutes. Remove the tart to a wire rack to cool, then refrigerate until fully chilled.

4 In the top of a double boiler, melt the chocolate with the coconut milk. Whisk until smooth. Pour the "ganache" over the cold tart and sprinkle the top with the peanuts. Refrigerate for at least 30 minutes to set, then slice while cold. Serve at room temperature.

485

14 oz /400 g canned/ tinned coconut milk

1 cup/200 g granulated sugar

¼ cup/30 g cornstarch/ cornflour

3 tbsp unsweetened cocoa powder

½ cup/120 ml almond milk

1 pinch salt

4 oz/115 g unsweetened/ baking chocolate, chopped

1 tsp vanilla extract

8 oz/225 g phyllo dough, thawed overnight in the refrigerator

6 tbsp/90 ml coconut oil, melted

6 tbsp/75 g turbinado sugar

SERVES 6

Pudding is great, but pudding in crunchy, sugar-crusted phyllo nests is even better. This dramatic presentation is easier than it looks, and once baked, the nests keep for a week, tightly covered.

Chocolate Custard Tartlets
in Shredded Phyllo Nests

1 Open the coconut milk and spoon off the solid, thick part into a small bowl; it should be about ¼ cup/60 ml. Refrigerate and reserve until serving. In a medium pot over low heat, whisk the remaining coconut milk with the granulated sugar and bring them to a simmer. In a small bowl, sift the cornstarch/ cornflour and cocoa powder to remove any lumps, then gradually whisk in the almond milk to make a smooth paste. When the coconut milk in the pan just starts to bubble, whisk in the cocoa mixture and salt and stir constantly until the mixture thickens, about 8 minutes. Do not boil. When the mixture coats the back of a spoon, take it off the heat and whisk in the chocolate and vanilla. Put the pudding in a bowl and cover it with plastic wrap/cling film, touching the surface to prevent a skin from forming. Refrigerate it to chill completely.

2 Preheat the oven to 400°F/200°C/gas 6. Slice the roll of phyllo dough in half across the roll, reserving half for another use. Unroll the phyllo to remove any paper, then roll it up again. Using a sharp chef's knife, slice across the rolled sheets in thin slices (less than ¼ in/6 mm wide). Drizzle all the slices thoroughly with the coconut oil, using your fingers to gently lift and fluff the strips. Divide the pile into six portions. Using six 1-cup/240-ml ramekins, or a sprayed baking sheet/tray, loosely coil the shredded phyllo to form nests. Sprinkle each nest with 1 tbsp of the turbinado sugar. Bake the nests until golden and crisp, about 20 minutes. Remove them to a rack to cool.

3 Place each nest on a dessert plate, fill it with ½ cup/240 ml pudding, and garnish with about 2 tsp of the reserved coconut cream. Serve immediately.

Vegetable oil spray

6 oz/170 g silken tofu

1 cup/245 g canned/
tinned or pureed
pumpkin

½ cup/100 g turbinado
sugar

1 tbsp cornstarch/
cornflour

1 tsp ground cinnamon

1 tsp ground allspice

½ cup/85 g dried
cranberries

1 tsp orange zest

9 sheets (about 12 by
17 in/30 by 43 cm) phyllo
dough, thawed overnight
in the refrigerator

1½ tsp brown sugar

SERVES 8

Ruffled, golden brown phyllo makes this a showy dessert that will impress and delight your friends. The smooth, spicy pumpkin filling, sparked with orange zest and tangy dried cranberries, makes this a great holiday-season showpiece. Bring one to the party and watch it disappear.

Ruffled Pumpkin-Cranberry Strudel

1 Position an oven rack in the lower third of the oven. Preheat the oven to 350°F/180°C/gas 4. Coat a 9-in/23-cm pie pan/tin with oil spray.

2 In a food processor or blender, puree the tofu thoroughly. Scrape down the sides and reprocess to get out all the lumps. Add the pumpkin and puree until completely smooth. Add the turbinado sugar, cornstarch/cornflour, cinnamon, and allspice and mix well. Stir in the cranberries and orange zest.

3 Unroll the phyllo and cover it with a sheet of plastic wrap/cling film, then cover that with a barely damp towel. Place a sheet of phyllo across the prepared pan and coat it all over with oil spray. Place another sheet at a 45-degree angle, pressing gently to fit it into the pan. Spray and continue, using five of the sheets. Scrape the filling into the pan. Layer four more phyllo sheets across the top, following the same alternating pattern.

4 Gently pull up the phyllo layers to form ruffles around the outer 3 in/7.5 cm of the pie. Coat with oil spray again.

5 Bake the strudel until the ruffled top is thoroughly golden and the filling puffs slightly in the center, 35 to 45 minutes. If the filling is still wet and the ruffles are browning fast, cover the top loosely with foil. Let the pie cool completely at room temperature. Garnish the center of the phyllo with the brown sugar. This will stay crisp in the refrigerator, uncovered, for 1 day. You can reheat it for 20 minutes in a warm oven.

DESSERTS

487

1 cup/245 g canned/
tinned or pureed
pumpkin

½ cup/100 g brown sugar

¼ cup/55 g tofu "cream
cheese"

1 tbsp cornstarch/
cornflour

½ tsp ground cinnamon

¼ tsp ground allspice

¼ tsp ground cloves

½ cup/120 ml coconut oil

10 sheets (about 12 by
17 in/30 by 42 cm) phyllo
dough, thawed overnight
in the refrigerator

¼ cup/50 g turbinado
sugar

MAKES 10 TURNOVERS

Freshen up your pumpkin pie experience and make these spicy, creamy pumpkin turnovers instead. This makes a big batch, enough to share or even to freeze some—if you can keep from devouring them all!

Pumpkin Spice Turnovers in Phyllo

1 Preheat the oven to 400°F/200°C/gas 6. Line a baking sheet/tray with parchment/baking paper. In a food processor or by hand, combine the pumpkin, brown sugar, "cream cheese," cornstarch/cornflour, cinnamon, allspice, and cloves and puree to mix.

2 Melt the coconut oil, if necessary, and put it in a cup with a pastry brush. Unwrap the phyllo, take out the ten sheets needed, and place them on a clean counter. Cover with plastic wrap/cling film and then a damp towel to keep them from drying out. Rewrap and freeze the remaining phyllo. Take a sheet of phyllo and brush half of it with coconut oil, and sprinkle with 1 tsp of the turbinado sugar. Fold the sheet in half lengthwise, brush again, then fold in half again, making a long strip. Place 2 tbsp of the pumpkin mixture on the bottom left corner of the sheet and fold it up like a flag, corner to corner, to make a triangular packet. Don't fold them too tightly, or they will explode in the oven. Place it, seam-side down, on the prepared pan. Repeat with the remaining phyllo and filling. Cut two small slashes in the top of each turnover.

3 Bake, uncovered, until the turnovers are browned and crisp, about 20 minutes. Let cool slightly on racks and serve warm.

2 cups/310 g blueberries, frozen or fresh

7 tbsp/90 g turbinado sugar

2 tbsp freshly squeezed lemon juice

1 tsp lemon zest

2 tbsp blueberry, apple, or berry juice

2 tbsp cornstarch/cornflour

6 sheets (about 12 by 17 in/30 by 42 cm) phyllo dough, thawed overnight in the refrigerator

3 tbsp coconut oil

6 tbsp/85 g tofu "cream cheese"

MAKES 6 TURNOVERS

I know these smell like blueberry heaven, but let them cool just a bit before biting into them since the filling is hot. Tofu "cream cheese" makes it easy to get a custardy base for the sweet berries, and the combo is just divine.

Blueberry "Cream" Turnovers in Phyllo

1 Preheat the oven to 400°F/200°C/gas 6. Line a baking sheet/tray with parchment/baking paper. In a 1-qt/1-L saucepan, combine the blueberries, 4 tbsp/50 g of the sugar, the lemon juice, and lemon zest. Bring to a boil over medium-high heat. Stir until the sugar is dissolved and the berries are bursting, about 5 minutes. In a small cup, whisk together the fruit juice and cornstarch/cornflour. Stir into the hot berries, and keep stirring until the mixture is thick and glossy. Take the pan off the heat and let it cool completely. Put it in the refrigerator to hurry it along.

2 Unwrap the phyllo, take out the six sheets, then rewrap the remaining sheets and put them in the refrigerator. Place the six sheets on the counter and cover with plastic wrap/cling film, then cover that with a barely damp kitchen towel to keep them from drying out. Take out one sheet, brush half with the coconut oil, and sprinkle it with ½ tsp of the remaining sugar. Fold the sheet in half lengthwise, brush again, and sprinkle with another ½ tsp sugar. Fold lengthwise again, making a long strip. On the bottom of the strip, scoop 1 tbsp of the "cream cheese" onto the bottom left corner of the sheet and cover with 2 tbsp of the blueberry mixture. Fold it up like a flag, corner to corner, to make a triangular packet. Don't fold them too tightly, or they will explode in the oven. Place each turnover on the prepared pan, seam-side down. Brush the top of each turnover with oil.

3 Use a paring knife to cut two small slashes in the top of each turnover. Sprinkle with the remaining sugar and bake until golden brown and crisp, about 15 minutes. Let cool slightly on racks and serve warm.

DESSERTS

489

8 ripe pears

2 tsp canola oil

¼ cup/50 g brown sugar

1 tsp ground cinnamon

½ tsp ground cloves

½ cup/120 ml coconut oil

16 sheets (about 12 by 17 in/30 by 42 cm) phyllo dough, thawed overnight in the refrigerator

Turbinado sugar, for garnish (optional)

MAKES 8 TURNOVERS

Roasting sweet, juicy pears until they reduce and condense makes a delectable filling for these crisp pastries. Use a ripe, but not overripe, eating pear like Anjou or Bartlett.

Spicy Roasted Pear Turnovers

1 Preheat the oven to 400°F/200°C/gas 6. Cut the pears into slices ¾ in/16 mm wide and long, then cut those into 1-in/2.5-cm pieces. Put them in a 9-in/23-cm square pan and drizzle with the canola oil. Toss gently to mix. Roast for 30 minutes, stirring halfway through, until the pears are tender and the pan is almost dry. Transfer the pears to a bowl; sprinkle with the brown sugar, cinnamon, and cloves; and mix gently. Let cool. Line a baking sheet/tray with parchment/baking paper.

2 Melt the coconut oil, if necessary. Unwrap the phyllo dough, take out sixteen sheets, and rewrap and refrigerate the remaining sheets for another use. Place the phyllo on the counter, cover with a sheet of plastic wrap/cling film, and place a barely damp towel on top to hold it down. Working with one sheet at a time, brush it with the coconut oil, and place another sheet on top. Fold the stack in half lengthwise, brush it, then fold it again to make a long strip. Measure ¼ cup/60 ml of the pear mixture onto the bottom left corner of the strip. Fold it up like a flag, corner to corner, to make a snug triangular packet. Don't fold the packet too tightly or it will explode in the oven. Brush again with oil and place the turnover, seam-side down, on the prepared pan. Repeat until all are finished and sprinkle the tops with turbinado sugar, if desired.

3 Use a paring knife to cut two small slashes in the top of each turnover. Bake until deep golden brown and crisp, about 20 minutes. Let cool slightly on racks and serve warm.

Vegetable oil spray

¼ cup/20 g unsweetened cocoa powder, plus extra for pan/tin

1½ cups/170 g unbleached all-purpose/ plain flour

¾ cup/150 g sugar

1 tsp baking powder

½ tsp baking soda/ bicarbonate of soda

¼ tsp salt

2 oz/55 g unsweetened/ baking chocolate, chopped

¾ cup/180 ml canola oil

2 tbsp almond butter

1½ cups/360 ml coconut milk

2 tsp egg replacer powder

1 tsp vanilla extract

1 tsp rice vinegar

½ tsp almond extract

½ cup/55 g almonds, coarsely chopped

4 oz/115 g semisweet/ plain chocolate

1 cup/115 g sliced/flaked almonds, toasted, for garnish

SERVES 8

Fudgy and moist, this cake is speckled with crunchy almonds and has a touch of almond butter baked right in. The rich "ganache" takes it to the level of a dessert you would have in a fine restaurant, but you can do this one at home—and not have to share!

Almond-Fudge Cake with "Ganache"

1 Preheat the oven to 350°F/180°C/gas 4. Coat a 9-in/23-cm round cake pan/tin with oil spray and dust it with cocoa. Tap out the excess. In a large bowl, whisk together the flour, sugar, cocoa, baking powder, baking soda/bicarbonate of soda, and salt. In the bottom of a double boiler, bring some water to a simmer, then reduce the heat to the lowest setting. Put the unsweetened/baking chocolate and canola oil in the top and stir until melted. Stir in the almond butter until smooth. Take the pan off the boiler and let cool.

2 In a cup, mix together 1¼ cups/300 ml of the milk, the egg replacer powder, vanilla, vinegar, and almond extract, stirring until the powder is dissolved. Quickly stir the mixture into the chocolate, then stir that into the flour mixture. Stir in the chopped almonds and scrape the batter into the prepared pan. Bake until a toothpick inserted in the center of the cake comes out with no wet batter attached, about 20 minutes. Let cool in the pan, on a rack.

3 In the top of a double boiler, melt the semisweet/plain chocolate with the remaining ¼ cup/60 ml coconut milk. Let cool slightly. Run a paring knife around the edge of the cake to loosen it in the pan. Carefully place a rack over the pan and flip it to remove the cake. Flip the cooled cake onto a cake plate, so that it's upside down. Brush off any crumbs, then pour the "ganache" over the cake, and spread it to cover. Garnish with the sliced/flaked almonds. Store in an airtight container in the refrigerator until serving.

Cake

Vegetable oil spray

2 cups/255 g unbleached all-purpose/plain flour

1 cup/200 g granulated sugar

2 tbsp lemon zest

1 tsp baking powder

1 tsp baking soda/ bicarbonate of soda

½ tsp salt

1¼ cups/300 ml vanilla rice milk or other milk

1 tbsp egg replacer powder

¼ cup/60 ml cold-press corn oil

¼ cup/60 ml freshly squeezed lemon juice

1 tsp vanilla extract

Filling

¾ cup/180 ml pomegranate juice

¼ cup/50 g granulated sugar

2 tbsp cornstarch/cornflour

Glaze

4 cups/400 g powdered/ icing sugar

5 tbsp/75 ml orange juice, plus more as needed

2 tbsp coconut oil, melted

½ tsp almond extract

½ cup/85 g fresh pomegranate seeds (arils), for garnish

SERVES 12

This light, lemony cake is adorned with both pomegranate filling and seeds, and an orange glaze that gives you three tasty fruits in every bite. The gemlike pomegranate seeds are a surprising and delicious garnish for a dessert, and are filled with antioxidants as well!

Lemon Cake
with Pomegranate Filling and Orange Glaze

1 TO MAKE THE CAKE: Preheat the oven to 350°F/180°C/ gas 4. Coat two 9-in/23-cm round cake pans/tins with oil spray and line the bottoms with parchment/baking paper cut to fit.

2 In a large bowl, whisk together the flour, granulated sugar, lemon zest, baking powder, baking soda/bicar-bonate of soda, and salt. In a cup, measure 3 tbsp of the milk and whisk in the egg replacer powder. In a medium bowl, whisk together the remaining milk, the corn oil, lemon juice, and vanilla. Whisk the wet mixture into the dry just until mixed, but do not overmix. Divide the batter between the two prepared pans and spread the batter evenly. Bake the cakes until the tops are brown, the sides are pulling away from the pans, and a toothpick inserted in the center of the cake comes out with no wet batter cling-ing to it, 30 to 35 minutes. Let the cakes cool in the pans on racks.

3 When the cakes are completely cool, run a paring knife around the edges and loosen them in the pans. Carefully place a rack over each pan and flip it to remove the cake. Peel off the parchment/baking paper.

4 TO MAKE THE FILLING: In a small saucepan, whisk together the pomegranate juice, granulated sugar, and cornstarch/cornflour. Over medium heat, bring to a boil, then whisk until thick and glossy, about 2 minutes. Transfer the filling to a bowl and refrigerate until cold.

5 TO MAKE THE GLAZE: Put the powdered/icing sugar into a bowl, then whisk in the orange juice, coconut oil, and almond extract. The glaze will be thick.

6 When the cake and filling are cooled, place one cake on a cutting board or counter. Use a long, serrated knife to split the cake horizontally, holding the blade parallel to the cutting surface. Lift off the top and place the bottom on a cake plate. Spread half of the pomegranate filling on the bottom layer, taking care to keep it about ½ in/12 mm from the edges. Place the top back on. Spread about one third of the glaze over the cake, then stir more orange juice into the glaze to make it pourable. Repeat with the second layer, splitting it, then topping the next layer with the remaining filling. Put on the fourth layer to finish the cake, drizzling the remaining glaze down the sides of the cake. While the glaze is still wet, sprinkle the pomegranate seeds over the cake and around it on the plate. Refrigerate until serving time.

Vegetable oil spray

1½ cups/170 g whole-wheat/wholemeal pastry/soft-wheat flour

1 cup/115 g unbleached all-purpose/plain flour

1 tsp baking powder

1 tsp baking soda/bicarbonate of soda

1 tsp ground cinnamon

½ tsp ground allspice

½ tsp salt

¼ tsp ground nutmeg

½ cup/120 ml coconut oil or cold-press corn oil

¾ cup/180 ml coconut milk

½ cup/120 ml agave syrup

1 tsp egg replacer powder

2 cups/220 g grated carrots

1 cup/170 g chopped dried pineapple

Frosting

2 cups/455 g tofu "cream cheese"

¼ cup/60 ml agave syrup

1 tsp vanilla extract

12 slices crystallized ginger, for garnish

SERVES 12

Pique your taste buds with the scents and flavors of tropical spices, sprinkled throughout a cake accented with bits of chewy pineapple and carrot. It's like a carnival in your mouth, all covered in creamy frosting.

Tropical Carrot-Pineapple Cake
with Tofu "Cream Cheese" Frosting

1 Preheat the oven to 350°F/180°C/gas 4. Coat two 9-in/23-cm round cake pans/tins with oil spray. In a large bowl, whisk together both flours, the baking powder, baking soda/bicarbonate of soda, cinnamon, allspice, salt, and nutmeg. Warm the coconut oil to liquefy it completely. In a small bowl, whisk together the coconut oil, coconut milk, and agave syrup; if the oil hardens in the liquids, heat the whole mixture gently just to liquefy, then let it cool slightly, stirring. In a cup, whisk 2 tbsp water with the egg replacer powder, then mix them into the oil mixture. Stir that into the dry mixture and then fold in the carrots and pineapple. Divide the batter between the prepared pans and spread to make a thin layer.

2 Bake the cakes until a toothpick inserted in a layer comes out clean, about 20 minutes. Let them cool completely in the pans on racks, then run a paring knife around the edges to loosen them. Flip one cake out by placing a rack over it and turning over the pan, then place it on a cake plate.

3 TO MAKE THE FROSTING: Put the "cream cheese" into a medium bowl. Add the agave syrup and vanilla and, mashing them with a fork, mix just until combined and creamy.

4 Spread a little less than half of the frosting over the bottom layer, then flip out the other cake and place it on top of the frosted layer. Spread the remaining frosting over the entire cake. Garnish the top of the cake with the slices of ginger at the edges. Refrigerate the cake until serving.

Vegetable oil spray

1½ cups/170 g whole-wheat/wholemeal pastry/soft-wheat flour

1 cup/115 g unbleached all-purpose/plain flour

1 tsp baking powder

1 tsp baking soda/bicarbonate of soda

1 tsp ground cinnamon

½ tsp ground cloves

½ tsp salt

15 oz /430 g canned/tinned or pureed pumpkin

1 cup/240 ml maple syrup

½ cup/120 ml canola oil (use half corn oil if desired)

½ cup/120 ml soy yogurt

2 tsp egg replacer powder

1 cup/170 g dried cherries, plus more for garnish

Glaze

2 cups/200 g powdered/icing sugar

¼ cup/60 ml cherry juice

½ tsp almond extract

SERVES 12

Pumpkin brings moistness and deep orange color to this cake, which is accented with tangy dried cherries. It's a perfect fall and winter comfort cake, with warming spices and discreetly disguised nutritious vegetable and fruit servings in every bite.

Pumpkin-Cherry Bundt Cake
with Cherry Glaze

1 Preheat the oven to 375°F/190°C/gas 5. Coat a 10-in/25-cm Bundt cake pan/tin with oil spray. In a large bowl, combine both flours, the baking powder, baking soda/bicarbonate of soda, cinnamon, cloves, and salt. In a medium bowl, whisk together the pumpkin, maple syrup, oil, and yogurt. In a small cup, whisk 3 tbsp water with the egg replacer powder until frothy, then stir into the pumpkin mixture. Stir the pumpkin mixture into the flour mixture, and when they are almost combined, add the cherries and mix them in. Scrape the batter into the prepared pan and smooth the top. Bake until a toothpick inserted into the center of the cake comes out with only moist crumbs and no batter clinging to it, 45 to 50 minutes. Let the cake cool in the pan on a rack.

2 Carefully run a paring knife around the edges of the pan to loosen the cake, then put a cake plate on top and invert the cake onto the plate.

3 TO MAKE THE GLAZE: In a medium bowl, whisk together the sugar, cherry juice, and almond extract until a thick glaze forms.

4 Drizzle the glaze over the cooled cake and sprinkle it with dried cherries while the glaze is wet. Store in an airtight container in the refrigerator until serving.

Vegetable oil spray

1 cup/115 g unbleached all-purpose/plain flour

1 cup/115 g whole-wheat/wholemeal pastry/soft-wheat flour

½ cup/60 g semolina flour

1 tsp baking powder

1 tsp baking soda/bicarbonate of soda

½ tsp salt

1¼ cups/300 ml agave syrup

¾ cup/180 ml rice milk

6 tbsp/90 ml extra-virgin olive oil

2 tsp cider vinegar

1 tbsp orange flower water (optional)

1 large orange, zested

SERVES 24

This cake is born of the Mediterranean, enriched with extra-virgin olive oil and bathed in orange-infused syrup. It's as delightful with a cup of mint tea in the afternoon as it is after a Moroccan-spiced meal. Orange flower water is a traditional flavor in Moroccan baking: it is a delicately perfumed liquid that adds an exotic touch, if you can get it.

Moroccan Semolina Cake
with Orange Syrup

1 Preheat the oven to 350°F/180°C/gas 4. Coat an 11-by-7-in/28-by-18-cm baking pan with oil spray. In a large bowl, mix together all three flours, the baking powder, baking soda/bicarbonate of soda, and salt. In a large cup, mix together ¾ cup/180 ml of the agave syrup, the milk, oil, vinegar, and orange flower water (if using). Quickly stir the wet ingredients into the dry, then spread the batter in the prepared pan. Bake until the cake is deep golden and a toothpick inserted in the center of the cake comes out with no wet batter clinging to it, 15 to 20 minutes. Remove the pan to a wire rack to cool.

2 While the cake bakes, combine the remaining ½ cup/120 ml of the agave syrup, the orange zest, and ¼ cup/60 ml water in a small saucepan. Bring to a boil over high heat and simmer to reduce to ½ cup/120 ml, about 5 minutes. Let the syrup cool.

3 When the cake is cooled, leave it in the pan and poke it all over with a toothpick. Pour on the syrup and spread it to cover the top. Let it stand until the syrup is absorbed (the orange zest will stick to the top). Slice the cake 4 by 6 to make 24 squares.

Cake

Vegetable oil spray

1 cup/115 g unbleached all-purpose/plain flour

1 cup/115 g whole-wheat/wholemeal pastry/soft-wheat flour

1 cup/200 g sugar

½ cup/80 g rolled oats

1 tbsp lemon zest

1 tsp ground cinnamon

½ tsp baking powder

½ tsp baking soda/bicarbonate of soda

¼ tsp salt

1 cup/240 ml soymilk or other milk

3 tbsp freshly squeezed lemon juice

1 tbsp ground flax seeds

1 tsp egg replacer powder

1 tsp vanilla extract

2 cups/220 g chopped Granny Smith apple

1 cup/115 g walnuts, coarsely chopped

Sauce

½ cup/100 g sugar

½ cup/120 ml maple syrup

½ cup/120 ml vegan creamer or soymilk, plus 2 tbsp

¼ cup/55 g Earth Balance margarine

2 tbsp cornstarch/cornflour

½ tsp vanilla extract

1 pinch salt

SERVES 12

If you need a cake so moist and delicious that nobody will suspect that it's vegan, this is it! The incredible caramel sauce poured over every slice will send you to the moon.

Apple-Walnut Cake with Caramel Sauce

1 TO MAKE THE CAKE: Preheat the oven to 350°F/ 180°C/gas 4. Coat a 10-in/25-cm round springform pan with oil spray. In a large bowl, combine both flours, the sugar, oats, lemon zest, cinnamon, baking powder, baking soda/bicarbonate of soda, and salt and mix well.

2 In a cup, whisk together the soymilk, lemon juice, flax, egg replacer powder, and vanilla. Stir the wet mixture into the dry until well combined, then fold in the apples and walnuts. Scrape the mixture into the prepared pan and smooth the top.

3 Bake until a toothpick inserted into the center of the cake comes out with no wet batter attached, 60 to 70 minutes. Let the cake cool in the pan for at least 10 minutes before running a paring knife around the edge and removing the springform sides. Transfer it to a platter or storage container and refrigerate.

4 TO MAKE THE SAUCE: Combine the sugar, maple syrup, ½ cup/120 ml creamer, and margarine in a small saucepan. Bring it to a boil over medium heat, then reduce the heat to a low simmer until all is dissolved, about 5 minutes. In a small bowl, whisk the cornstarch/ cornflour with the remaining 2 tbsp creamer, and then whisk them into the simmering sauce. Whisk in the vanilla and salt and simmer until thickened. Let the sauce cool to room temperature. Store at room temperature for 1 day, or refrigerate. In that case, it may need to be warmed and whisked to soften.

5 Serve the sauce over wedges of cake.

6 tbsp/85 g Earth Balance margarine

1 cup/200 g brown sugar or maple sugar

1 small pineapple

6 whole, frozen black cherries (not thawed)

1 cup/115 g whole-wheat/wholemeal pastry/soft-wheat flour

½ cup/60 g unbleached all-purpose/plain flour

1 tsp baking powder

½ tsp baking soda/bicarbonate of soda

¼ tsp salt

¾ cup/180 ml maple syrup or agave syrup

¼ cup/60 ml vegetable oil

½ cup/120 ml soy yogurt

2 tsp egg replacer powder

1 tsp vanilla extract

SERVES 8

When buying pineapple, look for as much yellow on the skin as possible. A green one will never ripen. You want a nice, sweet pineapple to top this luscious cake, bathed in sticky goodness.

Fresh Pineapple Upside-Down Cake

1 Preheat the oven to 375°F/190°C/gas 5. In an 11-in/27.5-cm round springform pan, melt the margarine by putting it in the oven for 5 to 10 minutes as it heats up. Sprinkle the sugar evenly in the pan. Wrap the outside of the pan with foil. Using a chef's knife, slice off the bottom and top of the pineapple. Set the fruit, right-side up, on a cutting board and slice off the skin, cutting deeply enough to remove the eyes. Cut the fruit into ¾-in-/2-cm-thick slices. Place each on the board and use a paring knife or apple corer to remove the round core, leaving the slices whole. Place the slices on top of the sugar in the pan, fitting them tightly together. Slice the remaining rounds into wedges and fit them into any spaces in a pretty pattern. Put a cherry into each of the holes where the pine-apple cores were.

2 In a large bowl, mix together both flours, the baking pow-der, baking soda/bicarbonate of soda, and salt. In a medium bowl, whisk together the maple syrup and oil. In a small bowl, stir together the yogurt, egg replacer powder, and vanilla, mashing any lumps, then stir them into the maple mixture. Mix the wet ingredients into the dry, stirring until they are well combined. Pour the batter evenly over the pineapple.

3 Bake until a toothpick inserted in the center of the cake comes out with moist crumbs, but no raw batter on it, 50 to 55 minutes. Let the cake cool for 10 minutes in the pan on a rack.

4 Run a paring knife around the edges of the cake to loosen it, then place a platter over the cake, and holding firmly, flip to invert the cake onto the platter. If any topping stays in the pan, quickly pick it out with a butter knife and put it in any gaps on the cake. Let the cake cool completely before serving.

Cupcakes

1 cup/115 g unbleached all-purpose/plain flour

½ cup/50 g unsweetened cocoa powder, sifted

1 tsp baking powder

1 tsp baking soda/ bicarbonate of soda

½ tsp salt

1 cup/240 ml soymilk or coconut milk

½ cup/120 ml maple syrup

¼ cup/60 ml canola oil

1 tsp vanilla extract

1 tsp rice vinegar

Filling

10 tbsp/145 g tofu "cream cheese"

¼ cup/20 g powdered/ icing sugar

20 whole, frozen black cherries (not thawed)

Frosting

½ cup/115 g tofu "cream cheese," at room temperature

2 oz/55 g semisweet/ plain chocolate

3 tbsp dark cherry juice concentrate or juice

MAKES 10 CUPCAKES

Everybody loves chocolate cupcakes, and when they bite into these tender, chocolatey gems and find a creamy, sweet cherry center, they will be even more delighted. The chocolate frosting will make you want to eat it with a spoon.

Chocolate-Covered Cherry Cupcakes

1 TO MAKE THE CUPCAKES: Preheat the oven to 350°F/ 180°C/gas 4. Line 10 muffin pan/tin cups with muffin papers. In a large bowl, whisk together the flour, cocoa powder, baking powder, baking soda/bicarbonate of soda, and salt. In a medium bowl, whisk together the soymilk, maple syrup, oil, vanilla, and vinegar, and stir into the flour mixture. Measure a scant ¼ cup/60 ml into each lined muffin cup.

2 TO MAKE THE FILLING: Mash the "cream cheese" with the sugar, then mold 1 tbsp around two frozen cherries and plop it into a cupcake. Repeat with the remaining filling and top each cup with more batter.

3 Bake until a toothpick inserted in the center of a cupcake comes out with cherry juice and melted cream cheese, but no moist crumbs attached, 20 to 25 minutes. Remove the pan and place it on a cooling rack until the cupcakes are completely cooled.

4 TO MAKE THE FROSTING: In a food processor or large heatproof bowl, put the "cream cheese." In the top of a double boiler or in the microwave, melt the chocolate, then pour it onto the "cream cheese" and quickly pulse or mix. Stir well, then stir in the juice concentrate.

5 Pipe or spread about 2 tbsp of the frosting onto each cooled cupcake. Refrigerate until ready to serve. Bring to room temperature before serving so the centers will be creamy.

Cupcakes

1¾ cups/255 g unbleached all-purpose/plain flour

2 tsp lime zest

1 tsp baking powder

1 tsp baking soda/bicarbonate of soda

¼ tsp salt

¼ cup/40 g mashed avocado

2 tbsp canola oil

1 cup/200 g granulated sugar

1 cup/240 ml almond milk or other milk

1 tbsp freshly squeezed lime juice

½ tsp vanilla extract

Frosting

½ cup/80 g mashed avocado

1 tbsp freshly squeezed lime juice

2½ cups/250 g powdered/icing sugar

MAKES 12 CUPCAKES

These intriguing cakes are green, and are even topped with a creamy green frosting, but their buttery avocado flavor will win over anyone who tries them. Avocados may be synonymous with guacamole in the United States, but in the tropical countries where they grow, they are often employed in sweet treats.

Avocado Cupcakes
with Avocado-Lime Frosting

1 TO MAKE THE CUPCAKES: Preheat the oven to 350°F/180°C/gas 4. Line 12 muffin pan/tin cups with muffin papers. In a large bowl, combine the flour, lime zest, baking powder, baking soda/bicarbonate of soda, and salt. In a medium bowl or a blender, puree the avocado until very smooth, then mix in the oil. Stir in the granulated sugar, then the milk, lime juice, and vanilla. Stir the liquids into the dry mixture, mashing if there are any lumps. Divide the batter among the prepared cups and bake until a toothpick inserted in the center of a cake comes out clean, about 20 minutes. Let the cupcakes cool in the pan on a rack.

2 TO MAKE THE FROSTING: In a small bowl, mash the avocado with the lime juice until smooth, then stir in the powdered/icing sugar. Cover and refrigerate until the cupcakes are completely cooled.

3 Spread about 1 tbsp frosting on each cupcake. Store, tightly covered, in the refrigerator, and let them come to room temperature to serve.

Cupcakes

Vegetable oil spray

2 cups/255 g unbleached all-purpose/plain flour

1 cup/115 g whole-wheat/wholemeal pastry/soft-wheat flour

2 tsp baking soda/bicarbonate of soda

1 tsp baking powder

½ tsp salt

1 cup/240 ml agave syrup

1 cup/240 ml vanilla soymilk or rice milk

½ cup/120 ml canola oil

½ cup/100 g creamy unsalted peanut butter

2 tsp vanilla extract

2 tsp rice vinegar

2 cups/340 g vegan chocolate chips

Frosting

½ cup/115 g Earth Balance margarine, at room temperature

2½ cups/250 g powdered/icing sugar

½ cup/50 g unsweetened cocoa powder

1 tsp vanilla extract

¼ cup/60 ml vanilla soymilk or other milk

¾ cup/85 g chopped roasted peanuts, for garnish

MAKES 12 CUPCAKES

Two great tastes that taste great together, peanut butter and chocolate make these moist cupcakes into the lovable bites of joy that they are. The creamy chocolate frosting takes it to another level, but if you want to eat them bare, they are just as tasty naked!

Peanut Butter–Chocolate Chip Cupcakes

1 TO MAKE THE CUPCAKES: Preheat the oven to 350°F/180°C/gas 4. Line twelve muffin pan/tin cups with muffin papers. Coat the top of the pan with oil spray. In a large bowl, combine both flours, the baking soda/bicarbonate of soda, baking powder, and salt. In a medium bowl or a food processor, blend the agave syrup, milk, canola oil, peanut butter, vanilla, and vinegar. Quickly stir the wet ingredients into the dry, then stir in the chocolate chips. Portion the batter into the cups, filling them to the top. Bake until a toothpick inserted in the center of a cake comes out with only melted chocolate and no batter on it, about 20 minutes. Let the cupcakes cool in the pan on a rack.

2 TO MAKE THE FROSTING: In a stand mixer with the paddle or with an electric mixer, beat the margarine until creamy. Add the sugar, cocoa powder, and vanilla and beat until the mixture is a thick paste. Adding the milk, 1 tbsp at a time, beat until the mixture is a creamy frosting.

3 Frost the cooled cupcakes with about 2½ tbsp frosting each and sprinkle the tops with the peanuts.

4½ cups/1 L soy or
coconut creamer

1 cup/200 g rapadura or
Sucanat sugar

10 tbsp/80 g cornstarch/
cornflour

2 tbsp vanilla extract

¼ tsp salt

SERVES 6

The natural flavor of pure cane comes through in this creamy pudding, with all its butterscotch notes and molasses undertones. Rapadura sugar is cane juice with the molasses left in, so it has much more character than white sugar. Simple, but subtle, this pudding will become one of your go-to comfort foods.

Butterscotch Pudding

1 Measure 4 cups/960 ml of the creamer into a medium saucepan. Add the sugar. Whisk over low heat until the sugar dissolves. In a small cup, whisk together the remaining ½ cup/120 ml creamer and the cornstarch/cornflour. When the sugar is dissolved and the creamer mixture is hot, whisk in the cornstarch/cornflour mixture, vanilla, and salt.

2 Whisk the mixture constantly over medium heat until bubbles start to come to the surface. Let it come to a boil just briefly, then take it off the heat. It will be very thick.

3 Transfer the pudding to a bowl or to individual serving bowls or goblets, then cover it with plastic wrap/cling film. Press down to the surface to keep a skin from forming. Refrigerate until set before serving.

Vegetable oil spray

12 oz/340 g silken tofu

1 cup/240 ml vanilla rice milk

½ cup/120 ml agave syrup or maple syrup

2 tbsp cornstarch/cornflour

2 tsp ground cinnamon

1 tsp vanilla extract

⅛ tsp ground nutmeg

⅛ tsp salt

5 cups/1.2 L cubed whole-wheat/wholemeal bread

1 cup/170 g dried apricots, chopped

Sauce

1 cup/200 g sugar

½ cup/120 ml soy creamer

⅛ tsp salt

SERVES 9

You can use up old bread for this recipe, but you will love it so much that you may find yourself making it whether you have extra bread or not. The dense, bready pudding is sparked with tart, chewy apricots, and the dreamy caramel sauce will have you wanting more.

Old-Fashioned Apricot Bread Pudding
with Caramel Sauce

1 Preheat the oven to 350°F/180°C/gas 4. Coat a 9-in/23-cm square baking pan with oil spray. In a blender or food processor, puree the tofu. Add the milk, agave syrup, cornstarch/cornflour, cinnamon, vanilla, nutmeg, and salt. Blend to mix, then pour it into a large bowl. Fold in the bread and apricots, and let it stand for 5 minutes to soak. Transfer the bread mixture to the prepared pan.

2 Bake until you can pierce the middle of the pudding with a paring knife and the knife is hot to the touch, 35 to 40 minutes. The liquid will be wet but thickened. Let the pudding cool slightly.

3 TO MAKE THE SAUCE: In a large pot, bring ¼ cup/60 ml water and the sugar to a boil, and cook without stirring until the sugar is melted and turning amber, about 5 minutes. Take the pot off the heat and pour in the creamer, being very careful because it will foam up and boil over very quickly. Return the pot to low heat and stir; the sugar will be in chunks that you will want to melt gradually into the sauce. Don't let it boil. Stir in the salt as you stir. Transfer the sauce to a heat-safe pitcher and let it cool slightly.

4 Serve the warm syrup over the warm bread pudding.

DESSERTS

503

1 cup/215 g short-grain brown rice

1½ cups/360 ml coconut milk

½ cup/100 g palm or brown sugar

3 oz/75 g dried mangoes, chopped

½ cup/75 g crystallized ginger, chopped

1 tsp ground cinnamon

1 tsp vanilla extract

1 pinch salt

1 tbsp cornstarch/cornflour

SERVES 8

Looking for a hearty dessert to follow an Asian meal? The exotic flavors of mango, ginger, and coconut will provide that perfect ending, setting off any spice and salt with smooth, sweet spoon-food.

Ginger-Mango Rice Pudding

1 In a medium saucepan, combine the rice and 2 cups/480 ml water and bring to a boil over high heat. Reduce the heat to low, then cover tightly and cook for 40 minutes. Stir in 1 cup/240 ml of the coconut milk, the sugar, mangoes, ginger, cinnamon, vanilla, and salt. Cover and cook until most of the liquids are absorbed, about 10 minutes.

2 In a cup, whisk the remaining ½ cup/120 ml coconut milk with the cornstarch/cornflour. Stir into the pot of rice and keep stirring until it is thick, about 5 minutes more. Transfer the rice pudding to a serving bowl or individual bowls and let it cool, or refrigerate if desired, before serving.

¼ cup/10 g agar flakes

3 cups/720 ml fruit-sweetened cranberry juice cocktail

½ cup/100 g sugar

2 large, ripe pears

3 cups/300 g fresh cranberries

½ tsp vanilla extract

SERVES 6

Kanten, the gelatin-like Japanese dish made with agar agar, is just as refreshing in fall and winter as it is in summer. This one is a perfect way to use cranberries and pears for a seasonal treat. Cranberries are superfoods these days, so you are bathing in antioxidants as you spoon up this tangy crimson treat.

Cranberry-Pear Kanten

1 In a medium saucepan, mix the agar with ¼ cup/60 ml warm water and let it stand for 10 to 15 minutes. The flakes will swell and soften. Add the juice cocktail and sugar to the pan and let them soak for 10 minutes more. Slice the pears, then divide them among six 1-cup/240-ml ramekins, or use one 6-cup/1.4-L bowl.

2 Over low heat, stir the mixture in the pan. Cook until the agar is dissolved, stirring often. Add the cranberries and boil until they pop. Add the vanilla. Portion the mixture into the ramekins or pour it all into the bowl and refrigerate until the kanten is set, at least 1 hour. Cover and keep in the refrigerator until serving.

3 cups/720 ml
unsweetened blueberry
juice

3 tbsp agar flakes

½ cup/100 g sugar

½ tsp almond extract

Two 6-oz/90-ml cups
vanilla soy yogurt

SERVES 5

Creamy soy yogurt makes this gelatin-like dessert a little more substantial, as well as smoothly melty on your tongue. Blueberry juice or a cocktail of juices should be easy to find.

Blueberry Yogurt Kanten

1 In a small saucepan, combine the blueberry juice and agar, and let them soak for 30 minutes. Stir in the sugar and almond extract. Bring the mixture to a boil over medium-high heat, then reduce the heat to a simmer and whisk until the agar is dissolved. Simmer for about 5 minutes. Take off the heat and let the mixture cool to room temperature. Put the yogurt and juice mixture into a blender and puree to mix.

2 Pour the mixture into a 6-cup/1.4-L bowl. Refrigerate until set, at least 1 hour. Cover and keep in the refrigerator until serving.

6 large kiwi fruits

3 cups/720 ml coconut water or white grape juice

3 tbsp agar flakes

Vegetable oil spray

¼ cup/60 ml agave syrup

1 tbsp loose-leaf green tea

SERVES 6

If you have fond memories of Jell-O molds, with their epic suspensions of fruit in gel, this will ring your bells. Bold kiwi spears are encased in a refreshing green tea kanten, and unmolded in individual servings for your spooning pleasure. Coconut water is the nutritious liquid from the center of the coconut, often sold as a sports drink, and not the same thing as coconut milk.

Green Tea–Kiwi Kanten

1 Peel the kiwi and slice them into vertical spears. Put the coconut water and agar in a saucepan and let them soak for 25 to 30 minutes. Coat six 1-cup/240-ml ramekins (or one 6-cup/1.4-L bowl) with oil spray.

2 Over low heat, stir the mixture in the pan and add the agave syrup. Cook until the agar is dissolved, stirring often. Add the tea and let it infuse for 4 minutes. Strain the mixture into a large measuring cup with a pouring spout. Divide the kiwi among the ramekins (or put them in the bowl). Pour the green tea mixture over the fruit and refrigerate until it is set, at least 1 hour.

3 To unmold, dip the ramekins carefully into a bowl of warm water, just to warm the outsides, then run a paring knife around the kanten and invert onto plates (or spoon from the bowl).

5 tbsp/12 g agar flakes

1 cup/240 ml cherry juice

1 cup/240 ml apricot
nectar

Vegetable oil spray

4 tbsp/60 ml agave syrup

1 large kiwi fruit, peeled
and sliced

1 cup/125 g fresh
raspberries

1 large banana, sliced

Coconut milk (optional)

SERVES 6

Burgundy cherry and golden apricot juices make firm, sliceable kantens, and when cubed and tossed together, they gleam like jewels. Mixed with fresh fruit, this is a satisfying and nutritious treat.

Cherry and Apricot Kanten-Cube Fruit Salad

1 Put half of the agar and the cherry juice in a small saucepan, adding ½ cup/120 ml water. Put the other half of the agar, the apricot nectar, and ½ cup/120 ml water in another small saucepan. Let them each soak for 25 to 30 minutes. Coat two 4-by-10-in/10-by-25-cm loaf pans/tins with oil spray.

2 Over low heat, stir the mixtures in the pans, and add 2 tbsp agave syrup to each pan. Cook until the agar is dissolved, stirring often. Pour the mixtures into the separate pans/tins, then refrigerate until firm, at least 1 hour.

3 To unmold, slice the kanten into cubes while still in the pans, then run a paring knife around the edges and invert the cubes over a large bowl. Add the kiwi, raspberries, and banana and serve as is or with a drizzle of coconut milk, if desired.

12 oz/340 g frozen or fresh peach slices

12 oz/340 g silken tofu, drained

½ cup/120 ml soy creamer

½ cup/120 ml agave syrup

1 tbsp vanilla extract

2 tsp orange zest

½ cup/120 ml raspberry all-fruit jam

SERVES 4

Frozen peaches puree to a smooth creamy base for this tofu-based "ice cream," adding more fruit to an already fruity dessert. Swirl in some raspberry jam for a brilliant sweet accent to the peachy "cream."

Peachy Berry-Swirl "Ice Cream"

1 In a food processor or blender, puree the peaches and tofu. When well pureed, add the creamer, agave syrup, vanilla, and orange zest and puree to mix. Transfer the mixture to a storage container and refrigerate in the bottom of the refrigerator for at least 4 hours.

2 Freeze in an ice-cream maker according to the manufacturer's directions. When it's ready, swirl in the jam with the motor on. Serve immediately or transfer to a storage container to freeze until firm.

2 cups/480 ml coconut milk or vegan creamer

½ cup/120 ml agave syrup

1 tbsp cornstarch/cornflour

½ cup/85 g vegan chocolate chips

2 tsp vanilla extract

3 oz/75 g silken tofu

¼ cup/20 g unsweetened cocoa powder

1 large vegan brownie, such as a Frosted Chocolate Bomb Brownies (page 475)

SERVES 4

Bake up a batch of the Chocolate Bomb Brownies and add them to this already super-chocolatey vegan "ice cream." It's intensely creamy and yummy—a chocolate-lover's dream cream.

Dark Chocolate "Ice Cream"
with Brownie Chunks

1 In a medium saucepan, combine the milk, agave syrup, and cornstarch/cornflour. Whisk and cook over medium heat until slightly thickened. Take the pan off the heat and add the chocolate chips and vanilla. Whisk until the chips are melted. In a blender, puree the tofu until smooth, scraping down the sides and repeating as necessary. Add the cocoa powder and process, then add the hot milk mixture and puree until smooth. Transfer the mixture to a storage container and refrigerate in the bottom of the refrigerator for at least 4 hours.

2 Freeze in an ice-cream maker according to the manufacturer's directions. When it's ready, chop the brownie into small chunks, sprinkle in the brownie pieces with the motor on. Serve immediately or transfer to a storage container to freeze until firm.

2½ cups/600 ml soy creamer

½ cup/120 ml agave syrup

½ cup/100 g crunchy peanut butter

1 tsp vanilla extract

SERVES 4

Vegan peanut butter "ice cream" is a delicious dessert, and the peanut butter has the side benefit of a strong flavor that hides any noticeable nondairy notes in the base. I'm sure that it would not take you long to figure out that a topping of vegan chocolate sauce or chocolate "ganache" (see page 485) would be fabulous on a bowl of this peanutty treat.

Peanut Butter "Ice Cream"

1 In a blender or by hand, whisk together the creamer, agave syrup, peanut butter, and vanilla. Transfer the mixture to a storage container and refrigerate in the bottom of the refrigerator for at least 4 hours.

2 Freeze in an ice-cream maker according to the manufacturer's directions. Serve immediately or transfer to a storage container to freeze until firm.

Base

1 cup/115 g raw cashews

½ cup/120 ml agave syrup

1 tsp vanilla extract

1½ cups/360 ml coconut milk

Sauce

½ cup/100 g sugar

¼ cup/60 ml coconut milk

1 pinch salt

½ cup/55 g toasted cashews, chopped

SERVES 4

The freezer case is filled with every conceivable conglomeration of ice creams—with chunks, swirls, and gobs of dough stirred in. This elegant coconut-based cream is streaked with sweet caramel and chunky cashews, for a taste as decadent as anything in the ice-cream shop.

Cashew "Ice Cream"
with Caramel Swirl

1 TO MAKE THE BASE: In a blender or food processor, grind the cashews to a fine powder. Add the agave syrup, vanilla, and a little of the milk and blend, gradually adding the remaining milk to make a perfectly smooth puree. Transfer the mixture to a storage container and refrigerate in the bottom of the refrigerator for at least 4 hours.

2 TO MAKE THE SAUCE: In a medium saucepan, combine the sugar and ¼ cup/60 ml water. Stir over medium-high heat until the sugar is dissolved. Raise the heat to high and don't stir, just swirl the pan over the heat. Heat the mixture until the bubbling liquid turns from champagne colored to an amber-caramel tone. Take the pan off the heat and immediately and carefully pour in the milk, a bit at a time, being careful because it will boil right out of the pot if you rush. Put the pan back over medium heat, add the salt, and cook, stirring, to dissolve all the sugar that formed lumps when the milk went in. When the mixture is smooth, take it off the heat and transfer it to a heat-safe cup. Refrigerate the caramel until cold.

3 Freeze the base in an ice-cream maker according to the manufacturer's directions. When it's ready, mix the chopped cashews into the caramel and swirl them in with the motor on. Serve immediately or transfer to a storage container to freeze until firm.

1 tbsp matcha tea powder

2 tsp cornstarch/cornflour

½ cup/120 ml soymilk or other milk

½ cup/120 ml agave syrup

2 cups/480 ml plain vegan creamer or coconut milk

SERVES 4

Green tea ice cream came on the scene to help Westerners enjoy desserts at Japanese and other Asian restaurants, where chilled lychee and mochi were just a little too foreign. Matcha is the antioxidant-packed powdered green tea of the Japanese tea ceremony, and it has a sweetness of its own.

Green Tea "Ice Cream"

1 In a small saucepan, whisk together the matcha and cornstarch/cornflour, then whisk in a little bit of the soymilk. Whisk until very smooth before gradually adding the remaining soymilk. Whisk in the agave syrup, then bring to a boil. Whisking constantly, cook the mixture over medium heat until thickened, about 3 minutes. Take the pan off the heat and whisk in the creamer. Transfer the mixture to a storage container and refrigerate in the bottom of the refrigerator for at least 4 hours.

2 Freeze in an ice-cream maker according to the manufacturer's directions. Serve immediately or transfer to a storage container to freeze until firm.

½ cup/100 g palm sugar or brown sugar

14 oz/400 g canned/tinned coconut milk

SERVES 4

We give thanks for the coconut, whose flesh gives us healthful coconut milk—the vegan version of cream. Simply infused with palm sugar, coconut sorbet is a perfect dessert to serve after Thai food. Or you can use it for a sundae, drizzled with your favorite sauces.

Coconut Sorbet

1 In a small saucepan, combine ⅔ cup/165 ml water and the sugar and bring to a boil over high heat. Stir until the sugar is dissolved, then cook for 2 minutes, lowering the heat to keep it at a vigorous simmer. Take the pan off the heat and let the syrup cool. When it is at room temperature, stir in another 1 cup/240 ml water and the coconut milk. Transfer the mixture to a storage container and refrigerate in the bottom of the refrigerator for at least 4 hours.

2 Freeze in an ice-cream maker according to the manufacturer's directions. Serve immediately or transfer to a storage container to freeze until firm.

2 cups/480 g avocado cubes (2 to 3 small avocados)

½ cup/120 ml agave syrup

½ cup/120 ml light coconut milk

¼ cup/60 ml freshly squeezed lime juice

2 tsp lime zest

SERVES 4

Creamy avocado makes this sorbet just a little richer than the usual fruity version. This makes a great dessert or palate cleanser for Mexican or other warm-climate cuisines. For an elegant riff on avocado desserts, serve this with Avocado Cupcakes with Avocado-Lime Frosting (page 500).

Avocado-Lime Sorbet

1 In a blender, puree the avocado, then scrape down the sides, add the agave syrup, and puree. With the motor on, add the coconut milk, a little at a time, and process until it is completely smooth. Add the lime juice and lime zest and process until everything is smooth and well mixed. Transfer the mixture to a storage container and refrigerate in the bottom of the refrigerator for at least 4 hours.

2 Freeze in an ice-cream maker according to the manufacturer's directions. Serve immediately or transfer to a storage container to freeze until firm.

3 cups/370 g chopped rhubarb

1½ cups/185 g fresh raspberries

1 cup/200 g sugar

1 pinch salt

¼ cup/40 g finely chopped crystallized ginger

SERVES 4

Springtime is when raspberries and rhubarb are both at their peak, so it makes perfect sense to put them together. Tangy rhubarb and sweet/tart berries make this sorbet bright red and dazzlingly palate cleansing.

Rhubarb-Raspberry Sorbet

1 In a medium pot, combine the rhubarb, 2 cups/480 ml water, the raspberries, sugar, and salt. Over high heat, bring to a boil, then reduce the heat to a simmer. Stir often, until the rhubarb is broken down and soft. Transfer the mixture to a blender or food processor. Put the lid on and hold it down with a folded kitchen towel so that no splatters will burn you. Process until smooth. Transfer the mixture to a storage container and refrigerate in the bottom of the refrigerator for at least 4 hours.

2 Freeze in an ice-cream maker according to the manufacturer's directions. Stir in the ginger. Serve immediately or transfer to a storage container to freeze until firm.

2 tbsp unsweetened cocoa powder

2 cups/480 ml vegan creamer or soymilk

½ cup/120 ml agave syrup

3 oz/75 g dark/plain vegan chocolate, chopped

2 tsp vanilla extract

MAKES 8 POPSICLES

Want a sweet, little lift while you are cooling off? These dark chocolate pops have enough antioxidant-rich cocoa and chocolate that they are almost like having sips of coffee, but sweeter!

Deep Dark Fudgesicles

1 Place the cocoa powder in a small saucepan, then very gradually whisk in the creamer. Whisk in the agave syrup, place the pan over low heat, and bring it to a simmer. Take the pan off the heat and add the chocolate; let it stand for a minute to melt, then whisk until the chocolate is all melted and incorporated. Whisk in the vanilla. Transfer the mixture to a storage container and refrigerate in the bottom of the refrigerator for at least 4 hours.

2 Pour the mixture into eight 3-oz/90-ml wax paper cups or popsicle molds. If using paper cups, freeze the mixture for 30 minutes to 1 hour before inserting sticks. Once frozen, put the cups in a heavy zip-top bag and store in the freezer.

DESSERTS

1 overripe banana

1 cup/240 ml mango juice

½ cup/120 ml coconut milk

MAKES 6 POPSICLES

On a hot day, these little pops are a refreshing way to energize with fruit and coconut. Sweet banana thickens, sweetens, and adds potassium to the vitamin-rich pops.

Coconut-Mango Popsicles

1 In a blender, puree the banana, then add the mango juice and milk and puree.

2 Set up six 3-oz/90-ml wax paper cups or popsicle molds. Pulse the blender again and then divide the mixture among the molds. If using paper cups, freeze the mixture for 45 minutes to 1 hour before inserting sticks. Once frozen, put the cups in a heavy zip-top bag and store in the freezer.

Resources

If you don't have a natural-foods store nearby that carries the special ingredients that you need, don't give up. Ask at the grocers near you whether they will carry or special-order the things you need. You may also be able to find a store a few towns over and make an occasional stock-up trip. It may also work out for you to order by phone and the Internet.

The Mail Order Catalog

Lots of groceries, including Asian and oils, faux meats
www.healthy-eating.com
800-695-2241

Vegan Essentials

Big selection of groceries
www.veganessentials.com
866-88-VEGAN

The Vegan Store

Vegan groceries and faux meats, clothing, shoes, etc.
www.veganstore.com and *www.pangeaveg.com*
800-340-1200

The Vegetarian Resource Group

Has a page linking to many sources
www.vrg.org/links/products.htm
410-366-8343

The Vegetarian Store

Faux meats
www.vegetarianstore.com
708-497-0167

Vegie World

Asian faux meats
www.vegieworld.com
212-334-4428

Ingredients Glossary

Achiote/annatto A deep orange seed native to South America, achiote is sold whole, ground, or in pastes mixed with other seasonings. It imparts a subtle flavor and a brilliant deep-yellow hue to foods, similar to saffron.

Acidophilus Acidophilus is a live culture, sold in capsule form. You can buy it in the refrigerated section at health-food stores. It's a dairy-free probiotic that helps populate the gut with good bacteria. In this book, it is used to culture nut purees, giving them a slightly tangy and cheesy taste.

Agar flakes/kanten Agar is a sea vegetable that behaves like gelatin. It is sold in bars, strips, flakes, and powder form and is sometimes referred to as kanten, the name of the gelatin-like dish it is used to make. In this book, agar flakes are used. Agar is a very healthful food often recommended for weight loss, containing 80 percent fiber and some protein with almost no calories.

Agave syrup or nectar Agave is the sweet sap of the blue agave plant, simmered at low temperatures to concentrate it and bring out the sweetness. Like maple syrup, it is a natural and unrefined product.

Amaranth The tiny seed that was once the central food of the ancient Aztecs. Like many ancient grains, it is high in complete proteins and minerals such as iron, magnesium, phosphorus, copper, and especially manganese. The tiny grains cook to a porridge or can be popped for use in cereals.

Barley, rolled Many grains can be rolled, a process in which they are steamed and then smashed flat. Rolled barley is actually higher in cholesterol-lowering beta-glucan fibers than oats and adds a nutty, chewy texture to granolas and baked goods.

Barley malt syrup Dark brown syrup made from sprouted, toasted, and then enzymatically processed barley is often used in beer and bread making. Unlike other sweeteners, grain syrups are high in maltose, a sweet molecule from whole grain.

Brown rice krispies Like the snap-crackle-pop white-rice cereal, brown rice can be popped for a crunchy cereal. Look for it in the gluten-free section if it is not in the cereal aisle.

Brown rice syrup Grain-based sweeteners are made by culturing cooked brown rice with enzymes that break down the starches into their sweet components, the main one being maltose. Brown rice syrup is considered a less refined sweetener, and it has a caramel-like, mild sweetness.

Brown rice vinegar The starches in brown rice can be fermented to make a flavorful vinegar. Regular white rice vinegar is golden and mild; brown rice vinegar is a little darker and stronger.

Buckwheat groats Buckwheat, the grain used to make kasha, soba noodles, and the classic pancake, is gluten free. Whole buckwheat groats are soft enough to eat toasted or raw in baked goods. Buckwheat is high in rutin, an anti-inflammatory flavonoid, as well as manganese, tryptophan, magnesium, and fiber.

Bulgur Whole wheat is parcooked in the husk, dried, and then hulled and chopped to make bulgur. The process drives the nutrients deep into the grain, as well as precooking it enough to make it a quick, high-protein, whole-grain option.

Burdock root or dock Often classified as a pernicious weed, in part because the root grows so deep and fast that it is difficult to remove once it gets going. For this reason, traditional Chinese medicine attributes it with a strong yang energy. It is high in fiber, calcium, amino acids, and polyphenols, which make it darken quickly when peeled. When preparing, peel and chop it, then soak it in cold water until you are ready to use it.

Chipotle, canned or ground The chipotle is a ripe jalapeño pepper that has been dried and smoked. From there, it is either sold whole, ground, or in cans/tins cooked in adobo sauce. Smoky chipotle adds great umami, heat, and flavor to dishes.

Chocolate, vegan or grain-sweetened Dark or semisweet/plain chocolates don't contain milk, but they are made with sugar, which may have been purified using bone char. Chocolates labeled as vegan have been made with vegan sugar. Grain-sweetened chocolate is made with malted grains like barley and corn, making it mildly sweet and giving it a slightly stiffer texture when melted.

Coconut oil, coconut milk, and coconut water Coconut oil has been much maligned, but its fats are actually good for you. It contains medium-chain triglycerides that burn like carbs, as well as antibiotic and antifungal lauric acid. It is a great fat for vegans to use, adding a mouthfeel that resembles shortening/vegetable lard or butter. Coconut milk comes in cans and can be used like cream in sauces and baking. Coconut water is the liquid that sloshes around in the ripe coconut, and it is sold as a high-electrolyte sports drink that is completely natural.

Corn oil, cold-press Only Spectrum makes an organic expeller-pressed corn oil. The rich corn taste gives baked goods a hint of buttery taste, especially when combined with coconut oil. Processed corn oil doesn't have the same flavor, so just use a buttery olive oil, nut oil, or canola if you can't find cold-press corn oil.

Curry pastes In this book, Thai red and green curry pastes are used, although there are all sorts of other ones. Read ingredients carefully, most contain fish or shrimp.

Dulse Dulse is a purplish sea vegetable that is harvested in the Pacific Northwest. It's thin and crisp and easy to enjoy as a sprinkle, or rehydrated and added to salads, soups, and sandwiches. It's available smoked or finely chopped as well, both great options for enjoying this mineral-rich plant.

Edamame Tofu and tempeh are made from yellow soybeans, but edamame is a different variety of soy that has been bred for a sweet, buttery taste. It's a classic snack in sushi bars, and the shelled, frozen beans are a great way to add convenient protein, fiber, and antioxidants to your meals.

Egg replacer powder When baking without eggs, it helps to have a powder to give your batter body and lift. I use Ener-G brand made with a combination of starches and leaveners. Easy to use, you just have to whisk it into a small amount of liquid to make a smooth slurry before adding it to other ingredients. Best in recipes that don't have too many eggs to replace.

Farro An ancient variety of wheat, usually associated with Italian cooking. It contains gluten, but some people who can't tolerate conventional wheat can eat farro.

Flax oil and flax seeds Flax seeds are the vegan's friend, providing essential fatty acids that omnivores get from fish and also standing in for eggs in baking. To make an egg replacer from flax, mix together 1 tbsp finely ground flax seed and ¼ cup/60 ml water to equal 1 egg. Flax oil should only be used in cold preparations, like salad dressings. It's not for cooking because heat damages healthful fats.

Flour There are many varieties of wheat in the world, but most people only eat one. Break out of the monoculture and try white wheat, an excellent flour made from a lighter colored wheat, with all the qualities that regular bread/strong flour has. Whole-wheat/wholemeal pastry/soft-wheat flour is made from soft winter wheat, a lower-gluten wheat that produces tender pastries and baked goods. Spelt, kamut, and farro are varieties of the wheat family that have gained popularity for people who are intolerant of regular wheat. They all contain gluten, just not as much as conventional wheat.

Flour, chickpea Finely ground chickpeas make this tasty, gluten-free flour. You can use Indian *besan* or garbanzo-fava flour, if those are easier to find.

Flour, gluten Gluten is the stretchy protein in wheat formed when flour mixes with water. Gluten flour is that protein without the starch and other components of wheat flour. It's high in protein, makes good mock meats, and acts as a binder in burgers and loaves.

Garam masala Indian spicing is a subtle art. What we know as "curry powder" in the United States does not exist in true Indian cuisine. Garam masala is a traditional finishing spice mix, usually made with warming spices like cinnamon and cloves, as well as savory spices like pepper.

Groat A general term for the hulled, whole form of certain grains and pseudograins, such as buckwheat, barley, or oats.

Gyoza and wonton wrappers Thin sheets of fresh pasta; many brands don't use eggs. Gyoza are round, wonton are square, and they can be stuffed and fried or poached.

Hemp seeds Hemp, the non-intoxicating cousin to marijuana, has very nutritious seeds. Because of marijuana laws, all the hemp sold in the United States is sterilized but retains its 31 percent complete protein, essential fatty acids, calcium, iron, and fiber. It is sold sprouted, hulled, ground, or made into milk or prepared foods.

Kaffir lime leaves Intensely citrusy leaves that impart a unique lime flavor to foods, and unlike lime juice, the flavor grows the longer you cook the dish. There is a movement to change the name to Makrut lime, because the name *kaffir* is a derogatory term.

Kale, lacinato Black cabbage, dinosaur kale, and Tuscan kale are a few of the many names for this attractive leafy green. The deeply curled, blue-green leaves are sturdy and sweet, stand up to most cooking methods, and are packed with iron, anticancer sulfur compounds, and plenty of fiber. You can call it anything you want, as long as you eat it.

Kamut A variety of wheat that was supposedly discovered in a tomb, preserved for thousands of years. Wherever it came from, it is a big, golden grain with a buttery taste, great cooked whole or ground for flour.

Kitchen bouquet When you are looking for an appetizing browned color and a little caramelized complexity, bottled Kitchen Bouquet sauce is a quick way to get it. Made from dark caramelized sugar, it is an easy way to make your mock meats a little meatier.

Kombu A sturdy seaweed, sold in dried strips and used most commonly for making Japanese stocks. It is also the original source for umami, and when heated gently in water, gives off satisfyingly mouth-filling glutamic acid.

Kumquats These tiny citrus fruits are less than 2 in/5 cm long and very fragrant. They are never peeled, but cooked whole or sliced.

Liquid smoke A touch of smoke flavor adds a grilled/barbecued taste to foods, as well as umami. This tiny bottle of concentrated smoky water is a way to add smoke without firing up the grill/barbecue, and it only takes a drop or two. To make liquid smoke, wood is burned and the resulting smoke is chilled to condense the water in the smoky air. The droplets are purified and aged in wood.

Margarine, nonhydrogenated/ Earth Balance buttery sticks Not all margarines are vegan, nor are they free of hydrogenated fats. Read labels carefully, or just buy Earth Balance sticks. They are beloved by vegans for their ability to stand in for butter with no bad fats or milk extracts.

Masa harina and masarepa Masa harina is the corn flour made in South America and Mexico. Whole dried corn is treated with slaked lime, soaked and ground to make a dough, then dried again to make a fine flour. Masarepa is not treated with lime and is used to make *arepas* in Venezuela and Guatemala. Because masa harina is more available, and the lime makes the nutrients in the corn more available, I use it in the arepas on page 163.

Matcha One of the prized teas of Japan, matcha is a specially grown green tea whose tips are carefully covered for its final ripening. It is then picked, steamed, dried, and finely ground, preserving all the healthful antioxidants, as well as the slightly sweet flavor. The powder is a great addition to ice creams, baked goods, and pasta doughs.

Milks, nondairy The choices in nondairy milks have expanded in recent years. Hemp, coconut, almond, hazelnut, oat, rice, and soy are just a few of the foods that are made into milk-like liquids. For most of the recipes in this book, you will want to select a neutral, unsweetened milk, or for sweet dishes, a sweeter one.

Misos An ancient food from Japan, made by culturing and fermenting cooked beans or grains with salt. The main ingredient is usually soybeans, but barley, wheat, and other beans may be used. White miso is sweet and mild, while red miso is heartier, and dark misos like *hatcho* and *muji* are the strongest. Miso is full of anticancer chemicals and probiotics, as well as great complexity and umami. It's also very salty, so just a little will do.

Mushrooms, dried The wide world of mushrooms is one that takes to drying very well. Just about every kind of fungus can be found dried. Dried mushrooms sealed in a heavy bag or storage container will keep for up to a year.

Nori The edible "paper" that forms the wrapper of sushi rolls, nori is a deliciously briny-tasting sea vegetable. Made by pulping the leaves of the nori sea vegetable and then molding them into sheets, nori is a mineral-packed vegetable that you can keep in the pantry. Don't reserve it just for sushi; it is great on salads, on sandwiches, or as a soup sprinkle.

Oats The familiar rolled oats we use for cereal are also available in whole groats, or chopped to make steel-cut or Scotch oats. They are a sweet, mild grain, and the groats make a tasty pilaf or addition to soups.

Orange flower water Middle Eastern and Mediterranean groceries will carry this aromatic flavoring. It's distilled from bitter orange blossoms, giving it an exotic citrus flavor.

Palm, hearts of The palm tree grows fat sprouts, which are then harvested and peeled down to the tender white hearts. These come canned, but if you do find some fresh, give them a try. They have a tender texture similar to canned artichokes.

Panko While plain old bread crumbs might do, you will find that you get a much crunchier, lighter coating for foods if you use this Japanese-style bread crumb.

Phyllo This tissue-thin pastry dough made from flour and water is sold stacked, rolled, and frozen and works best when thawed in the refrigerator for at least

24 hours. It's traditionally slathered with butter and layered to make a flaky pastry, but you can use healthful olive oil or margarine for a crisp vegan pastry.

Pimentón A smoked version of ground paprika, which adds great smoky flavor and umami to dishes.

Pomegranate molasses The name is a little misleading, since this thick syrup is made by boiling pomegranate juice. It gives foods a wonderful combination of tart, sweet, and fruity flavors and a boost of pomegranate nutrition.

Pumpkin seeds/pepitas These are not the seeds you scoop out of the pumpkin at Halloween, but from a variety of pumpkin with very long, slender seeds that are easy to hull. The resulting dark green seeds are a great source of essential fatty acids, minerals, and a unique flavor.

Quinoa, flakes Like oats, quinoa can be steamed and rolled flat, producing a quick-cooking cereal. Quinoa is so high in complete protein, calcium, and other goodies that it is a good grain to rotate into your baking, breakfasts, and other meals.

Rice Long-, medium-, and short-grain rices all have their best uses. Long-grain usually cooks up separate and fluffy, while medium and short can be softer and stickier. Brown rice has the bran layer left intact, so it will never be as sticky as white rice, and it takes longer to cook. It is much more nutritious. Sushi rice is the common name of short- or medium-grain white rice that is used to make sushi. It is a variety of Japonica rice and has lots of sticky amylopectin starch, which makes it hold together in the sushi roll.

Rice paper Thin sheets of rice starch are made into round, square, and triangular shapes. They are simply moistened to soften, then used to wrap a tasty filling. They make delicate, translucent soft rolls and should be consumed right away, because they become leathery as they sit.

Rice vermicelli and rice noodles Rice noodles, made from rice starch, come in infinite varieties. Rice vermicelli is the thinnest noodle, often sold bundled in skeins. Thicker noodles are used in pad Thai.

Rice wine, shao xing When you see a recipe for a stir-fry that calls for sherry, the writer is using it as a stand-in for shao xing. Shao xing is a fortified rice wine that gives Chinese food an authentic taste. It's easy to find, but if you must, use sherry instead.

Seitan Often called mock duck, seitan is a dough made from wheat protein. It was originally made by rinsing the starch out of a wheat dough, but now that gluten flour is available, it is much easier to make. It is also sold prepared and soaked in savory broth.

Soy sauce, Shoyu You can get by with one bottle of simple Chinese soy sauce, but you will gain a world of flavor if you expand your soy repertoire. Shoyu is Japanese soy-wheat sauce, a good all-purpose one. Tamari is a stronger Japanese sauce used in cooking. Light

Chinese soy is mild, while dark has molasses added. Explore soy sauces, but look out for added dashi or fish sauce.

Sriracha sauce A bright red hot sauce that was actually invented in California, Sriracha is a popular condiment at Asian tables around the world. It's made with red chiles and garlic.

Sugars Sugar terminologies are confusing, so just keep this in mind: If a sugar has big, golden crystals, it is turbinado. Dull, crumbly looking cane sugars are rapadura or Sucanat, a simply dried cane juice. Throughout Asia, Africa, Latin America, and the Caribbean, whole cane juice and palm sap are boiled down to make raw, concentrated sweeteners. Jaggery is made from both cane and palm and is found in Indian groceries. Palm sugar is a moist, grainy paste available in jars or blocks in Asian markets. Both retain the nutrients of their plants of origin and are unrefined.

Szechuan peppercorns Not a peppercorn at all, these are the dried flowers of an evergreen shrub. They are not hot like chiles or even black pepper, but have a mouth-numbing, tingly quality that is essential to real Szechuan and Tibetan dishes.

Tahini Like peanut butter, tahini is a ground paste, but made from sesame seeds instead of peanuts. It can be purchased in raw or toasted variations, the toasted having a little more nutty taste. It's a great source of calcium and protein and makes great dressings and sauces, as well as adding sesame flavor to hummus.

Tamari The original soy sauce, it was formerly a by-product of miso making. Darker and thicker than regular soy sauces, it can be made from all soy or have wheat as an ingredient. Loaded with umami, tamari is a vegan stand-by that adds both salt and great flavor.

Tamarind The tamarind pod grows in the tropics, and the part that we eat is a thick paste that plumps up the pods around the seeds. It is quite labor intensive to extract the paste from the fibrous pods, so it is sold in convenient puree and paste forms. The flavor is like a combination of lemons and raisins.

Teff The tiniest grain and an ancient food of Ethiopia and North Africa. It was traditionally ground for flour to make *injera*, the sour flatbreads of North African cuisine. It grows like a weed and is a great source of complete protein, calcium, iron, phosphorus, and trace minerals. It is gluten free and available in both white and chocolate brown varieties.

Tempeh Originating in Indonesia, tempeh is a cake of chunky, fermented beans and grains. Usually made with soy, it can have added veggies, seasonings, and grains like wild rice or brown rice. A culture ferments the beans and grains to make them more digestible, and it forms an edible mycelium (mold) that holds it all together. The resulting cake is chewy, nutty, and full of all the soy and grain nutrition you would expect.

Thai basil/holy basil One of the many varieties of basil, Thai basils are usually distinguished by purplish veins or stems and an anise-like flavor. If you must use sweet basil, you can.

Tofu All tofu starts as soymilk. Soybeans are ground with water and cooked, then the fiber is strained out to make a high-protein liquid. To make firm tofu, a coagulant like *nigari*, a mineral salt, is added, which makes the tofu form curds. The curds are fished out and pressed in a mold to force out the water, and the more water is removed, the firmer the tofu. Silken tofu is made more like pudding, and the soymilk is thickened without forming curds or removing any water. Silken tofu is much smoother and wetter than nigari tofu.

Tofu "cream cheese" Soy cheese technologies are advancing, and the first one to be a pretty good approximation of the original is tofu "cream cheese." It's not overly processed, just made with tofu and some gums and flavorings to give it the spreadable texture of cheese.

Turmeric, fresh This root was once only available in Indian groceries, but now natural-foods stores are carrying it. It looks a little like ginger root, but much smaller. If you can get some, use it in place of dried turmeric at about a 4 to 1 ratio. Turmeric has emerged as a potent protector of your brain and an anti-inflammatory.

Udon The Japanese noodle tradition gives us many tasty dishes, and udon is a buckwheat-based noodle that resembles a thin fettuccine.

Umeboshi vinegar and paste A traditional Japanese food, *umeboshi* plums are pickled in salt to make a tangy, sour, salty pink preserve. The plums are sold either whole or in paste form, and the liquid from the pickling process is sold as ume vinegar. Salty and full of umami, the plums are a source of enzymes that are thought to aid digestion.

Vegan protein powder While soy is the most common protein powder, many other plants—such as hemp, peas, rice, and various other foods—can be used to make protein-boosting powders. Many people are turning away from soy powders because of concerns about the solvents used to strip them of fat. Protein powders can be used in smoothies, ice creams, and added to baked goods and granola.

Vegenaise There are a number of vegan "mayonnaise" products on the market, but Vegenaise is the brand that has the most authentic taste. You can also make a great one with the recipe on page 113.

Wasabi Real wasabi is a Japanese relative of horseradish, a delicate plant that is grown in cold running mountain streams. Wasabi is notoriously expensive and hard to ship and store, so most American sushi bars and grocers sell wasabi that is really just horseradish with green coloring added in. Real wasabi is much subtler, more vegetal tasting, and less hot, but if you are accustomed to the American faux wasabi, it is fine to use it. Wasabi powder may also be horseradish as real powdered wasabi loses its flavor quickly.

Worcestershire sauce, vegan

Regular Worcestershire sauce is a complex blend of tamarind, spices, and fish sauce. Vegan brands make the same magic happen without the fish, and most people would be hard pressed to tell the difference.

Yeast, bread

Microorganisms that have been harnessed to ferment breads and beers, yeasts both break down grain and create gases to make breads rise. Active yeast is the conventional, slow kind, while newer varieties are called quick-rise or bread-machine yeast. Conventional yeast is best for overnight and slow-rise processes. Quick-rise is usually mixed with dry ingredients, and then hot liquids are added, and the method produces bread in half the time. All these recipes use granular yeast. Follow package instructions to convert to cake yeast.

Yeast, nutritional

A yellow powder or flake grown on a vitamin B_{12}–enriched medium, nutritional yeast is not active. It's purely for nutrition, as the name suggests, although you may find the cheesy taste addicting.

Yucca

A large brown tuber shaped like an oversized carrot, yucca is also called cassava root. The thick skin is peeled, and there is often a central core in larger yuccas that needs to be removed. Yucca is usually boiled to tenderness and can then be fried, mashed, or pureed.

Index